No Closure

No Closure

CATHOLIC PRACTICE AND BOSTON'S PARISH SHUTDOWNS

John C. Seitz

Harvard University Press
Cambridge, Massachusetts, and London, England
2011

Printed in the United States of America

Library of Congress Cataloging-in-Publication Data

Seitz, John C.
No closure : Catholic practice and Boston's parish shutdowns / John C. Seitz.
p. cm.
Includes bibliographical references (p.) and index.
ISBN 978-0-674-05302-1 (alk. paper)
1. Church closures—Massachusetts—Boston—History—21st century.
2. Catholic Church. Archdiocese of Boston (Mass.)—History. 3. Parishes—Massachusetts—Boston—History. 4. Boston (Mass.)—Church history. I. Title.
BX1417.B6S45 2011
254'.02—dc22 2010041632

Contents

No Closure

Introduction: Closings

A New Scandal

Like many Catholics of her generation, Susana lived life deeply connected with her parish. Sometimes her home seemed like an extension of Our Lady of Mount Carmel Church, which she could see just down the street from her tall brick row house in East Boston's Jeffries Point neighborhood. Her deep connection went beyond the sightlines. For one thing, vital supplies shuttled back and forth between home and church with regularity. In the years before she helped raise funds to install a new kitchen in the church basement, Susana used to cook great batches of macaroni and gravy in her own basement kitchen, running them across the street, with help from the church's young men, for the parish's many benefit suppers.

Church came into her home, too. She routinely entertained and fed priests, nuns, brothers, bishops, and, once, Boston Archbishop Bernard Law at her kitchen table. After the parish's nuns had left the parish in the late 1970s, Susana and her husband David seriously considered buying their former convent and turning its upper floors into their home. The lower floors, they imagined, could house a public shrine to Padre Pio, the twentieth-century Italian stigmatic to whom they had a devotion. The chancery never responded to their inquiry and they dropped the matter, opting instead to refurbish their own home.

The integration of church and home extended to business and economic survival. For a time, Susana and David owned a funeral home near Our Lady of Mount Carmel, and the community centered there was one important foundation for the business. With this business, and their involvement in numerous clubs and the parish council, David and Susana had gained prominence and some influence within the parish. With this power came a sense of responsibility, too. Susana and David were an effective fundraising team. They had even received a plaque from the church's pastor acknowledging their efforts.

Susana found herself frequently serving as a go-between, a mediator between priests and fellow parishioners on important and difficult occasions. She recalled stepping between the church and the rage of her fellow parishioners after evidence of clergy sex abuse and its cover-up began to emerge in January 2002. The parish had housed an abusive Franciscan brother in the 1980s, so Susana had her work cut out for her.[1] Despite this proximity, Susana defended the good name of innumerable innocent priests, cautioning her friends against unreflective anticlericalism. There are many "good priests," she told them, who "believe in God" and "believe in what they are doing."

When the archdiocese announced the closure of her parish in 2004, however, Susana and David experienced a deepened sense of scandal. Now victims of what they saw as the hierarchy's callousness, a form of outrage that others already knew hit home for them. Comparing the crisis to the clergy abuse, Susana drew a potent distinction: "That was sex abuse, but this is spiritual abuse, and this, I don't think this I'll be able to forgive." David added that the shutdowns had "caused people to lose their faith."[2] For Susana and David, who had long been out of the funeral home business, the toxicity of this new form of "abuse" radiated precisely from its affront to the neighborhood's Catholic past. The scandal Susana felt now was a symptom of a violation of the past. For Susana this past included her entire history in East Boston. Hardship and endurance, intimacy and commitment, were the keystones of this past. Her religious, business, and personal histories were inextricable from her relationship to the parish. In the closure, these stones were being removed and Susana felt a violation down to her core.

But weren't there other elements to this past that Susana's outrage obscured? Even if the overlaps were jarring—the announcement of Mount Carmel's shutdown arrived on the same day the parish's abusive brother pled guilty—was it really appropriate to compare sexual abuse and its cover-up with the loss of a parish?[3] Evidence of Catholic decline had surrounded Susana for decades. In 1953, the year Susana, aged 15, had arrived at Our Lady of Mount Carmel from Italy, the parish census counted 1,300 families. Although Susana and her soon-to-be husband found the community a lively and welcoming place for young Italian immigrants like themselves, this was already a decline from previous years. If in 1946 Mount Carmel was "one of the biggest parishes in the city of Boston," departures for the suburbs during the following years would begin a period of fitful declines. By 1953, the parish had lost 200 families. Over the decade of the 1950s, the total number of families would decline by 600. By 1980, however, the parish still claimed to be "one of the proudest Italian parishes in the Archdiocese of Boston," reporting a membership of 800 families.[4] Optimistic expectations of parish growth reverberated from this celebration, but it soon appeared that further expansion was perhaps beyond hope. By 2003, Mount Carmel had only 304 people attending mass each weekend.[5] In May of 2004, along with dozens of other parishes in the archdiocese, it ended up on the list of parishes that would be closed in the coming months.

Even beyond Susana's neighborhood the gradual consolidation of Boston's Catholic infrastructure was undeniable. Across the archdiocese, changes in Catholics' churchgoing practices, decline in priestly vocations, and shifting neighborhood demographics resulted in forty-five closings or mergers between 1985 and 2003. Of these forty-five transformations, over half resulted in the elimination of an ethnic parish like Mount Carmel.[6] So Boston Catholics, and especially Catholics associated with ethnic parishes, already lived amid decline and threat. Susana, David, and the others in resisting parishes around Boston had to have known closure might be coming. The struggles of the recent past must have put old expectations and hopes in a different light. What is the history of the scandal they felt?

A Dark Season in Catholic Boston

The immediate context of Susana's pain provides an opening to that history. In late May of 2004, the Roman Catholic Archdiocese of Boston announced that it would shut down sixty-five of its 357 parishes over the next six months. Seventeen more parishes were added to the list in subsequent weeks, bringing to eighty-two the total number expected to be either closed or merged with others within the year.[7] The large majority of these parishes would be "suppressed," a church legal term meaning that parish assets and liabilities would be transferred to the archdiocese, their pastors transferred, and their parishioners redirected to a new "welcoming parish."

Like many people in Boston in 2004, I marveled at the multiplying agonies that were testing the local church. In this latest bleak chapter, great numbers of Catholics—28,000 by the archdiocese's count—would be asked to leave their parishes.[8] I knew the importance of parishes for Catholics across the United States. Many Catholics still spoke fondly of the days when neighborhoods were named after the local parish's patron saint or other holy figure. In some cases, parish boundaries had been a marker of identity and community for Catholics across several generations.[9] Catholic parishes in some neighborhoods had provided reliable social services for people in need.[10] Now, I wondered how those people would weather the loss. Schools had been established alongside parishes in many cases. Where these schools had survived, they attracted families to neighborhoods that might otherwise have been taken over by absentee landlords or developers. It was becoming clear, moreover, that many church buildings would not survive being sold. They would be leveled, the space they had occupied filled with housing or perhaps a shopping center.[11] At the time of the announcement I was living across the street from a nineteenth-century Catholic church in Cambridge. St. Mary's would not close, but surveying its massive footprint in my neighborhood made it clear that more condos or additional commercial space would have radically altered my neighborhood. The same would be true for many others.

It was also clear that many of Boston's parish neighborhoods, some of which had once been the crown jewels of Boston's militant Catholic subculture, had gone through rough times in recent years.[12] Despite their strong neighborhood roots, many Catholics left the city of Boston for commuter communities in the second half of the twentieth century. Some of these neighborhoods became homes for new, predominantly non-Catholic communities. Naturally, Catholic parishes in these new communities often suffered during this transition.[13] Latino Catholics, as well as newer immigrant communities made up of immigrants from Haiti, Vietnam, Cambodia, Laos, and China, helped fill some of the abandoned urban churches.[14] But broader changes in patterns of churchgoing among majority Euro-American Catholics contributed to a diminishing sense of Catholic neighborhood presence and prominence. Even before the time of the closures in 2004, many urban parishes, and some of the newer suburban parishes as well, were experiencing occasional struggles with upkeep and attendance. These struggles often went in cycles, with parishes swelling for some years, and then falling off while a few core committed people kept the places afloat.[15] For those core people, the closures were particularly demoralizing.

Most pointedly, the closures came just over two years after the first major revelations about Boston's long history of clergy sexual abuse and its cover-up. Wounds from this profound betrayal of trust had not healed; new details about the extent of the abuse in the church were still emerging. Four months before the closings were announced, the United States Conference of Catholic Bishops (USCCB) had publicized the results of an independent report on nationwide sexual abuse patterns in the church. The report showed that 4% of Catholic priests who had taken their vows since 1950 had been accused of the sexual abuse of minors.[16] The Archdiocese of Boston released its own report at the same time, which indicated that 7% of Boston's priests had been accused of sexual assault since 1950.[17] The national report also reminded Catholics that the actual incidence of abuse was likely significantly higher, as abuse is often kept secret, especially among male victims. Both well-publicized studies made it clear that most of this abuse had taken place in the 1960s, 1970s, and through the mid-1980s. Catholics learned that most of the incidents had taken place in priests' homes, although many incidents happened in churches. A large majority of the victims were boys between the ages of eleven and seventeen; about half were between the ages of eleven and fourteen. Over six hundred million dollars had been spent across the United States for settlement and treatment costs related to sexual abuse.[18] Eighty-five million of that had been spent in Boston's recent settlement with five hundred victims.[19] These figures did not include money paid out to victims in private settlements over the years. With at least one thousand cases still unsettled nationally, estimates of a one billion dollar cumulative expenditure across the United States were in the air.[20] So the closures came at a time when Boston's Catholics were already in the midst of a dark season in their tradition.

There had been signs of a modest recovery. The archdiocese trumpeted the results of an audit released in January of 2004, which reported that most dioceses in the United States, including Boston, had complied with a 2002 USCCB charter on policies and programs for preventing and reporting sexual abuse.[21] Fierce criticism of this audit persisted, but the mere existence of checks like this was considered by critics as evidence of progress.[22] Voice of the Faithful, an organization of lay Catholics seeking transparency and greater democracy in the church, emerged as a powerful force in Boston and had spread nationally. VOTF's mission and motto—"Keep the faith, change the church"—were controversial, but the organization fostered animated discourse, especially among higher-income and suburban pockets of the Boston church.[23]

Despite these more positive developments, many formerly loyal Catholics still seemed to have hesitations about participation in the church. Child baptisms in Boston had remained more or less level in proportion to the Catholic population across the most tumultuous years, but other indicators were not as strong. Mass attendance, which had dipped below 20% of Catholics in Boston in the late 1990s, went lower still, from 17.5% in 2001 to 14.9% in 2002. Contributions to the archdiocese's annual appeal to parishioners took an even more significant hit, dropping from $17.2 million in 2000 to $8.8 million in 2002. By 2003, attendance and giving had ticked slightly up from their 2002 lows.[24] But significantly decreased donations, along with increasing evidence of archdiocesan budget shortfalls, signaled that additional days of reckoning lay ahead. Budget challenges were not new, just more onerous. In June 2001 the archbishop had launched the largest capital campaign in the history of U.S. dioceses, seeking $300 million from parishioners by the end of 2002. The goal was a long way off by 2002, and the abuse crisis made the hill that much steeper to climb.[25] Widespread parish closures, which in 2000 Cardinal Law had ventured to hope were behind the archdiocese, were now all but certain.[26]

In 2003 the recently installed archbishop, the Capuchin Franciscan Seán P. O'Malley, asked parishes to meet in their regional groupings (called "clusters") and come up with a recommendation about which one or two of them ought to close if he decided that an area could make do with fewer parishes.[27] O'Malley identified several factors that made the closures necessary. Shifting demographics meant that urban neighborhoods (and some suburban ones too) had more parishes than the Catholics there could support. Some parishes, the archbishop said, were running in the red and relied on the already strapped archdiocese for support. Others had buildings that were in poor condition and required expensive repairs unlikely to be made. The physical state of such churches would only get worse over time, their liability greater, repairs more expensive. Furthermore, the number of priests in Boston had already fallen significantly since the late 1960s, and small seminary cohorts now meant that replacements were not on the way. Finally, the archbishop admitted that the archdiocesan budget was in poor condition. The archdiocese could better support a smaller number of strong parishes and programs than a proliferation of small and possibly weak ones. With charitable giving down and with expenses already going unmet, the income gleaned from parish closures could prevent the archdiocese from having to consider filing for bankruptcy.[28]

Cluster groups were to consider a number of factors as they weighed the relative merits of the parishes in their group. No one factor should dominate the others, the archdiocese instructed. Instead, the group members—including lay people and pastors from each parish—were told to consider multiple factors to reach a consensus about which parish among them should close. The "sacramental index," a measurement of parish vitality amounting to the sum of the number of baptisms and funerals plus twice the number of weddings in a church, was a key metric. These numbers, along with data about mass attendance, confirmation cohorts, parish financial status, the existence of a parish school, the demographics of the congregation (especially whether or not the parish had foreign-language masses), the condition of the buildings, church social services, and the projected retirement of the pastor, were collected in aid of the effort to decide who should close. While cluster groups took these meetings seriously, everyone knew that the conclusions they reached were not decisions, but recommendations. The final word lay with the archbishop, who could and occasionally did overturn cluster recommendations.

This process met with varying levels of success. In some instances, clusters came to a common agreement about which parish should close; in others mutual suspicion and intrigue gave the process the feel of a game of strategy and subterfuge. Did a church over-report its attendance numbers? Did a friend of the bishop ally himself with another pastor to vote us out?[29] Almost immediately, skeptical observers and participants across the archdiocese were comparing the cluster process to the television reality program "Survivor," in which participants rely on guile and physical skill to avoid being voted "off the island" in the hope of winning prize money.[30] Some Boston Catholics, even if they did not think that the process was fatally flawed, initially tried to avoid selecting one parish over another, relenting only after the chancery insisted that they make a recommendation. Some even refused this ultimatum, leaving their fates entirely in the hands of the archbishop and his advisors.[31]

In the end, the clusters identified approximately one hundred parishes that could be considered for closure by the archbishop and a group of lay and clerical advisors called the Reconfiguration Central Committee. In consultation with this body, and with local vicars and bishops, the Presbyteral

Council then selected twenty-four parishes for the list from clusters that had refused to make a recommendation; they also added thirteen parishes based on their assessments of local circumstances. By early May of 2004, approximately 137 parishes faced possible extinction.[32]

On May 25, sixty-five of these were notified that they would close, with more announcements to follow. The day saw parishioners and pastors standing nervously by, anxiously noting the approach of mail trucks that might carry word of their fate. Stories immediately emerged of the celebratory ringing of church bells and of the tears and confusion accompanying the receipt of closure announcements. A documentary filmmaker caught pastor and parishioner anxiety and despair at the closure decree's arrival at a Charlestown parish. In Framingham, a pastor hung a black flag from the flagpole to alert parishioners of the bad news.[33] The *Boston Globe* (whose investigative team had won awards and the ire of some in the church for its reports on the sexual abuse crisis) and the populist-leaning *Boston Herald* offered dozens of stories of distraught pastors and parishioners contemplating how they would say goodbye to their parishes.

Demoralizing stories continued to emerge after the release of the names of closing parishes. On May 28 in Rome, Pope John Paul II officially appointed Boston's former archbishop, Cardinal Bernard Law, to oversee the basilica of Santa Maria Maggiore in Rome. Law had resigned in December 2002 after apologizing for mistakes in the shuffling of abuser priests from parish to parish during his tenure. Now he was taking over this "archpriest" position and would remain a cardinal, eligible to serve on the conclave that would select the next pope. Many in the archdiocese bristled at the details of Law's position. News of Law's "staff," his "car and driver," and the "two nuns" appointed to "manage his household" gave the impression that Law had suffered no major losses after his ambiguous service in Boston had ended in scandal. While they faced the closure of 20% of their churches, Law, one of the enablers of clergy sexual abuse, was handed a cushy position in a grand church in the "heart of Rome."[34]

Parish Shutdowns, Parish Occupations

As I read these accounts and listened to anxious and distraught Catholics in Boston, I began to see that this unhappy occasion offered a unique opportunity to learn more about how Catholics of all varieties dealt with changes in the church. It was not yet clear what would happen in the parishes that had been slated to close. The media was running stories about the majestic buildings that would be razed, the long traditions terminated. There were a few criticisms of the process in the air, mostly from members of Boston's active branches of the Voice of the Faithful. The Voice of the Faithful worried that the process was too swift, the appeals process too hierarchical, and the financial situation that made the closures necessary too obscure.[35] My wife, who had been hired as a temporary research consultant to the archdiocese-affiliated Catholic Charities, brought home stories of despondent pastors, angry parish secretaries, and at-risk social service programs that seemed to have no viable replacement in line. A few parish groups promised to appeal the decisions; others organized meetings to consider alternative ways of stopping their closure.[36] One group even let it leak that they might try to take over their church rather than allow it to close down.[37]

Several pastors from closing parishes publicly questioned the process.[38] Together, these openly dissenting pastors held a mass of support for closed parishes organized by Voice of the Faithful on August 15, 2004. The mass gathered Catholics from closed parishes in the hope that a show of solidarity would somehow influence a change in the church or perhaps even help them avoid closure. The Voice of the Faithful and the Globe estimated that nearly 2,000 Catholics attended the mass, which was held outdoors on the Boston Common. Criticisms of the bishops and the closures reverberated from this event. But amid these efforts, most parishes on the closure list began selecting closing dates and planning for their last masses.

In August 2004, I began the fieldwork that serves as the foundation of this project. For a time I waited to see what would happen and tried to remain open to promising avenues for research. I attended the "Mass on the Common," where I spoke with aggrieved parishioners and photographed the long line of white tombstone-like signs that lined the park walkway, naming the closing parishes. I visited several last masses, where pastors, bishops, and parishioners participated in closing rites and spoke movingly of the sorrows of loss and the opportunities of moving on. I sat in on meetings on parish closures held by local branches of VOTF. I spoke with some of the pastors and parishioners opposed to the extent or the pace of the shutdowns. Everyone was speaking of loss and mourning. On all sides of the process people compared the closures to death. Some spoke of the process of rebirth and joining a new parish as a spiritual journey. Closures might be borne with Christlike heroism and even triumph. The symbols at the Mass on the Common evoked tragedy. Everyone agreed that the transitions might be difficult and that it would take time for Catholics to recover.

It appeared that Catholics in Boston would follow a path both described and prescribed as typical of those going through the consolidation of their dioceses. As a 1988 study about "pastoral options" for "inner city" parishes put it, shutdowns were "undeniably difficult." But if closures were handled properly, those involved could pass through the various stages of grief toward "acceptance and peace." They could even come to see a shutdown as religiously meaningful: "one might find in parish closings and mergers a hint of the central Christian belief: it is only in dying that one is reborn." This idea could serve as a foundation for a "theology of dying parishes."[39] As the summer of 2004 came to a close, Bostonians seemed primed to apply this psychological and religious balm to their wounds.

By late August 2004, however, it became clear that in a few parishes around the archdiocese there were groups of Catholics who were going to reject this "process" altogether. They would not close. In conversations with allies in Voice of the Faithful and organized by a strong group of parish council members, parishioners at St. Albert the Great in East Weymouth moved into the church for what they called a perpetual vigil. With their physical and, they repeatedly insisted, "prayerful" presence they were going to keep the church open despite the decree against it. The group had thought ahead. Fearing preemptive countermeasures, they took over the church immediately after the last Sunday mass instead of waiting until the official closing date on the following Wednesday. In their planning they had been advised by a group of supportive Catholics from Worcester, Massachusetts, who were veterans of their own thirteen-month-long church occupation in opposition to a closure decree in 1992.[40] The St. Albert's resisters had planned to vigil in shifts, but they also stockpiled food and water in case replacements could not safely get inside the church. Copying the Worcester Catholics' approach, the St. Albert's parishioners filed a civil lawsuit claiming that the archdiocese did not legally own the parish, but only served as its trustee. In all this the dissenters were subtly encouraged by their pastor, Father Ronald Coyne. Dozens of parishioners took shifts day and night. Predictably, members of the media swarmed the church.

St. Albert's resisters had planned for religious services as well. With Father Coyne gone, the parishioners took responsibility for managing the buildings and directing the rituals for those who stayed on. Having been encouraged during Father Coyne's tenure to take leadership roles in the parish, parishioners did not face an extremely steep learning curve. At first they held simple daily prayer services and rosaries. Later, they added communion services, using a steady supply of consecrated hosts provided by sympathetic priests from the surrounding area. The names of these spiritual benefactors were kept in strict secrecy, in recognition that their careers could be in danger if they were known to have supported this outlaw endeavor. The basic goal of the resisters was to convince the archdiocese of its mistake in the original closure process and decision, get the closure decrees against them rescinded, and restore the parish.

The people occupying St. Albert's believed that their parish did not fit the criteria establishing eligibility for closing. They cited its full coffers, crowded Sunday masses, active adult and children's organizations, and the parish's charitable work to prove that they should never have been targeted in the first place. Suspicions about the chancery's motives and the jealousies of neighboring parishes added a personal element to the resisters' rejection of the closure process. Father Coyne had been actively supportive of the Voice of the Faithful, which had been banned from meeting in churches in many dioceses across the country and had recently been limited by the hierarchy in Boston. Coyne had also signed a letter calling for Cardinal Law to resign. All this made Coyne vulnerable to suspicions of disloyalty, but the archdiocese disowned any connection between these circumstances and the closure. A long process of vigiling, public relations efforts, meetings, and negotiations with the archdiocese began.

The protest struck an exhilarating chord. Eight other closing parishes eventually joined the effort at St. Albert's with their own round-the-clock occupations. A group at St. Anselm's in Sudbury began staying over in their church on September 12, 2004. For a time, the well-organized parishioners from St. Anselm's and St. Albert's provided advice and support to other groups who were considering occupations of their own. Noting these and other pockets of unrest, the archbishop asked two prominent lay Catholics to select and lead a committee to perform an external review of the closing decisions.[41] Their original mandate was to review only decisions affecting parishes that had not yet closed, but this was soon expanded. Over the course of the next several months the group met with parishioners at occupied parishes as well as parishioners from parishes that had appealed their closure but had not launched an occupation.

Five days after this review committee was created, another occupation began. After the last mass on October 12, 2004, parishioners at Our Lady of Mount Carmel, the Italian national parish in East Boston, began the third church occupation in the archdiocese. Less than two weeks later, they were followed into vigil by St. Bernard's in West Newton, where a group of parishioners took over the church despite having been told at the last minute that official masses would continue there indefinitely. They suspected this was a ploy to prevent an occupation; they would not be so easily duped. In late October, St. Frances Cabrini in the seaside town of Scituate began an occupation. Stories from this takeover reported that the locks on the church had been changed before parishioners had a chance to get inside. Testing all the doors, one would-be vigiler finally sneaked inside the church after finding that a side entrance had been left slightly propped open (apparently by accident). In Everett, the church's final mass on October 27 was followed by an all-night prayer vigil that turned into an occupation. A group occupied Infant Jesus-St. Lawrence Parish in Brookline on the 29th. On Halloween, parishioners at St. James the Great in Wellesley took over their church, bringing the total number of takeovers to eight. On November 6 the priest administrator of Immaculate Conception in Winchester asked police to remove a parishioner who would not leave after the last mass; apparently against the priest's intentions, this led to the parishioner's arrest, and the archdiocese later asked local prosecutors to drop charges. On Christmas Eve, a pastor's request that two parishioners be escorted out of Sacred Heart in Natick also led to their arrest and charges of trespassing (later dropped). Facing the same threat a day later, a group of five would-be vigilers left Sacred Heart and the church was locked and closed. In May of 2005, after a few reversals in the original closure decisions, a group at St. Jeremiah Parish in Framingham started an occupation.

By the early summer of 2005, fifteen parishes had submitted appeals to the Vatican, a total of nine had entered round-the-clock vigils, several had sued the archdiocese in civil court, and a few others were considering occupations. Each of these groups of resisters had different stories about the failures of the closure process and their particular circumstances. They had varying levels of support from among the ranks of parishioners. Some got by with just a few dedicated members; others enjoyed wide support despite archdiocesan critiques and pressure from former fellow parishioners.[42] A sympathetic media buoyed their spirits as well. The Council of Parishes, a group of Catholics from sixteen different parishes on the original closure list, had been advancing the causes of Catholics in occupied and resisting parishes. Its leaders cultivated relationships with the media and had become the main spokespeople in a public relations battle between resisting Catholics and the archdiocese.

The protests began to show results. External review led to reversals in the closure decisions at four occupied parishes and several other resisting parishes. A number of other parishes had had their closing dates delayed or indefinitely put off.[43] By May 2005, fifty-nine parishes had closed.[44] An archdiocesan estimate suggested that just twenty percent of the 4,000 Catholics who had been active at closed parishes had not signed up as members at a new parish, which was taken as an indication of success.[45] By early 2008, the number of closed or merged parishes had risen to seventy-five. The official appeals of several parishes to various Vatican bodies appeared to be failing. Despite most Catholics' acquiescence to the shutdowns in Boston, Catholics in five parishes continued to occupy their churches.[46] The times were unstable, the situation charged and in flux.

Contours of the Study

This book draws on fieldwork among resisting Catholics to explore and explain that energy and tension in light of Boston's social and religious histories, American Catholic history, and American religious history more generally. Just as Boston's shutdown plan was more extensive and faster paced than any other in American Catholic history, so too the resistance to shutdowns in Boston was more widespread and more sustained than the sporadic and ephemeral objections that arose (and continue to arise) amid other dioceses' efforts of consolidation. At one level, then, this is a study of the specific conditions and histories that prepared the way for the upheaval in Boston. But there are other pasts that Boston-area Catholics shared with other U.S. Catholics, and with others living in this country during the twentieth and twenty-first centuries. The controversy in Boston could have been much shorter-lived than it has been (occupiers still in churches nearly six years later) without diminishing the significance of the broader church and social tensions it revealed.

The occupations demanded—to a unique extent—that Catholics involved mark out the lines and limits of their engagements with the church. In doing so, Catholics were drawn to reconsider the past and its meanings; they struggled with changing notions of authority in the church; and they took up their responsibilities for the church buildings, and its rites, with new (or renewed) intensity—all of this in an atmosphere of challenge, scrutiny, and intrigue. The occupations brought new life to conflicts that had been lingering since the mid-twentieth century—over authority, sacrifice, sacred presence, and belonging—by pitting Catholics against some of their leaders on a matter of great mutual urgency.

Catholics in the occupations were not concerned as much with doctrine as they were with everyday theological questions of respect and memory, the relationship between religion, community, and comfort, and the meaning of the local church.[47] This is not to say that these Catholics did not participate in (or feel the weight of) the debates in the church about sexuality, for example, or women's ordination. They certainly did not ignore the questions that preoccupied the Voice of the Faithful, such as transparency in the church's finances and democracy in its decision-making. While not unmindful of these concerns, their dedication to preserving their parishes elicited a different set of theological questions and challenges in their relation to the church. If their struggle touched on these issues, it was sustained and energized by Catholics' affinity for their churches, neighborhoods, and communities. Study of the occupied parishes serves as a reminder of the variety of practices that matter for Catholics, of the importance of place and local solidarity.

Fieldwork in the occupied parishes offered the advantage of engaging Catholics as they took their parishes and religious lives into their own hands. Being in church was different than being out on the street or in a lawyer's office or a courtroom discussing legal strategies for the protection of a church. The churches themselves, the familiar spaces, sounds, smells, and images, provided opportunities and placed demands on people. Vigilers struggled about how best to take advantage of the opportunities the church provided them. How would they collect funds? What would worship services look like? How would they handle sacred objects? What kind of visitors would be welcomed? The challenges they encountered—for certain kinds of decorum, upkeep of the buildings, or certain responsibilities to the neighborhood, for example—were sometimes met and sometimes willfully resisted. I got to know Catholics as they took over their churches and made decisions about these kinds of questions, and in the process I gained better understanding of the ways those places meant something to them, about the nature of their Catholicism, and about the animating tensions of Catholic life in twentieth- and twenty-first-century America.

These sorts of questions did not relate uniquely to the effort to reopen the churches. It is true that the occupied churches were embattled places that nurtured the intense emotions bred of conflict. But they were not only that, and the Catholics who stayed behind in their parishes were resisters, but not only that. While their fight for their churches was the reason they were there, what they did, how they talked, and the ways they changed expressed their abiding connections to broader questions in the tradition. The conflicts evident in the occupations were not only those between the occupiers and the church leadership in Boston. They were also internal to resisting communities and to individual resisters themselves. Nor were the tensions exposed just of the moment; rather, conflicts over sacrifice and authority or sacred presence and material religion were built into the tradition as it had taken shape in Boston in the late twentieth and early twenty-first century. For the purposes of this project the resistance is both a central topic and the environment for inquiry into broader aspects of U.S. Catholic history and contemporary practice. It gives us a unique opportunity to see Catholics at work not only on their lives and faith in the present, but on the past and its role in the future of the tradition.

In the pages that follow I seek to answer two basic questions about this moment in Boston Catholic history. First, why did people resist the closure of their parishes? For some the experience of resisting closely resembled life before the shutdown. They arrived for Sunday communion services led by the occupying Catholics just as they would have for Sunday mass led by a priest. For others, the time commitment and anguish of the occupations were extensive and exhausting. But all these people made an explicit choice not to let go. This meant they stood in opposition to the expectations, values, and plans (if not demands) of Boston's Catholic leadership. Even those who combined attendance at services at the occupied churches with sanctioned masses elsewhere acted in conflict with, if not transgression of, the clearly stated goals of the hierarchy. The occupied churches were illicit; even if they hosted occasional or regular masses with the approval of the hierarchy, the archdiocesan leadership continually reminded Catholics that these parishes were "closed." By even the most modest support of these closed parishes, resisters perpetuated divisions in the Catholic community that the archdiocese wanted to erase. Moreover, they rejected the basic hierarchical structure of the church. The appeal of rebellion itself could have been a reason for the resistance, but this essentially avoids the question, whence the appeal of rebellion?

Among all varieties of participants in the occupied churches and among those advocating the closures there were many answers to the question of why the resistance happened. Some suggested that the reasons for their resistance were nearly self-evident: the outright rejection of their particular parish's closure, or wholehearted opposition to the overall closure process, were the only truly Catholic, just, or natural responses. Others (even these same Catholics in less confident moments) found themselves surprised by their involvement. The communities of resistance that I got to know all had gifted individual lay leaders willing to do most of the work in organizing a resistance. Some of the parishes also had well-organized parish councils (a Vatican II era innovation), a beloved pastor, or a history of survival in the face of hardship. Because they came from different circumstances (and they each insisted their situation was unique) it was impossible to isolate any single crux of their willingness to resist. These differences, moments of doubt, and ongoing reflection offer a chance to develop multilayered answers to the question of parishioner resistance. This book tracks these varied explanations.

The second question—what does the resistance to church closings tell us about modern Catholicism?—builds off the first. As I suggest below, the reasons for the resistance are rooted in Boston's Catholic past and in broader changes in the teachings and rites of the church since the mid-twentieth century. Understanding the depth of these Catholics' anger, confusion, and hurt at the closures requires an examination of their "formation"—a term with a distinctly Catholic usage, related to the mechanisms of training various members for their designated roles in the church—as parishioners during this time. The same is true of their hopefulness, energy, and care for their parishes and for each other. My study identifies origins in history and memory for Catholics' orientations to their parishes, neighborhoods, and the tradition more generally. If such work does not provide the last word, it does provide a beginning to understanding Catholics' resistance and its larger implications for Boston, the American Catholic Church, and the study of religion more generally.

This book is not an attempt to evaluate the propriety or impropriety of the shutdowns, nor is it an effort to re-establish the boundaries of "true" and "false" Catholicism. My focus on resisters is not a lionization of resistance or "popular" Catholicism (as if resisters could so easily be separated from the rest of their coreligionists). This is also not a text of policy or planning recommendations. As historian Thomas Rzeznik recently noted, there is probably no "'right' way to make" the "difficult, contentious, and often necessary decision" to close parishes. Even if there are better and worse ways to shutter parishes (there are, as Rzeznik and others have begun to show), my work addresses them only obliquely. Moreover, I am less certain than Rzeznik is about the meanings of the places, communities, and attitudes he disparagingly calls the "cocoons of parochial exclusivity."[48]

The project intends instead to understand resisters as they carried—in their thoughts, actions, and bodies—the imprint of wider struggles related to changes in the church and society across the twentieth century. Since I am interested primarily in these inner histories of resisting Catholics, I do my best to avoid getting caught up in the debate about which of the closures were appropriate and which were not. If some found the resisters' arguments and actions shortsighted, pathetic, or worse, it is precisely this divide—between various Catholic and American ways of imagining place, presence, authority, and community—that the shutdowns exposed for inquiry. And this divide existed not only between different parties in Boston, but also within resisters and their communities.

Those charged with the task of carrying out the shutdowns were likewise caught in these dilemmas. Regional bishops, the moderator of the curia, and the archbishop were all the targets of unstinting critique from resisters. These officials' expressions of distaste for the process and their sympathy for ousted Catholics were met with deep skepticism, their assurances of their good intentions often rejected out of hand. Their experience of such hard feelings was perhaps unavoidable, given their administrative role, but the prospect of consolidating an institution they themselves ultimately wanted to see grow certainly would have added its own kind of pain to the experience. Pastors (and the priests who helped them run parishes) were also charged with a difficult task. Pastors in particular were in the unenviable position of having to mediate between parishioners, whom they were often inclined to protect, and their bishops, who made decisions about priests' employment in the archdiocese and to whom they owed their obedience as well. Pastors had been charged with the preservation of these parishes for many years, and it must have been difficult when their efforts were erased by the closure decree. Their superiors urged them not to take closure as a referendum on their work, but the successes and failures of this reality among priests remain to be seen.[49]

Likewise, Catholics who did not resist the closure of their parishes faced challenges, although in this case, at least on the face of it, they came down on one side of the issue rather than the one I focus on here. In many cases, the efforts to integrate parishioners into new parishes went smoothly; in others, the relationship between parishes hardened and the new parishes suffered division.[50] Initial observations suggest that most of the active parishioners from closed parishes went with the program and joined the receiving parish. Although priests, bishops, and lay Catholics who were accommodating of change appear in the story, I direct attention mostly toward lay Catholics who took over their parishes. Other studies, of Catholics in merged parishes, of pastors, or of administrators involved in the shutdowns, can determine how resisters' stories relate to the experiences of these others. The fact that some people moved back and forth across boundaries between "resisting" and "compliant," and the fact that resisters themselves were not wholly comfortable with either of these categories, suggest that these terms may not provide the most pertinent or appropriate, or at least should not be the only, categories of analysis.

Methods: Occupiers and Their Histories

Fieldwork in resisting parishes constitutes the foundation of this project. The occupations were more than a convenient and congenial way to gain access to Catholics; they were rich religious and social environments. Occupied churches gave me, among other things, the chance to get to know Catholics who were, as a group, in church literally all the time. People talked with one another and with me at all hours of the day and often deep into the night. Fueled by the thrills of rebellion (and by copious coffee and sweets), they reflected on their parishes, their own histories as these connected with the churches', and on archdiocesan leadership. They considered the broader meaning of the shutdowns. As Catholics made themselves at home in their churches, the places acquired an air of experimentation, anxiety, and novelty of religious life in a familiar yet changed (and changing) locale. They became attractive not only to those who took part in them, but to me as a researcher.

Since I lived in the archdiocese, I had no obvious budget or time constraints for the research. I was relatively local, which enabled my research to stretch across three and a half years. Over this time, I combined fieldwork with teaching, archival research, and other daily responsibilities. I spent the majority of my time in the field at the parishes of Our Lady of Mount Carmel and St. Albert the Great. I got to know dozens of resisters. I visited their communion services, prayer services, business meetings, and social gatherings, and spent time talking with people on vigil "shifts" during the day and evening and occasionally overnight. At Mount Carmel, I began signing up for vigil shifts alongside parishioners as a way to get to know individuals and experience the flow of the occupied church. This also had the benefit of alerting the community that I would be at the church during a certain time.

Eventually, the few parishioners who bore the burden of covering vigil hours at Mount Carmel grew weary and shifts became thinner, with usually only one person in the church during a shift. For a time, I agreed to take over a shift on my own, in the hopes that I wouldn't actually be alone the whole time, but would have the chance to speak with people as they came and went. At the least, I would be able to talk with the occupier I replaced and the one that would replace me at the end of my shift. Often I selected the shift that led into the evening rosary, so I was guaranteed that at least a few resisters would show up for that time of prayer and conversation afterward.

To the extent that I was an occupier myself, I gained a sense of the thrills and anxieties (and also the routine chores) of being temporarily in control of a large and contested religious place. I did not take up this level of engagement and responsibility without some concerns. My ambiguous status as a participant-observer when I was one among a group in an occupied parish became even murkier when I was the only one in a church. This confusion revealed itself when on occasion a stranger arrived at the church doors. With what authority or integrity could I explain the occupation or monitor (as I had seen others do) the visitors' behavior in the church? As I fumbled my way through these encounters, or worried about what I would do in an emergency, or sat in boredom hoping someone whom I could "research" would arrive, I wondered whether I had made the right choice in agreeing to occupy the church alone.

On reflection, it seemed possible that the anxiety I experienced in potentially "breaking the rules" of ethnography by occupying Mount Carmel alone paralleled the anxieties felt by those who had taken over their parishes. Just as the contemporary rules of fieldwork range from strict observation and interview models to methods that fashion the fieldworker as an activist, so too had the rules of practicing parish been shifting and ambiguous over the last decades.[51] Resisters' own uncertainties—about whether the takeover was right, or about how to manage the occupations and negotiations with the hierarchy—witnessed to the abiding salience of a plurality of rules for being a good Catholic. We were both caught up in disciplines in flux. Perhaps this realization, of the complexity of practice (whether religious or ethnographic) within a field of changing rules, made my time alone at Mount Carmel worth the risks it entailed.

In most of what follows, I will ask readers to move back and forth with me between two churches, in the present and the past. In the process, we will traverse geographic, class, and ethnic divides. Mount Carmel is urban, ethnic, and older; St. Albert's is suburban, newer, and more American in ethos. I also visited Sacred Heart Parish, an Italian parish in Boston's North End, and spoke with resisters there. In particular, Sacred Heart's story helps give shape to the early history of Boston Catholicism; telling the story of resisters there also demands frequent oscillation between past and present. I also spent time among a group planning for resistance at the parish of St. Catherine of Siena in Charlestown and with occupiers at St. Jeremiah in suburban Framingham. I observed the rallies of a group organizing to protect a former Catholic school building in Brighton and sat in on meetings of the Council of Parishes, as its members discussed strategy and reported to one another on the status of the various vigils. This range opened possibilities for comparison and for thinking about the influence of Boston's twentieth-century urban and social history on Catholic life and practice.

I recorded conversations with over fifty resisters, pastors, and other Catholics surrounding the vigiling communities.[52] I also took notes both during and after my hours in parishes, or at meetings and events. Over time, I became a familiar presence in resisting communities in Boston, particularly at Mount Carmel and St. Albert the Great. Very soon, I could show up unannounced at these communities and join conversations, help with projects in the churches, or observe rites without noticeably disrupting the flow of events. I developed close relationships with a few individuals in each of these communities. These connections in particular enabled sustained dialogue between us about what was going on in these strange places. The resisting communities had access to my arguments both through ongoing informal conversations, a formal oral presentation in one case, and through my distribution of various drafts of my written work on the topic. These conversations shaped the final product, but it must be said that resisters will not agree with everything I write here about them. But despite appearances, this book is not the end of a conversation, but the opening of one.

Particularly at Mount Carmel (but also at St. Albert's and elsewhere), I found it was natural for me to chip in on cleaning and repair tasks around the church. This brought me close to Catholics' actual handling of the sacred and mundane objects and locales they were protecting and also helped bring me deeper into the flow of community life. My willingness to offer occasional help also gave me something to do, and in the process helped move the research beyond the recording of formal narratives and into documentation of the unusual phenomena of living in a church. Vigilers occasionally joked with me about my note-taking, and sometimes checked to make sure that I "got that down." I documented resisters' less-proud moments as well. In addition to their considered reflections and personal narratives, I sought to understand Catholics' frustrations and anger (not only toward the church, but also toward one another, toward the social world they lived in, and toward those who had left the parish), their management of their image under scrutiny, and their moments of absorption, boredom, and playfulness.

I could and almost always did return home at night. While there are benefits of completely abandoning home for a field site, recent reevaluations of the politics of fieldwork have opened space for a variety of ethnographic approaches. In particular, the idea of a single, cohesive, and unchanging field in which a scholar can (and must) be fully immersed has found critics who view such notions as too limiting of the variety and complexity of the lives of those we seek to understand.[53] The "locals" are not and never have been as fixed as field-workers have sometimes made them appear. While I made considerable efforts toward immersion in the resisting communities, I also found that the Catholics I got to know were not limited to a particular field wholly distinct from my own lifeworld. They were constantly seeking out ways to engage the world around them, making use of a variety of political, legal, and social networks and inventing new networks of their own. One of the initial contacts I made, for example, hoped that I could arrange a forum at Harvard on the shutdowns. Others referred me to canon and civil lawyers, politicians, and fellow scholars within the resistance across Boston with whom I could discuss the research. Both the resisters and I were encountering Boston's political, social, and religious landscapes anew. Such conditions warranted a somewhat looser notion of what constitutes a field.[54] Observing and interacting with Catholics in several churches (and collaborative organizations like the Council of Parishes) rather than just one opened up important similarities and differences across Boston's various social landscapes that would otherwise have been obscured.

There were other advantages to this kind of work. The extent of my time with Boston Catholics was one benefit of doing fieldwork in Boston. I was able to see, for example, how the thrills of occupying a church and standing in opposition to the church hierarchy lessened or flowed in cycles over time. As some people abandoned the effort, others petitioned the remaining supporters for greater commitment and help. I became aware of the strain that the occupations placed on Catholics, and I witnessed communities fighting, dividing, and uneasily reconciling.

Furthermore, as conditions outside of the occupations changed, the meanings and goals of the occupations shifted in response. As resisters' lawsuits made their way—mostly unsuccessfully—through the Massachusetts and Vatican court systems I observed how Catholics adapted their thinking and reoriented their approach. My extended time in the field also coincided with changes in the leadership of the church. Pope John Paul II died and was replaced by Cardinal Joseph Ratzinger, Benedict XVI. Archbishop O'Malley was promoted to the cardinalate. The archdiocese gained a new second-in-command when Father Richard Erikson replaced Bishop Richard Lennon as Vicar General and Moderator of the Curia in 2006. There were more immediate changes too. Supporters or participants in the vigils died, became ill, lost their jobs, or encountered other life challenges. After a two-year period during which fieldwork occupied most of my time, I began spending more time writing. The ability to continue to visit these communities after this initial, more intensive period of fieldwork helped prevent static portrayals of these Catholics and their resistance.

The research also entailed an historical component. The cues for the kinds of historical sources I sought out came from my fieldwork in the resisting communities. I sought the historical grounds for what I was learning of resisters' Catholicism in their parishes' pasts. Throughout Boston Catholic history, parishes have been the crucial center of clerical attention and parishioner practice. There were other sites of Catholic worship and practice—shrines, monasteries, convents, schools, chapels—but parishes were the mainstay of Catholic life (and sometimes included these other spaces too, such as the school and convent at Mount Carmel). Parishes warranted special attention from nearly every corner of the church. The stakes of the closings could not have been much higher. By all accounts the church's health depended on the survival of its parishes, its status and place on their grandeur. What it meant to be a good parishioner had been a topic of great concern for lay and clerical Catholics for decades. It was in the parish that most priests' training was tested. It was in the parish that lay Catholics received much in the way of instruction, guidance, and opportunity to be good Catholics.[55]

As Mount Carmel's Susana described it, a parish is "practiced" by its parishioners.[56] Bulletins, parish correspondence with the chancery, parish censuses, sacramental records, and special event program books offered a glimpse of the concerns and needs that occupied pastors and people at St. Albert's and Mount Carmel over the years before the shutdowns. These documents unearth the rules of "practicing parish" as they were communicated through pastoral language, modes and mechanisms of giving, memorials, family choices, rites and liturgies, and parishioners' own initiative in the face of conflicts and tests to their parishes. But since most of the written material that exists in parish archives is best suited to understanding parish finances, and since parishes are not only distinct from but are deeply embedded in the broader social world, getting a sense of the full spectrum of the shifting rules of parish practice required going beyond these immediate local sources. Broader diocesan history and changes in Boston's urban and suburban landscapes influenced Catholics' orientations to their parishes.

The Second Vatican Council

Other sources for exploring the rules of parish practice emerged as well. The most important among these were documents related to the transitions in the church connected to the Second Ecumenical Council of the Vatican.[57] The more I got to know the situation in Boston, the more I realized that resisters' struggles, pain, hope, and excitement could not be comprehended outside of an appreciation for the history of the Council and its legacy. I want to offer an entry point into that history here, and in the process begin to show the place, in the broad sweep of American Catholic history, of the resistance to shutdowns in Boston. Along with preparatory meetings and other partial intervening sessions, the Council consisted of four several-weeklong gatherings of the world's bishops in Rome from 1962–1965.

Practically speaking, the end product of these meetings was a set of sixteen major documents (called, in order of authoritativeness, "Constitutions," "Decrees," and "Declarations") on various issues about church definition, structure, liturgy, and mission and about the church's relationship to the rest of the world. Official documents explicitly created to interpret, clarify, and implement the Council's recommendations are considered "postconciliar." In some cases these postconciliar documents, because they are more concerned with the application of new rules, were more important than the conciliar documents themselves. Taken together, the texts precipitated changes in the ways Catholics worshiped and prayed, and suggested new ways for Catholics to talk and think about themselves, about the church, and about the world.

Catholics continue to debate the implications and significance of these documents and the postconciliar documents produced in the late 1960s and 1970s to clarify and assist in the implementation of their messages. On one side of the debate stand those who contend that the documents of the Second Vatican Council should be read in light of their "continuity" with older documents and traditions in the church.[58] Thinkers on the other side suggest that the event needs to be embraced as a moment of genuine transformation, if not in the specific content of dogma, at least in the tone or approach of the church to the challenges and opportunities of the contemporary world.[59] For both parties, everything that has happened in the church since the Council is necessarily read for what it might say about the direction ("positive," "negative," "revolution," "reform," "renewal," "continuity," "fracture") established for the church by the Council.

Understanding the process entailed in constructing the conciliar documents helps explain the ongoing debate and confusion. In short, the documents, for whatever else they achieved and symbolized, are also records of contention inside the mid-twentieth-century church. Angelo Roncalli (Pope John XXIII) had surprised Catholics in 1959 when he announced the Council only a few months after he had been elected to the papacy. Most observers and Vatican insiders expected John XXIII to be a passive "interim" pope, who because of his relative old age, his lack of theological expertise, and his rustic upbringing would remain content to serve as a bridge to a longer-term pope rather than assert himself as a catalyst of change in the church. Conservative insiders among the Roman Curia saw great risks in such a major undertaking, and immediately began planning to establish a relatively modest agenda, aiming mainly toward the reiteration of the last council, an abbreviated (1869–1870) gathering referred to as the First Vatican Council, or Vatican I.[60]

This previous gathering is primarily remembered for making official the principle of papal infallibility: when commenting officially on matters of faith, Roman Catholic popes speak without error. Papal infallibility offered a direct and prickly retort to those nineteenth-century critics who accused the church of being too authoritarian, dogmatic, and insular, characteristics which ran precisely counter to the emerging "modern" principles of representative governance, scientific method, the separation of church and state, and the philosophical and religious embrace of individual experience. Pushed to its extreme, papal infallibility suggested that the pope functioned wholly apart from the rest of the hierarchy, as a sort of supreme dictator whose statements overrode all contrary evidence, regardless of its source. While this interpretation sometimes prevailed both inside and outside the church, the main purpose of the infallibility statement was to shore up confidence in the church as the final and divine arbiter of truth.[61] In this way, then, the First Vatican Council was of a piece with the explicit critiques of modern theology, science, history, philosophy, and economics that emerged in documents like Pope Pius IX's "Syllabus of Errors" (1864). After Vatican I, these critiques would be reiterated and extended in debates about "Americanism" in the 1890s, in documents such as Pius X's own list of modern errors (*"Lamentabili Sane,"* 1907), the encyclical *"Pascendi Dominici Gregis"* (1907) concerning the mistakes of modernism, and the "Oath against Modernism" (1910) to be sworn by all clergy, seminary professors, and religious superiors.

Many inside the church saw little need in the late 1950s and early 1960s to let up in the church's battle against modernism. After all, hadn't the modern secular promise of "progress" proved as unreliable as these previous church condemnations had warned? By the time John XXIII called for the council, Communism appeared to be stronger than ever. The Second World War had made it clear that the promises of modernity were gravely inadequate to meet the challenges of fascism and Nazism.[62] The world's postwar democracies, while laudable in their resistance to Communism, could not be relied upon to prevent a new, nuclear holocaust. Catholic critics also looked carefully at capitalism, which, while not condemned in most Catholic circles, continued in its extremes to be seen as a force for selfish acquisitiveness and individualistic competition. Theologically, these traditionalists saw a growing vogue for relativism, therapeutic self-improvement, and pragmatism masquerading as morality. As important, this group, made up mostly of Vatican insiders carrying over from the long papacy of Pius XII, envisioned their hold on power in the church slipping away into the hands of an unpredictable mass of diverse bishops who would come to Rome clamoring for a fundamental shift toward more decentralized, collegial decision-making.[63]

But in 1959, John XXIII famously opened the Council in Rome with a statement declaring it time for the church to use the "medicine of mercy rather than that of severity" to engage the modern world. He announced the opening of the Council with the suggestion of a need for a new spirit of collaboration and partnership with the societies outside of ecclesiastical borders. This was a radical shift from the church's previous posture and self-understanding. With this opening, the pope moved official conversations in the direction of a minority of theologians whose labors in the 1920s, 1930s, and 1940s had been directly critiqued in Pius XII's encyclical *Humani Generis*, as "false opinions threatening to undermine the foundations of Catholic doctrine."[64] These Catholic intellectuals, particularly in the lead-up to the Second World War and the Shoah, had called the church to engage both the modern world's promises and pathos in terms other than simple condemnation or embarrassed silence. (Consider, for example, Jesuit theologian Henri de Lubac's vivid description of the church's condition in 1942: the church, he said, was obsessed with identifying the heresies of modernity, on the one hand, while on the other it exiled the faith to the obscure technical theology of experts, where it was left to die.)[65]

When Pope John XXIII joined theologians like de Lubac to reorient the church's relationship to the modern world, they produced a set of documents that contained astonishing theological innovations for the church. Among the most significant challenges to previous church teaching were the claim that the church rejects "nothing that is true and holy" in other religions of the world, and the assertion that "the human person has a right to religious freedom."[66] These conclusions were hard-won, and hotly debated at the Council in part because of the thorny questions they implied: if the church is to endorse the rights of conscience and religious tolerance, what happens to its claim to provide unique access to salvation? Does opening the way to a robust form of tolerance lead to the conclusion that the church is no more than an equal player in the realms of culture, society, and politics? If the church is to stand behind the freedom of conscience for non-Catholics, can it deny that same freedom to Catholics? Can a resolutely hierarchical church give meaningful support to a representative system of governance?

The most basic questions, however, had to do with history and tradition and in particular with the limits and possibilities of "development" in the church. To what extent could core matters of church teaching and practice change? If change was indeed possible on some level, how should Catholics talk about it and explain the relationship of old to new? And finally, who has the power to implement change or control behavior in the church?[67]

Since much of what happened in Boston in 2004 was related to the ways Catholics related, physically and emotionally, to Catholic places and the rites and sacraments they housed, it is important also to attend for a moment to the Council as a circuit for change in the liturgy. The basic questions about "development" also animated debates that would come to the surface in the Council about the transformation of liturgy. Here too there was a longer history that informed what was happening at the Council. Advocates of the renewal of Catholic ritual, dating as far back as the 1830s in France and the 1860s in Germany, had been advocating heightened attentiveness to the proper performance of the liturgy as the center of Catholic worship and as the source of both transcendent mystery and this-worldly power. For these liturgists, advancing people's appreciation for and understanding of this mystery and power required making changes in the way the mass was experienced, and in some cases the way it was performed. This involved careful study of Catholic tradition, the mining of resources from medieval, patristic, and biblical periods in search of elements that could enliven Catholic ritual without deviating from officially approved forms. This confidence in the past among liturgical reformers paralleled and sometimes actively drew from the emerging confidence in the nineteenth century on historical methods. As biblical scholars were showing in their historical-critical rereadings of the Hebrew Bible and New Testament, what was "handed down" might not necessarily be the same as what was "original" or "pure"; for liturgists interested in faithful renewal of the church's life of prayer, disciplined historical research could remedy the problem.

The efforts of this interconnected group of scholars, monks, and priests from various European countries, and, after the 1920s, the United States, are referred to as the "liturgical movement." The movement continues to this day, with the greatest concentration of energy in this country still radiating from its historic U.S. center, the Benedictine seminary at St. John's in Collegeville, Minnesota. At various points, and always with origins and fidelity to a particular past in mind, participants in this movement called for the restoration of Gregorian Chant, the shifting of the Holy Week calendar, the streamlining of certain rites, the advancement of liturgies such as the dialog mass (people respond to the celebrant's prayers), the reduction of popular devotions such as feast days and private, mid-mass recitation of the rosary, the "turning around" of the Catholic altar to face the congregation, and, particularly in the United States, the use of the vernacular in the mass, and the general encouragement of lay involvement both as comprehending participants and, later, as active performers of certain parts of the mass. Another fixation in the U.S. branch of the movement was related to its rise during the economic struggles of the Great Depression. Leaders of the movement in this country insisted on a connection between the performance of the mass and the social world. Properly understood, mass could instruct and spiritually empower Catholics toward solidarity and selflessness in social and economic relations.

These changes had been tolerated in pockets, and some changes even officially endorsed in the years leading up to the Second Vatican Council.[68] Advocates eagerly sought Roman support for changes that were often considered controversial because they upended accepted patterns of prayer and worship. Virgil Michel, O.S.B. the American leader of this movement from the late 1920s until his early death in 1938, routinely cited Pius X's 1903 *motu propio* on sacred music, *Tra le Solecitudini*: "Active participation in the sacred mysteries and the public and solemn prayer of the Church is the primary and indispensable source of the Christian spirit." Michel also pointed to Pius' admonition toward frequent communion in order to convince scrupulous Catholics of the orthodoxy of this relatively rare practice. Another favorite citation of American reformers was Pius XI's 1925 encyclical, *Quas Primas*, where liturgy is identified as the source of social regeneration. The concept of the church as the "Mystical Body of Christ," to which these liturgists were profoundly and controversially devoted, received papal endorsement in 1947, in Pius XII's encyclical *Mystici Corporis*. *Mediator Dei,* Pius XII's 1947 encyclical on the sacred liturgy along with the 1955 restoration of the Easter Triduum marked two high points in the history of the movement.

But certain aspects of the movement faced hostility. The potential for the social focus of American reformers to lead toward a kind of mystical Catholic socialism along the lines of Dorothy Day and Peter Maurin's Catholic Worker Movement posed a threat to Catholic bishops with a more moderate approach to the problems of modern liberal capitalism. Other mid-twentieth-century conservatives in the church resisted the idea of celebrating all or parts of the liturgy in the vernacular. They saw this as a threat to tradition and a disruption of the unity, dignity, and solemnity of the mass. Beneath these concerns were worries about blurring the distinctions between lay and clerical members of the church.[69]

In calling for the Second Vatican Council, John XXIII echoed those yearning for change in the church. Drawing from liturgists and theologians who had been largely at the church's margins, John's solution was two-pronged—on one hand, what the church and world needed was for the church to go through a process of *aggiornamento* or "bringing herself up to date where required." Previous councils were not perfect or complete, even if the deposit of faith and the fundamental dogmas of the church remained steady. The title the pope had chosen for the current council implied as much.[70] The world had changed, and the church needed to make every effort to make sure it could communicate its truths to meet the needs of contemporary humankind. Indeed, in the spirit of the social encyclicals *Rerum Novarum* (1891) and *Quadragesimo Anno* (1931) (both of which Angelo Roncalli, before he became pope, had studied and considered deeply), the church could use its wisdom to mold and transform, rather than merely contest and condemn, the contemporary age. As such, the church asserted its ability to communicate not only to Catholics, but to all humans' experience of modern conditions. The pope's two major encyclicals *Mater e Magistra* ("Mother and Teacher," 1961) and *Pacem in Terris* ("Peace on Earth," 1963) take a similarly constructive and social-justice-oriented approach.[71]

But *aggiornamento* could not stand alone without suggesting the church's succumbing to faddishness or relativism. The French term *ressourcement,* or "return to the sources," directed attention to practices and concepts of the distant past that could be recovered and restored in the contemporary church. Instead of abandoning tradition, then, change would entail the discovery and application of a more genuine version of tradition. Reformers like de Lubac and Michel had turned to the patristic period and to the imagined ethos of Jesus and the primitive church to find this purer past toward which the church could now turn as a source of renewal. In affirming, in his statement formally opening the council on October 11, 1962, that history is the "teacher of life," Pope John XXIII chided those in the church who would look skeptically upon the possibility of discriminating useful from less useful Catholic pasts. *Ressourcement* had been moved definitively from the margin to the center of power in the church.

So while they never conceded power entirely, the Roman Curia and their small group of allies of the early 1960s were forced to contend with this powerful rationale for change. Also aligned against them were a large, if shifting, proportion of the world's bishops, who soon made it clear that they were eager to work under the sign of the pope's openness to change (as *aggiornamento* and *ressourcement*) rather than succumb to the cautious worriers the pope had called the "prophets of doom" inside the church.[72]

But if *aggiornamento* and *ressourcement* were suggestive and inspiring, they were also vague and imprecise. In part, this openness was an asset for those seeking change; instead of condemnations and the explication of precise, legalistic policies, the Council operated more freely, producing documents with broadly metaphorical language and passionate pastoral challenges and consolations.[73] But such language was also a sign of compromise, leaving questions of implementation and specific changes for future discussions. The double-sided language of the Council's first major document, *Sacrosanctum Concilium* ("The Constitution on the Sacred Liturgy," 1963), signaled the church leaders' dilemma: they hoped, they wrote, that "sound tradition may be retained, and yet the way be open for legitimate progress." This dual aspiration, along with contentious divisions among players at the Council, resulted in documents that contain "both 'traditionalist' and 'progressive' statements side by side," with no effort to "resolve the contradictions." The result has been "profound ambiguity" and "different interpretations."[74]

A confluence of social changes in the 1960s and 1970s further complicate the question of the meanings of the Council's documents in the United States. The possibilities for interpreting the documents as continuous with tradition or as somehow breaking from it took shape inside of, not apart from the social tumult of the period. In the United States, Catholics' rising social status, their educational accomplishments and their gradual post–World War II move into white-collar jobs and suburban neighborhoods impacted the way the Council made sense in their parishes and in the archdiocese. A well-educated, higher-income population of Catholics, many of whom had at least partially cut ties with their ethnic roots and taken up a more "American" ethos, might hear conciliar discourses on "the freedom of conscience" and the "common priesthood of the faithful" with a different ear than would denizens of a more embattled or separatist subcultural community.

The Civil Rights Movement and Black Power, especially as these related to questions of equal housing and access to education for African Americans in Boston, also transformed Catholics' experience of the city and the parishes that had once defined their neighborhoods. With these new pressures, the teachings of the conciliar and postconciliar documents about authority and place took on distinct shades. The rise of second-wave feminism, stimulated in part by the publication of Betty Friedan's *The Feminine Mystique* in 1963, also added new lenses through which to view Catholic teaching about authority, sexuality, the role of the laity, and the status of women religious. The battle with communism reached a heightened intensity during the Council's meetings. The discussion in the Council on the separation of church and state would be received differently in light of one's attitude toward the terrifying nuclear arms race and policy of "containment" related to the Soviet Union. Americans in the mid and late 1960s were also facing up to continued expansion of the Vietnam War, and in particular worried over the question of bombing industrial areas in North Vietnam, along with the specter of conscription and the possibilities of conscientious objection so central to protests of the war. Boston, with its many nationally prestigious colleges and universities, witnessed more than its share of protest and debate surrounding these issues. Here again, the Council's endorsement of "freedom of conscience" would have different meanings for people on various sides of these debates.

Present Lives of the Past

If the Council offered continuity amid change as a description of its accomplishment, others faced it as an ongoing puzzle to be solved. This book explores the ways that this broad dilemma has been felt among a relatively small group of Boston lay Catholics, past and present, who faced this puzzle in their lives as parishioners, workers, parents, children, citizens, siblings, and neighbors. This distinction does not imply that there are indelible lines differentiating average from "professional" Catholics and scholars: there are not. Catholics experienced these challenges in conversation with their pastors, Catholic school teachers, catechism instructors, mission priests, and with other experts and professionals in the church. But it does highlight the fact that these theological dilemmas have profound personal and social implications and are felt at the most intimate levels of experience. Often, it must be said, such problems can be considered with leisure and without obvious controversy or impact. In the case of the church shutdowns, formerly academic or merely private struggles suddenly had dramatic real world influence. This book, then, makes an effort to illustrate the connections among Catholics' "week-to-week" religion and the "vivid" experience of the shutdowns.[75]

Despite their ambiguities, the conciliar and postconciliar documents undeniably added new idioms to the range of possibilities for Catholic self-understanding. Some of the Catholics I got to know in Boston had read one or two of these documents and actively sought to align themselves with the messages they read in them. Even if they hadn't read the documents,

"Vatican II," as the Council is often called, had been a major part of their formation as parishioners. Key phrases from the Council—especially the affirmation of "conscience" found in *Gaudium et Spes* ("The Pastoral Constitution on the Church in the Modern World," 1965) and the notion of lay empowerment entailed in the assertion from *Lumen Gentium* ("The Dogmatic Constitution on the Church," 1964) that the church is "the people of God"—had been a part of parish conversations in Boston for several decades.[76] In most cases, parishes had started a parish council, a Vatican II innovation designed to involve lay parishioners in parish decision-making. These were only sporadically successful. But even in cases where pastors remained less consultative, lay people in most parishes were more involved in running day-to-day operations than in the decades before the Council. This is explained in large measure by the gradually diminishing number of priests and women religious (who were technically "lay" Catholics with vows) who would have done this work in previous years, but the thrust in the liturgical movement and in the Second Vatican Council toward a wider definition of "ministry" opened the way.[77]

The rewritten rules about parish practice embedded in these documents gave shape to everyday life in parishes in varying measure over time. Just as the conciliar documents could be ambiguous, open-ended, and self-contradictory, so too were the changes in parish life and Catholic self-understanding they facilitated. Despite well-documented radical shifts in Catholics' prayer lives, devotions, and confessional practice, the ways of being Catholic that these new rules were meant to replace did not vanish altogether.[78] For one thing, those among church leaders who had seen the Council as a "trauma" went directly to work to scale back the reforms and contain their practical implications.[79] In some cases in Boston, as in other locales across the United States, the implementation of the various reforms were fitful and chaotic.[80] Moreover, neighborhoods and buildings still mattered to Catholics, even if the bishops now called the church a "pilgrim."[81] Lay Catholics did not altogether give up on the embattled and separatist sensibilities of the early and mid-twentieth century, nor did the newly animated goals of social justice and ecumenism completely overpower the values of comfort, familiarity, and stability. And it was not the case that there were always lively and widespread complaints about this: these older ways succeeded and remained part of U.S. Catholicism in part because they felt right. It was a sign of the appeal, durability, and power of these older ways of imagining American Catholic life that they could even be articulated and cultivated by people whose earliest memories should have been "postconciliar" and suburban. And of course all of this was understandable given the church's complex and challenging ambition to combine continuity and change.

The unanswered questions from this time of transition opened the space for the resisters to parish shutdowns in Boston.[82] Divisions and confusions over the meanings of the changes in the church during the 1960s and 1970s (as the Council's practical recommendations were fitfully implemented) created the space for varying responses to church shutdowns. Resisters' creative or habitual play within the variety of rules of parish practice enabled them to sustain and justify the resistance as truly Catholic. Analyzing the occupiers' negotiation with and combination of these rules sharpens our understanding of contemporary Catholicism and its relationship to the Catholic past. This kind of analysis also opens up questions about the work of memory, the significance of religious places, and the meanings of modernity in the study of religion.

In their combinations of postures toward sacrifice and authority and in their endorsement of multiple ways of relating to sacred presence, Catholics were not deviating from sophisticated theology. Rather, they were living inside its tensions. This was true as well for those charged with the task of supporting the shutdowns. All would have to face the question of the meanings and power of multiple and sometimes opposed ways of being Catholic in the new circumstances in Boston. Both sides sought to control the high ground by making the conflict a matter of backward pre-Vatican II Catholicism versus modern and sober post–Vatican II Catholicism. They also competed over the Second Vatican Council's claim to have realigned the church with Jesus and the primitive Church. Obviously, they selected and vetted the past in their own ways.

This book explores those relevant pasts and analyzes Catholics' witting and unwitting engagements with them in their resistance to the shutdowns. As I hinted above, the following chapters are organized with the themes of sacrifice and sacred presence in mind. Two initial chapters take up these themes chronologically as they took shape and changed in the histories of parishes that would end up on the closure list in 2004. Stories from the present (from occupied parishes) in these chapters suggest the problematic character and ongoing significance of these histories for Boston Catholics. The final two chapters take a more synchronic approach. They enter into the experience of occupying a church and evaluate the power and meanings of Catholics' contested pasts in the resistance to church closures in Boston. This structure advances my argument that complications and confusions in the rules of practicing parish explain the resistance. Changes in church teaching and rites, along with shifts in the social and economic standing of Catholics, parishes, and the archdiocese, helped produce those who would defend their parishes. It is precisely the incompleteness of the changes that explains the resistance and links it to broader issues in Catholic and American religious history.

A word about the two broad themes guiding the discussion is warranted here. Sacrifice has been an issue of signature importance in U.S. Catholicism. In particular, it has been a key idiom through which Catholics faced parish life. Parishes have been embattled places for much of U.S. history. Calling on a seemingly endless set of narratives of sacrifice in the tradition, twentieth-century U.S. pastors and other leaders made it clear that parishioners had to emulate Christ's self-giving if the parish was to survive. Pastors were desperate, because they were often overwhelmed, that parishioners were to suffer willingly—sacrificing particularly of their time and money—for the defense of the parish. It was not just a place where people gathered for worship, but was "the Church in miniature," "a family," an outpost of hope against secularism, immorality, anti-Catholicism, and other threats in the wider culture—for U.S. Catholics, the parish was the beating heart of the tradition.

Chapter One begins with Archbishop O'Malley's 2004 call for Boston Catholics to emulate their ancestors' selflessness by giving up their parishes. Catholics in resisting parishes did turn to the past amid the shutdowns, but what they found was more complex than the archbishop averred. They found histories that affirmed local autonomy and distance from the hierarchy. The idea of the archdiocese as a united whole crumbled under the weight of these histories of division. But there were also stories that tied Catholics to a broader moral world, a powerful endorsement of the local parish as the site of universal Catholic glory and grandeur. Church buildings themselves played a part in the construction of this shared moral world of Catholic abundance. Churches became unique and inviolable sites on the landscape through elaborate rituals and through the postures of reverence and expectation enjoined upon those who frequented them. Narratives of abundance gained power and resonance in part because they seemed to confirm Catholics' difference and separation from the social diffusion, individualism, and personal isolation Catholics have long diagnosed as unique American ills.

Resisters' desires to keep their churches open witnessed to the power of this way of imagining Catholicism in relation to "America."

Chapter 2 addresses the challenges resisters faced in drawing on the more recent past in their defense of their parishes and in their efforts to define themselves as Catholics. Momentous changes in the church and in U.S. society during the latter half of the twentieth century, and competing notions about what those changes meant, energized and complicated Catholics' efforts of resistance, which often became projects of memory. A context of increasing need helped keep sacrifice at the center of Catholic parish life, in both urban and suburban locales, throughout this period. But the ways sacrifice for the parish was explained and explored by Catholics changed during the twentieth century. The emphasis in the post–Vatican II church on the idea that the church is "the people of God" took on a life of its own in parishes. The idea had various and complex meanings inside the conciliar documents, especially *Lumen Gentium* and the "Decree on the Apostolate of Lay People" (1965). These meanings resonated powerfully in parish life, but in a variety of ways. It was simultaneously a powerful tool to encourage parishioner giving and a promise of greater lay control of the church. But as those in threatened parishes would find out, it also suggested a new universalism. In the rationale for the shutdowns, the idea of the church as the people of God identified a universal people, not a local congregation. Despite what might have been said over the years as leaders sought to engage parishioners, the motif, it now appeared, never referred to those in the pews. It had always meant the entire Christian community, extending across place, time, and even the barrier of death. Local sacrifices were simply added to those in the storehouse of the communion of saints, they had no particular value or meaning *as* local sacrifices. Accordingly, advocates of the shutdowns could argue that sacrifice for the church meant the opposite of what it had seemed to mean up to the eve of the shutdowns: giving up the parish, not protecting it for the good of the church. The shutdowns animated these competing ways of thinking about "the church" and brought broader struggles over the meanings of modern Catholicism into sharp relief.

Late-twentieth-century upheaval in Boston also changed what it meant to be a Catholic. As the lived environment changed around them and as many of their family members and friends left for the suburbs, urban Catholics gained new narratives of sacrifice related to survival in a changing city. Urban Catholics in particular had heard the call to sacrifice for the benefit of the greater good before, since this had long been the rationale for projects of "modernization" coming from city officials and urban planners. When these projects seemed only to benefit the economically elite while diminishing the local quality of life, these city Catholics developed deep suspicions about officials' calls for transcending the local. When the shutdowns showed that the church could not be counted as an ally in defending their neighborhoods against upheaval, resisters saw disconcerting connections between the church and other forces of corporatization and bureaucratization.[83]

But Catholics were not wholly hostile to change. Their time-honored separation and otherness proved unstable, especially as Euro-American Catholics across the twentieth century became successful navigators of, and, eventually, captains on America's educational, political, and economic seas. As their status and position improved by the measurements of education and income, the uncertainty of Catholics' ability to sustain the idioms of otherness became more evident. Alongside the otherness cultivated through the idea of a Catholic subculture ran a powerful current linking them to America. This was manifest in the extent to which Catholics affirmed that there was no significant difference between their own beliefs, aspirations, and social posture and those of non-Catholics.[84] This Americanized Catholic posture had become more convincing after the Second World War, when Catholics proved they were eager not only to 'go with the flow' in terms of suburbanization, public and higher education, and Cold War militarism, and also willing to lead the charge in articulating a patriotic hyphenated (Judeo-Christian) American religiosity.[85]

Resisters found many ways to channel a powerful current of American identity against the shutdown plan. They repeatedly highlighted the connections between the Boston hierarchy and "Rome," essentially turning the chancery into a foreign country and local officials into Vatican stooges. Their turn to the American civil courts and local politicians also suggested that the conflict about shuttered churches hinged on a contrast between American and "foreign" values. The same was true of their efforts to school the archdiocese on matters related to the local real estate market and business management. If you're going to run the archdiocese like a business (shutdowns as downsizing), why not allow actual business experts—the laity themselves, or perhaps a professional consulting firm—manage the effort? But resisters' experience with and embrace of Catholic separatism made these propositions delicate and ambivalent. They could not, of course, wholly embrace a religion of legal or bureaucratic proceduralism or market efficiency, and they could not give up on Catholic transcendence of national borders. Just as resisters played and struggled across the divide in Catholic history and memory between older and newer ways of talking about sacrifice and presence, their occupations need to be understood in light of this longstanding puzzle of U.S. Catholics' troubled relationship to the nation.

The postwar period also presented Catholics with puzzles related to new rules about the meaning and power of the objects and locales of Catholic life. The reform of liturgy in the Second Vatican Council was the decisive step in a larger project of recalibrating Catholics' interactions with the material objects and ritual forms of their tradition. Reformation of the rite of church dedication, and new instructions about how to construct churches, invested *people,* not the buildings and things themselves, with holiness. Behind this change was the assumption that Catholics entertained an overly instrumental version of their faith. Instead of unique sites for contact with efficacious sacred presence, churches, the revisions emphasized, were simply the "house of the church." This shift was not only negative. It validated the idea that churches are made not out of actual consecrated stones, but out of "living stones"—the people, whose presence as community manifested God's presence. This change both drew on and diverged from the liturgical movement, which had its origins in Europe but took off in this country after the late 1920s. These reformers, whose efforts were largely, if gradually, embraced both by the U.S. church and by the Vatican, had retained a robust appreciation for churches as unique sites of sacred presence while also calling for lay people to appreciate the lively action of the holy spirit in them during worship, and while highlighting the connection of the life of worship to life in the world.

As these changes illustrated, sacred presence is a contested category of religious practice.[86] Like the parish, presence does not just exist: it is practiced by people who are informed by rules, disciplines, and experiments that change and compete over time and in particular contexts. The various histories of presence to which resisters were witnesses and participants signal different "strategies" for cultivating certain dispositions for being in church. Indirectly, and through repetition of their forms, the rites I analyze here sought to produce two different kinds of "ritualized body."[87] This divided history of the meaning and power of church buildings gave resisters multiple and sometimes contradictory vehicles for the expression of their love for the places and things they were protecting.

As I show in chapter three, the Catholics in resisting parishes had inherited a variety of competing orientations to presence and place. Ideas about churches that circulated in their early years were not really ever abandoned; they remained part of practicing the parish. A range of approaches to Catholic material culture and ritual were alive, not only in vigilers' living memory, but also in the ways pastors and bishops talked about churches, and their rites and special locales. The tendency, among supporters of the shutdowns, to refer antiseptically to closing churches as "buildings" captured one aspect of this division. Juxtaposed with a memo I saw in several resisting parishes entitled "How Can You Evict God from God's House?," this rhetoric suggests the discrepant orientations to sacred presence circulating in Boston. Resisters were not ignorant of the liability of appearing to be attached to special objects, places, people, or communities, but they also appreciated the comfort and solemnity that came from the long traditions treating these things as inviolable. Understanding the character and history of this braiding undermines teleological approaches to the question of Americanization, modernity, and sacred presence.

Chapter four explores the ways the combination and conflict of modes of thinking about sacrifice and authority in the church played out among the resisters. What I found was that occupiers cobbled together an uneasy mix of Catholic ways of thinking about sacrifice and authority as they took over their churches. The resisters represented an uncomfortable third way between those in the parish who had left the church altogether and those who had moved on as the diocese instructed. They were not ready to wash their hands of the church but also hostile to any whiff of obedience that might be read as retrograde lay Catholic passivity. They faced a complex but not uncommon challenge: resist, but do not separate. Their very position as vigilers exemplified this. They were fighting—in some cases giving years of their lives to the struggle—essentially to regain their place in the church. The divided histories of sacrifice and authority, combined with the complex relationship of Catholics to "America" and to Boston, guided this mix. As parishioners they were possessed by the church as much as they possessed it. Understanding the delicacy of these moves of belonging opens a window onto why and how so many of those who feel torn in the tradition remain within it. It also offers a chance to reconsider American Catholic modernity as something other, or perhaps simply more, than a lay-led march toward greater freedom and more democratic church management. A fifth chapter addresses these latter issues, situating the resisters' experiments inside broader conversations about U.S. Catholicism and the study of religion.

As these chapters illustrate, the title of this book, *No Closure*, refers to more than Boston Catholics' efforts to prevent the shutdown of their parishes. It is also meant to entail and transcend the resisters' implicit rejection of the psychological model of mourning prescribed by their leadership for handling loss. The title does not seek to imply that pursuing emotional closure in the wake of loss is somehow unsophisticated or merely obedient. It does suggest that finding peace in religious upheaval may be more difficult than some in Boston presumed. It is a self-serving title, in some ways, in that it affirms the historian's efforts. If one can show that the book on the past has not been closed, then there will always be a need for clarifying and explaining that past to others. But the need to identify the origins of occupiers' complicated versions of Catholic practice only became pressing in light of their own pursuit of clarity on the question of the relationship of the church (and themselves) to its past. Simply being in churches—in the haunting presence of their memorials and their evocations of sacramental experience—directed attention backward.

But there were competing versions of the tradition. The struggle over church closures was also a struggle over the American Catholic past. In this competition resisters situated themselves at the edges of the legitimating authority of the church. This position at the margins gave them the freedom to draw upon multiple ways of practicing parish and multiple ways of being American and Catholic. But it also meant that they could not simply rest in the knowledge that they were "begotten" of tradition; they had to will a history for themselves.[88] The occupations themselves did some of this work. In tying themselves to their churches, the resisters literally controlled a crucial link to the Catholic past. If churches' power as the key to Catholic truth had diminished in the social and theological upheavals of the 1960s and 1970s, the notion of a specific group of people as "living stones" could just as easily be put to use in defense of the parish. Resisters, however, did not have to choose between these divergent ways of talking about a church. They did not have to choose between conflicting ways of talking about sacrifice, or different orientations to sacred presence, or citizenship. Instead, they could and did combine these. These combinations were not only strategies in the resistance, but also manifestation of U.S. Catholics' ongoing struggle with unanswered questions from the Catholic past.

1

The Pasts Living in People

The Church of Boston has a great history forged in persecution and sacrifice. We will have a great future if we do not flee from the cross. Reach out to one another in prayerful support. Let our love for our faith help us overcome our pain and help us focus on our mission.

—Most Reverend Seán P. O'Malley, O.F.M. Cap., "Remarks of Archbishop Seán O'Malley on Parish Reconfiguration," May 25, 2004.

In our country today, so much about history has sort of been blotted out.

—Ralph, businessman and parishioner of Sacred Heart Parish, North End, Boston. August 24, 2004.

"People kept saying, 'We own the church! We own the church!'" Ralph explained. "But what the hell were they talking about?" In 2004, Ralph, a middle-aged businessman and lifelong parishioner of Boston's Sacred Heart parish, seized on this enticing but vague piece of parish oral history as a spur to the effort of resisting its closure. At first there seemed to be very little reason for hope. Like many Boston-area parishes, Sacred Heart had lost much of its previous luster. Mass attendance was down, the number of marriages and baptisms had dropped off, some of the parish clubs had ceased functioning, and most of the regulars were older, their children and grandchildren having stopped attending mass or left the old neighborhood for the suburbs. It also appeared that the Scalabrinian Fathers, who had served the parish since its beginnings in 1890, were ready to leave for other missionary fields. The Scalabrinis' special charism to serve migrants meant that this North End parish of second-, third-, and fourth-generation Italians no longer fit their specific missionary model. Like East Boston's Our Lady of Mount Carmel, Sacred Heart was an Italian national or ethnic parish, meaning it had no particular territorial boundary. In the parish's early years, there were more than enough neighborhood residents to fill the church and help it grow. In later years, it relied on attracting parishioners from across the archdiocese with Italian-language masses and devotions. Italian Catholics from around Boston, and even those dispersed in other parts of the country, still returned to the North End for the tremendous summer saint's feasts and processions. Some also came back to receive their sacraments at Sacred Heart. But as families who had left the city for the suburbs had their own children, the strength and number of bonds back to the mother parish decreased.[1]

The neighborhood around Sacred Heart was changing, too. Instead of multi-generation Italian families taking up residence in rented flats or entire buildings, many of the North End's densely packed three- and four-story residences had been condo-ized or transformed into "luxury" apartments. Real estate in this formerly poor and working-class neighborhood had boomed over recent decades, the higher rents supported by young professionals who were attracted to the North End's charming narrow blocks, its lively Italian restaurants and cafés, and its easy access to the waterfront and downtown Boston.[2] With these changes and the reconfiguration mandate in mind, the cluster group recommended that Archbishop O'Malley close Sacred Heart. He complied, leaving the one-square-mile territory of the North End with one parish, St. Leonard of Port Maurice. With East Boston's Our Lady of Mount Carmel also on the list of parishes to be shuttered, the proposal completed the slow demise of Italian national parishes in the City of Boston.[3]

The refrain Ralph heard among his fellow parishioners in the North End in 2004—"We own the church!"—would be repeated among parishioners in closing parishes across the archdiocese. In ethnic and territorial churches, in suburban and urban locales, people were finding ways to articulate an immutable claim on their churches. Inevitably, these claims rested on resisters' urgent and purposeful turn to the past. As the archbishop's comments implied, parish shutdowns were an invitation to just this kind of reflection. In particular, they were an invitation to the histories of "persecution and sacrifice" that he suggested sat at the center of the making of Boston Catholicism. But the meanings of these pasts could not be taken for granted. In his comments explaining the shutdowns, the archbishop argued that Catholics should replicate the selfless perseverance of their forebears in the pursuit of a "great future," a future to be inaugurated in this case by the painful process of shutting down parishes. Your ancestors did not put themselves first, the archbishop averred, and neither should you.

As resisters accepted this invitation to the past, they uncovered and reanimated histories that were much more complex than this model implied. The story behind the North Enders' claim to own Sacred Heart church offers one powerful example. Upon hearing of the closure, Ralph, along with his business partner and brother, Phillip, and the parish business manager Carla, faced a dilemma. They felt that closing Sacred Heart was wrong, and they worried about the losses that would accompany the closing. They knew, for example, that priests from Sacred Heart had long been committed to offering weekly mass during Boston's cold weather months at a nearby home for seniors. They had heard the residents' plaintive questions about who would "wear the vestments" the priests stored there for the occasion. They also worried about subtle matters of access that could easily be overlooked in the transition to a new parish. "A huge percentage of our parishioners are elderly," Carla reminded me as we talked in a café across from the church in North Square. Even if they could walk the few blocks to St. Leonard's (and this was not a given), once they got there the place was not easy to navigate. The only bathrooms, Carla noted, were located in the basement, down a treacherous set of stairs.

Practical concerns about accessibility hinted at more fundamental disorientations entailed in the upheaval. Carla recalled listening to a parishioner wonder about the fate of a beloved statue at Sacred Heart. For years this woman had tended to the statue, changing its clothes to match the seasons of the church calendar. There was no way the new parish could accommodate the many statues that filled the uniquely dense devotional environment of Sacred Heart's upper and lower churches. Some of the devotions that thrived at Sacred Heart would not make the transition to a new church. Ralph worried about the group of elderly parishioners who gathered each evening to recite the rosary in the lower church before the seven o'clock mass. "You take this away from them, you're taking away part of their lives," Ralph asserted. He meant this quite literally, and interpreted the daily gathering as a chance for these neighborhood old-timers to check up on one another. The people of this informal group, Ralph said, structured their existence with the evening rosary in mind: "They wait for this every night." If a regular didn't make it one night, they were sure to get a call making sure everything was OK.

The weight of these kinds of parish stories pressed upon people like Ralph, Phillip, and Carla as the closure approached. As middle-aged parishioners in an aging parish, they felt that they had a responsibility, along with the resources and energy, to actively oppose the closure plan. But they did not think of themselves as agitators. The brothers described themselves as "shy," and Ralph said that they had never "stepped out in front" on anything like this before. Ralph and Phillip were clearly active, however, in neighborhood issues and had even co-written political opinion pieces for the *Post-Gazette*, an Italian-American weekly based in the North End. So despite their worry about shouldering the community's expectations, they were in command of important details and well positioned to take action. Carla's job deep inside the church's organization made her lack of compliance a more momentous personal reorientation. It also put future prospects for parish work in jeopardy. After an initial period confirming that they would have wide support and adequate funding from the community, the trio put aside their hesitations and set about the task of undoing the shutdown plan.

Histories of Division

Sacred Heart parishioners' puzzling claim about church ownership sent Ralph, Phillip, and Carla into parish and neighborhood history. They sought to furnish details that would clarify this murky picture of the church's origins. If it was somehow true that someone other than the archbishop actually had a legal claim to the church building, then they could hope that appeals to civil authorities might disrupt or even prevent Sacred Heart's shutdown. Ralph and Phillip had a sense of where they might turn for the answer. Sacred Heart, they knew, had an unusual relationship with a lay organization called the San Marco Society, a men's charitable group they had themselves joined years ago. Parishioners knew that the group had played a crucial role in the founding of the parish, but beyond this information, details were vague. Moreover, since parish archives had been destroyed in a mid-twentieth-century fire, records of this organization's past were not easy to come by. While old-timers in the group insisted that the society held some ancient legal rights to the church, no one really knew what this piece of memory really meant. A trip to the county archives, where Ralph and Phillip dug through piles of real-estate records, unearthed a startling document which resisters would herald as the key to their winning case against closure.[4]

The complex story of this document and its emotional and legal power begins in the particular religious, ethnic, and class histories of the North End. But the broader lessons extend beyond North End Catholicism, Italian-American Catholicism, or even urban Catholicism. The story shines a light on the historical meanings and power of parishes for lay and clerical Catholics and on the significance of Catholic parishes in American religious history. More specifically, it shows that the rules of parish life—in this case who could say mass there, what kinds of people would be welcomed there, who would control its finances, devotions, and rites—were established with intention and discipline. It demonstrates the complex motives and meanings of Catholic sacrifice, and the mutable lines of division between local parishes and the church. The story also establishes the groundwork for an understanding of parishes as sites of Catholic distinctiveness in America. As such, it offers a fitting beginning to the effort to understand the meanings of resistance to parish shutdowns as a part of modern U.S. Catholicism.

The document Ralph and Phillip held in their hands at the county archives was the deed for the land on which Sacred Heart stood. Its power in the present day rested on the late-nineteenth-century struggle behind its creation. As Italians began to arrive in Boston in numbers in this period, the North End became the regional center of Italian Catholicism.[5] With Irish Catholics fitfully making their way into the upper reaches of city and state government (the first Catholic mayor of Boston, an Irish-American, was elected in 1884, the first Catholic governor of the commonwealth, also of Irish descent, in 1913), the newer Italian-American Catholics were often regarded with unease and even disdain.[6] Middle-class Irish Bostonians fretted that their hard-won gains within the city's Protestant establishment were vulnerable to nativist notions of Catholic unreliability.[7] Well into the twentieth century, Boston's Irish Catholic leaders felt a need to demonstrate and affirm their political and religious maturity to a shrinking but still powerful Yankee elite.

Like the Irish before them, Boston's Italian immigrants were considered superstitious, religiously fickle, and overly emotional. Moreover, in their relative lack of means they were seen as a threat to Irish Catholic aspirations for respectability.[8] Because of the overwhelming Irish majority among Boston-area Catholics by the time southern Europeans began to arrive, ethnic mixing and equal opportunity among Catholic nationalities proceeded more slowly in Boston than it did in places like New York, Philadelphia, or Chicago.[9] Boston's Italian immigrants adapted the practices of their homelands and developed religious and social networks alongside those of their Irish counterparts. This included clustering in places like the North End, and later, East Boston. Italian-language parishes were established in these areas, and intimate communities of commerce and religion began to thrive in a world at some remove from the centers of ecclesial, economic, and political power.

As in other urban centers across the country, Italian Catholics in Boston had an early and persistent interest in maintaining distinctly Italian places and traditions. Ethnic mixing, of course, was never wholly avoidable or undesired, but as their numbers grew, Boston's Italians could command and support relatively independent social and religious structures.[10] Originally sharing a parish with a Portuguese congregation, the North End's growing Italian population soon ventured out on its own, supporting a Franciscan priest in buying land and building St. Leonard of Port Maurice Parish.[11] St. Leonard's was the first Italian parish in New England. After it was dedicated in 1876, this parish grew rapidly and became an attractive worship site not just for Italians but also for a number of Irish Catholics who, according to Franciscan accounts, appreciated the distinct devotional practices encouraged by the friars.[12] Even though many of these Irish participants were no more than occasional visitors, the parish grew crowded.[13] This growth, the pastor's wide responsibilities (he was asked to care for Italians across the archdiocese), and conflict both between ethnic groups and among Italians from different regions of Italy contributed to tensions between a group of northern Italians and the pastor. Archbishop Williams asked the pastor to hear confessions only in English, which may also have enhanced tensions.[14] When the pastor refused to support this minority group seeking to establish a new parish in the North End, the group broke off from St. Leonard's and began collecting money from its members for a new church.[15]

The group, calling itself the *Societa Cattolica Italiana di San Marco*, immediately posed a challenge to the Franciscans and to Archbishop Williams. After purchasing a Seaman's Bethel a few blocks away from St. Leonard's the group added an Italianate sloping roof façade to the plain square meeting house and began to fix it up to host religious services. In 1885 they asked the archbishop to dedicate it as a church. National (ethnic) parishes were becoming a staple of Catholic growth in Boston, so Archbishop Williams was not wholly unwilling.[16] In these years ethnic churches were not considered ideal: they were "tolerated" in Boston and elsewhere in the U.S. as a way to retain Catholicity among recent immigrants. Ethnic difference would gradually fade, bishops reasoned, making room for the emergence of a more uniform, and perhaps more American, Catholicism in this country.[17] But if ethnic parishes like the one the San Marco Society proposed were an acceptable compromise, the idea that they would be independent of diocesan control stretched the case too far. The San Marco Society's proposal—they would start a Roman Catholic parish while keeping the deed to the property in the name of their organization—seemed unworkable from the beginning. By this time American Catholic bishops had established a tradition of insisting that church titles rest in the name of the local bishop or archbishop. This policy eventually became civil law in Massachusetts in 1897, when the Archbishop of Boston gained official designation as a corporation sole. Lacking the legal compulsion that would come later, the San Marco Society had some justification in resisting this arrangement in the 1880s.

Their resistance echoed battles over church ownership and management that were common in this country in the late eighteenth and early nineteenth century. Tracking this history establishes one important ground for making sense of the conflicts over shutdowns, and in particular the civil and canon law arguments they stimulated in contemporary Boston. Labeled the "tensions of trusteeism" by historian Patrick Carey, the struggles crystallized the difficulty of adapting Catholicism to a country where legal precedents presumed a Protestant or congregational structure and where the royal patrons who had funded new churches in the old world did not exist.[18] Lacking support of this kind and fearing the power of anti-Catholic laws to prohibit Catholic institutional ownership, colonial-era church leaders, including (with reservations) the first U.S. bishop John Carroll, began to endorse a form of collective patronage—under the legal title of trusteeship—for new churches. Under this system, a group of lay Catholic benefactors would hold parish property in their names, under the proviso that they would hold it in trust for the good of the local church. The arrangement protected property from seizure under anti-Catholic laws and enabled Catholic expansion in the years before the church could afford to shed its reliance on the wealthy few. Soon, advocates of lay trusteeship began to make the case that the practice could promote a more successful

Catholic integration into this country; after all, the trustee system resembled a kind of church democratization, including lay management of parishes' temporal affairs. What had begun as a way to protect and preserve Catholicism in an anti-Catholic country had become, at least in part, a vehicle of Catholic accommodation to and even embrace of American ideals. But just as they would in controversies to follow, Catholic Americanizers faced powerful opponents who were more interested in building a strong Catholic subculture than in molding an American Catholicism.[19]

From the perspective of church order, American lay trusteeism posed new problems. In Europe patrons traditionally held certain privileges over the churches they endowed, including control of church assets and a voice in who would pastor the new church. In these cases, one or two wealthy individuals might be carefully selected for their reliability and willingness to cooperate with church leadership. In the American case, the relative poverty of church and citizens meant that bishops could not be so choosy. The number of trustees expanded, and "reliability" could not be so easily guaranteed. For its entire existence bishops fretted over what they saw as abuses of the trustee system by "unreliable" lay trustees.

With these concerns in mind, some bishops in the U.S. church, many of them trained in Rome and resistant to adapting church norms to national circumstances ("Gallicanism"), began in the early nineteenth century to take an active stance in American courts to establish more centralized control of parishes as part of the nation's civil law.[20] As new parishes came into being, bishops with an interest in limiting lay claims of ownership refused to bless new churches unless the deeds were in their names. This principle of a bishop's ultimate responsibility for all goods and obligations in his diocese gained the title "corporation sole." This was a legal designation which made the local ordinary—whoever was in charge of the diocese at any given time—the sole trustee of the goods and obligations of churches in his diocese.[21] Relying on the loyalties and donations of waves of Irish immigrants, those opposing lay trusteeship gradually eliminated the practice and advanced the policy of corporation sole in both church and civil courts. Except in local pockets, the pro-trustee efforts to translate European patterns of lay trusteeship into the American system gradually came to a stop over the course of the nineteenth century.

While the "tensions of trusteeism" became muted as diocesan consolidation efforts succeeded across the country, the San Marco Society, holding the keys to a popular worship site in Boston's North End, offered a relatively late counter-effort. Citing the Italian system of patronage called *fabbriceria*, under which parish patrons held control over the temporal matters of church management, the group refused to hand over the deed in exchange for official recognition as a parish and assignment of a priest.[22] The archbishop refused to bless the building, leaving it without a consecrated altar for the Eucharistic celebration, and without a pastor. From 1885 to 1890 the society and the archdiocese remained in a deadlock. During this time those associated with the San Marco Society continued to meet and pray in their new building. Lay leaders hosted services in the building, and community members "read and expounded the gospel of the Sunday and led in the recitation of the rosary or litanies." Considered "rebels against legitimate authority," these Catholics found little flexibility on the part of the archbishop.[23] For his part, Archbishop Williams was a mild but persistent advocate of Catholic accommodation. He was sympathetic to an older, Yankee Catholic tradition that took a more cautious approach than the militancy that arose later in Boston Catholics' official relations with Protestants. Williams extended this caution to his own career path: he turned down the opportunity to become a cardinal to avoid undermining his fragile collaborations and friendships with Boston's Protestant elite. Such caution did not always sit well in Rome; Williams came in for criticism from Leo XIII for this kind of moderate accommodationism.[24]

This subtle undercurrent of unease between Boston's Catholic leadership and the Vatican helps explain the conflict and its eventual resolution in the North End. It also connects the story there to an intra-church controversy that would flower in the coming decade related to so-called "Americanist" tendencies rising in the church. As in the earlier trusteeship debate, the lines connecting this "Americanist crisis" to the struggle over shutdowns in 2004 must be drawn with care. These were complex problems, and despite their own claims to the contrary, Boston's resisters cannot be described as the carriers of one distinct tradition inside American Catholicism. But their resistance suggested the continuing relevance of the dilemmas U.S. Catholics faced in the nineteenth and early twentieth centuries. Commentators and historians of U.S. Catholicism refer almost by instinct to the period following the Second World War and to the rise in the late 1950s and early 1960s of the "two Johns" (John F. Kennedy and Pope John XXIII) as the decisive moments in American Catholicism. Despite subtle historical analyses of Americanization as an ongoing question, American Catholic history often treats these decades as a point of no return. Along with Catholics' economic and educational mobility and the return to grace of a third John—the American Jesuit, political theorist, and theologian John Courtney Murray—these turning points symbolized the final erasure of American Catholic otherness. After this point, Catholics were not different from their fellow Americans, but shared and contributed heartily to a pared down, pro-American, anti-Communist, consensus Judeo-Christian faith. According to this argument, this was the time during which the undercurrents of Catholics' American-ness flowed clearly and confidently into the light of day.[25]

But the question of what Catholics held onto and what they discarded in this transitional period is not so easily resolved. The shedding of old selves is rarely quite as final as we might think. Tracking the contours of the 1880s dispute in Boston's North End—and resisters' 2004 evocation of it—brings the ongoing complexity of Catholics' American-ness into sharper view. The 1880s struggle positioned Boston Catholics at the intersection of two controversies. The first was the issue of lay trusteeship; the San Marco Society Italians sought to retain control over a property they had purchased and hoped to turn into a church. They cited Italian tradition to make this case. Archbishop Williams resisted this arrangement as a violation of an emerging consensus about the propriety of more centralized control.

The second issue concerned Americanization. Williams was not insisting that these Italians give up their aspirations for a "national" parish. Like other American bishops, he recognized the peril of insisting too forcefully upon the immediate transcendence of ethnic Catholicism, particularly the desire among new immigrants to have sermons and confession in native languages. But even amid this pragmatic concession—the "tolerance" of ethnic parishes—controversy could arise. Williams' insistence on English-only confession at St. Leonard's, for example, may have added to the desire of the San Marco Society for a place of their own. Certainly the San Marco Society's regional loyalty (in contrast to "national" Italian identity) proposed to move the diocese in the direction of an increasing, rather than decreasing number of distinct pockets. And of course it had also to be clear that the members of San Marco Society did not desire their own parish as a merely temporary expedient that would eventually give way to the erasure of their ethnic and religious distinctiveness. This is one point where the two controversies intersect: these North End Italians lobbied for church ownership and management precisely in order to nurture and retain this cohesive otherness in contrast to the homogenizing aspirations of Boston's religious leaders. If Williams hoped to help make the American church an ally of the established order, then these North End Italians' insistence on distinctiveness would have been unwelcome and unsettling.[26]

They were not alone in articulating the value of Catholic difference. The dilemma in Boston's North End was just a small slice of a larger story unfolding in America and Europe related to the question of Catholic accommodation: should the church adapt its outward forms and doctrines in order to be better positioned to win favor among the citizens of liberal democracies and students of contemporary philosophy and science? Or should the church insist on its own unique purity amid these competing claims, with Catholics around the world taking their cues from Rome? In the 1890s a few intellectuals in Europe actively embraced the position of a vocal minority of U.S. Catholics in favor of much greater openness to accommodation on the part of the church. The intra-church disputes that resulted are called the "Americanist" crisis, a title that referred to the errors supposedly endemic in American Catholicism.[27]

It is important to remember that both sides in this debate desired greater prominence and power for the church in the modern world—they differed about how best to accomplish this goal. Accommodation could allow the church to harmonize better with the political and social tendencies of a particular place. Those leaning in this direction (led by Father Isaac Hecker and his advocate Walter Elliott, and later by Bishop John Ireland in America and Abbé Felix Klein in France) worked under the sign of cooperation and communication, not distance and difference from modern societies and their distinct political and philosophical orientations. They held that the conditions of social and religious life in America were, far from a hindrance to the health of religion, uniquely welcoming of Catholic growth, expansion, and religious health.[28] In America, advocates also thought certain compromises with liberal political principles might undermine Protestant critiques of Catholicism, and ease the road for Catholic integration and success. They also sought, usually subtly and cautiously, to distance themselves from Rome, which they saw—through the eyes of American critics—as a hindrance to Catholic acceptance in America. For these accommodationists, there was often an accompanying anxiety about the Catholicism of newly arrived immigrants, which smacked too heavily of the old world, of the kinds of otherness (foreign languages, elaborate popular rites, intense communalism) they sought to soften or downplay in their efforts to forge a winning American Catholicism.[29]

Others in the church, in arguments crystallized decisively in Leo XIII's 1895 encyclical *Longinqua Oceani* and in his explicit 1899 condemnation of "Americanism" in *Testem Benevolentiae*, made the case for resisting the concessions Catholics might be tempted to make to national mores and, in particular, liberal political theory and theology. *Longuinqua* acknowledged the freedom available in America for the church to prosper, but cautioned against overestimating the value of this situation. God's grace and Catholics' hard work, not separation of church and state or the free rein of individual conscience, had allowed the church to prosper in America; Catholics should not forget the church's legitimate claim to temporal power and should not stop seeking "the favor of the laws and the patronage of the public authority." While no one wished America to fail, the document pointed clearly to the final source of America's potential success: Americans "can in no better way safeguard their own individual interests and the common good than by yielding a hearty submission and obedience to the Church." Rome and its faithful agents, not America and its republican system, merit Catholics' final loyalty. American Catholics should not, Leo XIII warned in *Testem*, presume that the church in America should be "different from what it is in the rest of the world." If America fostered "self-reliance" as a contrast to obedience, this should not become a spiritual value for Catholics. Characteristically American "endowments of mind" certainly exert an influence on the country, but Catholics should not "exalt" these qualities and tendencies; like all "real Catholic[s]," Americans are ultimately and willingly "bound in fellowship with Your Holiness," the pope. These calls for obedience struck at the heart of the controversy, since Catholic obedience was precisely the worry of Catholic and non-Catholic Americans alike.[30]

But this is also where issues of theology intersect with the ethnic controversies that were at play in late nineteenth- and early twentieth-century American Catholicism. In the minds of both Protestant critics and more affluent and assimilated Catholics, ethnic Catholics were uniquely unreachable by the (supposedly bedrock) American values; it was easy to assume that they were connected not to America and its democratic principles, but to Rome and its frequent calls for obedience. These suspicions created a situation of conflicting authorities: lay Catholics who were in dispute with their local officials found it natural to turn to Europe, and particularly to Rome, for help. This was less a matter of obedience than of strategy. American resistance to Roman assertions of authority had as much to do with bishops' eagerness to protect their own control of their dioceses as it did with any active animosity toward particular theologies, doctrines, or policies. But bishops' ultimate obedience to the pope made efforts to protect their turf a delicate proposition.[31]

In the case of the San Marco controversy in the North End, the foreign advocates came in the form of a fledgling missionary group from northern Italy. Against the friars of St. Leonard's and the archbishop, the San Marco Society had turned to the homeland for help. Petitioning Rome for influence and seeking aid from across Italy, the group managed to attract the attention of the Scalabrinian Fathers, an organization of Italian missionaries with the specific goal of enhancing Italian Catholicism in the New World. Founded in 1887 in northern Italy, the group was called the Missionaries of St. Charles Borromeo (later called the Pious Society of the Missionaries of St. Charles [P.S.S.C.]) often shortened to the Scalabrinians, after their founder, Giovanni Battista Scalabrini. Here too there were dilemmas about "national" versus Roman loyalty to be overcome. For a time, Scalabrini's Italian-nationalist vision put him at odds with the Vatican, within which the pope had declared himself a "prisoner" beginning in 1870, when the Italian army conquered Rome. This separation made Italian nationalism an un-Catholic position. Scalabrini's winning vision, however, was of the preservation of Italian Catholics abroad. These Catholics, he argued, could serve as a saving remnant. The group received papal approval, and soon began sending missionaries around the world.[32]

When they arrived in Boston, the Scalabrini fathers' well-known aspirations for rigorous training and refinement may have been an advantage. This pedigree, perhaps even more than their Roman imprimatur, allowed them not only to forge a strong connection with the North End society but also to negotiate successfully with Boston's Catholic elite, who desired to make both Irish and Italian parishes the grounds for the production of genteel, "orderly," "decent" and "proper" Catholics.[33] After a year-and-a-half of negotiations, during which the San Marco group agreed to abandon their building and meet instead at a separate chapel, a solution emerged. The San Marco Society turned the deed over, with the express stipulation that the land would be used only as a religious home for the Catholic Italians of the neighborhood. The archbishop saved face by not allowing the society to keep the deed, but recognized the formerly outlaw group and affirmed the parish's distinctly Italian character as endorsed by the Scalabrinians. The archbishop approved the dedication of Sacred Heart Parish under the pastoral care of the Scalabrinians in 1890.[34]

A Victory Bred of Catholic Separatism

One hundred and fourteen years later, in the summer of 2004, lawyers representing the San Marco Society called upon this unusual deed in an effort to halt the archdiocese from seizing nearly two million dollars from parish accounts as a part of the shutdown plan. By this time, a host of civic offices had expressed concern over the management of the assets the archdiocese would gain in the closures. One issue concerned the charities and public services that were associated with many closing parishes. The mayor's office had established a task force charged with studying the question of how the city could help prevent gaps in social service left by the parish shutdowns. From the perspective of the commonwealth's attorney general, the key question was the proper fate of charitable donations made to now-defunct organizations. By the time the San Marco Society brought its case to county court, the archdiocese had already agreed to a limited oversight role for the attorney general with respect to certain gifted assets collected from closed parishes. Reassured by this agreement and trusting that the archdiocese would be responsible in its use of the funds, the county judge rejected the San Marco Society's demand that the parish money be kept out of chancery hands.

It was the beginning of a long string of defeats awaiting civil and canon lawsuits brought against the archdiocese by parish groups aiming to undermine the shutdowns. Civil court judges were hesitant to get too involved in what the archdiocese's lawyers argued were the internal affairs of a religious organization. The meaning of the deed had not been fully tested in court, but it appeared that its initial power would be somewhat limited. But when I spoke with Carla, Ralph, and Phillip just a few days after this decision, they rejoiced at the news that the archdiocese had veered away from the plan to shut down the parish and had even agreed, for the time being, to leave the money untouched as well. They praised their ancestors for their foresight, and saw divine providence in their discovery of the deed.

At the time of their long battle over church ownership, Sacred Heart's founding generation may have seen the 1890 conclusion as a mixed result. The San Marco Society did, after all, give up its claim to the property. But the concessions included in the deed—the stipulation that the land entrusted to the archdiocese would be used "for divine worship for the use and benefit of the Italian Roman Catholics of Boston who may desire to worship with the parish of the Sacred Heart"—had provided a stunning twenty-first-century victory.[35] The church would remain open as a "chapel of ease" of the parish of St. Leonard's. Becoming a "chapel" deprived Sacred Heart of its juridical status in the church (it could no longer officially appeal any future closure decisions within canon law), but it affirmed that Sacred Heart would remain a legitimate site of Catholic worship. In the agreement parishioners would keep their seven o'clock daily mass, the weddings planned for the church could go forward, and the list of masses to be said for parishioners' loved ones would be fulfilled at the church, in the presence of those who paid for them.

Despite these gains, Carla, Ralph, and Phillip worried that chapel status was little more than a step toward eventual closure; a later round of shutdowns could scoop up the now-defenseless Sacred Heart. This was the fear, along with a restrictive mass schedule, that prevented East Boston's Mount Carmel from accepting a similar "chapel deal" in 2005. More immediately, the arrangement meant that the original impetus for Sacred Heart—the San Marco Society's desire for a place distinct from St. Leonard's—had finally been undermined. Noting that the St. Leonard's pastor and Parish Council would now control what happened at Sacred Heart, Ralph lamented that "the people we were running away from are going to be administering like God in heaven!" Old wounds and rivalries between the two parishes had not disappeared over time, and the team leading Sacred Heart's resistance effort remained committed to reestablishing the place's status as a parish. They thought that winning this partial victory would at least buy the group enough time for their canon law appeal to make its way to more sympathetic minds at the Vatican.

But even more fundamental doubts had been unearthed in the process. Resisters had mobilized in various ways to halt the closure. Ralph and Phillip had distributed three thousand pre-addressed, postage-paid cards in the neighborhood, directing people to send their messages in support of the parish to the archbishop. They claimed to have collected receipts indicating that at least two thousand of these had been mailed. Carla had encouraged people worried about the closure, and in particular those concerned about already-scheduled masses and weddings, to bombard the regional bishop with phone calls. Members of the community had even agreed to violate the unwritten (but serious) rule against overexposing their special and historic statues. Typically held in reserve until their feast days, the North End saints were brought out and paraded around the neighborhood in support of the effort to prevent Sacred Heart's closure. The funds collected in this unusual procession were channeled into the resistance.

Despite all these efforts and more, resisters concluded that without the legal weight of their unique deed, the archdiocese never would have wavered from its original plan to shutter the church. After all, similar efforts had done nothing to help dozens of other parishes across the archdiocese. While Ralph said that he wanted to believe that the archbishop had changed his mind with respect to Sacred Heart "out of the goodness of [his] heart," he knew that the decision to keep the space open as a chapel would "always be colored" by the parishioners' discovery of the San Marco document. It seemed more likely that the archdiocese was making the pragmatic decision to keep the parish open as a chapel in order to avoid further controversy in the North End. The resolution repeated, in other words, Boston bishops' historic "tolerance" of ethnic communities as a passageway to integration.

These deeper suspicions on the part of Boston's resisters were bred of the violation of the histories of sacrifice that made possible the 2004 decision to shutter Sacred Heart. The sacrifices that were meaningful to resisters at Sacred Heart were not the same sacrifices the archbishop had in mind when he described Catholics' ancestors as models of compliance. At Sacred Heart, the relevant sacrifices had been made precisely in the face of what others expected and demanded of them. The archbishop asked Catholics to consider their ancestors' persecution, but at Sacred Heart and elsewhere, the church itself was seen to have been one agent of persecution, which made further sacrifice on its behalf even less palatable. Furthermore, it was not lost on Catholics that the ancestral sacrifices to which the archbishop drew their attention were not necessarily made on behalf of the greater mission of the church, but instead on behalf of the local parish, the neighborhood, and the family, with the universal church gaining existence and legitimacy in and through these local communities of meaning.

With Leo XIII's 1899 condemnation of "Americanism," and Pius X's 1907 promulgation of the Syllabus of Errors and condemnation of modernism, what there was in America of robust "Americanizing" came to a halt.[36] Catholics' nineteenth-century turn toward Rome, called "ultramontanism" in reference to the journey "over the mountains" to Italy from the rest of Europe, came decisively to America. This did not mean American Catholics stopped believing in the possibility of a deep concordance between their religion and their citizenship.[37] But obedience to Rome and renewed assertions about the purity of the church and its "deposit of faith" meant that America, not Catholicism, would be called upon to do the adapting. In the process American Catholic distinctiveness had a new imprimatur.

This outcome helped establish ethnic parishes as a staple of Catholic growth, but it radiated beyond ethnic parishes into a broader emphasis in the American Catholic church on separation.[38] Catholics learned that they were (or should be) different from other Americans—in their moral discipline, in their loyalty to family, tradition, and place, in their relationships with saints, and their reverence for unchanging truths. With this discipline and training, Catholics could not only be American, they could help guide and transform America, bringing it to its full potential.

Boston's new archbishop, William Henry O'Connell, soon became America's torchbearer for this new, more aggressive Catholic position. He had gained the lead job in Boston in 1906 (first as coadjutor, then as archbishop in 1907, and as cardinal in 1911) in part by promising to turn Boston toward orthodoxy, antimodernism, and "triumphant papalism." This appointment distinguished Boston as a key battlefront in the church's struggle with the related enemies of Americanism and modernism. Coming at a time when the church had a new, even more assertively antimodernist leader in Pope Pius X, the appointment of O'Connell to Boston marked the "decisive nail in the Americanist coffin." O'Connell shared American bishops' tendency to view ethnic parishes as a workable, but imperfect and temporary solution to the challenge of 'churching' America's new immigrants. But he was more comfortable with ethnic variety than most others, suggesting that managed properly it posed no real threat to the unique catholicity of the church. Rather than Americanization, O'Connell sought above all the emergence of a unified, aggressive, and decisively *Roman* Catholicism. Along with the schools sometimes attached to them, parishes were the sites where this "militant and triumphant" separatism could best be cultivated.[39]

Pieces of this Catholic separatism abided among 2004's Boston resisters. They carried it with them into their efforts to preserve their parishes. The triumph with which Ralph, Carla, and Phillip discussed the San Marco deed celebrated parishes as sites of Catholic distinctiveness. One aspect of this distinctiveness was the unique Italian devotionalism and community life that the parish made possible. But more than this, the victory, however partial it may have been, affirmed the values of stability, tradition, and endurance amid a changing neighborhood. For them, shutdown would have signaled the final ascendance of distinctively non-Catholic values—bald marketplace logic, desacralization of landscape and architecture, destruction of community, the relativization of formerly stable truths. It would have signaled the final abandonment of the fight American Catholics had been enjoined to take up as a special kind of citizens. Parish defense had been a key idiom in the creation of that kind of American.

The Shared Moral World of Parish Defense

The willingness of Sacred Heart's would-be parishioners to maintain the church for five years between 1885 and 1890 while they agitated and waited for archdiocesan sanction speaks to their willingness to sacrifice and to the value they placed on having a Catholic place of their own. But it was not a battle for total independence. Just like those who resisted parish shutdowns in 2004, the people occupying the place that would become Sacred Heart were not seeking freedom from the church. They sought unity with the church alongside local control of their finances and their religious lives. Despite the conflicts, as these Catholics fought for their local place they also fought for their share of the church. Whatever might have been their hostility toward the archdiocese, there could be no clean break between the parish they hoped to create and the church. The Scalabrinis offered a bridge by legitimating care for the Sacred Heart parish as care for the church as a whole.

Understandable twentieth-century efforts to enhance the meaning of local sacrifices by linking them to "the Church" made twenty-first-century shutdowns a tenuous proposition. The rules of practicing parish built a bridge between defense of the parish and good Catholicism. We must recognize that Catholics have always worked creatively within those rules. They frequently shifted, for example, the location of "the local" according to a host of other demands and interests, such as the need for a good homilist or the desire to live away from dense urban streets. But these shifts only made it harder to leave once a satisfactory local had been found. Catholics in resisting parishes in Boston had absorbed too well the lesson that a vibrant parish was the lifeblood of neighborhood, church, and the nation. A history of consensus and collaboration among laity and church officials around the issue of parish defense had as much to do with the creation of resisters in 2004 as did the histories of intra-church conflict. Priests, bishops, and laity had shared a commitment to local parishes as the quintessential sites of Catholic presence and promise in the metropolitan landscape.[40]

This shared moral world—flowing out of Catholic separatism and with a healthy neighborhood parish as a central value—constituted another aspect of the complex past that 2004 resisters unearthed as they sat in church halls and considered the meaning of the shutdowns. Resisters often shared with me the story of how they found themselves among those who refused to accept the closure mandate. They often expressed surprise, suggesting that it was not in their character to buck the system. The trope certainly had the powerful effect of positioning the resisters as average; it also branded the shutdowns as an extreme measure that demanded an uncharacteristic response. But resisters' hesitations also carried the imagination and memory of a unified Catholic past and the hope for a unified future. They signaled resisters' confusion at the apparent rupture of a moral world they thought they still shared with the church as a whole. In hesitating or in chastening their rebellion, resisters signaled their appreciation for the universal glory available to local parishes that had been the hallmark of their training as parishioners.

Val, a parishioner at Our Lady of Mount Carmel in East Boston, narrated his entry into the resistance as a story of willing compliance undermined by a dawning awareness of the violation of the past at the heart of the shutdowns. The story moves from Val's present to his past and into his family history; in the process it points to the connections between the resistance to parish shutdowns and the means and manner by which Boston's Catholic church grew from the early to the mid-twentieth century. As such, it moves our story forward in time from the late nineteenth century conflict at the North End's Sacred Heart into a period of tremendous Catholic growth and change.

Before the shutdown, Val had been an active member of the parish. He was a regular mass-goer, and also attended other parish events. The pastor at the time of the shutdown was one of his distant cousins, a relationship that would cause Val deep consternation when suspicions about his cousin's management of parish funds circulated among the resisters and splashed across the pages of the *Boston Herald*.[41] Before these embarrassments, as the parish prepared for closure, Val had been asked to serve on a committee that would help plan the last mass. At first Val agreed to join the group, but the committee's direction soon became a source of profound inner conflict. While the committee talked about post-mass balloons and pastries in the church basement, Val had imagined a somber gathering marking the "death of the church." Outnumbered and deeply distressed, Val promptly quit the group, telling the leader that he "didn't like what he was hearing" and that he "couldn't handle" the thought of hosting a "feast" on such a grim occasion. Remembering the conflict later, Val reasoned that the others on the committee had adopted the attitude of the pastor, who was taking a new assignment at a parish on Cape Cod—"What did he care? He was moving on, and we were the ones who were going to be left without a church." The other committee members moved on too. They had their celebration as planned, "said their goodbyes" and then "completely left the church and that was it."

Val told his story as a rejection of this simple finality. If at first he was perhaps ready to mourn the loss of the church, the stark opposition of his imagined church "funeral" to others' "feast" alerted Val to broader incongruities entailed in the closure. Just as he wanted "no part" of the party and its "cookies and cakes," Val realized that he could no longer digest the shutdown. The history of sacrifice for the parish and a militant Catholic spirit informed this decision: "We wanted to continue to fight to keep our church open, not to close it," he told me. The implied obviousness of this formulation rested on the word "continue." In protecting the church from closure, Val understood that he was carrying forward the attitude and posture proper to committed Catholics. For him, the proposed shutdown was just another among a long sequence of challenges that Catholics in East Boston had to overcome. Just because it was the church that was now asking Val to adapt did not mean that the core lessons of the past—in this case the value of fighting for the church—could be swept away. For Val, the tone of the planned post-mass event struck a note discordant with this truth. He attended the mass, but avoided the party afterward. He soon found that others shared his disdain for manufactured closure.[42]

Later in the week following the last mass, word spread that two parishioners had decided to start an occupation. Val jumped at the opportunity. He joined the resisters and soon began spending long hours in the occupied parish. At first he was one among relatively large groups of six or eight people in the church at any given time. Later, as initial passions cooled and others meandered back to their pre-vigil routines, he was often there alone. He became a core member of the group, one of three or four "regulars" in the vigil who spent many hours every week sustaining the occupation and keeping the church secure and accessible for others who showed up for parties and services but could not donate so many hours to the cause.

Val had also volunteered to lead the community's evening rosary, a duty that made him an essential figure in the only regular daily gathering of resisters at the church. Such tasks were a significant burden, but they also had their rewards. Val said that leading the rosary brought him deeper into the tradition than he had been when his participation consisted mainly of simply fulfilling his "Sunday obligation." Regular rosary recitation was a new practice for him, but the duty at the church inspired him to bring the practice even further into his life. He began saying the rosary at home night and day in addition to leading the prayer in the evenings at Mount Carmel. "My faith has gotten stronger, not weaker," Val explained, "I've gotten closer from trying to protect our church from being closed." The rosary responsibility literally kept Val close to the church as he waited, sometimes late into the night, to lock up while others visited after the prayer.[43] He bore these responsibilities quietly, but he sometimes mentioned his worry that he was spending too much time away from home, where his ailing mother relied on his help around the house.

He took solace, however, in his mother's support for the occupation. This kind of family support could not be taken for granted. Others in the occupation had been alienated from family members because of their unwillingness to abandon the parish. In keeping the church open, the resisters knew that in some cases they prevented these others from resting easy; the continuation of events and services inside and around the supposedly closed church served as a constant reminder of community divisions. Official pronouncements and casual asides from archdiocesan officials combined with the rites surrounding closure and the words of priests at receiving parishes to signal clearly that resisters, not those who moved on, were the perpetrators of fissure. This meant they became targets of recrimination and critique, even from within their own families. Some of the resisters' families worried about them and at times accused them of living in the past; in the process, they signaled the power of the past living uneasily in all of them.

Just as family members could provoke this discomfort, they could also inspire confidence with their support. Having his mother behind him—and also having her writing checks to the community of resisters—helped Val confirm the morality of his stand against the shutdown. Val's mother never appeared at the church—it was his affirmation of her support (and other resisters' similar suggestions about their own absent parents' approval) rather than its precise character that interested me. For Val, the accumulated years of his mother's presence in the neighborhood and at Mount Carmel added weight to the cause. Others saw the preponderance of oldtimers as a sign of the resisters' backwardness; after all, an aging parish population—signaled by the lack of a parish school and few marriages and baptisms—was an obvious demerit in the process that decided which parishes should close. Those occupying the churches chose to interpret their collective old-age differently. They made a virtue out of a perceived liability. No one spurned the participation of young families, but young families did not carry the same weight of experience and memory thought to abide among the older members of the community. To describe this value as "nostalgic" would put a gauzy layer across what was actually closer to respect for durability and character in the face of genuine upheaval. Resisters like Val cherished the marks of validity granted by the approval of those who had witnessed previous changes and the passage of time.

"The Church is growing everywhere": Abundance and Character in Catholic Boston

Val saw his mother's support as an access point to the shared moral world that confirmed the validity of the occupation. Her story seemed to tell the story of the church and the neighborhood, and their broader connection to Boston's Catholic history. Val's grandparents had arrived in Massachusetts from Italy in the early twentieth century. First arriving in the factory town of Lynn, they found themselves looking with longing toward the Italian center in the North End. His grandmother, Val remembered learning, soon demanded that she and her husband move to the North End, where they could more easily communicate with their neighbors. Soon other communities in Boston offered the same opportunity. Like many second-generation Italians, Val's mother had decided to leave the crowded streets of the North End when she had children. She settled in East Boston, an island separated from Boston by a harbor and connected to it by way of underwater rail and automobile tunnels.

By mid-century, the time when Val's mother moved to East Boston, the place had already been established as an airy alternative locale for Italians seeking relief from the density (perhaps also the smothering intimacy) of Boston's North and West Ends.[44] East Boston's island setting had helped establish the community first as a resort for wealthy Bostonians, and later, in the second half of the nineteenth century, as an important port and maritime manufacturing center. Shifts in shipbuilding technology had undermined the neighborhood economy in the 1870s. This transition prompted real estate speculators to buy up cheap land on the island and to build tenements and triple-deckers to house workers in the light industrial and clothing manufacturing plants that were taking root in the area.[45]

While East Boston's isolation along with its industrial character would prevent it from becoming a genteel "streetcar suburb" as Dorchester and Roxbury had in the late nineteenth century, its uniform grid, its many trees, and its sea breezes did offer a contrast to longer-settled parts of the city. By 1898, East Boston even boasted a tremendous seaside park, one of many outdoor spaces designed for Bostonian's recreation and moral rejuvenation by Fredrick Law Olmsted.[46] Noting these assets and the neighborhood's good schools, Val's mother joined thousands of Italian migrants and immigrants making the transition to East Boston in the early and mid-twentieth century.

Our Lady of Mount Carmel Church, which also attracted Val's mother to the Jeffries Point section of East Boston, grew up amid this change. Distantly related to the North End's Sacred Heart by way of various missionary enterprises, the church opened in 1905 with little of the controversy that had surrounded the North End parish.[47] The addition of Mount Carmel gave the one-square-mile Jeffries Point area three parishes, and established in the neighborhood a Catholic density that had already proven sustainable in places like Boston's North End, South End, and Charlestown. It took the parish fifteen years (from 1905 to 1920) to finish the Romanesque church building with both an upper and a lower church. By this time the parish had overcome typically tenuous beginnings to become a thriving part of the neighborhood.[48] These were years of heavy Italian immigration, with Jeffries Point receiving a good share of these newcomers and Mount Carmel a good share of their donations. By the early 1920s, the parish was baptizing several hundred children and marrying one or two hundred couples each year. By 1930 the parish had its own school, with housing for the sisters on the top floor. They amassed enough capital to build a new convent in 1951 and a new rectory by 1955.[49]

The ability of the parish to pursue these projects rested on the willingness of parishioners to understand the church as a local and universal good. A 1930 address celebrating the school's dedication conveys the pressing demand pastors and parishioners felt in relation to the parish. The community's success in building the $125,000 school became an occasion for self-scrutiny and moral testing. Expansion should not become an excuse for laxity, as a notice distributed at the school dedication celebration made clear. The responsibility for parish growth had rested on too few and there were multiple missed opportunities, the pamphlet reported, for parishioners to join in the church's future glory. Mount Carmel's Third Order of St. Francis and the Christian Mothers were going strong, but they could always use new members. Each of these groups offered unique opportunities for Christian formation. The Third Order, which boasted three hundred members at Mount Carmel, encouraged "humility" by helping members reject the "spirit of the age" which "revolts against authority, secular and religious, and proclaims man a law unto himself." The two hundred members of the Christian Mothers, with "bead in hand," were "continually giving witness" to the efficacy of the rosary as this prayer was "revealed to S. Dominic by the Blessed Virgin Herself." The Children of Mary had "the best way of spiritual development" and were the "best aid to the priest, in his anxiety for the well being of his flock." This group seemed to be seeking members: "Miss Parishioner," the notice asked, "are you a Sodalist?" "Mr. Parishioner" came in for this same query in relation to the Holy Name Society.

In these years, lay initiatives were increasingly encouraged, but only as they were monitored and incorporated under the guidance and control of the newly disciplined and disciplinarian chancery.[50] On the level of the parish, where affiliation with the hierarchy was a necessary precondition of existence, this consolidation of authority and intensification of oversight was accompanied by the rhetorical alignment of "parish" with "Church." Just as the eventual dedication of Sacred Heart endorsed the efforts of the North End's San Marco Society, this tendency had the effect of aggrandizing local sacrifices by blurring the differences between local and universal church.

This precedent helps explain the even more direct interrogation of Mount Carmel's parishioners in the 1930 celebration program. "The Church is growing everywhere, thank God!" the document began, "but are you doing anything to further that growth?" The parish's organizations, it continued, were "arteries" through which the "life blood of the Church" would flow to "ever widening regions." Linking personal and collective religious health, the address suggested that only those who were "affiliated" could take pride in the "growth of your faith." This was a pointed charge, especially because it was issued on the day of the school's blessing. Those who had "been standing aloof" from active membership in the parish could "take no real part in the joy of the Church over the increase of her members." Instead, they "stand lonely and unnoticed, outside of all the splendid activities of a militant Church," and they shared "none of the glory which goes to the workers in the vineyard."[51] This celebration of the parish's accomplishment belonged only to those who had taken active part in the church. In the shared moral world taking shape at Mount Carmel, the stakes of parish participation extended to the very existence of the universal church. Sacrifice for the parish was sacrifice for the church. Participation in the parish was participation in the church. In times of relative strength, there was no reason to distinguish the two. The committed practice of parish assured Catholics of a piece of the "glory" of the church.

Although Val's family history had its share of mobility and change—his grandmother's move away from Italy and Lynn and his mother's move out of the North End, for example—he thought of it more as a story of stability and commitment. He let me know, for example, that once his grandmother arrived in the North End, she almost never left. Although he never met his grandmother, he learned from his mother that she stayed in the North End even as her health declined and her children invited her to move in with them in East Boston. "That is where she wanted to be," he explained. This stubbornness impressed Val, who said he "fell in love" with her through stories he learned from his mother. For Val, she was an example of everything that was right about the Catholic past. She was "a very holy woman" and "a good mother," and she was also "a very religious woman" who visited the church three times a day according to family lore. This last characteristic—her nearly constant presence in church—touched precisely on the difference between present and past, according to Val. Linking his own experience with his grandmother's, Val asserted that Catholics "didn't have the problems that we are facing now." While he acknowledged that there was some truth in the critical view of the past that said Catholics simply used to "pay, pray, and obey," he couldn't bring himself to dismiss the past as a time of ignorant obedience. "I mean, we had problems then, but it was different." For Val, the critical difference was the abundance and vitality of the church's events.

This recollection—"packed" churches, when you had to arrive a "half hour to three-quarters of an hour early in order to get a seat" at one of the parish's many Sunday masses—is familiar to anyone who studies contemporary American Catholicism.[52] Familiarity, however, should not numb us to the core values such remembrances evoke. Val said that he used to simply show up for mass regularly and give as much money to the church as he could afford. He didn't think of this as "pay, pray, and obey"; it was just a matter of being a "practicing Catholic." Now, as a member of the vigil, Val still attended mass at a nearby parish in order to fulfill what he thought of as his Sunday obligation. But he said that he had changed as a result of the vigil. At this mass, which Val attended regularly before making the trip back to Jeffries Point for Mount Carmel's Sunday service, he listened closely to the announced purpose of any "second collection." He had become a discerning giver: "If it is about the Propagation for the Faith, it's out. If it's for the archdiocese, it's out, I will not contribute a dime to them." Central Catholic offices, whether in the Vatican or the city, were—temporarily at least—cut off from Val's Catholic universe. He was proud to report that he had returned the archdiocese's annual fundraising form with a note reading "Keep Our Lady of Mount Carmel Church open, then I will make a contribution." He returned his mother's form with the same note.

Val's struggle to define himself as a Catholic in relation to the needs of the present and the ambivalence of the past finds resolution in the values underlying the narrative of Catholic abundance. Obviously, crowded masses and full coffers across the archdiocese would have prevented the need for widespread shutdowns. But the narrative of Catholic abundance Val invoked carried with it a deeper longing for the cultivation of what Richard Sennett has called "personal character." Sennett, who writes about the lived experience of class and work relations, suggests that the new versions work in capitalist economies overemphasize flexibility and mobility. Where old models of promotion rewarded durability and longevity, the new capitalism sees these as potential hindrances to innovation and market adaptability. In the new "flexible capitalism," he discovered, workers are rewarded more for "immediate capability" than for "seniority." The real freedoms these new models offer come with their own set of rules and limitation. Teamwork, which proposes to open workplaces to fresh ideas, also deflects responsibility from any one individual and undermines accurate assessment of success and failure. The demise of lifelong "careers" in favor of multiple temporary jobs across one's working years exacerbates the modern condition of "drift" in place of the opportunity to cultivate "mastery." The ever-present possibility of being "downsized" as firms try to stay ahead of trends adds a new and fearful sense of vulnerability to the work experience.[53]

All of this, Sennett writes, has a dubious effect on productivity and also serves to undermine the "long-term aspect of our emotional experience."[54] For Sennett, the new regimes of work threaten to stifle the development of character, which is made up of those traits we most respect in ourselves and for which we want others to respect us. As a distinctly relational quality of the self, character depends on the opportunities available to individuals within a given social world. Val's embrace of the shared moral world with the narrative of Catholic abundance at its center was a call for a social reality friendly to the development of personal character. People in church, the seats filled, constant activity and buzz—all of these suggested that the parish was a reliable social site where commitment, durability, and longevity were given their due.

In contrast, in their prioritization of parishioner flexibility and mobility the 2004 parish shutdowns echoed the values of the new capitalism. Church buildings were to be sold, after all, on the open real estate market, with few official constraints outside of blocking any buyer with a "sordid" use in mind for the property.[55] Other aspects of the shutdowns could be read in light of the new capitalism. In describing the archdiocese as a unified whole, where everyone had to take responsibility for the dire condition of the Boston church, reconfiguration officials drew on longstanding ecclesiology. But this description also worked to deflect blame for the church's failures onto an amorphous collective. For some of those in closing parishes, this effort to spread responsibility was particularly hard to swallow in light of the immense debts incurred as a result of past officials' criminal negligence in cases of clerical sexual abuse.

Even more significantly, in suggesting that one parish was as good as the next for satisfactory worship life, the church became another agent of the "fragmentation of narrative time."[56] The church wanted people like Val to create new stories in new parishes, to reclaim narrative time by connecting themselves to the longer story of Christian redemption and by starting a new chapter of their lives as Catholics in new communities. As the pastor of Mount Carmel's "receiving parish" told me, the shutdown was a chance for parishioners "to start with new memories and to start with new lives." For Catholics, he argued, time is ever and again refreshed:

> Every time we come to the altar it's not [the] point that [we say] 'I've been in this parish for seventy-eight years, or seventy-eight days.' It's every time we come to that altar it's our first day. And everything starts from that moment on, until the next time we come.

With willingness to undergo this constant rebirth in Christ, Catholics could appreciate the core message of the shutdowns, which was that "there's something bigger out there than yourselves in this church, and we have responsibilities to it." This pastor blamed "distrust" of the church for the problems the archdiocese encountered in sending this message home.[57] But for Catholics like Val, the fact that it was not his first day at the altar was precisely the point. The stories of his mother and grandmother and their sacrifices were tied up in his sense of reverence and meaning at Mount Carmel.

The distrust the pastor diagnosed, then, was an outgrowth of resisters' worry about the kind of people and church they would become if they accepted the pastor's version of an infinitely renewable Catholic selfhood. Val turned to the universal church, but also to the language of stability and continuity, to articulate the larger truth he aimed to represent as a resister. "As a Roman Catholic" he told me,

> I still believe in the teachings of Christ. That's one thing they can never take away from me . . . and I don't think that the archdiocese today, and I even may have to extend to the Vatican, is what Christ really wants. It's completely different. He said to bring our lost sheep back into the flock. What they are doing is they are scattering us.[58]

The scattering Val loathed applied as much to individual Catholic selves as to the community. Traditions encouraging them to count themselves "worthy" of the church's glory through their sacrifice for and participation in the parish had strengthened the link between wider responsibilities and local realities. Instead of cultivating what Sennett calls "postmodern" "pliant" selves, resisters—in their resistance and in the stories they told about it—opted to enact and narrate the more connected version of selfhood they inherited from the shared moral world of Catholic abundance. Churches were the embodiment of that moral world; they provided "refuge" and an alternate "scene of attachment and depth."[59]

If former versions of Catholic abundance had long been absent from Mount Carmel, Val was still able to think of his experience as a Catholic in terms of that narrative. Relaying his grandmother's story of perpetual presence in church and stubborn commitment to her parish neighborhood provided a perfect opportunity to express the kind of traits Val cherished. As he had never met her, Val's love for his grandmother was a love for what she stood for, what she represented. Val expressed this love and developed in himself the kinds of traits he respected in his grandmother by making occasional visits to Sacred Heart parish with his mother. When he arrived at the North End church Val made a point of sitting in the exact seat his grandmother used to occupy so often. He put himself in the place, again, both in this action and in telling me about it, of an intimate form of Catholic abundance. In the process, he was reclaiming the values of durability, longevity, and connectedness underlying that story.[60] In the hours it demanded and in the attentiveness it required, occupying Mount Carmel offered another opportunity to express these traits and to sustain the emotional bonds that those traits enabled.

Consecration and the Production of Parish Inviolability

Alongside pastoral invocations of the glory and joy awaiting active parish participants, Catholics in the first seven decades of the twentieth century encountered church buildings themselves as imposing structures on the moral landscape. The rules of practicing parish aimed to establish churches as singular locales, places worthy of the greatest reverence and respect. Church buildings and the things inside them warranted this special attention because they were unique sites of God's presence and efficacy. The Roman Catholic rite of church and altar consecration—the ceremony that began the official life of a church—made this uniqueness and opportunity very clear; a brief look at the character of this ancient rite helps explain Catholics' hesitation to give up their churches.

In the next chapter, I point to a 1978 version of the rite of consecration, which was a product of the liturgical and theological changes emerging from the Second Vatican Council. This latter rite, and the attitudes and postures it encouraged, both challenged and offered new possibilities for Catholic engagement with the locales and objects of their tradition. Comparing these two rites to one another provides a compelling picture of the adjustments Catholics were asked to make in relation to Catholic material culture over the course of the twentieth century. As we will see, the shutdowns relied heavily on the revised version of Catholic attitudes toward the meaning and power of churches and the things in them. Resisters did not wholly reject these newer ways of thinking about Catholic material culture, but they also gave witness to the abiding power of older ways of thinking about presence and efficacy embedded in the objects and locales of their religious lives.

The rite that accomplished the consecration of Sacred Heart (in 1890) and Our Lady of Mount Carmel (in 1920) was the same rite, with only very minor changes, that would have been performed in churches around the world for the preceding five centuries.[61] The various parts of this rite (along with instructions for its performance) were compiled into a single volume in English by Father A. J. Schulte, a liturgy professor at Pennsylvania's Overbrook Seminary, in 1907. This document was rewritten with slight adjustments in 1956 and 1961. The result was a text known as a "pontifical"—a complete set of directions and prayers for the entire performance of the rite. This particular pontifical, called *Consecranda*, was just the first of a series of manuals Schulte would produce in order to aid priests and bishops in the performance of their ritual functions. In one sense, such work anticipated the spirit of the liturgical movement that would grow in influence in this country in the 1930s; it provided, like latter publications from Virgil Michel's Liturgical Press, practical how-to guides for making liturgy smoother, more precise, more edifying, and more elegant.[62]

But the document and its revisions contrast interesting ways with the liturgical movement that would follow—Schulte's work was not about finding and highlighting select aspects of the liturgy from favored parts of church history. Moreover, no explanation of the history or origins of the various aspects of the rite is offered. It was simply a matter of preserving accurately and precisely the tradition as it had been handed down. The text and the series of which it was a part also differed from the liturgical movement in its focus on the hierarchy. The document expresses only a vague concern that lay onlookers see the rite at all, much less that they understand and appreciate its meanings. And the connection of ritual to social justice, solidarity, or communalism plays no part in this compilation.

While the "manual" genre and its timing certainly limited the scope of the documents in Schulte's series, these contrasts nonetheless help explain why reformers working on a comprehensive overhaul of the rite in the 1970s found central aspects of the tradition upsetting; crucial actions in the establishment of an official church contained "accretions" from portions of church history they would sooner forget.[63] Fidelity is fine, but purity is better, and understanding is crucial. We should not just blindly perform inherited traditions; we can use history, biblical study, social science, psychology, as well as spiritual reflection and discernment to discover rites that are faithful to the past while remaining meaningful in the contemporary world. In this the reformers, some of whom were also creators of the Second Vatican Council's document on liturgy, drew directly on the liturgical movement, especially as it had developed, by the 1950s and 1960s, into a movement concerned primarily with a "stronger lay voice in church affairs."[64] But updating through the discovery and explication of pure sources is a fraught enterprise. The thick history of the rite (and reformers' discomfort with it) confirms the potency and durability of the ideas and postures it enacts and enjoins.[65] Although some of them were wary of it, resisters in Boston also understood the potency and durability of these older ways of imagining and being in Catholic places. Their occupations were a manifestation of that understanding. They lived inside the lingering dilemmas of liturgical reform in this country.

By their very nature, dedication ceremonies are rare. The Catholics in Boston's resisting parishes may never have witnessed a church dedication. What was said and done at these ceremonies may not have firmly determined practice at churches afterwards, but the manuals for such events provide indispensible clues about how Catholics were instructed and cultivated in the practice of their faith in relation to objects and locales. The bishops and priests who performed these rites and the Catholics who took part in them encountered the church's best efforts to ritualize the proper orientation to places and things of worship. These attitudes and postures carried forward in daily movements in and around church buildings. Vigilers' idea that they were protecting "God's House" carried with it the legacy of this abandoned rite and its instruction about the power and meaning of the places the archdiocese was asking Catholics to give up.

Understanding some of the specific contours of this rite and its history will help clarify the point. Until the revisions of the 1970s, the rite of church consecration aimed to establish churches as sites of unique spiritual efficacy and inviolable sacred presence. For several centuries in the early church, a place could legitimately be consecrated simply with the celebration of a mass on its altar. But the momentous event of the establishment of a new church called out for more elaborate and richer ritualization. The rite of church dedication that developed drew upon pre-existing funerary and baptismal rites.[66] Just as incoming church members were sprinkled or submerged with holy water, so too the new building was sprinkled in the dedication rite. By the ninth century, the ceremonies had developed a full-throated sacramental character, treating "the new building as a human—one who is to be baptized and made a pure receptacle of the presence of God and made a member of God's universal *corpus*."[67] The practice of anointing walls, altars, and floors was likewise a remembrance and evocation of those same actions during the blessing and consecrating of persons.

From an early time it was also ideal to dedicate churches with the installation relics if they could be obtained and verified.[68] The dedication rite that took shape over the medieval period was largely focused on the installation of relics, whether whole bones or otherwise, into the new buildings' altars. Unsurprisingly, given nineteenth- and twentieth-century Catholic anti-modernism, the 1907, 1956, and 1961 translations of the rite carried this tradition forward. The first stages of building a church included not only securing permission, funding, and architectural plans, but also obtaining verifiable relics. Once these tasks had been completed, the planning for the ceremony could begin. The pastor, the consecrator (usually the local bishop), and—for parish churches—parishioners were all asked to observe a fast the day before the consecration. This posture of vigilance not only alerted the community to the coming event, but also acknowledged the arrival of the relics in the neighborhood. On the eve of the ceremony, the consecrating bishop brought the relics to the parish and set them in place near the church where the relics would be attended by two burning candles and, in some cases, "two, four, or six lay persons" overnight.[69] The bishop's task was to pray before the relics, formally confirm their legitimacy, insert a statement to that effect, and seal them in a case of lead, silver, or gold.[70]

The placement of relics enhanced the religious potency of the new place. The prayers of martyrs were considered particularly efficacious in reducing the just temporal punishments awaiting sinners at their deaths. In this economy (grounded in the idea of the eternal communion of saints) relics and indulgences had long been in close connection. Following this tradition, the bishop's note enclosed with the relics specified that a one-year indulgence would be granted to those who attended the consecration ceremony. A somewhat shorter indulgence was available to those who came on the anniversary in subsequent years. Announcements about these opportunities were made to the parishioners in the weeks preceding the event.[71]

The rite included the mass mainly as an afterthought. While the rite could be considered a series of acts preparing the church for mass, the actual celebration of the eucharist did not play a part in the ceremony.[72] Instead, it entailed a long sequence of processions, circumambulations, lustrations, anointings, and incensings, all accompanied by the recitation, in Latin of course, of psalms and prayers. The manual aimed to ease bishops' execution of the ceremony, which at three to four hours was among the longest and most elaborate in the church.[73] In 1907 the rite called for the participation of forty people—among them deacons, priests, masters of ceremonies, cross-bearers, chanters, holy-water bearers, censers, bier-carriers, a mason, altar boys, and torchbearers. The 1956 revision reduced this number by about ten leaving the number of torchbearers, for example, up to local discretion. In both versions the assistants' duties were the same: they were to attend the project of relic installation and aid in the exorcism and blessing of various parts of the building.

Along with a formal deed or title exchange, these were the two main accomplishments of the ceremony. The rite began in a darkened church, with only the bishop and his ministers. After prayers, the bishop signaled for the lighting of twelve evenly spaced candles against the church's side walls. The next step was an ordered procession to the place where the relics had been kept overnight. There, the bishop and others prayed before the relics and recited the seven penitential psalms.[74] Leaving the relics behind in order to prepare the church for their installation, the group then moved to the front of the church for a singing of a saints' litany provided in the appendix. Then the bishop exorcised and blessed salt and water and combined them.

The prayers accompanying this action dated back at least to the ninth century.[75] Like prayers that would occur at a later moment over the "Gregorian water" used to bless the altar, these petitions called for "infestation," "defiled spirits," and "the terror of the venomous serpent" to be expelled wherever the sanctified mixture was sprinkled.[76] The bishop then sprinkled himself, the clergy and the bystanders before circling the church three times to sprinkle the lower, middle, and upper parts of the church walls in sequence. This sprinkling was not only a replication of baptism, but was also a "grand and complex exorcism . . . meant to put the evil one to flight." The sprinkling, performed on both the inside and outside walls, was intended to remove demons and other evil powers from the actual stones of the church building.[77]

Between each circumambulation of the outer walls the bishop performed a rite of knocking and dialogue (based on Psalm 24) with a "guard" who had been left inside the church. After these events and the dramatic opening of the door on the third go-around, the bishop and his assistants entered the church. The "bystanders" and visiting clergy remained waiting outside until later. After praying in front of the altar(s) and invoking the names of the saints whose relics they would hold, the bishop inscribed with his crosier the letters of the Greek and Latin alphabets in diagonal lines of ash spread in a cross shape across the church floor.[78] Later, the bishop would anoint twelve crosses, evenly spaced along the church walls, as the definitive gesture accomplishing church consecration.[79]

The remaining steps for the consecrating bishop, all accompanied by prayers, chanting, and singing, included additional blessings, anointings, incensings, and sprinklings of altar, walls, floors, doorjambs, and other objects. The bishop uttered a consecratory preface, led a procession with the relics, and offered an exhortation for those in attendance. Relics were installed and sealed in the altar with cement mixed with holy water. The bishop also burned wax and incense in five locations atop each altar. In this perhaps most dramatic part of the rite, the altar "became a field of fire from which arose dense clouds of smoke and fragrant balsam."[80] In all, there were 144 steps, all laid out in painstaking detail.[81]

The tremendous effort and expense, along with the mystery and grandeur of the event, certainly marked church buildings as special sites on the landscape. The liturgical movement, which is clearly a source of the kinds of changes in liturgy that would transform the mass and also this rite of consecration, had not, at the cusp of the council, moved wholly away from the profound invocations of presence and power that would dissipate in the reforms. At least among this influential circle of theologians and reformers in the mid-twentieth century, the prayers and actions associated with the rite of consecration had yet to be labeled arcane performances from a bygone, magical, or pagan age. Later efforts—in the postconciliar period and during the shutdowns in Boston—to obscure, minimize, or downplay this kind of robust affirmation of presence had to overcome mid-century liturgists' endorsements of it and Catholics' consistent tendency to think about their churches in these ways.

One example from the liturgical movement illustrates the resilience of Catholics' willingness to invest locales and objects, and not just people and their actions, with divine potency. In 1958, just one year before the announcement of the Second Vatican Council, the Liturgical Press published a sympathetic theological analysis of various dedication rites in its "Popular Liturgical Series."[82] One article, drawn from a Catholic Action journal called *Sponsa Regis*, explained the "meaning of the altar" in terms that perpetuated the messages about presence and efficacy embedded in the consecration rite. The author, Father Paschal Botz, O.S.B., was a protégé of Alcuin Deutsch, O.S.B., the abbot (from 1921–1950) of the center of liturgical reform in this country, St. John's Seminary in Collegeville, Minnesota. After education in America and Germany, Botz became a professor of theology and later dean of the graduate program in theology at St. John's. He compiled and edited the first edition of *A Short Breviary*

(1941) for the Liturgical Press and went on to publish several books for the Liturgical Press and St. John's Abbey Press. Throughout his long career he published and gave talks about liturgy, "victimhood," the sacraments, and sacramentals. Botz was an important player in the core Benedictine cohort of the U.S. liturgical movement, and a close confidant and colleague of Gaylord Diekmann, O.S.B., who in 1938 took over the leadership of the important liturgical renewal journal *Orate Fratres* from the movement's great force, Virgil Michel, O.S.B.[83]

In this document, Botz concerned himself with educating his readers about the potency and permanence of Catholic altars. The altar, Botz argued, was a symbol of "God's special presence localized."[84] In contrast to pictures and statues, altars were efficacious symbols. They actually endowed the things placed on them with holiness: "bringing things to the altar sanctifies them." Religious efficacy and symbolism were not mutually exclusive. For Botz, the relationship of the symbol to its referent was so close as to nearly close the distance between them. "A symbol stands for something. Symbols have power, either earthly or heavenly, to put us in contact with spiritual reality. . . .the altar has the power of sanctifying us by contact with its inherent holiness." The altar during mass provided a "complete picture of Christ," and was a perfect reenactment of Calvary in an "unbloody" mode. Like the Ark of the Covenant and the "Old Testament altar," the "New Testament altar stands in God's presence, only in a far more perfect way." Accordingly, the presence localized in the altar offered more than a reason for reverence, repentance, or awe—it offered relief, refuge, and healing for a suffering people.

Ritual memories confirmed this interpretation. When it was consecrated, Botz reminded his readers, each altar was "set aflame by the Bishop in sight of all the people." This tradition of lighting incense in five locations on an altar would be curtailed in revisions of the rite of consecration that were only a short time away. For Botz, however, this act during the altar's consecration was integral to its holiness and power. The altar covered in fire presented a "vivid picture" of the "fire of the Holy Spirit," which in "fulfillment" of the fire "of old" "consumes, sanctifies, and glorifies our gifts placed on the altar." At the consecration, "it becomes permanently sacred with the sanctity of Christ."[85] For these reasons the altar was the site of a special commerce; it was a "crossroads," a meeting place for human and divine in a "wondrous exchange." This should matter to Catholics because it was especially at the altar that their needs would be heard. In fact, Botz suggested, "[n]o place on earth is more efficacious than an altar for the hearing of our prayers."

Botz was not so enamored of the altar as to disregard the long tradition of recognizing God's presence throughout the world. But he did not hesitate to single out the altar as a particular site of God's grace. If being "out in the open on a bright spring day" elicited greater feelings of devotion, or if a "statue of the Sacred Heart" was more affecting, nonetheless the altar was "more effective." "[A]ngels are there," Botz reported, "carrying our prayers and offerings to the throne of God's Majesty most surely." He cited approvingly the "old world piety of people venerating the altar, for instance in Palestine and Italy, where people 'take a blessing' by touching the altar with their hand and then their lips."[86] This appreciation of an intimate relationship between people and object led Botz to anticipate that soon "more altars will again face the people."[87] His hope for altars facing the people flowered, of course, in the reforms of the Second Vatican Council. But Botz's brand of enthusiasm for an altar's religious efficacy would not survive that transition unscathed.

Botz's discourse—and indeed the consecration rites themselves—must be considered as contributions to a long debate within the Catholic tradition about the meanings of religious locales and objects. It was not the case that before the Second Vatican Council there were no questions about the efficacy of Catholic locales and objects. Catholics have perennially struggled with the desire to endorse churches and shrines as uniquely holy places and an equally powerful need to downplay their significance in light of truer, universal, or invisible versions of those places beyond the normal range of the human senses. Variation on these issues was no doubt often related to local contexts, such as the need to sustain a place of worship in the face of nearby competition, or, as in the closures in Boston, the need to detach people from a particular place. Variation also related to fundamental theological concerns. St. Augustine's careful differentiation of the City of God from the City of Man is one version of this need, emphasizing that the City of Man—including even ecclesial structures and communities—was always finite in comparison to the transcendent and eternal City of God.[88] Ceremonies for the dedication of a church and an altar took up these questions in an immediate, practical, and liturgical way. What did this new place on the Christian landscape mean? What were its powers and its limits? How would these meanings relate to the people who performed the rite and to those who paid for its upkeep and filled it with their prayers?

Memory Loss

Boston Catholics in the 1940s and 1950s maintained a robust commitment to participation in church organizations, charities, and liturgies. The Knights of Columbus, the League of Catholic Women, the Catholic Youth Organization, the Holy Name Society, and other organizations thrived during these years as they had never before. Masses, novenas, and parish missions were all well attended. Weekly communion and confession were common. Public rites such as processions and "holy hours" also thrived. If Catholics were moving more confidently into the public sphere, parishes remained Catholics' world.

At the center of these parishes was the parish church.[89] Resisting Catholics were caught up in at least three distinct discourses about these places in which they and their families had spent so much of their time and money. The ancient rite and its continuing use and relevance into the 1950s and 60s suggested the literal holiness of Catholic objects and locales. The ceremony did not simply create a metaphorically rich set of instructive symbols or a site for people to gather in holy solidarity, it created a uniquely and specifically holy site on an otherwise undifferentiated landscape. Botz and his confreres at St. John's were clearly more interested in developing Catholics' understanding of these places and rites than were Schulte and his supporters at the *American Ecclesiastical Review.* But despite these differences, and despite its links to reforms that would come later, the liturgical movement had not abandoned the rite's unapologetic affirmation of churches' efficacy and permanence. Later changes in the rite of dedication would move decisively away from this set of meanings. But resisters in Boston, living in the opportunity and confusion of "continuity amid change," saw little reason to choose one over the other.

These rites and theologies—affirming the reality of sacred presence embedded in specific churches with the power to heal and provide succor—added another layer to the complex history behind Boston Catholics' unwillingness to leave their churches. When a group of resisters found abandoned relics sitting in drawers and closets in the sacristy at Mount Carmel, they responded with a combination of reverence and unease. The relics were at once potent sacred objects and sad reminders of a time when the parish needed multiple consecrated altars to fulfill demand for masses. Presumably they had been stored in the sacristy for safekeeping after the downstairs chapel and upstairs side altars had been dismantled. Regardless, the resisters were offended at the thought of these sacred objects gathering dust behind closed doors. They blamed their pastor for leaving the relics behind instead of making arrangements for their proper relocation after the shutdown. Of course, this ignored the likelihood that they would have been more offended had the relics been removed. But now they worried that certain members of the resisting group might abscond with one or more of the relics. Indeed, the vigil leader Annetta suspected that one of the people who had left the group had made off with two of the more portable relics. This worry encouraged her to warn others against telling Jake, a teenage member of the group who had a particular penchant for snooping around the church and the abandoned rectory, that the remaining relics were there. Annetta thought he might try to sell them for his own profit.

The uncomfortable and exhilarating discovery of these saintly objects reminded parishioners of the power of the buildings they suddenly possessed. When Annetta lifted up the altar cloth to show me the relics still embedded in the church's active altar, she wondered aloud if we were committing a sin. Annetta knew that of course the altar cloths were routinely changed, and that—at least in the period after the Second Vatican Council—lay people routinely stood upon the dais near the altar. But her caution and scrupulosity carried the imprint of the notions of presence and efficacy Catholics had worked so hard to build into their sacred objects and locales.[90]

The same was true of Annetta's response to a "Walk for Life" procession sponsored by a man from outside the community who had recently joined the resistance by attending (and often leading) the evening rosary. The plan had been for this pro-life march to make its way around East Boston, stopping along the way inside Mount Carmel for a prayer in front of the parish's statue of the Madonna. Although not everyone in the vigil was a supporter of "Right to Life" activism, they were happy to have marchers visit the supposedly closed Mount Carmel instead of the other nearby parishes. Hosting such a devout group of Catholics could provide Mount Carmel resisters with implicit endorsement and validation of their occupation.

But as the planning went forward Oscar, the walk's organizer, decided that he could not defy his pastor and the archbishop by leading the procession into the closed church. Annetta described Oscar's change as a hypocritical offense against the sacred character of the church building and the things in it: "You came here to say the rosary," she said she told him, "Why did you do that?" Answering her own question, Annetta said she reminded

Oscar about the sanctifying presence of Jesus' body in the form of consecrated hosts left in the tabernacle by the departing pastor: "You know the consecrated host is here." When he replied that he came because he had a devotion to Our Lady of Mount Carmel, Annetta rejected the suggestion that one could separate out the sacred presence and spiritual efficacy embedded in the church from that available from Our Lady. "*You* have a devotion?" she scoffed, implicitly comparing Oscar's cautious approach to the supposedly full-bodied devotion of the vigilers. Oscar's plan to lead the group in prayer on the street in front of the church building gave Annetta an idea: "I'll stand out [on the church portico] and when you say your prayers out in front of the church I'll take rotten tomatoes and throw them at you, even though they're expensive."[91] Annetta would rather that Mount Carmel had nothing to do with the "Walk for Life" than have these activists insult the sanctity of the church by refusing to respect the power and legitimacy of prayer made inside its walls. The church-front prayer went forward without the tomato-hurling, but Oscar soon stopped arriving at Mount Carmel for the rosaries. Oscar had no history at the parish before the shutdown, which perhaps made it easier for him to distinguish between his devotion to Our Lady of Mount Carmel and the affirmation of the inviolable sanctity of the church in East Boston that was one of her houses.

This was not the case for people like Celia and Sam, a husband and wife team who were two among the most die-hard members of the resistance. Neither Celia nor Sam shared the fervency of Oscar's devotion to Our Lady, although Celia did pray the rosary in front of her almost every evening. The couple's story offered another angle on the question of the meanings of the histories of sacred presence in the church. In the summer of 2005, seven months after Mount Carmel's official last mass, Celia and Sam celebrated their sixtieth wedding anniversary in the church hall. Although it had since been refurbished as a bingo hall (and later as an explicitly gambling-free gathering place), the basement where we toasted their anniversary was once the "lower church" where Celia and Sam had celebrated their wedding mass in 1945. This remarkable overlap seemed all the more notable in the context of the church occupation. When the closures were announced, it certainly would have seemed far-fetched to suggest that Sam and Celia would be celebrating their sixtieth anniversary seven months later in a priestless, outlaw church.

The church's longstanding endorsement of parishes as unique locales of sacred efficacy and presence became manifest in sacramental memory and hope. To newspaper reporters, to bishops, to one another, in memory books, and to me, Catholics in Boston again and again recited the names of people in their families who had received sacraments in the closing parishes. I also heard Catholics in resisting parishes fantasize that someday their children or grandchildren might get married there, or that they themselves would be buried from there someday. These sacramental histories and hopes were often among the first things I heard from people when I introduced myself to them as a researcher. It was as if these stories were enough, by themselves, to justify the protection of the building.

In the warm glow of Sam and Celia's anniversary, this certainly seemed to be the case. Celia took the opportunity to offer the group some general advice about marriage ("It gets easier"). Sam beamed about the community's affection and basked in its attention. If the occupation often seemed hopeless, here was an opportunity to justify having stayed with it thus far. Sacraments were markers of the intervention of the sacred power of the church in people's lives. In this case it was clear that it was not the church in general, but this specific place—the basement which had once housed an altar with the relics now in the closet upstairs—that solidified and gave meaning to that intervention. The church's continuing existence mirrored that of Sam and Celia's marriage, and indeed their lives. Certainly there was change. In recent years the couple's aging had not been easy. Celia suffered from severe back and leg pain, and Sam was occasionally hobbled by a bad hip. Their two sons had left East Boston, although one still returned frequently and made occasional visits to the occupied church. The "lower church" had gone from a site of sacramental practice to an unadorned meeting hall. The number of marriages still performed at Mount Carmel had plummeted.

But adaptation and decline were different than rupture. Sociologist Danièle Hervieu-Léger has suggested that changes in religious practice and structure in modern capitalist societies can be understood as a product of the "disintegration of collective memory." The genuine liberation that came with post-Enlightenment challenges to authoritative and official truths carried with it the potential to destroy the ability of discrete social groups to transmit their knowledge from one generation to the next. As modern people pursue the dynamic and fluid ideal of self-realization, memory ironically becomes "homogenized" by aligning mainly along the lines available in the "sphere of production." In this realm, memories are "technical, functionalized, and neutral" and thus lacking in depth, sharpness, normativity, and "creative capacity." At the same time, the flood of information available with advanced systems of mass communication also undermines collective memory by subjecting people to a never-ending sequence of disconnected snippets of news.

Alongside homogenization, then, modern societies tend toward the "fragmentation" of memory into the "isolated recollection and scraps of information which are increasingly incoherent." For Hervieu-Léger, understanding the fragmentation and homogenization of memory advances what we can say about secularization. Loss of religion is in part a loss of memory, the waning ability of people to imagine themselves as part of a "chain" extending back meaningfully into the past and forward into the future.[92]

Sam and Celia's anniversary party was not a dramatic event. The resisters scheduled the brief moment of celebration to immediately follow one of the group's Monday night meetings, when leaders of the group would update the others about various happenings in the resistance and discuss how to proceed. Shoehorned into the schedule like this, the party's setting was simple and sparse: fluorescent lights overhead, folding chairs and tables on the linoleum, paper plates, cake, champagne, and coffee. No big speeches or grand gestures were performed. But even in its simplicity the moment testified to the complex histories that made the shutdown of places like Mount Carmel and the North End's Sacred Heart something more than a difficult necessity for the good of a struggling diocese. For the resisters the shutdowns were an attempt to shut down memory, and therefore a subversion of religion. This is what Val meant when he accused the archbishop of sinning and what Susana and others meant when she compared the closures to sexual abuse and cover-up, and what David meant when he explicitly called the archbishop to account for making people lose their religion. The shared moral world of Catholic abundance, the idea of the universal church living in and through the individual parish and its supporters, and the profound inviolability built into churches at their consecration, all of these components of Catholics' past served to specify and deepen Catholic memory and the possibilities for meaning, even as neighborhoods and the church itself changed across the twentieth century.

Divergent Histories: Change and the Making of Resisters, 1950–2004

First-time visitors to Our Lady of Mount Carmel church in East Boston could easily miss the small saints' room tucked in the corner immediately to the right upon entry. From the beginning of the church's existence, this room had been a site for intimate devotional prayer. Along its main wall, there were several alcoves cut out of green marble, each housing a different saint. Since the church's beginnings, petitioners would light candles in front of a particular saint, dropping perhaps a few coins, a dollar, or more as a donation and offering. Income from these and other candles around the church ranged from a high of about $424/week in 1945 to about $250/week in the mid-1990s.[1]

By the early 1980s, the relatively luxurious and languid economy of this back room—individual parishioners making small anonymous sacrifices on good faith—had to be augmented with a new mode of exchange. Because of a continuing need for maintenance and a relatively small base of regular parishioners, a new plan emerged to fund needed renovations. Having already emblazoned their names (or the names of their ancestors) on the church's pews, windows, doors, and many of its statues, the parishioners were now offered the chance to purchase a plaque to be mounted in the saints' room. Many jumped at the opportunity. From 1980 to 1997, the open spaces on the remaining walls were gradually covered with small wooden plaques with names, dates, and small crosses on them. These plaques were mounted in uniform rows, evenly spaced from one another and clustered tightly around preexisting wall hangings. The saints—the Redemptorist St.

Gerardo in a black robe, blind St. Lucia of Syracuse holding her eyeballs in a dish, royally clad St. Liberatore, St. Maria of Monte Viggiano (dated September 1925), among others—were now joined by their benefactors as fixtures in the back room.

By comparison, the new windows at St. Albert the Great Parish in Weymouth are hard to miss. As part of a late 1990s parish improvement campaign, the pastor at St. Albert's had proposed replacing the church's dusty yellow arched windows with colorful stained-glass windows depicting the saints. The finance committee and the pastor had already taken out loans for other church and rectory improvements, and the general offerings could not support the expense, so the windows would have to be funded by direct parishioner donations. This plan was a tremendous success, with parishioners rushing to claim their favorite saints and commissioning fifty-six windows at a cost of $2,500 to $3,000 each. Together with her daughters, thirty-five-year parishioner Catharine secured St. Anthony in memory of their husband and father. This was a fulfilled dream for Catharine, who remembered that she had always wanted to find a way to memorialize her husband in the church. Her appreciation of the opportunity speaks to the immediacy of the investment that parishioners at newer churches like St. Albert's felt.[2] Instead of recalling loved ones from several generations ago or families who had moved elsewhere over the years, the windows at St. Albert's and the plaques at Mount Carmel carry a much more proximate memorial.

In addition to joy or the memory of loss and the honor of becoming a donor, these raw, living memorials could evoke shame, embarrassment, or anger. Plaques at Mount Carmel memorializing families that had left the parish were a sad emblem of change and loss. One of St. Albert's new windows memorializes Cardinal Bernard Law, who helped dedicate the new windows and received one in his honor.[3] In 2002, Cardinal Law would step down and leave Boston after he admitted making mistakes in his handling of cases of clerical sexual assault. If they were suddenly "surrounded by the saints," mass-goers at St. Albert's were also now in the potent presence of the not-so-distant past and the corruptible present.[4]

Parishioners looted Mount Carmel's saints' room shortly after the closure announcement in 2004. With the pastor's blessing, many of the plaques that lined the walls were pried loose and taken home by donors or their families. This left the room with a strange appearance; the neat rows of donor plaques were broken occasionally where a family had reclaimed what was left of its gift to the parish. Where plaques had been removed, however, they left a light outline of themselves, delineated by the clean wall-space they had protected from smoke and dust. These traces of sacrifice, jarring alongside plaques forgotten or left behind out of defiance or indifference, remained evident during the years of church occupation.

The whole room provided a map of the long and changing history of sacrifice that had shaped Catholics in Boston. Just as the proliferation of plaques alongside saints signaled the growing need for the church to become "the people" more and more literally, their imperfect and unfinished removal spoke to the complexity of sacrifice as a guiding Catholic ideal in the period of church closings. Sacrifice remained; how and why it related to the rules of practicing a modern parish remained abiding questions.

Bernard Law's name among the names of St. Albert's parishioners' loved ones on church windows prompted similar questions. If the windows represented the objective transformation of the local church into the people of God, Law's name among them put the meaning and weight of that theology in doubt. The abuse crisis in Boston shone a light on the self-serving secrecy, intimate power, and insularity that the structures and fears of the late twentieth-century church made possible.[5] If the people of God ecclesiology signaled a new humility in a church chastened by the dramas of the first half of the twentieth century, then perhaps Law's presence in St. Albert's windows served as a dark reinscription of that teaching: the church is the people of God, not an infallible institution.[6] But if, as seemed to be the case in Boston, the teaching had more to do with the softening of status differences in the church and the encouragement of lay ownership of the church, then Law's presence served as a reminder of the limits of that vision and a bitter encouragement to church occupiers, who saw Law's negligence as a crime and a precursor to church shutdowns.

Tumultuous Years for a Pivotal Generation

As these abiding questions built into Boston's churches suggest, resisters' pasts were both contested and divided. This is why so many of their stories and so much of their activity concentrated on the meanings of recent history. The future of their parishes depended on achieving a proper understanding of their pasts. Since the past was itself unstable, resisters faced a complex challenge. The struggle in Boston was in part a struggle over Catholic memory. As such, the episode reaches beyond its immediate context and into larger questions facing U.S. Catholics. As Robert Orsi has argued, contemporary Catholics are both seduced and repulsed by the recent past, particularly by the heyday of parish and family-based devotionalism in the several decades leading up to the Second Vatican Council.[7] How Catholics remember says a lot about their place in and sense of the present. The shuttered churches became one battleground in that larger struggle to define the possibilities and promise of the Catholic future by deciding how and what to lift up from its past. Major changes in the language of sacrifice and authority, in the urban environment, and in teachings about the meanings of Catholic locales and objects provided both opportunities and challenges to Catholics' efforts to answer those questions.

This chapter moves from 1950, when St. Albert the Great was founded, through 2004, when it, along with Mount Carmel, Sacred Heart, and dozens of other Boston parishes, ended up on the closure list. Like the older narratives of local autonomy, Catholic abundance and separatism, and overflowing sacred presence, memories from this more recent period emerged forcefully among Catholics as rationales and justifications for the resistance. As before, there were challenges to marshaling these recent memories to upend the closure plan. For one thing, defenders of the reconfiguration took hold of these same pasts as they explained and justified the shutdowns. And resisters themselves, both individually and as groups, struggled with the meanings of the various pasts the occupations highlighted.

Another difficulty facing resisters, who relied so much on reconstituting community memory, rested in the momentous changes across this period in the ways Catholics encountered their parishes, the church, and their neighborhoods. But resisters were not just passive recipients of these changes, they were among the prime witnesses, instigators, and interpreters of those transformations. They were part of a pivotal generation. The majority of those associated with resisting parishes were above middle age, born between 1930 and 1960.[8] They grew up with at least some familiarity with the mass as it had been performed for centuries, in Latin. And they witnessed the transformation, in response to the major and most intricately debated innovations of the Second Vatican Council, to a fully vernacular mass after the mid-1960s. They saw the sacrament of penance fall into almost complete disuse and once robust Marian devotions decline.[9] They experienced rapid declines, beginning in the 1970s, in the number of priests, nuns, and brothers in Boston's parishes and schools.[10] They were part of a church that took stances in the public realm (of varying vigor) during their young adult years against communism, divorce, contraception, and abortion, and in favor of busing.[11]

Social changes were also dramatic during the resisters' formative years. They moved into young adulthood between the 1950s and 1970s, a time of change in Catholics' patterns of work, their sense of civic engagement, and their residential tendencies.[12] They were educated during a time when Catholics were much more likely than before or after to attend a Catholic high school, college, or university. Partly for this reason, they were more likely than their predecessors to achieve middle- or upper-middle-class economic status.[13] Catholic schools started to close in the late 1960s and early 1970s, just at the time when the resisters were beginning to have school-age children of their own.[14]

Broad changes in patterns of parish participation also entailed significant adjustments for those who remained loyal churchgoers. Boston pastors in the first half of the twentieth century could be confident that they would fill their churches for several masses on Sundays. They could count on strong attendance for novenas, missions, rosaries, holy days, bazaars, and other parish events. This vitality continued into the 1950s.[15] As we have seen, this did not prevent church leaders from articulating the challenges facing their parishes or from prodding those who had not contributed to the vitality of the parish. Later, extra-parish movements such as the "charismatic renewal" and "centering prayer" offered alternatives for a number of Catholics, but for the most part the territorial or national parishes remained the center of Catholic practice.[16] In the short term, parish growth and decline were not uniform, but oscillated unevenly in local places depending on the appeal of the current pastor, the vitality of certain clubs, or generationally clustered demand for rites of passage. But in the longer term, after a period of significant urban flight and suburban growth, both suburban and urban parishes faced the challenge of an overextended and under-attended Boston church. Catholic expansion joined with decreasing parish participation to make financial struggles a defining feature of parish life in the latter half of the twentieth century in Boston.[17]

The lived environment of Boston was changing in this period as well. In the immediate post-war period America's cities were badly deteriorating. Infrastructure that had sustained them in the early part of the twentieth century had crumbled during the lean years of the 1930s. The post-war boom and suburbanization left many cities behind while also demanding more of their transportation systems. Boston felt the pressure to modernize with unique urgency. Changes in maritime and other industries meant that the city had suffered mightily in the 1920s and into the Great Depression. By the time of the Second World War the city's infrastructure was nearing complete collapse.[18]

In addition to the broader national economic downturns, Boston's atmosphere of suspicion and rivalry had contributed to its catastrophic decline. The administration of Boston's longtime mayor James Michael Curley was widely suspected of corruption, and New Deal agencies and private businesses punished the city by diverting investments elsewhere. Curley's counterpart in the church, Cardinal William Henry O'Connell (Archbishop of Boston from 1907–1944), exacerbated the impression of Boston as an embattled place with his assertive claims about the rise of a triumphant Catholicism in the former heart of Protestant America. Where other U.S. cities had been able to channel post-war investments more successfully into their urban centers, the image and reality of Boston's internal divisiveness hindered its recovery. The city's urban poor and its infrastructure suffered the results of this dysfunction. Its streets and bridges deteriorated, industrial centers closed down, and civic spaces became rough and disordered. As a result, outlying regions began to attract post-war business and real-estate developments.[19]

The desperate need to modernize Boston transformed what it meant to be Catholic in the city. As the urban environment changed around them, city Catholics encountered new challenges to their efforts to maintain livable and sustainable neighborhoods. As historian John T. McGreevy has shown, neighborhood change had direct and powerful theological entailments. In Catholic urban centers across the North and East, "the community came to be church within a particular, geographically defined space." This early and mid-twentieth-century "theological emphasis on the local" invested not only parish mortgages (which when paid were often ceremoniously burned on the altar) with religious meaning, but also gave religious significance to the less manageable problems posed by the bulldozers, highways, tunnels, and airplanes of Boston's modernization.[20]

As Boston changed, the church changed with it. Following its parishioners into the suburbs, the archdiocese entered a second building boom between 1940 and 1960. During these years, the archdiocese gained sixty-five new parishes outside of Boston, Cambridge, Lowell, and Lawrence. Within these urban centers the archdiocese gained only eight new parishes over the same period. A longer view highlights the expansion of Catholic suburbs: beginning in 1917 only nine new parishes were to be added in the archdiocese's urban zones. In contrast, 149 new suburban churches would be built between 1917 and 1984, when the archdiocese had a high of 299 suburban churches.[21]

A combination of immigration, migration, and especially increased birthrates meant that approximately 600,000 new Catholics came into the archdiocese between 1940 and 1960. This tremendous growth matched the kind of expansion in Catholic Boston that had been seen during the heaviest years of European Catholic immigration.[22] Expansion continued into the late 1960s, with growth centering in the expanding number of parishes outside of the city. While the archdiocese's Catholic population continued to grow, most of the new Catholics lived in the suburbs, leaving urban parishes to survive with fewer and less wealthy parishioners. Changes in the urban population did not result in the church's abandonment of the city. For decades through the mid-twentieth century, the number of urban parishes remained steady despite shifting populations and limited neighborhood resources and participation. While suburban churches started to close in the mid-1980s, it was not until the late 1990s that the number of urban parishes began to drop.[23]

For this reason "hierarchy" should not be understood as a term of contempt. The church's hierarchical organization has been both an asset and a challenge in the maintenance of local parishes across American Catholic history. As Gerald Gamm and others have pointed out, centralized management, along with the territorial connotations of the parish system, allowed dioceses and various religious orders to make the kinds of commitments of money and personnel to urban parishes that other, more congregationally organized religious organizations could not. Churches like East Boston's Our Lady of Mount Carmel, nearby Our Lady of the Assumption, and the North End's Sacred Heart were getting smaller and less wealthy, but they were not yet in danger of being closed.[24]

But the relationship of the center to the periphery in the modern church was more complex than this notion of redeeming hierarchical stability suggests.[25] The location and form of authority in the church had been called sharply into question by the Second Vatican Council's *Lumen Gentium* ("Dogmatic Constitution on the Church," 1964) and its "Decree on the Apostolate of Lay People" (1965). In particular, the notion of the church as the people of God provided opportunities and challenges for Catholics who had been accustomed, in the years before the Council, to an explicitly and unapologetically top-down model of decision making in the church and at the level of the parish. Appearing prominently in *Lumen Gentium's* second chapter (after an opening chapter on the "Mystery of the Church" and before a chapter called "The Church is Hierarchical"), this notion of the church as "the People of God" advanced the idea that the church could not be contained solely by its hierarchy, its doctrines, or even its tradition. "The symbolism of the change was potent," historian John W. O'Malley writes, "the first reality of the church is horizontal and consists of all the baptized, without distinction of rank."[26] This was a more open notion of church than had prevailed in previous decades, when centralization of authority, suspicion about "modernity," and moral, linguistic, and liturgical uniformity and permanence had been the defining features of the "culture" of the church, which had offered itself to the fallen world as a perfect society.[27]

In contrast, the notion of people as the church extended the structure horizontally; the church moved outward into the world as a "pilgrim" sharing in the broad human effort to realize together the mystery of Christ's announcement of the Kingdom of God. In addition to suggesting an opening up of universal church decisions to greater input from the world's bishops (collegiality), the emphasis on the people of God entailed a softening of the boundaries separating lay from clerical Catholics with respect to the church's role and mission in the world. Lay Catholics, *Lumen* asserted, shared in a "holy priesthood" which was ordained by God and signaled their real "consecration" toward acts of sacrifice and bearing prophetic "witness to Christ." As the title of the following chapter, "The Church is Hierarchical," made clear, however, although all members of the church share in a "common priesthood of the faithful," there are differences "not only in essence but also in degree," among ministerial and hierarchical priesthoods (priests and bishops) and the priesthood of the baptized. While all participate, for example, in the offering of the Eucharist, only those of the ministerial priesthood do so with "sacred power" and "acting in the person of Christ." This "sacred power" was also reserved to bishops in their guidance and instruction of others. In other words, they acted with the authority of Christ in their management of the church.

Despite these important constraints, the emphasis in *Lumen Gentium* and "The Decree on the Apostolate of the Laity" on lay Catholics' priesthood attempted to gather up lay Catholics into the common mission of the church. Their very worldliness was cast as an attribute, making them ideal workers "for the sanctification of the world from within as a leaven." In parishes, this language helped make possible the implementation of lay Eucharistic ministers, lectors, cantors, and musicians during mass and opened the door widely for lay pastoral assistants, school principals, and teachers, whose numbers would grow impressively in postconciliar years.[28] These kinds of commitments and parishioner acceptance of their responsibility, not only in the preservation, but also in the management and "ownership" of the church would become crucial in the latter three decades of the twentieth century.

The next pages track parish calls for the sacrifices of the people of God amid the toughening economic climate of this period. The story takes us back and forth between suburban St. Albert the Great and the urban, ethnic parish of Our Lady of Mount Carmel. Parishioners learned in these years the potency of the people of God ecclesiology as a call to both opportunity and responsibility. The lessons of this kind of parishioner formation, despite being laced with reminders of the basic hierarchical structure of the church, posed distinct challenges to the effort of reconfiguration begun in 2004.

"There is a cost": Scarcity and the People of God

Founded in 1950, St. Albert the Great Parish grew up directly within the demographic shifts troubling Boston's urban parishes. Along with other towns on Boston's South Shore, Weymouth became an area of growth after the war. With a naval air station established in South Weymouth in 1941 and subsidized housing for war veterans going up in the 1950s, Weymouth's population expanded rapidly. Between 1945 and 1960, Weymouth gained 21,000 new residents, a number equal to over half of its 1960 population.[29] Although Weymouth was an old town with some light industry, its growth was not the development of urban density, but the more measured expansion typical of post-war bedroom communities. Weymouth's position straddling Route 3 made it especially convenient for commuters. This bisection also meant that Weymouth would remain more of a working-class town than its more secluded and sheltered neighbors such as Hingham and Scituate. Along with greater affordability, Weymouth's relative proximity to Boston made it an attractive option for a significant portion of Boston's mid-century migrants.

Naturally, the church itself was understood to be a permanent part of Weymouth. A newspaper photograph and caption documented the April

29, 1951, groundbreaking ceremony and promised that with St. Albert's, "the spiritual welfare of Weymouth is ensured for the future."[30] In January 1954, the first pastor, Father Connors, received authorization to perform the dedication on the completed church. A month later, the church had received its solemn blessing and benediction.[31] A new place had been established on Boston's Catholic map. Like the old places, it beckoned for the loyalty of its Catholics. At first, the parish experienced steady growth and unquestioned stability. Between the groundbreaking of 1951 and 1962, the parish nearly doubled from 465 to 950 families. But by the 1970s, St. Albert the Great suffered from the kind of financial strain that was testing many of Boston's urban parishes. While the number of baptisms remained steady at about ninety per year in the 1960s, a pattern of decline soon set in. Between 1968 and 1973 the number of baptisms fell from ninety-three to sixty-nine. In 1981, only fifty-nine were baptized.[32]

This slackening was accompanied by financial and political struggles. A telling controversy during 1970–71 appears briefly in the parish correspondence files at the archdiocesan archives. The exchanges reveal the challenges Catholics faced in the implementation of practical reforms associated with the Second Vatican Council. The conciliar call for greater lay involvement in parish finances and planning met with uneven success across the United States. Many dioceses, including Boston, established offices particularly designed to mediate between pastors and the newly created parish boards or councils.[33] After just over a year in existence, St. Albert's board called upon Boston's "Moderator of Councils" to use his authority to encourage greater cooperation from their pastor. The board's letter to Cardinal Humberto Medeiros, signed by eight lay members and two priest assistants who were listed as "Spiritual Director[s]" to the council, expressed dismay at the pastor's refusal to join board meetings. Officially the "Council Board Chairman," the pastor had only attended the first meeting and had not responded to the meeting minutes sent to him or to their many invitations. The pastor "mistrusts the Board," the letter said, "does not approve of the Board, and refuses now to speak to any Board members about any matter." Factors beyond the breakdown in communication also created this occasion for writing. According to the board members this was a "crucial period in St. Albert's history":

> The majority of parishioners in St. Albert's parish share the knowledge that the parish is in a state of decline. They are discouraged and disillusioned and are confused as to where they should turn now. The only chance for

> survival for the future of this parish is through cooperation with the pastor. We need the guidance and direction of the Pastor as recommended by the writings of Vatican II.

Motivated by this broad sense of urgency and eager to incorporate the latest church teachings on lay participation, the board and other St. Albert's parishioners would find themselves placed under even greater demand in the coming years.[34]

Money became a constant theme at the parish. A new pastor offered greater transparency, but this openness came with even more frank and alarming assessments of the parish's financial straits. The 1973 implementation of an envelope system for parish giving made it clear who among the parishioners had given what amounts to the upkeep of the struggling church. A thin yearly budget and abiding debts to the archdiocese spurred a series of fundraising drives.[35] Financial strain had a way of trickling down from the chancery as well. In early May of 1974 parishioners listened to a tape recording of Cardinal Medeiros reflecting on "present diocesan problems" and the need for parishes to pay their "'just debts'" to the archdiocese. Medeiros had inherited a forty million dollar budget deficit, even after his predecessor, the gregarious Cardinal Richard Cushing, had significantly cut archdiocesan debts.[36] Wider economic struggles started to manifest nationally. Whispers of a problem with inflation related to spending for defense and the war in Vietnam worried economists in the boom years of the 1960s. After 1973, the nation faced a severe economic downturn, with rising unemployment hitting hardest in the lives of baby boomers and racial and ethnic minorities. If these changes made it harder for St. Albert's parishioners to meet the parish's needs, parishioners were consistently made aware of their abiding responsibility as Catholics. Shortfalls become a "double burden," the pastor noted, "because eventually the parish has to pay it" out of the general revenue, thus delaying "needed repairs."[37]

In these years the bulletin repeatedly directed parishioners' attention to details of debt and to calls for help coming from the local pastor, the chancery, and the Vatican. Medeiros wrote to parishes in early June of 1975 outlining the residual challenges of the recent growth of the Boston church and noting that the entire church was "tightening our belts" in order to restore the church to solvency:

> during the years of expansion when new parishes and institutions had to be established, the diocesan debt rose to eighty million dollars. We have

> been paying substantial sums on this debt and it is now down to twenty-two million.[38]

An "increased income appeal" at St. Albert's in late 1976, sent at least one hundred parish volunteers out to residences to distribute new envelopes and a census form to parishioners. The pastor explained the project by focusing on the future and appealing to parishioners' business sense:

> Please remember this Appeal represents a SOUND INVESTMENT in our wonderful parish with its excellent programs and fine facilities that will reflect the love and generosity of ALL parishioners. It will guarantee a renewed and fiscally-sound St. Albert's parish. The parish is counting on YOU!"[39]

While this effort resulted in a significant temporary boost for the parish, four years later it was clear that the parish would "scarcely keep even" if the weekly collections were their only source of income. Like urban Mount Carmel, by the mid-1970s St. Albert's was relying on church-hall gaming to stay afloat. By 1980, parishioners were warned not to let the few committed "Beano" volunteers get overworked, for revenues from the game had "paid for all our major improvements and supported the various programs of the church."[40] Vatican II calls for lay involvement often meant a willingness to make serious financial sacrifices to keep the parish afloat.

In East Boston, Mount Carmel had arrived at 1980, its 75th year as a parish, with similarly pressing concerns. Like St. Albert's, Mount Carmel was not meeting its yearly assessment bills from the archdiocese and was having trouble paying its dues to a new multiparish Catholic elementary school.[41] While the story is inevitably one of decline, the parish's survival through this period of broader transition speaks to the sacrifices of its remaining members. Since Mount Carmel was a national parish, it could not be as agile in adapting to new neighborhood demographics. If local territorial parishes had a claim on the neighborhood and whoever was living in it, Mount Carmel—like Sacred Heart in the North End—offered a distinctively Italian Catholicism. This did not mean that it gave up all connection to the neighborhood, but it did mean that the parish relied on attracting people from neighboring communities. Since many of those who left East Boston over the years were among the upwardly mobile, retaining their loyalty became even more important to parish survival.[42] If revenues declined and buildings crumbled, the church nonetheless persisted on the gifts of a dedicated few. As ideas of church changed, the accent of sacrifice would shift too.

Our Lady of Mount Carmel's long history aided its leaders in communicating the message that the church warranted the sacrifices of its members. As it had at St. Albert's, the language of church as the people of God enhanced the message by clearly signaling the need for each person's involvement. It also made it possible to lift up local values and to affirm a community ethos that was distinct from the broader archdiocese. A 1980 jubilee address from the provincial head of Mount Carmel's Franciscan friars makes use of the local past and contemporary church teachings to make the case for Mount Carmel as a precious site of intimate local truths. The vicar provincial, The Rev. Cletus J. Dello Iacono, OFM, JCD, began the address by evoking the sacrifices of the previous generations of parishioners:

> The men who established this parish were of Italian birth and of Italian parentage. They did not possess much in the way of material goods, but they counted as the foremost of their possessions their Catholic faith.

Because of this faith, he reminded the people, "they were willing to make the financial sacrifices necessary for providing a means to fulfill their obligation to worship God."[43] Drawing on the legacy of the ancestors to give a new perspective to present hardships, Rev. Dello Iacono urged unflinching devotion: "in deference to their memory, we pledge that we cannot let their work die."[44] But there were multiple challenges to consider. The flowering of "many ideologies" and the "rapid changing lifestyle of the neighborhood" posed great threats and explained, at least in part, the several defeats the parish had felt over the past years. Among other hardships noted were loss of parishioners and the closure of the school and the convent.

Dello Iacono also listed and tried to correct various false "categories" of opinion on the teachings of the Second Vatican Council in relation to the meaning of a parish. The Second Vatican Council, Dello Iacono urged, did not signal a diminished need for a "stable parish." Those who cited the Council's "Pastoral Constitution on the Church in the Modern World" to suggest that the money spent building churches instead should be put to humanitarian causes had taken the reforms too far. Others who grew "impatient with compromises" and those who, "appealing to Church Tradition," said that "certain things can never change" also missed the essential point. The Council offered renewal, not revolutionary reform. Some clung too tightly, Dello Iacono continued, to the way things were; they saw too many changes and remained "fearful" of losing the church as their "symbol of security."

To all of these understandable misconceptions Dello Iacono added an endorsement of Mount Carmel as a "living community" that must "continue to grow." Despite the skeptics, the parish "will undoubtedly continue to be the normal way most people live as members of the church." Other movements and groups may offer "particularly engaging preaching" or "more inspiring" celebration of the liturgy, but the parish is the essential core of Catholic living. Despite struggles, conflicts, and confusions, the parish as the center of Catholic practice was not going anywhere.[15]

Moving from this "blueprint" toward more personal realities, Dello Iacono did not hesitate to endorse Our Lady of Mount Carmel as a particular place on the Catholic landscape. "Mount Carmel," he told his listeners, "remains the place" for your sacramental moments, for celebrating your faith, for hearing Christ's message, for confronting your "bad choices," and for contacting "the mystery of God." "There are no better means," Dello Iacono urged, "by which people can better understand and live their Christianity than in their parish community." The promise of this place meant that "when you gather as *Church*, as the People of God, in Mt. Carmel you are assured that the message and life of Christ is brought to you." As a provincial head, Dello Iacono had probably uttered similar words about the various parishes associated with his Franciscan province. In this case at least, the ecclesiology of the church as the people of God only bolstered the value of the local parish in a specific part of a community. Dello Iacono's words aimed explicitly to undermine the notion that the new ecclesiological emphasis signaled a diminished need for the local parish.

Dello Iacono's paean to Mount Carmel also included consideration of the unique position of a parish on the social landscape. The place was not merely there to advance a vision of the church's mission, it was there to provide an alternative community, free of the constraints and alienations of the modern world:

> The parish, then, is the Church in miniature. It is Christ living in His members at a particular place and time in human history . . . a parish is not merely an exclusive group of individuals who happen to live in the same geographical area; it is a family in which the members are united to one another by strong spiritual bonds, especially the bond of love.

This love circled within the community, but also extended beyond it. In this light, Dello Iacono outlined Mount Carmel's duties and its importance in the city. The three Catholic churches within just a few blocks notwithstanding, "Mount Carmel today, as it has been for these seventy-five years, is responsible for the life of the church in this area of East Boston." This approach combined guilt over the lost glorious past with a promise that the parish could still be a community where inviolable values could overcome material trials and the pressures of secularization. Commitment to this place was as good as commitment to the church.[46]

A 1984 booklet from Mount Carmel also drew directly on the Council. Entitled "My Parish," it emphasized rules related to participation and the rewards of a measure of parish ownership. Its cover letter is worth including in its entirety:

> Dear Parishioners:
>
> The Second Vatican Council tells us that the CHURCH is the "PEOPLE OF GOD." The Church of our Lady of Mt. Carmel then is
>
> YOUR CHURCH. . . . . .
>
> YOUR PARISH. . . . . .
>
> YOUR HOUSE OF WORSHIP. . . . . .
>
> The Franciscans, who have been assigned to YOUR CHURCH are there to help you and to serve you in every way possible.
>
> The purpose of this Booklet is to offer you a handy source of reference to the different LITURGICAL SERVICES AND ORGANIZATIONS of your Parish, with the hope that YOU may become still more involved with its spiritual and social growth.[47]

The capital letters and underlining of these notes at both Mount Carmel and St. Albert's work simultaneously to enjoin lay sacrifice and to signal the limits of clerical capacity and responsibility to keep the parish going. In one respect this was an old narrative: the church thrives on the lifeblood of parishioner engagement. But the language of church as "the People," along with the threats of Catholic decline gave the message a new edge. Encouraging ownership of "my parish" required a seamless connection between the church as the people of God and the local, physical church buildings.

Just over ten years later, in November of 1996, the archdiocese and the pastors in East Boston and elsewhere began reshaping this message in light of ongoing struggles and the looming need for consolidation. This was the process of "clustering" of parishes, which happened across the archdiocese after Cardinal Law mandated the process in a pastoral letter issued in 1994. The aim, according to the announcement letter in East Boston, was to strengthen local Catholic communities by helping them avoid the unnecessary "duplication of programs and expenditures." Justifying the necessary transitions required a rethinking of ecclesiology. The letter in East Boston signaled the transition: instead of highlighting the parish as the "Church in miniature" as had been done at Mount Carmel as recently as 1984, it was now clearly best to de-emphasize parish boundaries and instead highlight the breadth of the church. After listing problems such as crumbling (but still "beautiful") churches, decreasing populations, under-attended masses, and the aging and declining numbers of priests, the letter outlined a difficult, but necessary solution:

> For years, we have been conditioned to think of our particular parish as our home, and rightly so. Such identification with out [*sic*!] parish is a source of strength and should not lightly be set aside. However, our Cardinal has now asked us to expand our vision. He has asked us to consider how we can best serve the needs of all of East Boston with the resources we have at hand.

The letter goes on to valorize "collaboration" over "competition" and solicits the help and "constructive suggestions" from the people of East Boston's parishes. The process of parish clustering was in part designed to prepare the ground for reconfiguration. The "clusters" that were created in the mid-1990s would meet during the 2004 shutdowns to decide which of their member parishes should close. Competition between parishes, then, was difficult to erase from the picture entirely.[48]

Concern for intra-parish sustainability persisted and grew even more intense as clustering signaled potential shutdowns of weak or redundant parishes. Across the years, appeals for cash and more parishioner help ranged from strident and accusatory, to cajoling, encouraging, and businesslike. At St. Albert's in Weymouth, a 1999 bulletin masthead reveals that the principle of giving had been woven directly into the parish title: "St. Albert the Great: A Stewardship Parish." The call for parishioner engagement had become a defining characteristic of the church. These bulletins also contained a regular feature called "Stewardship Corner" where readers learned of special acts of giving or requests for further contributions in support of "your parish, your spiritual home."[49] In 2001, the pastor and the finance committee offered a quarterly financial report outlining the church's health and its prospects:

> Father Nichols and your parish Finance Committee want to thank you for your generous response to our request for increased offertory contributions. We are not surprised as you have always responded when we asked.

Appreciation quickly turned into accusation and a reminder of the rules of practicing parish:

> Asking for money is always difficult and really should not be necessary. We all have a personal obligation to support the church as would be appropriate given our individual circumstances, as Disciples of Christ. Just as there is a price to pay to live as free Americans, so too there is a cost to worship where and how we chose [*sic*].[50]

The recrimination and urgency of this report surely related to the recent loans the church had taken out from the archdiocese for church improvements. Just as paying one's taxes and abiding by the law undergird the U.S. democracy, contributions and parish participation ensured the future of the St. Albert's community. This comparison suggested that the people had the final say, through their choice either to fulfill or neglect their obligations, in the contours of their parish life. If parishioners were naïve to believe such claims in the context of a hierarchical organization, little from the histories of these parishes suggests that anyone did much work to disabuse them of these notions. And how could they? One cannot simultaneously lead people toward sacrifice for growth and prime them for loss and detachment.

News revelations on the Feast of the Epiphany, January 6, 2002, may have done the trick. This was the date investigators at the *Globe* chose to reveal the first wave of findings from their inquiry into the cover-up, across several decades, of clerical sexual abuse in the Archdiocese of Boston. The issue was not entirely new. Questions about clerical abuse and the proper response to it had occupied the U.S. church off and on since the 1985 revelations in Henry, Louisiana, about the serial abuse by Father Gilbert Gauthé.[51] In 1992, the United States Council of Catholic Bishops, following the model already established in Chicago under Cardinal Bernardin, addressed clerical sexual abuse and the problems of cover-up with a five-part plan. In 1993 it established an ad-hoc committee on sexual abuse in the Church. Pope John Paul II formally addressed the issue twice in 1993 and again in 1999.[52]

In January of 1994, Cardinal Law issued a letter to be inserted in parish bulletins about the crisis and the proper archdiocesan response. While isolating "some priests" from "[m]ost priests," the cardinal offered a vision of the church as a united entity, collectively in need of healing:

> I encourage local parish leaders to gather with parishioners for prayer. Let our prayers be shaped by our mutual need to ask for mercy and forgiveness,

> by our need to express repentance for deeds committed or interventions not made, and especially, by our need to overcome all forms of abuse be it in the family, the Church or society.[53]

This letter deflected attention from the church's problem with secrecy and insularity, but the archdiocese had begun more actively to address the kinds of behavior that would explode as scandal in Boston eight years later. One year earlier, for example, Father John Geoghan had finally been removed permanently from active parish ministry by Cardinal Law. Law had known about Geoghan's abusive actions since 1984, but his last chance, at St. Julia's in Weston (Geoghan was there off and on from 1984–1993), had proven another disaster.[54] Widespread acknowledgement of the problems in the American Catholic Church certainly contributed to his final removal in 1993 and his defrocking in 1998. It wasn't until the 2002 revelations in Boston, however, that the issue accelerated and gathered widespread momentum as a full-blown crisis.[55]

As the crisis grew heated, St. Albert's received a new pastor. By all accounts, Father Ronald Coyne transformed the parish. His particular message was a direct gospel of love and an endorsement of more democratic church. He was known for rejecting the existence of hell and for urging older Catholics to abandon their attachments to the overbearing guilt and anxieties of their Catholic upbringings. Personalization and ownership became themes that carried forward into the parish's sense of itself in the early twenty-first century. If the new stained-glass windows made the church "the people" even more literally than before, the new pastor drove this message home with constant reminders. When he took over around Easter of 2002, Father Coyne struck a note that would resonate through his teachings and continue in the voices of the vigilers. "You are gifted and you are the church," he told them immediately, and offered to make good on this philosophy by holding "listening sessions" where anyone could make suggestions to him and to the parish council, which he hoped would also attend.[56] The theme of stewardship returned as well, not in the bulletin masthead, but in the mission statement, which described stewardship as the giving of "time, talent, and treasure to further the goals of our commitment to the service of God's people."[57]

Directly addressing the sexual abuse crisis and yet still having to seek parish financing and debt reduction, Coyne spoke of the church as a local institution with the people at the center:

> This is not an easy time to contribute to the Church, but your generosity assures me that you trust the leadership of our parish. Your investment financially and spiritually guarantees a healthy future.[58]

Part of ensuring this healthy future required paying down the $150,000 parish debt accrued in the recent church and rectory renovations. With increasing numbers of parishioners the parish managed to eliminate the debt within two years. Coyne's guarantees, however, and his repeated promise that "it is your church!" would be profoundly tested when St. Albert's ended up on the list of parishes designated for closure.[59]

A comparable history at Mount Carmel gave its arrival on the closure list a similar sting. In 2001 a Mount Carmel parishioner named David was scheduled for a heart transplant. Asking for help from his beloved Padre Pio, David promised to erect a statue in the saint's honor should he survive the ordeal. David was not new to parish fundraising and devotional life. Over the years, David had been a consistent advocate of Mount Carmel's traditions. He spearheaded the effort to sustain the parish's Feast for Our Lady of Sorrows by arranging processions with the statue and celebrations in the Blessed Mother's honor each September. As we have seen, David and his wife Susana were among the most active fundraisers in the parish.

After David emerged from surgery and had made a full recovery, he took up the project of erecting not just a statue, but an entire shrine to Padre Pio across the street from the church. He had long wanted to "bring Padre Pio from Italy" but had not received permission from the pastor until now. He convened a party in the church hall and requested pledges from his fellow parishioners for the effort. From the approximately 180 people at the meeting that night David secured pledges of $13,800. Immensely encouraged, David solicited help from local contractors and established various donation grades through which parishioners could have memorials or their own names embossed on plaques at the shrine. Gathering $500 (for a name under the altar), $1,000 (for a name beneath Padre Pio), and thousands of dollars worth of services, David and his committee raised $150,000 to commission a statue and erect a shrine.[60] The end result was an altar, lamp lights, and a large Padre Pio statue inside a fenced-in stone and grass courtyard in front of the abandoned convent.

Later, local media seized on this effort (and Mount Carmel in general) as a poignant symbol of the heartbreak of parish closures.[61] More than a story of personal devotion betrayed, however, the story is also indicative of the parish's ability to raise a large amount of money and gather in-kind services given the right cause. Such evidence gives weight to their later claim that, if given the option, they could have raised the money needed to repair the parish instead of closing it. It also speaks to the distance that had developed between the pastor and his parishioners. After he gathered the first pledges, David recalled, the pastor marveled at David's ability to solicit funds: "Father Francis grabbed me outside and said, 'How the hell did you do that? If I asked they wouldn't have given me a dime!'"[62] If donors at Mount Carmel were fickle, when they were given the right pitch they continued to show an interest in making improvements to the spiritual and aesthetic health of the neighborhood.

The late twentieth-century context of continuous need brought the notion of sacrifice to the center of what it meant to be a parishioner. Without their consistent giving and participation, parishioners learned, their parishes would fall deep into the red, physically disintegrate, and perhaps vanish altogether. Such dire conditions spurred a change in expectations. If previous training urged that the parish could extend the glorious reach of the mystical body of Christ, parishioner formation in the latter half of the twentieth century centered more on parish survival. Where entire neighborhoods once took their name from their parishes, some parishes were now struggling to keep just one corner of their neighborhoods. In this atmosphere, the idioms of parishioner sacrifice took on a new, urgent inflection. This urgency came through in documents from the Second Vatican Council: "present circumstances" the Second Vatican Council's "Decree on the Apostolate of Lay People" diagnosed, "demand from [lay people] an apostolate infinitely broader and more intense" than during the church's "early days."[63] Such calls were carried forward in local diocesan and parish language, which routinely used the "people of God" idea to encourage parishioner giving.

Changes in the orientation to sacrifice for the parish complemented the history of sacrifice from the early part of the twentieth century. Narratives of abundance that blurred the boundaries between "Church" and parish would survive these seasons of more tenuous parish existence. While the conciliar texts drew on the biblical "people of God" concept to encourage input (John W. O'Malley calls it "charism" or "initiative" as a contrast to structure or "law") from the peripheries of the church, this was only one of its uses in the practice of parish.[64] Even more than a cautious but real broadening of authority, the motif became an instrument for deeper loyalty and attachment to local places. These two connotations of the people of God notion of church are not wholly contradictory: authority demands commitment, and commitment repays authority. But a third connotation of the phrase—the replacement of particular churches with a universal church—sat very uneasily with the values of authority and commitment. So while it may have hinted at a shift away from parochialism and toward universalism, the teaching that the church is the people of God ended up adding another orthodox rationale to loyalty and attachment to the home parish. Because they combined these multiple notions of sacrifice, resisters to parish shutdowns had a potent and fluid history of sacrifice to work with.

Already Agitated: Urban Upheaval and Parish Stability

One spring afternoon during the occupation, as two parishioners and I sat in the tiny narthex of Our Lady of Mount Carmel Church, a neighborhood couple parked in front and began unloading groceries. Noting that the leader of the group, Annetta, was in the church, the man took the opportunity to mention a complaint. The church bells, he explained, were waking his family up at eight in the morning every day; couldn't Annetta stop the bells from ringing? As was often the case when vigilers encountered unsupportive outsiders, hostility was just below the surface in the exchange. Annetta's nerves were frayed at this moment and the dismissiveness of the man's question—"Is that really necessary?"—only added to Annetta's feelings of isolation, anger, and despair.

Clearly, not all Our Lady of Mount Carmel's neighbors shared the sense of the inviolability of the church as a glorious site of Catholic abundance, sacred presence, and ancestral sacrifice. If the church had once been the dominant center of the neighborhood and the pride of its parishioners, it now threatened to become a nuisance. Annetta, who could be remarkably warm and charming, also had a fiery side that made her a formidable leader. She rarely backed down from a perceived slight, and this occasion was no exception. It used to ring at six in the morning, she reminded the couple, further cautioning them not to forget that the church was still open. The couple's bitter and repeated denial of this latter fact aggravated Annetta and sealed the event in the vigilers' memory. Like Oscar with his Walk for Life, the couple had established their infamy with their bald denial of the vigilers' most basic truth. Ringing bells, which had probably annoyed the family while the church was officially open, had no warrant in a closed church. Annetta contained her anger, but afterward she realized that the woman was the granddaughter of a deceased parishioner. This connection to the past gave her frustration a new edge. "I should have told her that her grandmother was turning over in her grave," Annetta lamented. The couple had not only offended the sanctity of the occupied church, but had violated their own family history. Their attitude highlighted the frailty of the neighborhood's intimate bond with the church and with the past.

As the couple walked away, Annetta jibed that the foundation of the couple's home, which was very close to the church, would be the first to disintegrate in the demolition and construction that would attend the church's sale to a developer. Annetta drew on recent history to affirm this point, explaining that work on adjacent tunnels and construction on a nearby Embassy Suites hotel had rattled foundations across the neighborhood.[65] The couple was guilty, then, of a self-destructive disloyalty to the neighborhood as much as they were of offending the church. They were acceding to the undermining of their own foundations. Instead of hearing the church bells as a signal of the neighborhood's connection to its past or to the sacred, they were irritated. They had aligned the church with the other encroachments that had disrupted life in East Boston across the century; like construction trucks rumbling through residential streets or airplanes flying low overhead, it was a source of unwanted noise. Their annoyance echoed painfully in the ears of those who were protecting the church. So many of the parish's families had left for the suburbs, and now even these remaining children of parishioners had disowned the church as just another urban annoyance. From the vigilers' perspective, opposition to the church's struggle to survive was an embrace of the unchecked development that had encouraged urban flight in the first place.

The heated exchange between Annetta and the neighborhood couple (and the lingering sour taste it left in the mouths of Mount Carmel's resisters) suggested the complexity of parish defense amid significant changes in the neighborhood and city. In Boston's urban settings, the shutdown plan ran up against the lingering pains and exclusions of Boston's class and ethnic histories. In the North End and East Boston, these were felt primarily as upheavals associated with changes in the lived environment. In both of these communities, development and displacement have gone hand in hand. Neighborhood memories of these changes are inseparable from parish histories. This was the bitter truth behind Annetta's reference to highway tunnels and airport hotels near the East Boston church. Battles won and lost against these forms of upheaval informed these Catholics' attachments to their parishes. As they considered the shutdowns, Catholics reanimated stories of broader neighborhood struggles against unwanted change. In both East Boston and the North End, these histories were dominated by a sense of geographic, class, and ethnic outsiderhood. Closure proposals only exacerbated and animated those feelings while adding the additional sting of betrayal, a feeling that was not, of course, absent from the suburbs. But urban parishioners had longer neighborhood histories to contend with and draw upon as they determined the meaning and plausibility of the shutdowns. Because of this local knowledge, resisters had wide appreciation for the kinds of histories that were relevant in determining the right course of action when it came to defending parishes or moving on.

For Sacred Heart's Ralph, the proposal to close his North End church was only the latest test in a long history of a neighborhood defined by challenge.

> It goes so far beyond 'the church is closing'; it goes way way way beyond it. And for people who are not of the neighborhood, no one could ever understand it. No one could ever understand it. And here, things seem to be even much more deeply rooted, much more exaggerated, much more everything. And we kept saying, this not a suburb. The cities are different, and when you're into the ethnic parts of the city things are *really* different . . . they're making no distinction. And they are painting everything with a broad stroke. Be sympathetic to the particular areas that you are going into.

Locally inflected Catholicism, Ralph asserted, doesn't "just go away" because a vicar or archbishop has decided the neighborhood could make do with one less parish. For all the validity of the "argument on paper," that pointed out "that less than a block and a half away there is another Catholic church," resisters in the North End were still puzzled at how officials could not understand that as an Italian parish, Sacred Heart had "a different function." In place of broad strokes Carla (the parish business manager) and Ralph called for attention to real histories of sacrifice which, in this case at least, extended beyond the narrative of parish upkeep and sacraments into a social history of the neighborhood.[66]

The local manifestations of Boston's twentieth-century "development" offered one opportunity for others to begin to comprehend the unwillingness of Sacred Heart parishioners simply to accept officials' assurances about their vision for the great future of Boston's Catholicism. Social and political realities had tested Sacred Heart and helped put sacrifice at the center of the ways the parish was remembered and practiced. North Enders have many stories about the city and state using their power to try to override neighborhood concerns. Even before Italians dominated the place, nineteenth- and twentieth-century planners and city officials looked with a combination of suspicion and desire on the neighborhood. Adjacent to Boston's government and business center and to the narrow streets and crowded tenements of the West End, the North End was often seen as ripe for transformation. The West and North Ends were lumped together in these visions, which sought to renew Boston by eliminating its trouble spots. One early twentieth-century plan envisioned transforming the North and West Ends into "first class residential sections." A post–World War II plan envisioned the clearance of the West End, the South End, and the North End in one swift stroke.[67]

As these plans germinated, Boston's transportation needs had already taken a toll on the North End. From the mid-twentieth century forward the North End had been cut off from the rest of Boston by an elevated highway, a looming and noisy "Central Artery" cutting through Boston and known as the "green elephant." The road represented one side of Boston's desperate attempt to modernize in light of its loss of residents and income to competing suburbs.[68] But construction of the highway had its own costs. The project had decimated a major portion of the North End, destroying scores of homes and uprooting 900 businesses.[69] An exit ramp from a related project in the mid-1990s dug even deeper into the North End while lining the pockets of one of its politically connected undertakers.[70] The damage might have been even worse; only protests and lobbying prevented even greater losses.[71] "They almost got rid of the North End," Ralph remembered.

As preposterous as this suggestion might sound today, the annihilation of the neighboring West End in the late 1950s confirmed for North Enders the possibility that well-intentioned plans for general uplift can be easily derailed by political expedience, backroom bargaining, and disregard for ethnic, class, and racial outsiders.[72] Ralph and Carla imagined Catholic officials as the same kind of detached idealists who supported the razing of the Italian, black, and Jewish West End on the strength of half-baked promises that the new development would provide for the displaced. By the early 1960s, when it became clear that the new "West End" would offer housing only for the economically elite, Bostonians had their eyes opened to the fantasies and biases driving so many projects of "urban renewal."[73] Many credit the West End debacle with the stiffening of resolve across Boston against officials' best-laid plans for development and neighborhood change.[74] The publication in 1962 (and a second edition in 1982) of sociologist Herbert Gans's *Urban Villagers* brought specific attention to the West End's displaced Italian community. In this popular community study Gans described the West End not only in terms of its poverty and filth, but also as a site of warm ethnic solidarity amid a city of cold bureaucracy and constant transitions.[75]

If the West End history was not enough, Sacred Heart parishioners could simply walk two blocks toward downtown Boston to confirm their initial hesitations about the shutdown. There they would find a giant hole in the ground where the Central Artery had been. The "Big Dig"—as the plan to put the highway underground had come to be called—was the culmination of doubts about the Central Artery that had arisen in the 1950s, even before the elevated highway was finished. Even as it was being built, planners could see that it would be insufficient and they were already wondering if it might be feasible to put it underground.[76] In 2004, that plan was under way—the intrusive rumbling "elephant" was in the process of being dismantled and series of tunnels were taking shape to replace it. This welcome improvement also added to the bitterness of the memory of loss. During the long and disruptive process of reclaiming the former highway land as a tunnel and then as a park, North Enders had constant affirmation of their suspicions about the limits placed on vision by bureaucratic structures.

The neighborhood's distinct ethnic past added to the anxieties about the shutdowns. Boston's divided history meant that the question of ethnic difference remained close to the surface. For Italian-Americans in the North End, and in East Boston as well, it was impossible to ignore the prevalence of Irish-American leaders in Boston's ecclesial and civic life. Ralph listed the Irish surnames of all the people with whom they were dealing in the hierarchy as they resisted closure—"O'Reagan, Lennon, O'Malley, Boles, Coyne"—and drew a line connecting the proposed shutdown and previous episodes of ethnically targeted displacement. The proposal to shutter the few remaining Italian parishes in the archdiocese suggested that the idea that ethnic discrimination had "disappeared entirely" was just a fantasy. The alliances between an Irish-dominated church and city in the mid-twentieth century seemed to be returning in the closing of ethnic parishes. "The Italians have been through this before," Ralph complained. "You know, it existed 100 years ago, and then it went away a little bit and then it resurfaced in the fifties again, and then we thought it went away and now it is resurfacing." Again today, Ralph continued, the Italians encountered

> an Irish clergy, with an Irish hierarchy, in an Irish city, facing a neighborhood that is somewhat in a siege mode, and then [they're] going to come in and tell you 'We're going to take your church, get out of there. We're going to send you to a place that you don't want to go to.' And then you say, 'Wait a minute, who are these people?' We built the church; they never put a penny into it.[77]

Themes of sacrifice and ethnic conflict merge here to create a definition of parish that is resistant to the historical narratives of humble selflessness which the archdiocese offered to those in closing churches. Having withstood many decades as the target of reformers' desire and having suffered some effects of the plans they carried out, people in the North End found ways to add political and urban history to the stories of meaningful Catholic sacrifice. This meant that their narratives of sacrifice were made up as much of perseverance and resistance as they were self-abnegation and humility.

Ivan Strenski's theoretical reflections on religious sacrifice offer one perspective for making sense of this difference. Strenski highlights the moral and religious differences between thinking of sacrifice as the prudent "giving of" the self versus thinking of it more radically, as the unbridled "giving up" the self. He ventures the opinion that "giving up" best characterizes contemporary common usage of the term. Strenski argues that the liberal desire, expressed in the late nineteenth century by Durkheimians Henri Hubert and Marcel Mauss, to replace self-destructive sacrifice with more prudent and controlled versions of the act seems pallid and unsatisfying in the face of the secret longings of the "undomesticated" side of human nature.[78] The liberal version of sacrifice never took off, Strenski argues, because people seem to crave the paradoxical freedoms that come with the unbridled abandonment of self to outside powers. In Strenski's reckoning, the Catholic version of sacrifice Hubert and Mauss were contesting, which enjoined sacrifice on the model of Christ's crucifixion as the "total annihilating surrender of the self," better satisfies the religious and social need for expiation and redemption.[79]

But the resisters to Boston's shutdowns—at least as they stood in opposition to the particular version of "giving up" the archdiocese asked of them—challenged this conclusion. The wide, albeit passing, media embrace of the resisters would suggest that others too understood the legitimacy and value of the more limited, or what Strenski calls "tidy bourgeois," notion of the term.[80] By linking endurance through hardship and the ongoing commitment to parish and neighborhood with sacrifice, resisters in Boston rejected the notion that self-abnegation is the only true, or even the only truly Catholic sacrifice. Giving did not have to be self-annihilating in order to "count" in the Catholic cosmos. There were limits to the sacrifices the church could ask of them. Was it sheer pragmatic calculation that allowed these Catholics to formulate and defend such a supposedly "bourgeois" notion of sacrifice? Were they rebelling against the church's longstanding hostility toward America's "perverse individualism"?[81] Writing off resisters' actions as cynical strategy or crass selfishness misses an opportunity to understand the layered histories—Catholic, American, ethnic, and local—underlying their actions and narratives.

Resisters at Our Lady of Mount Carmel had neighborhood precedent to work with in nurturing their hopes that officials would respect their claim to their church. But like the Sacred Heart parishioners, people at East Boston's Mount Carmel were acutely aware of the potential for misguided idealism, and even abuse, inherent in the call for local sacrifice on behalf of the greater good. As Mount Carmel grew with steady Italian migration and immigration in the early twentieth century, East Boston itself was expanding and forging more direct connections with Boston. At the time of Mount Carmel's founding in 1905, East Boston had just recently become one terminus of a sophisticated underwater tunnel. This passageway connected Jeffries Point beneath Boston Harbor to downtown Boston by trolley. While ferry service between the two ports would continue until the 1950s, the development marked the beginning of more fluid commerce between Boston and East Boston.

Capital and other resources did not always flow equally between the two locales. Politicians, bishops, educators, and developers dealing with East Boston knew well that part of the East Boston community ethos was a sense of alienation from the wealthier centers of commerce and politics across the harbor. Its previous life as a resort community speaks to this sense of distance, as do the continual acclamations in the late twentieth century and early twenty-first century of East Boston as the next 'hot spot' for contemporary real estate speculators. Despite these perpetually renewed hopes, real estate values climbed at a slower rate than those of Boston, Charlestown, and South Boston, and the long-expected "arrival" was continually delayed.[82]

Part of the challenge was that East Boston's location—close to the heart of Boston, but also isolated from it by the harbor—had become a liability as the city's transportation needs changed. Landfill had closed the gaps between harbor islands to create East Boston, and this process could be repeated over and over again to extend the land mass out into the harbor with relative ease. This made East Boston an ideal site for industrial expansion. In 1923, three years after Mount Carmel was formally dedicated, the first planes began flying in and out of a new airfield a short distance from the church on the island's eastern mud flats. As the 1924 Johnson-Reed Immigration Act slowed the traffic of Italian immigrants into Boston, East Boston's population began to even out. The airport's growth, however, did not even out. Soon landfill alone could not produce enough terrain for the rapidly expanding airport. In some cases, whole blocks of houses were bulldozed to produce the level runways and flat foundations of what became Logan International Airport. Tunnels and highways expediting travel through and to East Boston and its growing airport displaced hundreds of families over the years.[83] In their promise to connect this isolated community to the rest of the world these developments would also dismantle East Boston from the inside.

Over the course of the mid to late 20th century, cherished portions of East Boston fell victim to Logan's expansion. Community activism has centered primarily on the effort to halt or mitigate the impact of various projects related to Logan. Resisters at Mount Carmel referred frequently to the 1968 blockade of a trucking route used by Massport, the "quasi-public" firm responsible for airport management.[84] In this episode, residents insisted that Massport send its trucks along property it already owned rather than running them along the more direct route right through a major residential and business district of East Boston. Massport resisted, insisting that there were no viable alternatives. For years, approximately six hundred trucks a day spewed dust and rumbled noisily through streets not far from Mount Carmel Church. After presentations and political lobbying failed to get results, residents organized a sequence of protests on the trucking route. They maximized their impact by encouraging women in particular to take over the streets. The baby carriages these women brought with them heightened the effect, and after a few days and threats of "riot," the protesters managed to convince the mayor to secure promises of a new trucking route for Massport's construction. In the big scheme, this was a minor victory. A year later, in 1969, Logan had finally overtaken the last remaining acres of Olmsted's East Boston park, along with a tree-lined residential street called Neptune Road leading up to it. Airport-related controversies, including protests over noise pollution, and arguments about the placement of a third automobile tunnel into East Boston, continued throughout the latter decades of the twentieth century. Today, two-thirds of East Boston's land area is occupied by Logan.[85]

Community and chancery responses to a string of changes in the 1970s at Mount Carmel and nearby Our Lady of the Assumption parish convey the importance of the airport in defining the neighborhood ethos and a broader sense of the struggle that has shaped the meanings of parish. Founded in 1869, Our Lady of the Assumption is a traditionally Irish parish located on the hill above Our Lady of Mount Carmel in East Boston's Jeffries Point neighborhood. Sharing a neighborhood and a large proportion of their parishioner base, the two parishes have been tied together for better and for worse over the course of the last fifty years. Details from Assumption's saga of survival speak to the sense of sacrifice and ownership encouraged and rewarded among Catholics in this tumultuous period.

Over the first half of the twentieth century Assumption had been transformed from a mostly Irish parish to a mix of Irish and newer Italian families. With this change, upkeep of the parish became difficult. Italian families who were part of the parish were often drawn to perform sacraments at Mount Carmel. Of 154 funerals at Mount Carmel in 1975, 100 were at least nominal members of Our Lady of the Assumption. This mobility deprived Assumption of much-needed income, and the church and school fell into disrepair.[86] The tendency for Jeffries Point residents to attend masses at both the national Mount Carmel Parish and the territorial parish of the Assumption was not a new challenge. A lay review of Assumption in 1972 noted that people "feel free to worship at one Church or the other," and remarked that this tendency made it "difficult to give exact figures on the size of the membership at the parish." Suggesting that only four or five hundred people were "directly involved," this review went on to suggest that any new pastor at Assumption had a difficult task in front of him.

Citing "pastoral neglect over a period of time" the author described a church and community at the brink: "[t]he Church is no longer the focal point for people's lives. The rectory, attached to the Church is a distant place for most people." The assessment made social and psychological observations as well: "Economically the poorest in all of East Boston," the people of Jeffries Point had a "weak" family structure and felt a "sense of powerlessness in determining the future of their community" in the face of airport expansion. They needed a pastor who would "at least become involved if not take a leadership role" in the people's ongoing fight to "rehabilitate the community" and continue the struggle against Logan's growth. He need not be or speak Italian, the review continued, but he should be willing to work to unite the various factions in the community, including, presumably, the "growing number of Spanish-speaking people moving into the area because of many low-rent apartments."[87]

Assumption's new pastor did not seem to fit the bill. By August 1972 he had already run into controversy when he closed the school after learning from the state inspector's office that it was unsafe for occupation. With worries about Catholic school and parish closures thick in the air, the school's principal contested this decision, suggesting that the pastor had unilaterally shuttered the school without reference to any inspection.[88] With the pastor's integrity called into question and parishioners clamoring for a quick solution, Assumption seemed to be caught in a downward spiral. As the pastor complained to chancery officials about the waning value of "authority" for "these people," the bishops quietly confirmed the school closure.[89] Plans were already being made to create a single consolidated Catholic school located on Jeffries Point's flatlands.

This change was part of the official chancery response to the shifting populations and economic struggles of the city and its churches. In 1969 Boston's Cardinal Cushing had established a Planning Office for Urban Affairs (POUA). This branch of the archdiocese aimed to address "urban problems" and their relation to church institutions with the goal of enhancing the church's ability to reach urban Catholics.[90] In May of 1970, Catholics in East Boston learned that their city would be among the first communities in the archdiocese toward which the new urban office would direct its attention. East Boston was singled out on ethnic and economic grounds: As "an ethnic, blue-collar community which is very similar to many of the other blue-collar working communities," East Boston was considered a valuable site for the testing of the POUA's mandate. Other representative communities included Haverhill (an "old industrial city"), Dorchester ("a community in great transition: from white to black and

Spanish-speaking") and Acton ("a growth suburb"). In East Boston, the office directed its attention to Catholic schooling and sought to launch an "urban education research" project to determine how best to utilize East Boston's six parish schools.[91]

The intervention of outside agencies like the POUA made residents and pastors ill at ease. Correspondence at Our Lady of Mount Carmel signaled pastoral and parishioner suspicion about the organization's mandate and the potential upheaval entailed in its findings. After confirming that the POUA was indeed an official archdiocesan office, the pastor subtly cautioned the chancery against taking radical steps in East Boston. "There have been rumors," the pastor warned, "that certain parishes in East Boston will be closed. Some of my parishioners are up in arms thinking that it will affect Mt. Carmel." The chancery responded with confirmation of the POUA's mandate and an ominous silence on the question of closures.[92]

The concerns of Mount Carmel's pastor and his parishioners were partially validated when the POUA's study group, organized "to develop insight into working class groups," soon put its lessons to use by proposing a consolidation of parish elementary schools in East Boston. By 1971, the POUA was planning to combine Mount Carmel School with the school from nearby Sacred Heart parish under the title "Community Center for Christian Education." This first combined school turned out to be only a temporary stopgap. In 1973 parishioners from the two parishes met to discuss their mutual inability to pay their agreed-upon assessments for the combined school. They decided to raise tuition and increase their fundraising efforts.[93] These measures did not resolve the problem for Mount Carmel, which by December 1974 again was having trouble paying its portion.[94] Meanwhile, a more comprehensive plan was being put together for East Boston's struggling Catholic schools. With Our Lady of the Assumption, Holy Redeemer, and Sacred Heart, Mount Carmel had committed itself to a new $10,000 yearly assessment for a new Catholic school that would combine their parishes' elementary students. Called East Boston Central Catholic, the school was underwritten in part by the Office of Urban Affairs.[95] With parishioners leading much of the planning, the school opened its doors in a building of the Holy Redeemer parish in September of 1974.[96]

Trouble with Catholic schools came at a particularly bad time. In the mid-1970s Boston was the site of vicious controversy and occasional violence over a plan to racially integrate public schools through federally mandated busing.[97] Busing was one among other incidents to follow pitting the archdiocese explicitly against large and diverse groups of lay Catholics. Although Charlestown and South Boston saw the most active resistance to busing, this was one issue on which Italian East Boston and the people of these Irish neighborhoods saw eye to eye.[98] Our Lady of the Assumption was the epicenter of East Boston's anti-busing efforts, since it was the home of activist Elvira "Pixie" Palladino. In the fall of 1974, a few months after judge W. Arthur Garrity's decision to implement busing became official, Palladino petitioned Assumption's pastor to allow the parish color guard, a group of about fifty or sixty eight- to twelve-year-old girls, to attend an antibusing rally at East Boston's Suffolk Downs racetrack.[99] Rumor had it that Palladino had recently spit in the face of a monsignor from nearby Most Holy Redeemer parish. In the midst of other threats to the parish, the pastor did not savor the possibility of offending the popular community leader. Loath to alienate himself from parish parents any further (and himself opposed to busing) the pastor wrote the chancery seeking backup for his reluctant decision not to allow the children's participation. Officials received this letter as a pitiful if understandable attempt to displace blame away from the pastor for the church's unpopular position.[100]

But the note also signaled the desperation of pastors in places like East Boston in their attempts to preserve their parishes. The anxiety about shutdowns expressed at Mount Carmel cropped up at Assumption in 1976, when pieces of the church ceiling began crashing down into the nave. Restricted to once-a-week masses in the hall in the church basement, the pastor now began to take heat both from his bosses at the chancery and from his parishioners. This episode, documented in memos sent within the chancery and in letters sent to the cardinal by concerned Assumption parishioners, reveals something of the neighborhood's contentious past. It also highlights the seriousness of the prospect of closing a parish, both for church officials and for parishioners.

Even though Assumption had clearly not been raising enough money even to keep its buildings in safe condition, officials supported the remaining parishioners in their attachment and eager devotion to the parish. This support flew in the face of expert recommendations. Estimating basic repair costs in 1976 at between $85,000 and $120,000, the Archdiocese Building Commission recommended to the cardinal that the closed building "not be restored." Internal chancery reports, however, informed the cardinal that despite small and shrinking weekend mass numbers, "there are those who want the church opened and repaired because they were baptized there and grew up there, etc." The information came with a note of warning: "it would be most difficult to convince the people to go along with the decision to dismantle or take down the Church building."[101]

The cardinal had plenty of voices to take into account, as the parish seems to have rapidly mobilized a targeted letter-writing campaign to protect their church. These voices, almost exclusively women's or married couples', defended the sanctity of the parish and pled for its survival. Parishioner Anna Porrazzo told officials that "closing the church would be a tragedy and a disservice to the Catholic community."[102] Miss Lena Matera added personal detail, telling the cardinal that she was a "paralyzed individual" and that any "thoughts" other than those related to "maintaining and restoring this Grand Church" would "upset and depress" her. "You can count on me" and others she urged, "to assist in any way possible."[103] Likewise, forty-year parishioner Mrs. Jennie Ioro acknowledged that the church needed fixing, but reminded the bishop that it was "so handy to attend mass in cold and stormy weather." Even if Ioro may have jaunted down to Mount Carmel for special events or during the warmer months, she still cherished having Assumption only a "2 minute walk" away.[104] Others simply reported their families' history in the church, citing baptisms, first communions, marriages, requiem masses, and attendance at the now-closed school.[105]

Letters addressed to the cardinal from Assumption parishioners also speak to a determination and resilience that would echo a few blocks away at Mount Carmel thirty years later. Several portrayed a battle-tested community threatened on multiple sides and eager to restore Catholic grandeur. Officials' concern that the people might not "go along" with a closure decision reflected their awareness of the struggles in East Boston over the gradual expansion of Logan Airport. Jeffries Point is a neighborhood of about two square miles in the southeastern portion of East Boston. The territory borders Boston Harbor and holds Mount Carmel, Our Lady of the Assumption, and Holy Redeemer Parishes. As noted, the neighborhood had been particularly impacted by airport expansion and noise disturbances since the airport's opening in 1923.

Mrs. Mary Ellen Welch relayed this history and the "beleaguered" community's bonding through their defiance of outside forces.[106] The airport's "unchecked expansionist policy," she wrote, led to the destruction of many Jeffries Point residences and turned the area into a "bombed out city." Welch described how "a strong community group" helped "turn the tide" of airport encroachment, and secured the building of a "beautiful waterfront park" where the airport had envisioned transportation infrastructure. Such successes spurred residents to invest in their properties, Welch contended, and bolstered the commitment of the "tight-knit community of long term residents" whose "phone lines are humming" with talk about the "future, or non-future, of the parish." She joined others in blaming the pastor for the parish's "wasteland" condition, and petitioned the cardinal to remove him and his "negative attitude toward parish life." Joining this theme, another correspondent reported that the pastor had not called any "Lay Board meetings" in 1976 and had thereby undercut the possibility of organizing fundraisers or taking action on the deterioration of the building.[107] Another parishioner added to the list of complaints by reporting that the pastor authorized the sale of a church organ to St. Therese's in Everett without running it by the parishioners who had contributed to a "special collection" to purchase the organ in the first place.[108]

Using reasoning that would return in the struggles later over reconfiguration, Welch ended her letter with a comparison between her parish and others, offering a class interpretation of the threat to the parish: "We are poor and working class. We may not have an acre of land around our homes. But we have proved we have faith and hope. And most people love the Church dearly." Along with recognition of their faith, hope, and love, Assumption parishioners demanded respect despite their distance from the channels of power. For Welch this distance translated into leverage with church administrators:

> We feel like we're the forgotten ones—for whatever reasons. You know it's really discrimination to ignore our situation here and enrich other parishes by giving them the opportunity to choose options like the team ministry approach to parish organization. If we all had an equal opportunity our parish would be revitalized and would spring to life like Lazarus did from his grave.

Welch's reference to innovations in parish management illustrates her willingness to combine appeals based on attachment and loyalty with a contemporary understanding of the need for the people of God to take up responsibility for their parishes. Chancery officials were convinced or at least worried about violating this potent mix of neighborhood solidarity, parish attachment, and contemporary ecclesiology. The chancellor reported to the cardinal that the people are "already agitated" and "feel like they are whipping boys and that they 'get it' from State, Massport, etc."[109] By December an internal memo suggested that the cardinal was "not about to suppress the parish" and urged that even if the church had to be dismantled, "an alternate structure or place for the parish to function must be obtained."[110]

Eventually, the parish was repaired and reopened. The chancery's willingness to take a chance on Our Lady of the Assumption Parish would be repeated in 2004 when the archbishop rejected the East Boston cluster's recommendation that Assumption should close.[111] He named Mount Carmel to the closing list instead.[112] If parish defensiveness, the emotional recollection of sacrifices and sacraments, and professed willingness to "be the church" paid off for Assumption parishioners in the mid-1970s, the same approach at Mount Carmel fell on deaf ears in the context of the hardships of the early 2000s.

But resisters there shared the embattled perspective of Assumption's 1970s letter-writers. Val, the rosary leader among Mount Carmel's resisters, had a long history of activism in the face of encroachments on the neighborhood. Even though he had worried that his involvement might raise the ire of his bosses in city government, Val decided again and again that the protection of the neighborhood warranted the risk. On many issues he had worked with Annetta, who had also taken an active interest in protecting the neighborhood from truck traffic, tunnel construction, and the proposed demolition of a neighborhood footbridge. Their history of working on committees, courting and lobbying political officials, blocking streets, and attending community meetings offered a kind of preparation for the work of the occupation.

The connections made in these earlier projects carried over into the question of the shutdown of Mount Carmel. For one thing, Annetta's involvement was one important spur encouraging Val to join the resistance. Her very active role in many of the neighborhood's struggles helped make the occupation, which she led along with a few others, more visible and formidable. Annetta's past was not wholly uncontroversial, but she was respected by many as a person willing to stand up for what she believed in. She earned this reputation not only as a community activist but also as a vocal critic of the area's Catholic leadership. Along with her husband Mark, Annetta had been active in ensuring a lay voice in the reorganization of the neighborhood's Catholic schools in the 1970s.

Even more recently, she had made a splash in the parish after she critiqued the pastor's support for a developer's plan to convert a nearby building (a former gumball factory) into condos. Annetta's earlier criticism of the pastor—she thought he gave a sweetheart deal to a developer who bought the parish school—added to the hostility between them. When Annetta and Val showed up to distribute fliers supporting congressman Joseph P. Kennedy at a church function in the mid-1990s, the pastor threw her out, while allowing Val to continue. After this dustup Annetta reported that the pastor told her husband that he felt sorry for him, being married to a "bad woman." After this incident Annetta gave up further parish involvement. The shutdown plan upended that promise, bringing Annetta back into the now-priestless church. If the reversal was sudden—from church exile to church leader—Annetta's long history of leadership and organizing made her new role as the leader of Mount Carmel's "Survivors" a good fit.

This was true because people in the parish saw a connection between defense of the community's streets and buildings and the defense of the church. As Val explained in relation to his own history as an activist: "this was our neighborhood . . . which is different from the church, but it's similar. It's doing the same thing as when you're fighting for the church." Battles of their middle age against the city had become struggles in their "old age" against the archdiocese. More than simply preparing them for the current struggle, the experience of having been "alienated" from the structures of city and state power had an impact on Catholic life and the practice of parish in East Boston. As it had at Our Lady of Assumption thirty years before, the attempt to shutter Mount Carmel touched nerves still raw from an ongoing sense of "siege" in the neighborhood.[113]

The origins of the resistance lie in the experiences that shaped Boston's Catholics' understanding of the meanings and value of their parishes. In the early years of Sacred Heart and Mount Carmel, these lessons centered on sacrifice for the parish as a vehicle to Catholic glory and grandeur. The local church carried the imprint of parishioner sacrifices. Its durability and beauty spoke to the devotion and generosity of its members. At these national parishes, the history of sacrifice was inflected with the triumph of Italian Catholicism in Irish Boston. In both locales, the church's stability amid economic threats and industrial development added another layer to the history of sacrifice. It was easy to feel beleaguered in these neighborhoods, but the glory of the local church offered a reminder of community resilience. This local vibrancy tied Catholics to the broader glory of the church. Parishioner sacrifice helped make the church's place in the neighborhood seem inviolable.

In the effort to understand the resistance to parish shutdowns religious and social histories cannot readily be extricated from one another. The challenges and upheavals of neighborhood change informed Catholics' devotion to their parishes as much as changes in ecclesiology. It makes sense, then, to think of resistance to parish shutdowns as a defense of neighborhood stability, or as fear of memory loss, or as loyalty to ancestors, or even as sheer hostility to change. But such understandings are acceptable only if they are not opposed to religious explanations, as if these commitments and fears somehow took shape in a realm untouched by the symbols, idioms, and power of the church.

Dumb Stones and Living Stones: Revising Presence and Efficacy

Even if many suburban parishioners from places like St. Albert's did not share these histories of upheaval with their urban counterparts, resisters all across Boston did contend with abiding questions in the tradition about the meaning and power of church buildings and the objects in and around them. As noted, the church has long been vexed by a tension between affirming the efficacy and holiness of church buildings and a competing tendency to restrict Catholic attachment to locales and objects by emphasizing their strictly symbolic importance. An episode from St. Albert the Great's 2004 occupation animated the resisters because it tapped into this debate and seemed to confirm the occupiers as caretakers of a sacred history that officials were willing, if reluctantly, to destroy.

As did so many of the vigilers' stories, this one begins with a visit from an outsider. Not long after resisters had taken over the church, the community came to realize that their church had powers about which even they were unaware. The story begins with the visitor approaching Margery, "obviously very emotional" and with "her eyes all welled and full of sadness." The problem, Margery learned, was that the woman was fearful that the church closure and the vigil would mean she would lose access to the parish's Blessed Mother grotto, which had stood in the corner of the church parking lot as long as parishioners could remember. Despite being a Baptist, this woman's visits to this Mary over the course of many years had helped her through the death of a young son and her husband. She had even told several of her non-Catholic friends about the grotto, some of whom had begun visiting it too. Although she said she "couldn't explain it," the woman told Margery that they all felt "tremendous peace and comfort" in front of the grotto, where a small Mary stood perched on a ledge, adored by a stone child kneeling at ground level and tucked inside an arched stone cave.[114]

Margery's response to the woman was protective, understanding, and warm. She told the woman that the vigilers welcomed her and her friends anytime. They could even come inside the church if they wanted. She promised that the vigilers were not going to let anything happen to the grotto, that they were "doing a lot of praying" and taking an "activist" stance in protecting the property. When the woman told Margery that she was confused about her attraction to this obviously Catholic figure, Margery reassured her that it was all right. "It is not just about the Catholic church," she told her. "It is about God's community and our community, and what is at the root of us all: our faith."

Margery's response clearly relied on changes in the attitude of the church toward non-Catholic religions. These changes had been codified in *Nostra Aetate*, which had overturned previous church attitude by affirming Catholic respect for the wisdom available in other religions. The realization that the grotto transcended traditional Christian boundaries gave the grotto and the story its resonance. The fact that a non-Catholic could understand the efficacy of a Catholic shrine while the church's own leaders were in the (unenviable) position of proposing to remove it seemed to validate the occupation. As it was relayed to me, however, the story was also about the ability of Margery and the vigiling community at St. Albert's to position themselves as guardians of the overflowing sacred presence enshrined in Catholic tradition. Margery's assertion that the grotto was built "stone by stone by the parishioners," and her evaluation of it as "very Gothic" and "beautiful" reinforce the importance of the themes of community memory and sacred presence. The grotto, inasmuch as it was considered somehow "Gothic," was appreciated as a small reminder of the church's not so distant past, when Boston-area parishes were built with aspiration for historic grandeur. It contrasted with the modern style of St. Albert's parish church, which is low-slung, carpeted, intimate, and aesthetically modern.[115]

The excitement in telling and retelling of this story at St. Albert's, like the drama over discarded relics at Our Lady of Mount Carmel, emerged from the flux and tension around ideas and practices related to sacred presence in the church. Occupiers saw presence as an issue of the emotional life. The relationships enabled through the possibilities of an enchanted space on the landscape sustained Catholics (and others, it appeared) in their pursuit of meaningful lives in the midst of change and hardship. Were the emotional bonds carried in this Blessed Mother grotto transferable if the statue moved somewhere else? Did such risky and charged relationships with the tradition's saints even belong in a modern church?

The history of the excitement about the Baptist visitor and the questions it provoked resides in post–Vatican II efforts of liturgical reform. Inspired by the Second Vatican Council's document on the liturgy, reforming clerics of the 1970s turned their attention to the messages the church's various rites were communicating about sacred presence. With the new mass well established in most locales, in the late 1970s reformers endeavored to bring other aspects of church life in line with the history and reasoning behind the central liturgical innovation of the Council. The reformed rite of church and altar dedication laid out for Catholics—perhaps more powerfully than any other document—the arguments of the contemporary church about the meanings and limits of the objects and locales of Catholic practice. If most Boston Catholics encountered these reforms only obliquely, those in closing parishes felt the full force of the rite's revisions when defenders of the reconfiguration used the same reasoning to coach them about the true meanings and the limits of church buildings.

Called the *Dedication of a Church and Altar,* the new rite was published in 1978. In this document, reformers aimed to simplify and streamline the ancient rite as it had been performed over the last several centuries. They excised what they saw as unnecessary accretions from the medieval and other periods and sought to make the rite more legible and instructive to modern participants. The idea of the church as the people of God aided reformers in their efforts to shift people's attention away from what they might "get" out of being in the physical space of the church and toward their own roles as members of a universal communion.

Changes in the rite suggested changes in the proper Catholic orientation to churches and the things in them. The installation of relics, for example, went from being the dramatic core of the ceremony and long-term source of solace and healing to being an optional part of the ceremony after 1978. The rite offered no indulgences as it had before. Instead, the authors of the new rite wanted people to know that saints' bones were used primarily because they could remind us of exemplary Christian lives. If relics once enhanced the holiness of a place, now they merely offered moral lessons.

The *lustratio*—that elaborate repeated ritual sprinkling of the building and the altars—was more closely tied to baptism and its human participants. The action as it related to the walls was purely symbolic—walls and people were to be "sprinkled together" and dedicators were to emphasize the metaphor of the people as the "living stones" of the "Church." Holiness or sinfulness in the building has no bearing on the real meaning of the rite and the church it produces. Other rites of claiming and purifying the place were severely curtailed or even eliminated. The 1978 rite did away with the somewhat mysterious practice of sketching the Greek and Latin alphabets in diagonal lines of ash laid out across the length of the church. Likewise, reformers saw the recreation of Christ's "harrowing of hell" through the elaborate ritual of knocking on the door and calling out for the scattering of evil spirits as too "theatrical" and subject to mockery for its dramatic elements.

One reformer, in a note reminiscent of Father Botz's 1958 paean to the altar for the Liturgical Press, noted wistfully that the dramatic high point of the old rite for many was the moment when the top of the altar was set aflame using wax and incense.[116] But reformers ultimately deemed the copious smoke and fragrance to be too closely associated with what they called Israelite religion. Indeed the prayers in the old rite made this connection unapologetically. But now, the "mystic functions" of the "Priests and Levites" were no longer considered good models.[117] For the new rite, such connections fostered misconceptions about Christ's relationship to the world. Christ came, as one historian summarized the reformers' argument, not to set particular places aside as holy, but to "abolish the traditional boundaries between the holy and the profane." The flames and copious smoke of this ceremony distracted from this message and threatened to overpower, in the minds of the observers, the more important message of "desacralization."[118] In the new rite, then, smoke and flame would be curtailed, the spirit would not be invoked as it had been, and people would no longer be asked to kneel during the moment.

Another new feature of the reformulated rite was an emphasis on explanation and instruction. The implication here was that the old rite was too shrouded in mysteries, often including actions for which no explanation or origin could be given. Reformers constructed the prayer of dedication as a key moment in that project of instruction. Comparison of the "consecratory preface" from the 1956 manual and the parallel "prayer of dedication" from the 1978 rite gives a clear picture of the adjustments liturgists hoped to make in Catholic attitudes toward locales and objects. In the new rite the prayer had been entirely rewritten to reflect, as one commentator put it, "not only changed understandings of the church building, but the new self understanding of the Church itself."[119]

The new prayer makes reference to the place being dedicated primarily for the ways "the mystery of the Church is reflected" there. Capital 'c' Church, which is not mentioned even once in the earlier version, is the subject of almost half of the fifty lines of the new prayer.[120] In addition to encouraging reflection on the relationship between local and universal church, the new prayer directs attention to the activities of people rather than God's action. After it calls on the Lord's "Spirit from heaven/ to make this church an ever-holy place," the new prayer lists activities in the place that the *congregation* shall carry out. The body of the prayer includes several stanzas that begin with the phrase "Here may. . ." these petitions call on the people to "celebrate" the Eucharist, "be fed," pray "for the world's salvation," and offer "justice" for the poor and "true freedom" for the "victims of oppression." These petitions are more like instructions to the people preparing to support a new church than they are invocations of divine aid or affirmations of holiness.

If the new "prayer of dedication" highlights the universal church and the activities of Catholics, the old "consecratory preface" called more directly upon God's activity and referred to the local church without metaphorical overlay. The pre-reform consecratory prayer specified the responsibilities and benefits awaiting the new church's members. After urging priests and laity to devote themselves to the place, the prayer called directly and confidently upon God's intervention in the lives of the parishioners. This call referred to the local church as a place from which the "Lord, by the grace of the Holy Spirit" would accomplish a variety of reconciliations and healings, the absolving of sins, and the hearing of prayers. In "this house," the petition suggested, the sick may be healed, the weak restored, the lame begin to run, lepers may be cleansed, and demons expelled. By the "gift" of the Lord, the prayer continued, "all who enter this temple" may have their sufferings relieved, their prayers answered, and every bond of sin absolved. The final four lines again make reference to the issue of the work the people are to perform. In this case this work is directly in response to the Lord's gifts: the prayer suggested that the people, having "all their prayers answered," should "rejoice." Finally, there was the work of representing the Lord's goodness to the world. Having received "the mercy they had begged," all who enter the church "may be perpetually engaged "in glorifying your generosity."

This economy of give and take grounded in a particular place is missing from the newer prayer. The new rite removed all efficacy from this aspect of the ceremony. There are no promises that prayers will be heard and acted upon by God, only requests that the peoples' prayers might "resound through heaven and earth." If efficacy was the first thing to go, presence was close behind. Comparison of the two prayers' opening lines makes this clear. The new prayer begins with a reference to God's distance and concludes with a statement of injunction:

> Father in heaven,
> source of holiness and true purpose
> it is right that we praise and glorify your name.

These lines establish that the prayer is "a lyrical act of pure praise."[121] The theme of human initiative continues as the prayer sets out to explain the activity of the moment:

> For today we come before you,
> to dedicate to your lasting service
> this house of prayer, this temple of worship,
> this home in which we are nourished by your word and
> your sacraments.

One feels the weight of the manual's change of name—from "consecranda" in 1907 and 1956 to "dedication" in 1978—in this passage.[122] Unlike consecration, dedication comes wholly from within. To dedicate a place to God puts the onus on the people of the congregation to keep the place whole and pure. Presence is not gone, but it is now located in the people of God. The church is the people of God, and the small 'c' church is nothing more than the "house of the Church," to use a phrase common in the documents of reform.

The opening lines from the older "consecratory preface" convey a very different sense of the character of the new place. The tone is not timid. "Be present to our prayers," it begins and repeats a formula calling for presence:

> be present to the sacraments
> be present also to the holy works of your servants,
> and to us who beg your mercy.

> Pouring out the richness of his seven-fold grace,
> let your Holy Spirit come down into this church. . .

These lines lay the groundwork for a long description of the various aspects of God as they might hear the prayers of the people "in this house." They also express the hope that through the "deep devotion" and "lowly service" of the clerics uttering the prayer, God might "consecrate this church." The theme of presence and efficacy go seamlessly together. Consecration adds holiness to a place, and with that comes the promise of answered prayers and healing.

The commentator who presented the two prayers side-by-side for his readers in 1983 hoped that the comparison would show the benefits of the rite's revisions. The new rite, with this prayer at its center, is "one of the jewels of postconciliar reform." The author's appreciation of this rite did not prevent him from offering a few critiques. While the new rite had significantly reduced the time commitment (the old rites "seemed to go on forever!"), this observer wondered if they could not be cut down still more. Dedications for secular buildings, he enthused, are "extraordinarily brief." Their ribbon cuttings, deed exchanges, and speeches efficiently accomplish the goal of acknowledging a special moment in civic life. An even shorter dedication rite might reduce the remaining "danger that the length and complexity" might still "obscure, rather than highlight, the important symbolic role" of the ceremony.[123]

The author also critiqued the new rite's mention of "cleansing of these walls and this altar," which misleadingly suggests that "these 'dumb stones' are in need of purification." The problem with even this single reference to the previous rite's focus on exorcism is that it risks causing confusion. It is "essential" that all who participate in the rite understand the symbolic function of the washing and anointing of the walls. "The building is in some sense a recognizable symbol of the people who gather in it"; speaking of cleansing its walls, however, takes the metaphor one step too far. "The holiness (and the sinfulness) of the building is entirely derivative." The core metaphor [of the rite] is deeply rich and biblical, but remains underappreciated as metaphor. "The problem," this writer speculated, relates to a shared inability to grasp symbolic language and action: "we are accustomed to taking everything so literally."[124] In order to reduce this risk, this author recommended that the rite be only an opening point for catechesis. The rite's message for the people of God should not end after the dedication of the building.

One finds the same interest in liturgical instruction in *Environment and Art*, a 1978 United States Bishops' document on the design of Catholic places. It calls for the "opening up of symbols."[125] Reformers of the dedication rite sought measured attention to the meanings of the core liturgical actions, not the piling up of "arcane" rites in a sequence of formulaic or mysterious steps.[126] Meaning mattered more than effect. This extended to the daily liturgy and church design: "[c]ausality and efficacy," *Environment and Art* worried, "have been emphasized at the expense of sacramental signification."[127] Interestingly, and in a nod to the dynamism of the church's ongoing separatist stance in America and "modernity," the manual goes on to relate efficacy to a modern desire for "efficiency." As it had in the secular world, overemphasis on "efficiency" in the liturgical realm diminished possibilities for meaning. Petrified and shriveled symbols may be "more manageable and efficient," but they do not "signify in the richest fullest sense."[128] As in the rite of dedication, the crucial meanings were related to the Eucharist and the community of Christians.

The notion of "living" carried tremendous weight for both reform manuals. In the dedication manual, "living stones" took precedence over actual stones in the church walls. The church, it asserted, is "a special kind of image of the church itself, which is God's temple built from living stones."[129] As we have seen, the purification rites had these living stones as their target. For *Environment and Art*, the term "living" centered attention on "action" as the core of Catholic truth:

> The most powerful experience of the sacred is found in the celebration and the persons celebrating, that is, it is found in the action of the assembly: the living words, the living gestures, the living sacrifice, the living meal.[130]

Because they are associated with the holy through a "quest for the beautiful," these actions call upon and support the "whole person" in ways that counter the deadening hyper-rationality of the modern social realm.

In such formulations there is a palpable eagerness to undo or subvert misunderstanding about the meanings of Catholic locales and objects. The church should offer a "more total approach" by nurturing "feelings of conversion, support, joy, repentance, trust, love, memory, movement, gesture, wonder."[131] These kinds of experience had to be more a matter of community than of place. The true object of design decisions, they insist, is not the building, but the congregation. This orientation is reflected in the opening sentences of a contemporary manual for church dedications tellingly entitled *Holy People, Holy Place: Rites for the Church's House*. This 1998 training publication included a copy of the 1978 dedication manual and offered commentary on the rite and its history and meanings:

> When a community constructs a new church building or renovates an older one, the basic question in the process is, "Who is the Church?" From this follows another question, "What is a church building?"[132]

The rhetorical surprise of the pronoun "Who" in the first question minimizes the "What" of the second question. The aim is to prioritize the invisible communion of souls over the visible building and people's interactions with it. In the design handbook, the parallel history of efficacy is more clearly noted as a problem to be excised:

> The historical problem of the church as a *place* attaining dominance over the faith community need not be repeated as long as Christians respect the primacy of the living assembly.[133]

Awareness of this historical problem led the writers of the design handbook to argue that the use of the term "church" to describe the building in which Christians worship is "misleading." Church, *ecclesia*, meant 'Christian people' for the ancient Christians. When they spoke of their place of worship it was *domus ecclesia*, "the house of the Church." A year 2000 revision of the non-binding *Environment and Art* handbook incorporated that text's primary theme in its title: *Built of Living Stones: Art, Architecture, and Worship*. Quoting the dedication rite, the design manual agrees that a church is "'the building in which the Christian community gathers to hear the word of God, to pray together, to receive the sacraments, and celebrate the eucharist.'" It did, however, offer a less stark approach to the question of presence. It encouraged those planning a new building to consider that they are creating a place where God will be especially present:

> That building is both the house of God on earth *(domus Dei)* and a house fit for the prayers of the saints *(domus ecclesiae)*. Such a house of prayer must be expressive of the presence of God and suited for the celebration of the sacrifice of Christ, as well as reflective of the community that celebrates there.[134]

This gesture to the "house of God" signaled ongoing discussion among liturgists about the relationship of postconciliar reforms to the preconciliar liturgical movement. The reformers of the 1920s, 1930s, 1940s, and 1950s were not as vexed about presence and efficacy as were those working on the new rite. But acknowledging that churches are the "house of God" did not give way to a full endorsement of presence or efficacy. In planning the construction or remodeling of a church, some versions of presence are more important to consider than others. There are "central" and secondary signs, with the Eucharist accorded "supreme prominence."[135] In general, this new handbook for church design reiterates the notion that the sacraments now contain what was once "visible of our Savior."[136] The concentration of presence into the sacraments means that these liturgical functions have both a teaching aspect and an affective aspect. They "encourage full, conscious, and active participation, express and strengthen faith, and lead people to God." But they "also touch and move a person to conversion of heart and not simply to enlightenment of mind."[137] Things like "incense, ashes, holy water, candles, and vestments" (which were offered in such bountiful measure during the pre-Second Vatican Council consecration rite) now had meanings primarily related to immediate experience, not the abiding efficacy of the objects they blessed or touched.[138]

Along with this attention to affective experience, the new design manual amplifies "mystery" as a cherished value that can and should be built into church buildings. Here too the preconciliar liturgical movement, with its heightened attention to the mystical power of the church's ancient traditions, seemed to have regained some influence among American bishops. Divine presence is a mystery that must be nurtured and sustained in church. "Without a meditative dimension," to church design, the manual concludes, "Christian architecture risks reducing the mystery of divine presence to either social action or to a comfortable domesticity." The idea is to encourage, through design elements, a "contemplative attitude" in everyone who encounters the place.[139]

These gentle notions of the significance of Catholic locales and objects are far removed from the kinds of efficacy hoped for in the 1956 translation of the consecration rite. Presence itself had changed with the times. Presence once held out promises of healing, forgiveness, and sanctuary. For a time symbols overtook this kind of efficacious presence. Didactic and elegant, they were available in both the new and old rites of dedication for anyone who did not take the old versions of presence too literally. These symbols were not "efficacious" in the way Father Botz had contended in 1958; they were instructional and richly informative for the well-schooled interpreter. Church buildings were practical in that they put a roof over the head of a community. But more importantly, they were metaphors. In this formulation, presence was most real as it was manifest in the actions of the community of believers. In the most recent church design manual, the church maintained this "living stones" metaphor in full force. It also sought to augment this understanding of buildings with the idea of presence as a "mystery." The presence of Jesus Christ is a mystery available for affective and experiential exploration in the harmony, beauty, and dignity of churches as they facilitate and enliven the sacraments. This kind of presence does not strike or impose; it "unfolds."[140] As a mystery, it has time on its side.

"More than a symbol"

The "dedicatory exercises" preceding the ten o'clock mass at Our Lady of Mount Carmel on November 28, 1920, most certainly followed the traditional rites of consecration. These rites not only transformed the building into a symbol, but also established it as a uniquely efficacious place to seek healing and forgiveness. The events were well attended and lasted all day. After the dedication exercises, the church hosted two masses, special afternoon services for the children, and a recitation of the rosary by about 1500 people. The evening included Vespers and the "Benediction of the Most Blessed Sacrament."[141]

The February 27, 1954, dedication of St. Albert the Great took place in a very different Catholic Boston. The *Pilot*'s description of the modest church conveyed one aspect of these changes: "conveniently located on Route 3, St. Albert's attracts the attention of those traveling along the South Shore."[142] Instead of the image of crowds "throng[ing]" as they had in Mount Carmel's "great auditorium," the paper conjures images of commuters turning their heads to see the church as they sped home from work, or stopping in for mass before heading into Boston for some weekend shopping.

The obvious differences between urban, Italian Mount Carmel and suburban, multiethnic St. Albert's may be misleading. Both parishes inherited the parallel, competing traditions in the church's teachings about locales and objects. Both were dedicated during the time when the church's rite of consecration included unapologetic exorcisms, the door-knocking and alphabet ceremonies, the sevenfold anointing, copious incense, and the field of fire atop the altar. These rites signal an orientation toward locales and objects that is not exhausted by the term "symbol" and is not satisfied with vague "mystery." This orientation to locales and objects expected presence and efficacy, and it did not vanish with the revision of the rite of dedication or the reevaluation of church architecture.

This orientation prompted the creators of the Mount Carmel's 1980 Diamond Jubilee program to include a photo and caption from a newspaper about the church's altar. It lauded the altar as "splendid" and "unparalleled even in this modern world." The altar, it continued, was the place where "thousands upon thousands of worshippers sought religious comfort, generation after generation where they kneeled in solemn prayer." The same confidence encouraged the day's speaker, the Rev. Cletus J. Dello Iacono, OFM, JCD, to reject the idea that religious places were only symbolic of something beyond themselves. "Your church," he told the crowd,

> has always been more than a symbol. It has been a house of Prayer, and into the various buildings, which have housed the worshippers through the years, have passed the old and the young, the newborn and the dead, seeking to make contact with Jesus Christ and His teachings.[143]

The special opportunity for contact, across lifetimes and generations, could not be contained by the metaphor of "living stones" or the actions of the church as the people of God. It was the promise of this same kind of contact that urged a pastor at St. Albert's to remind his parishioners that the men of the Nocturnal Admiration Society had the opportunity to sit directly before the Lord. The host they admired, he said, was

> not only a symbol, not only a figure, not only a sign even so sacred a sign as a sacrament—but a living person—the second Person of the Blessed Trinity—the word of God made Man.[144]

The protest embedded in these rejections of a merely symbolic interpretation of Catholic locales and objects illustrates the autonomous voice of the church's parallel history of efficacy.

This voice can also be heard in the bulletin announcements at St. Albert's for a novena to the "Miraculous Medal" and in the timeline of Boston-area expositions of the "Pilgrim Statue of Our Lady of Fatima" to whom "many miracles" had been attributed.[145] The idea that God is manifest in the individuals gathered in community was just one among many possibilities for bringing presence into practice. The objects and locales defended by Catholics in Boston's resisting parishes were more than "bricks and mortar," and they were more than symbols or repositories of mystery. They had been endowed with efficacious presence. Whether this presence was in the walls, the altar, the tabernacle, or even strictly in the people as they gathered there, some felt that it was inalienable from that place.

There is nothing new in the church's distancing itself from objects and locales. The competition between efficacy and symbolic meaning in the church's relationship to locales and objects is old and ongoing. The Second Vatican Council and the liturgical reforms that followed it made a significant contribution to the debate by adding volume to the side of meaning. Catholic locales and objects don't act, they mean; they point to something beyond themselves, the way symbols represent some other aspect of reality. Exorcism of objects is a non-authentic remnant. Relics are interesting, but mainly for what they teach about exemplary lives. Buildings are primarily metaphors for the universal church.

But things and places also continued to act. The Council's dialogue with modernity could not undo the church's long history of efficacy. Perhaps the ongoing give and take in relation to the efficacy of locales and objects is itself the "mystery" that makes these places worthwhile for so many. But the question is not always benign, and play with varying ideas has to end when decisions have to be made and enforced. There is confusion, especially for those who grew up with efficacy and grew old with meaning, like most of those in the resisting parishes in Boston.

Conclusion

As witnesses to and instigators of the momentous changes of the late twentieth century, resisters, like other Boston Catholics of their generation, were heirs to divergent histories. What the church and city became over the course of their lives seemed to be radically different from what they had been, and what they imagined they had been, in their early years. For those in occupied and resisting churches, this divided past provided both opportunity and challenge. In mounting a case against the shutdowns, it was not always clear whether histories of parish abundance or more recent histories of perseverance through scarcity offered the best case for preservation of the parish. In addition to providing a source of emotional solace and empowerment, narratives of overflowing sacred presence in Catholic churches seemed to offer a persuasive and orthodox rationale for halting the shutdowns. But more recent arguments about holiness abiding not in buildings but primarily in the "people of God" seemed to contradict this past while also offering yet another way to justify the occupations.

Vatican II–era language about lay leadership in the church also had a double edge when it came to the shutdowns. Past and present affirmations of a lay-led church seemed to militate against shutting down parishes against lay Catholics' wishes. This was one lesson behind resisters' invocation of pastoral descriptions of parishes as "your church."[146] But resisters' references to the important role of pastoral leadership in either bolstering or undermining a parish suggested the limits of more horizontal models of church organization. Catholics still sought out inspiring and gifted individual leaders, and some were willing to travel across parish lines when they found one and to fight to retain him. Changes in the lived environment also posed questions to the meaning and value of parishes. The idea so common among urban resistors about the closures as another siege upon their neighborhoods witnessed to the uncomfortable links between the values of neighborhood stability and ownership, and Euro-American Catholics' history of racial exclusiveness and hostility to difference. Resistance to parish shutdowns did not carry the same hostility to outsiders—indeed, vigilers in East Boston actively, although unsuccessfully, tried to recruit Spanish-speaking parishioners and the few young neighborhood newcomer professionals who walked by the parish on their way to another parish nearby. But all forms of ownership carry with them the indelible mark of exclusion as part of the search for stability and control over life. As such, white Boston's past of hostility to racial integration provides a reminder of the more painful aspects of Boston's history of neighborhood solidarity and the principle of subsidiarity that justifies it.[147]

But enclaves are not only reactionary hiding places, they can also be rare sites of comfort and relief in an otherwise taxing and soulless landscape. Even in suburbs, as St. Albert's vigilers discovered, set-apart places like their grotto could offer an antidote to loneliness and sorrow. Additional highways, runways, or housing, while not unwelcome in themselves, strengthened attachments to the places they threatened. Protecting these places amid threat suggested the possibility of a kind of sacrifice that fell somewhere between the selfish and the self-annihilating. In the shutdowns Catholics' past bubbled up and presented these kinds of untenable choices. In the resistance that followed, Catholics had no choice but to take up the challenge.

3

"What do we have?" Locales and Objects in the Hands of the People of God

Sunday, October 12, 2004, was scheduled as the day for the "Last Mass" for Our Lady of Mount Carmel Church in East Boston. Two days later the parish was permanently to shut its doors. The church and surrounding properties would soon be sold and perhaps leveled to create room for new developments. The "Last Mass" was a chance for the community to offer a collective ritual goodbye to their ninety-nine-year-old Italian national parish. As in other locales around the archdiocese, however, things would not go as planned in East Boston.

Shortly after the mass ended, as mournful parishioners listened to an organ refrain of *Ave Maria* and slowly headed for the exit, a statue of the parish's patroness, the Blessed Mother as Our Lady of Mount Carmel holding the baby Jesus, tumbled to the floor. According to the story, no one was near Our Lady at the time she fell. Churchgoers heard a sudden crash and turned to see their patron saint chipped and prone on the dais. Parishioners and news reporters, hearing cries in Italian ("La Madonna!") and in English ("Our Lady fell!" and "It's a sign!"), rushed up the aisles to get a closer look as others struggled to lift the nearly life-sized plaster statue up off the ground.[1]

Immediately after the Madonna fell at Mount Carmel, the process of interpretation began. Some explained that the repeated touching of the statue by distraught departing parishioners may have inched her slowly back on her platform, where she teetered until she finally went over. Others enhanced this story and added an element of blame for the church custodian, noting that the statue's platform was nothing more than a narrow and fragile crate on which he had set the Madonna in order to make her more visible for the last masses. Still others, remarking that no one could find this suspicious crate, rejected naturalistic explanations, instead preferring to leave what was immediately called a "miracle" open to supernatural explanations. Whether they held to the natural or supernatural explanations, vigilers considered the event special, even deeply significant: later, a sign hanging prominently at the back of the occupied church read "Our Lady of Mt. Carmel Has Sent a Message."

The event's precise message was up for debate. This fluidity became a cause for concern among those in the parish who feared, accurately as it turned out, that observing officials would find it easy to critique the occupation if they appeared credulous and susceptible to suggestions of overflowing sacred presence in their church.[2] As if to highlight the balance they were seeking between control and celebration of this dangerous event, the "Survivors" (as Mount Carmel's occupying group called themselves) soon moved the Madonna to the center of the dais directly in front of the altar, but also locked the statue inside a new glass box. If other statues could still be touched, kissed, and easily moved, this Madonna had found both a new isolation and a new centrality. She had the most prominent position in the church; they framed her with electric devotional candles and illuminated the statue with several lamps pointing up from the floor. But it was clear that she would not be moving—whether jumping or falling—anymore. The fractured pieces from her back would no longer be carried off in people's pockets as relics.

This doublesided response to the fallen Madonna captures occupiers' need to walk a fine line in relation to sacred presence. The church's history of efficacy embedded in locales and objects animated the event and gave it power to shape people's lives. The Madonna was not a symbol here, but an active, present reality with an opinion on the church closure. Some even used the event as a reason for joining the parish's occupation. The parallel history emphasizing the symbolic interpretation of churches and its things limited this exuberance. The community considered seeking some kind of official recognition of the event from Rome, but cautious occupation leaders thought it judicious to avoid identifying their effort wholly with the Madonna's fall.

Governing sacred presence was particularly important and difficult in the context of the church closures. This chapter examines the ways the shutdowns highlighted stresses in the tradition related to sacred presence in locales and objects. The competing histories outlined in the previous chapters came into conflict in Boston during the shutdowns. Forms of presence and efficacy that had been removed from the 1956 rite of dedication persisted for people in occupied churches. These Catholics were not, however, insensitive to the arguments of the reformers. Resisters understood and even appreciated the notion that God's presence was in the congregation. Because they read "people of God" in local and antiauthoritarian terms, they could afford to add this idea of presence in the community to other ways of thinking about presence in the church. As it would with the question of sacrifice and authority, the Second Vatican Council's "people of God" ecclesiology moved in multiple directions in relation to sacred presence.

"Our home is in you:" Controlling Presence with the Closing Manual

Caution about the church's history of presence and efficacy in objects and locales reverberated through the manual presented to pastors of parishes on the closure list. This 168-page document, *Archdiocese of Boston Parish Closing Manual: "Rebuild My Church," Version 1.0*, described to the pastors and staff of closing parishes the rules of the closure process. It offered theological resources for managing grief, suggested liturgical options to mark the communities' final celebrations, and provided numerous checklists, forms, and questionnaires for organizing and sequencing practical matters related to shutting down and transferring parish resources. The document sought ways to inculcate detachment among parishioners of closing churches by asserting a symbolic and metaphorical rather than literal presence in parish things. The manual presumed that a struggle with shutdowns was inevitable, but argued that maturity and properly managed mourning would clear the path for the tremendous changes the archdiocese sought to facilitate and control. A review of the key features of the *Closing Manual* establishes the essential foundation for understanding resisting Catholics' engagements with questions of presence in their churches.

As suppression decrees were issued to parishes in May of 2004, the archdiocese provided pastors with copies of the *Closing Manual*. Comparing the closures with the death of a loved one, the manual acknowledged what the archbishop called the "sorrow, frustration, and anguish" of the closing process. In a gesture that simultaneously expressed empathy and authorized the shutdowns, the archbishop opened the manual with a reference to his own suffering as the initiator of this process. "Closing one parish makes me sad, but closing many is truly heartbreaking."[3] Such an opening was significant given the heightened attention to the new archbishop as the replacement for Cardinal Bernard Law, who had left the diocese in disgrace after being shown to have covered up clergy sexual abuse in the diocese.

The subtitle of the *Closing Manual*—"Go, Francis, rebuild my church, which you can see is well nigh in ruins," the command St. Francis had heard from a crucifix before his radical abandonment of privilege—likewise directed attention to the archbishop, whose Franciscan vows of poverty had caused a stir for the first months of his tenure. Upon his arrival in Boston in the summer of 2003, the archbishop's brown robe, sandals, and beard, all omnipresent in the media, were immediate, obvious, and powerful symbols of sacrifice and asceticism. These emblems of poverty received nearly obsessive attention from local news sources and later became the target of lampooning among resisting Catholics. But in the meantime the archdiocese, laity, and media worked together to put forth the image of a humbler Boston Catholicism as a contrast to the excesses of the Cardinal Law regime.[4] Reports of Law's opulence, which at one time in Boston's history would have signaled to Catholics their influence and power in the city, now became confirmation of the pomposity, elevation, and self-serving isolation of the hierarchy.

The *Globe* reported that many Boston College students seemed to have warmed to the new archbishop almost immediately, citing his "down-to-earth persona" and his reputation for humility and empathy.[5] Before O'Malley's installation as archbishop, a former Maryknoll priest and member of the gay Catholic organization Dignity gave voice to the message he wanted O'Malley to send:

> All reports about the new archbishop are positive, that he is modest, humble, not coming to Boston with the baggage of pomposity and elevation. It would be nice if he moved into the cathedral [residence in the South End]. It would be symbolic, but symbols can be a means of communicating ideas.[6]

This expectation appeared to be fulfilled when O'Malley sold the archbishop's residence and other property at the chancery to neighboring Boston College, one of his first major decisions as archbishop.

The *Globe* echoed the former priest's evaluation when it editorialized on the "symbolic" meaning of the move:

> On a personal level, the newly arrived archbishop, Seán O'Malley, revealed much about himself last summer when he shunned the fancy quarters in Brighton in favor of more modest surroundings in the rectory of the Cathedral of the Holy Cross in the South End. That move signaled that O'Malley wished not to fall victim to the poor judgment common in leaders who isolate themselves from their followers.

The editorial went on to predict that the archbishop's decision would stave off distress and bitterness anticipated as a result of the upcoming meetings on parish consolidations.[7] As it happened, most parishes closed without vocal complaint, but Boston's officials also faced widespread and bitter opposition to the closures. Nonetheless, the archbishop's demonstration of the new Franciscan spirit of humility and sacrifice would be an important resource later for the justification of closures and the rebuttal of resisters. In his letter explaining the closures, O'Malley wrote that the decision was difficult but necessary, and not catastrophic. "I know from my own experience of being uprooted many times in life that the Church's faith can be as alive in one place as it is in another."[8] His experience of sacrifice gave legitimacy to his request of it from others.

This is the context in which the *Closing Manual* appeared. Much of its advice centered on the ritual mediation of change. Invoking the archbishop's prerogative to sanction special "Masses for Various Needs and Occasions," the *Closing Manual* listed possible liturgies for parishes' final ritual acts.[9] These plans for a "Last Mass" described it as an occasion for acknowledging the challenges of a painful but necessary transition. The Office for Worship urged pastors to prepare a celebration to "express the people's grief while allowing for a sense of solace" and to communicate that:

> [t]he change is a transition, a 'journey:' There is a 'from where, 'to where,' and 'through what' dimension of this change. The liturgies will not accomplish that journey, but they will symbolize and nurture it.[10]

To facilitate this journey, pastors were to be sensitive in their homilies and to avoid "preaching which ignores feelings (e.g. stressing God's will without acknowledging God's understanding of uncomfortable feelings)."[11] Managing their relationship to objects was crucial to protecting parishioners' feelings. Homilies should acknowledge how the "church moved from being a building to being the center of our lives."[12] But now Catholics should recall that this center was always mutable, and that its power remains fixed in the memory of worship and life there, not in the place itself. Abraham's willingness to leave his homeland and the paschal mystery of Christ were the exemplary narratives of obedience and suffering that, through faith and togetherness, produce positive change.[13]

The Last Mass was also a time to channel energies and interests toward the universal church as embodied in the "welcoming parish." The potential conflict between the local and the universal played out in the description of Last Mass "Option A" (titled "The Mass for the Local Church") which

> was chosen because its prayers and readings remind us that the Church is something larger than one particular parish. Rather, the Church is the people who have been created by the Spirit in baptism and formed through the gospel and Eucharist. As important as the parish is to the lives of the people connected to it, we must always recognize that we are part of a community.[14]

The *Closing Manual* encouraged pastors to elaborate on this understanding of church with particular emphasis on the difference between material and spiritual truths. Whether a pastor chose Option A or B (with the title "The Mass for Thanksgiving"), the manual had recommendations for appropriate opening remarks:

> Although this is our last celebration in this Church, we will continue to hear God's Word and share the Lord's table because as a people of faith we know that who we are in God's eyes and what we believe in cannot be limited by bricks and mortar and human structures. In a spirit of gratitude, then, let us prepare ourselves for the Eucharist by seeking God's mercy and forgiveness.[15]

The manual warned that parishioners might misconstrue the building and its objects as somehow essential. Extending this theme and seeking to illustrate its viability, the archdiocesan reconfiguration website promoted the poetic response of a "devout" lay Catholic:

> Quite naturally our hearts are sad,
> As we gather together at Mass each day.
> To say goodbye to Blessed Sacrament Parish,
> Our special place for us to pray.
> After many years in the parish fold,
> Our church is one that has to close,
> But after praying I faced the truth:

Our allegiance is to our religion and not
A parish roof.
So, though I know my heart will grieve,
I'll attend each service before we leave,
Until the day when we depart
With love for God, our new parish,
And faith in our hearts.[16]

This model response offered a critique of religion that is associated too closely with the church building. It identified and sought to dam up undercurrents in Catholic thought in relation to objects and locales.

The manual's list of points to emphasize in the last mass addressed similar concerns:

> The community of the people and their personal, spiritual journey are more important than a building and things. Rather, reference to things should help people gather their memories and make their transition.

Another point made the remarkable argument that the "things" of the church should become "images":

> Regarding the things of worship, emphasis is on central images: the Word of God, the altar around which Christ gathers his church, the baptismal call and dignity of the Catholic people, and the images of being gathered in prayer and then sent in mission.[17]

Here the particularity and materiality of the essential "things of worship" vanished. The Word of God was clearly a reference to the Bible, but it was not a specific Bible. The altar was the altar one sees at the front of the church, but it was more crucially the altar of a mystical communion, that universal ritual table around which Christ's church gathers. Even more dramatically, the baptismal font became the "baptismal call" and the actual gathered community was dispersed and disassembled through the image of a missionary church. The symbolic and metaphorical understanding of church buildings showed its utility in mediating changes in Boston.

The manual's optional closing ceremony included a procession out of the building with "a few tokens of our history" as a gesture of incorporation into the receiving parish. Here the receiving parish loomed larger than the universal church. But the manual still downplayed particular material objects. The registers (parish record books listing sacraments of initiation, marriages, and deaths) were the tokens named as appropriate for this ritual.

These books are rarely part of a parish's material life. The registers are not items of worship nor are they a physical part of the church, but things which the manual suggested "represent what we bring to St. Y Parish, which so many of us will soon call our own."[18] These documents are essentially confidential, moreover, and the manual warns pastors to make sure that the books are not available for public perusal before or after the procession.[19]

The emphasis on the sacramental documents in the homily recommendations and in this optional ritual directed attention to the possibility of family continuity and highlighted special moments of memory that would continue to have a place in the new parish. Other liturgical items—crosses, "a special chalice," contents of the cornerstone, altar candlesticks—might be added to the procession if, as was usually the case, the building would no longer be used as a worship site. But the manual recommended that these be taken up "without comment" and suggested that "only a few such items should be included—those with special meaning. (This is not the time to empty the church)."[20] If the receiving parish was within walking distance, other items, like a special statue or a parish banner, might become part of another procession, led by incense, out of the old parish and into the new one.

The pastor could also choose to hold a "procession for remembering," a ritual walk to sites of special significance within the closing church such as the baptismal font, the Stations of the Cross, and the altar.[21] The manual provided a set of prayers of remembrance for this "out-of-the-ordinary event."[22] The prayers in each special site trod delicately with respect to presence, but nonetheless acknowledged the history of efficacy that once gave those places their power. The rite particularly identified transformations wrought through the sacraments celebrated at the specific sites. Prayers in front of the confessional or reconciliation chapel, for example, highlighted the combination of consecrated place and sacramental action: "We thank you and we praise you for the healing and reconciling love that has been given through the sacrament of penance in this church." The opening lines of the rite's final prayer reestablished the core message of detachment and symbolic meaning: "God our refuge, our home is in you. You are greater than any temple, church or cathedral that can be built by human hands." The remaining lines nodded to the history of efficacy, but moved swiftly toward a different meaning of church:

> yet in this place we have met your divine majesty. This church building has been a place of blessing for us. Protect us on our way. Lead us to new friends in another faith community. We ask this through Christ our Lord.[23]

God's majesty and blessings at the altar gave way to "new friends," highlighting the communal meanings of the church. The final remembrance might also elevate the objects of parish life, with a special emphasis on their mobility:

> If the entire community is being transferred to another church, delegate one or more members (the parish council president, the oldest member of the parish or the youngest) to carry an object (or objects) that can and will be used in the new place (such as a sacred vessel, a small icon or the book of the gospels). This person will be presented with the object.

During this transfer, the presider reassured the witnesses that the "life of this community will continue in another place" and offered instructions to the selected parishioner:

> [Name], receive this [name of item] that will be used at [name of new church]. Take it (directly) from this place to [name of the new pastor/pastoral administrator] as a sign that our journey of faith will continue there.[24]

The essence of church is not in objects or locales but in the community. In turn, the community is not limited to a particular place, but identified with the broad communion of Catholics making up the people of God. Moreover, the receiving parish would be just one stop on the parishioners' "journey of faith."

The things of the churches were also on a journey. As symbols of something beyond themselves, Catholic objects could be mobile and remain meaningful. But things were also meaningful for their value on the market. There were definite policies established to manage the redistribution of parish objects. Fear that objects would fall into the wrong hands and cause scandal to the faithful meant that the manual took a strict tone with pastors urging them to follow the instructions in order to protect Boston's Catholic assets.

On this matter Bishop Richard Lennon, the archdiocese's second in command, acted as a sort of administrative disciplinarian in contrast to the archbishop's more pastoral opening letter. In a letter following O'Malley's, Lennon encouraged pastors to be particularly careful to avoid sloppy management of the "patrimony of your parish":

> Be vigilant so that nothing in your parish disappears. Inventories of your financial books and your material goods must be taken accurately and these assets must be protected. There is a process for the redistribution of these

> items and it must be followed closely. Otherwise, chaos will abound and the assets of your parish will be lost. Any deliberate distribution of the assets of your parish outside of canon law or the system created here without express permission will be handled strictly and appropriately.[25]

The manual is rife with warnings along these lines; procedures for marking and tracking items are spelled out with great detail. The archdiocese even sent teams of appraisers to closing parishes with color-coded stickers: red stickers for sacred items, green stickers for non-sacred items worth more than $500, orange stickers for non-sacred items for auction, and no stickers for items under $500, to be sold or distributed at the pastor's discretion.

Sacred items not going to the receiving parishes after two weeks were made available for pastors from parishes anywhere in the archdiocese. After another two weeks, the archdiocese planned to "aggressively market" remaining sacred items to *"bona fide"* resellers. After ninety days, unclaimed items would be destroyed on site, sold in bulk, or stored for later sale.[26]

The emphasis on the mobility of Catholic objects and people presented in the *Closing Manual* is an ancient part of the tradition. But as Lennon's warning about items vanishing suggested, local efficacy and inviolable sacred presence had their living histories too. The *Closing Manual* and the 1978 *Rite for the Dedication of a Church and Altar* both sought to undo versions of Catholic presence and efficacy that had been woven into Catholics' lives before (and in many cases after) the Second Vatican Council. For those who had grown up before the Council, such changes were not wholly unwelcome, but neither were they necessarily comprehensive. The ritualization of place they had grown up with had disciplined and accustomed them to revere and protect Catholic objects and locales as holy in themselves. The *Closing Manual* suggested the congregation and its memories were the proper sites of holiness; resisters could not help but agree. But some memories were inalienable from local places, and forging meaningful communities through coercion or the obliteration of boundaries proved untenable for some in Boston.[27]

"It's the building you're in:" Sacraments, Memories, and Emotion in Church Buildings

Narratives of proper mourning, detachment from objects, and the universalism of the church combined in the manual to make anything but a dignified, if mournful, transition to a new parish less than Catholic. It is possible to feel warmly toward "things," but a mature Catholic understands that they are passing, and that the core of the tradition resides in the invisible and intangible. Resisters were not ignorant of these arguments, and in fact, did not wholly disagree. Many times I heard resisters renounce attachment to "the building" as the reason for their occupation. They understood that such arguments attempted to flatten their opposition and portray them as naive, stubborn, or selfish.[28] They parried this argument with evidence of their broader efforts, such as advocacy of a democratic church, appeal to canon law, civil court filings, and statistics contradicting archdiocesan neighborhood studies. This work spoke to fundamental concerns, not naive attachments, and, they hoped, would establish a precedent of lay Catholic engagement for future generations. They argued that the process of the closures was flawed, and claimed to stand up to the hierarchy on behalf of other Catholics who would not or could not do so themselves.[29] Yet they also retained the idea that in Catholicism buildings and the things in them matter beyond the symbolic interpretations offered in the *Closing Manual* and in the kinds of teachings reflected in the 1978 dedication rite.

Ralph, from the North End's Sacred Heart, built this idea into a theoretical conversation with "the priests" about the prospect of closing the church. Justifying the closures, Ralph said, the authorities forwarded the argument that one church is as good as another, so long as it offers the essential rites. "Well, what's the difference?" Ralph's hypothetical opponents asked. "'You do the sacraments, you have the mass, and that's the end of it.' And I said 'It isn't the end of it, what are you talking about? You're destroying a family unit.'" If the reconfiguration manual and archdiocesan officials were not quite this insensitive to loss, Ralph's narrative still accurately captured their fundamental message. Officials hoped Catholics would look beyond their previous lives to make new companions with whom they could continue their journey of faith.

In arguing that community was more important than bricks and mortar, they seemed to gloss over Catholic traditions where the two come together. Ralph captured something of this combination as he offered his thoughts on the true meaning of religion:

> The artistry that goes into making these churches is part of the emotional fabric of the church. To just say that it means nothing is insane. Religion is about emotion. I mean it is about emotion. It is about praying for your

> parents that might not be there any more. The thoughts that you had when they took you to church years ago. It's all about emotions. It is what holds you together in the church.[30]

Here emotion takes precedence to obedience as a source of religious meaning. While this formulation lifts up the periphery over the center, it is not the unvarnished triumph of the individual over the collective. The emotion Ralph describes takes shape out of the web of various relationships made possible through the parish church. The connections between artistry, emotion, meaning, and memory meant that his particular church—its bricks and mortar and everything else—was inalienable from the truth of the tradition.

Even the suburban box-like churches Ralph so vehemently disdained had their own communities of memory and sense of a spiritual exchange enabled in a particular place. Many of them had been around for fifty years or more by the time of their closing. This was the case at St. Jeremiah Parish in suburban Framingham, where reflections on the building and its relationship to true religion were not dissimilar to those of their urban counterparts. After having heard one non-vigiling member of the resistance describe the vigil as unnecessary given the roadblocks to closure contained in the community's legal battle, I asked Art about his reasons for staying in the building. At first, he suggested that occupying the building provided "another layer of protection" against the unpredictable archdiocese. The following morning, as we woke up and prepared to leave, Art approached me and suggested that "comfort" was perhaps a better explanation of the occupation. When I came back a few days later, Art approached me again and reported that he'd talked with another vigiler about my question and wanted to offer a refinement to his previous answers. Occupying the building, they had decided, was the only way that they could "keep the community together." Without it, they would be subject to an even more profound exile, having to "meet in the parking lot or something."[31] The hard work of sustaining the resistance would have been nearly impossible without possession of the building. In this sense, the building was both the means and the end of the resistance. If this practical reasoning was not the same thing as Ralph's appeal based on artistry and emotion, it nonetheless invited the same question: what is the proper relationship between community (past and present), building, sacred presence, and the core of the tradition?

Louis, a St. Jeremiah vigiler in his late forties, approached this question with the suggestion that "the community is the building." "I hate to say it," he told me, "it's the building you're in." His rhetorical reticence reflected an awareness of his vulnerability to what he called "the party line" which he said, amounted to "Don't make it about the brick and mortar." Join the receiving parish and "The community will resurrect itself and merge into one bigger, stronger community." But he insisted, "No, we won't have our community. It's going to be a different community. It's going to be a larger community. And you're not going to have that same feeling." He knew the community of St. Jeremiah's would itself be a "new community" after the vigil, but the combination of core members and the building might help it retain "that same feeling." When I asked him to explain what he meant in joining community and building he worked toward a different concept entailing togetherness and memory of the sacraments:

> How can I say it? It's not just the building, it's a gathering place. It's memories, you know. I've [only] been at this parish twelve years, [but] I've taught here, my daughter had her first communion here. It's a lot of memories you know? Yeah, you can say mass at another place, but it doesn't give you the same sense of community, I think.[32]

While the *Closing Manual* portrayed orientations toward presence as a choice between community and building, for Art, Louis, Ralph, and the other resisters, they were linked. Appreciation of the vivid sacramental memories instantiated in the buildings themselves was a characteristic feature of those who stayed behind.

No one denied, of course, that these sacraments had taken place there. The *Closing Manual*'s emphasis on the sacramental books signaled their awareness of the importance of these life passage moments. But for these resisting Catholics, the memory of sacramental action warranted deeper respect than the simple preservation of its written record. The manual's suggested procession of remembrance to sacramental sites in the church, if pastors chose to perform it, only tried to "symbolize and nurture" change; this approach could not, for some at least, disentangle specific sacramental memories from the essence of the tradition.[33] The resistance showed that the action of the people of God, so deeply embraced by those reforming church rites and aesthetics in the 1970s, was not as alienable from the places in which it happened as these reformers had suggested. This was not just a matter of attachment, comfort, or conservatism. The church's history of endorsing local places as inviolable and uniquely efficacious still spoke to Catholics.

Beyond one's own family's sacraments, the accumulated history of sacraments freighted particular church sites with a sense of their unique efficacy. For Abigail, a St. Albert's resister, others' sacramental experiences lived on in evocative ways in the material goods of the church. Her overnight hours in the parish reconciliation room stirred reflection on these experiences:

> And . . . where my little bed is is the chair where the priest sits to hear confessions, and I was sitting there thinking of all the feelings . . . the conversations, the opening up. [They] were probably very painful conversations with the confessors . . . and I'm thinking of all of the absolution that was given at those times, and all of those people that walked out of that little room . . . feeling renewed.

Abigail was one of the few people I met who told me that she was close to someone who had been abused by a priest. As the church's "little room" where one-on-one contact with priests offered absolution and renewal rather than shame and pain, the reconciliation room may have had special resonance for her.

Comparing her sleep at home to her sleep at the church, Abigail described the "strange peaceful feeling" she had in the church. Like others, Abigail acknowledged the truth of the universalizing message of the diocesan officials, but she could not get away from asserting the continuing relevance of the local:

> God is everywhere, and he is as at home in my bedroom as well as he is in this building, but this is a consecrated house of God, and that's another thing that bothers me. How can they desanctify this building? This is holy ground. It will always be holy ground, and I don't want it to be condos. Or anything else. If it had to be closed and it had to be something else, it should be a church or a temple, or something for God.[34]

Abigail's movement here—from the intimate imagining of others' confessions to the affirmation of God's limitless presence and back to an affirmation of the holiness of particular places—characterizes resisters' tense and sometimes strategic weaving of multiple idioms of presence and place in explanation of the proper means of practicing parish.

The ability to imagine past and future movements in church spaces enhanced resisters' commitment to the histories of reverence surrounding them. I noticed this during a goodwill tour launched from St. Albert's to fellow occupied parishes. Caravans of St. Albert's parishioners fanned out across the archdiocese to pay their respects and buoy the spirits of the groups who had taken up vigils in their own parishes. The pilgrimage prompted some mild competitive instincts from those I traveled with, who saw their own cozy and perpetually bustling parish as superior to the quieter and more spacious parishes they visited. Mostly, however, the trip spurred mutual appreciation and reflection on the beauty and power of the archdiocese's churches. At St. Bernard in Newton the visitors admired the building and allowed the hosts to point out its best features. They also swapped horror stories with their hosts about the fate of former Catholic church buildings. One resister conjured the image of the church turned into a gymnasium, with basketballs pounding across the floor. Another described a former church that had been turned into a bar and now had a beer vat on the altar.[35]

These imaginative exercises captured vividly what was at stake in the occupations. A similar speculation about a parking lot in the church basement hushed the normally boisterous crowd at Mount Carmel one evening. An archdiocesan property manager had recently visited the church, and observers noted that he had been particularly interested in the space beneath the front stairs. Some guessed he was investigating whether this could be a possible egress to parking in the basement for condominiums above, in the former church. As a few hard-of-hearing resisters strained to catch the flow of this conversation, I noted that the others brushed off their inquiries in an attempt to shield them from the bleak possibility of cars parked where we were sitting.[36]

Although frustrated Catholics in closed parishes might not agree, their pained imaginings and experiences were perhaps similar to the feeling that prompted the archbishop to compare himself, as the leader of a dramatically contracting archdiocese, to Jesus bearing his cross. In a letter asking for understanding from parishioners, O'Malley conveyed the deep suffering entailed for those affected by the process. "At times," he wrote, "I ask God to call me home and let someone else finish this job, but I keep waking up in the morning to face another day of reconfiguration."[37] Expressions of sympathy and the executioners' own suffering did not go far among the resisting communities.[38] Nonetheless, the archbishop's vivid image conveys the potency and resonance of church buildings among Catholics. Even as O'Malley emphasized the universal church, the reality of the close bond between local place and the truths of the tradition could not be erased. The extreme language of the archbishop's lament carried the weight of both a loss of presence (from the Boston landscape) and a lack of control (in his own role as leader). If it were up to him, churches would not diminish, but would multiply across the landscape. But circumstances made the difficult closures necessary. He could not dictate the situation as he wished and Catholics' access to presence embodied in their familiar Catholic churches would suffer for it.

The angst expressed by the archbishop, of course, was amplified and particularized among communities facing the closure of their churches. They felt the combined loss of control and presence even more acutely, since their churches created the context for both as part of their religious lives. Ralph expressed the link between a church's sacred presence and aspects of control in a rebuttal of the ritual and psychological remedies presented in the *Closing Manual* and other official statements. Ritual and psychological remedies struck Ralph as incongruous with the ways he had come to understand the tradition. He chafed at the suggestion that understanding the stages of mourning could heal the wounds of parish closure:

> . . . this is a family group and it took 116 years to develop that. And they say, 'Oh, you just migrate there.' And some [say] 'Oh, it is like losing a relative.' No, it is like losing an entire family. This is what is not understood. Consequently, you go there, and you go there as an orphan. And you'll never be anything but.[39]

Going from "here" to "there" between the North End's parishes was a journey of some four blocks. Living members of the "family" of Sacred Heart, or major portions of it at least, could have made the journey to St. Leonard's without too much trouble. But such explanations missed Ralph's point. Losing the church building was paramount to losing the family. For Ralph, the tradition gained meaning precisely in its local textures and relationships. The emphasis in the American church on "family"—in the Christian Family Movement of the 1940s and 50s, for example, in the Marriage Encounter movement of the post Vatican II church—established a foundation for this kind of appeal. While the emphasis and approach differed widely, the centrality of family in twentieth-century lay Catholic formation made resisters' appeal to the language of family understandable. Whether "the core of Catholic social thought," a symbol of the fundamental unity of all people in the "Mystical Body of Christ," or the foundation for a healthy spiritual life, the Catholic family ideal resonated across twentieth-century American Catholic experience.[40]

With these family ideals in mind, Ralph thought the transformation called for in the shutdowns was more fundamental than its supporters allowed. In Ralph's passionate critique, the gap was like the difference between suffering through a single family member's death and the loss of an entire family. One is a natural, everyday occurrence; everything comes to an end. The other is the kind of devastating, unnatural tragedy that does not easily fade from view. The difference resides not in the quantity of the loss but in the sense of subjection and powerlessness in the face of tragedy. The proposed loss of sacred presence from North Square and loss of control of the situation combined to create the outrage Ralph felt.

Another resister in a suburban parish put it less dramatically as he tried to explain the ongoing resistance. "People don't just attend a church," he told me, "they put their heart and soul into it."[41] Defenses like those the occupiers presented in legal briefs, press releases, and power-point presentations did not advertise this same core commitment. In linking community, sacramental memory, reverence, and control, the commitment to churches as unique places of sacred presence underlay the resistance. Defense of presence defined in these ways gave the resistance much of its energy. The history of efficacy and the ample endorsement of sacred presence in locales and objects from the church's past made this commitment an enduring and fundamental aspect of the resistance.

Presence and the Marketplace

It was in part these histories of presence that caused the chancery to share Abigail's hope that the buildings it sold would go to other religious or social services organizations.[42] There were practical concerns, too. For one thing, religious groups might be willing to pay more for former church buildings because they would not have to invest as much in renovation as would developers seeking to transform church buildings into housing. Rectories, convents, and schools posed fewer challenges than churches, which often had to be leveled instead of renovated to create housing.[43] A commitment to advancing social justice were among the promised checks the church would place upon its marketing of the properties. But disciplined selling practices also conveyed the idea that sordid use of former church land could scandalize the faithful by offending people's sense of remaining holiness there. Each press-release by the archdiocese about the sale of church buildings detailed the elaborate process of vetting possible buyers, with scrutiny of potential deals reaching all the way to the Holy See "where needed."[44] There were no promises, of course, that churches would be sold only to these groups, and Abigail's speculation about condos reflected the economic realities of Boston-area real estate.[45]

The inability of the archdiocese to control who took over their former churches was revealed in East Boston when the archdiocese sold a building to a local photographer who "flipped" the property twenty days later for a substantial profit.[46] Unsubstantiated suspicion of a secret kickback to the church gained energy after the *Herald* reported that the second buyer was an anti-Catholic religious organization seeking to make inroads in heavily Catholic East Boston.[47] If the archdiocese knew that this other group wanted the building, but did not want to appear to support an anti-Catholic organization, selling first to the original buyer offered a shield from critique. The archdiocesan chancellor denied knowledge of the photographer's plan, and expressed frustration that the original buyer and not the archdiocese had earned maximum profit on the property. But this did not assuage resisting Catholics. Details of the "flip" (the photographer was reported to have met with the East Boston church's neighbors to announce his fictitious plan to turn the church into an art studio on the same day that he met with the Pentecostal group to confirm their purchase of the property) incensed observers.[48]

Not only had the archdiocese squandered its assets and sold to a shady businessman, but it had (apparently) unwittingly abetted a group with which Catholics in Brazil had battled for years. Resisters in Boston played an active part in the media's coverage of this transaction. The Council of Parishes called for further investigation of the matter in a letter to the Vatican's representative in the United States. The letter suggested that the archdiocese's sloppy appraisal and bidding systems and its failure to insist on deed restrictions against resale to a "hostile religious denomination" violated canon law.[49] Soon the archdiocese also faced criticism on this matter from an independent archdiocesan review board called the Parish Reconfiguration Fund Oversight Committee (PRFOC), which had been chartered in September of 2004 to review and make recommendations related to the reconfiguration funds. Though they were somewhat less suspicious of the chancery's motives, the PRFOC confirmed the Council of Parishes' assessment and lamented the "financial loss and grave embarrassment" it had caused.[50] The archdiocese published a clarification of policy for future transactions.[51] For their part, resisters circulated a web video that confirmed their sense that the chancery just didn't care. It showed one of the leaders of the denomination that eventually bought the building kicking a statue of Mary on Brazilian TV.[52] That some Catholics in Boston suspected the archdiocese of secretly selling a church to an anti-Catholic group signaled the level of suspicion and distrust that had taken root in relations between lay Catholics and the hierarchy.

This episode was not only a debacle on the grounds of asset management, but also because of the questions it re-raised about Catholic objects and locales. Who deserved to own a Catholic building? What uses were fitting for former churches? What are Catholic objects, after all? A popular story at Mount Carmel held that a bishop had reprimanded a group there by reminding them that statues were "just pieces of chalk" or "only carved marble."[53] The story lived on in the community because it captured a fundamental disconnect between parishioners and planners of the shutdowns on abiding questions in the Catholic tradition. Susana offered her critique of the bishop's charge by raising some of these questions:

> [the bishop] told them that the statue of Padre Pio over there is a piece of carved marble. OK, if that's what you think of it, let's go to Rome, let's take all the statues out, and let's sell all the churches, because they are nothing else but buildings. What do we have? Why do statues cry, why do pictures cry? Why?[54]

Susana's cry brought the church's history of efficacious locales and objects up against its history of symbolic meaning in these things. Her husband's response tried to mediate between these histories:

> Maybe it's not wrong to say that Padre Pio is carved marble. It *is* carved marble. It's the thought behind; the idea. You look up at Padre Pio, to his face, [it] looks like him, feels like him; you remember him. Sure it's carved marble, but it's got a meaning for me. For him to say it's 'only carved marble,' that was a dumb thing for a bishop to say.[55]

The statue in question was the same one David had promised he would install if he made it through his recent heart transplant. His rebuttal was grounded in the power of objects to activate specific meanings rooted in personal relationships and memory. This assessment is not hostile to the idea that Catholic objects are not themselves holy, but rather symbolize truths. But it also takes seriously the history of sacred presence in things.

For someone like David, who told me that he had once met the healer-mystic-stigmatic-saint Padre Pio in Italy, the statue offered an intimate recreation of contact with holiness.

The proximity of the statue for David and Susana (it was only about two hundred feet from their front door) certainly added to its power and significance. But as we have seen, reverence for special places like the Padre Pio Shrine was not limited to dense urban places like East Boston. If the East Boston shrine offered residents constant reminders of the wondrous stories of this old world saint, neighbors of Framingham's St. Jeremiah's encountered a distinctly new world version of Catholic presence. St. Jeremiah's was the family parish of teacher-astronaut Christa McAuliffe. Her death along with six other astronauts aboard the space shuttle Challenger in 1984 prompted the parish to install a state-of-the-art bell system as a memorial. The bells' dedication ceremony, which featured church and political dignitaries, lived on in the parish memory. "Christa's Bells" could be heard in the surrounding blocks, including in the backyard of McAuliffe's mother, who became a plaintiff in the church's doomed civil suit against the archdiocese.[56]

Whether it was condominiums, a strip mall, or another religious community that was to have replaced these sights and sounds in East Boston, Framingham, and elsewhere, the concern among Catholics for their buildings echoed the archbishop's oft-repeated critique of the dominance of the marketplace in American life. If religious places could be sold to the highest bidder, what kind of resistance to the culture of consumption could the Church legitimately offer?[57] In the North End, Ralph wondered if the church leadership could really appreciate the meaning of an old neighborhood parish, where being in the church was just as "easy" as being "in another room in our house." "It wasn't like it was 'over there,'" Ralph said, ". . . there were just people and priests floating in and out of this place." If the church was like another room in one's house, then watching while someone else sold it off certainly would have given the feeling of helplessness in the face of the overbearing dominance of market values. The fluidity of sacred and profane in the integration of home, street, and church did not make the church less special. Instead, it meant that the church stood against what Ralph saw as the prevailing trend of corporatization in Catholic America. Defense of "flavor" (Sacred Heart's "garlic" versus "white bread" as Ralph's taste of the suburbs) extended to an evaluation change in society and the church:

> instead of the personal feeling that you get out of a church, it is going to be like a supermarket—the Wal-Mart of the church. You process people [in], you process people out, what is that? What are you going to get out of it?[58]

Ralph's lament rests on what we might call a thicker notion of time than we are normally accustomed to imaging possible in modern contexts.[59] Wal-Mart (and the spirit of Wal-Mart) is the antithesis of thick time—it removes the past (in the form of smaller, locally owned businesses) and the future (by making and selling products oblivious to the demands of durability and sustainability) in the interest of the present. The fact that many of us can only afford to buy things from places like Wal-Mart means that thick time has become a commodity available only to the rich. Ralph saw the shutdowns as the church's submission to the broader American project of mass consumption. This was not willful ignorance of economic realities. Ralph was himself a businessman, and had even proposed raising money to support the church by establishing it as an official stop—with souvenir shop and all—on Boston's Freedom Trail, a popular historical walk that goes right past the church's front door on its way from Paul Revere's house to the Old North Church.[60]

Even when resisters argued that it was "not about the building," the significance of local place and God's presence there remained important. At St. Catherine of Siena in Charlestown, for example, a sense of place grounded in a social and neighborhood vision gave urgency to the resistance. In describing her response to ongoing merger meetings with another parish, Stephanie expressed her sense of parish place in terms of its current and possible future influence on the struggles of life in the public housing units surrounding the church. Accepting the possible loss of the building as a church, Stephanie continued to argue for the preservation of the place: "what would be the real tragedy is if the presence of the church was taken out of this location." "If this church needs to close," she added, the community could "keep the upper church as a social services place." Stephanie went on to describe the airiness, quiet, and sanctity of the upper church as she envisioned it filled with publicly accessible computers, vocational training courses, and youth meetings. This rendering of the value of the parish echoed the message of the previous pastor, whose commitments to a parish food pantry, AA meetings, and local youth clubs gave the resistance at St. Catherine's its particular social-justice character. The gentrified surroundings of Charlestown's other two parishes and a recent stabbing a few blocks from the church enhanced the resisters' investment in St. Catherine's as the last stronghold of Catholic social justice in the embattled town.[61]

Across the archdiocese resistance groups offered compromise solutions. They insisted that portions of church land could be sold, or alternate sources of income could be found. Most often, these plans included selling the church rectory or convent for use as housing. As in Weymouth and in Scituate at St. Frances, parishes in the suburbs sometimes had undeveloped land that resisters were ready to sell as needed. The archdiocese saw these offers as unworkable or simply insufficient stopgaps. Episcopal documents and guidebooks chalked such proposals up to the "bargaining" stage of grief as articulated by Elizabeth Kübler-Ross. Resisters understood themselves simply to be creative, flexible, and pragmatic. The helplessness on the part of the church in face of these proposals caused some to wonder whether the shutdowns were a symptom of some bigger fundamental problem with the direction Catholicism had taken in America. Whether it was a product of America's social dynamism, America's comparatively short history, or its relatively strict standards for separation of church and state, the dilemma in Boston sometimes appeared to resisters as a uniquely American problem.

Resisters in East Boston often repeated the idea that churches never close in Italy, even after they sit empty for decades. In the North End, Carla recalled a visit to a town in Sicily with "no less than seven churches" for just over 30,000 people. While this ratio is not out of proportion by Boston standards, Carla's larger point was about the propriety of respect for tradition and the patient sacrifices that made that respect both worthy and real. "Some of them are closed, because they need repairs," she admitted, "but they won't sell them, they'll raise funds, and it could take them forty years. But they'll restore them and reopen them again. Not what we are doing here." Here in the United States, by contrast, the archdiocese could propose permanently shuttering a parish like Sacred Heart, which was in good repair and had money in the bank.[62] The lament over Americanness among these parishioners of national Italian parishes was perhaps more acute than it was elsewhere, as loyalties to the old world were more intense. But their sense that "in Italy it's religion, here it's business," was not unique.[63] One suburban resister's recollection of a trip to Italy included the revelation that neighbors of a crumbling village church had volunteered to have their wages garnished for its lavish renovation.[64] Such stories certainly disregarded the long histories of conflict and warfare between church and state in Italy, but the basic point remained unchanged: what was happening in Boston was a disordered anomaly, connected somehow to local conditions, culture, and norms.

As it stood in Boston, the need for cash was seen as too dire to entertain anything but the fire-sale approach they had undertaken. The gradual revelation, over the course of the shutdowns, of the archdiocese's grave financial situation aimed to justify this sense of urgency. In 2003, the archdiocese announced that the central fund was operating at an annual $10 million deficit. A leaked report from 2004 indicated the annual deficit was double that amount. Making matters worse, the archdiocese had not made contributions to its clergy pension fund between 1986 and 2002, leaving $80 million in unfunded liability. Explanations for the closures such as the shortage of priests and the crumbling of church buildings eventually seemed secondary in light of the "severe shortfalls" in the archdiocesan budget. The news only became bleaker. By 2005, the reported pension liability had grown to $135 million.[65] Despite the shutdowns, in 2006 72% of cash and equivalents were still locked up in parishes, suggesting that additional closures might be the most expedient way to stem the archdiocese's "bleeding."[66] In January 2008, the archdiocese still noted "significant financial challenges" and revealed that maintaining shut churches occupied by parishioners and those with appeals pending cost the archdiocese $880,000 per year.[67]

By this time the projections for a tremendous windfall from church closures were completely exhausted. In closing or merging seventy-five parishes since 2004, the archdiocese had netted only $62.7 million. All of these profits had already been spent by 2008 without alleviating the general sense of financial crisis. Although there was still approximately $31 million tied up in occupied or appealing parishes, the net from closures would be less than half of the $200 million anticipated when the process began.[68] Although the archdiocese's finances were still bleak, the archbishop had promised Catholics that without church closures, the situation would have been even worse.[69] The archdiocese continued to seek ways to balance its budget. In 2007 it announced that it would sell an additional $65 million in property to Boston College.[70] As these details slowly emerged, it became clear that the shutdowns were as much an attempt to restore the diocese's financial solvency rather than, as officials originally insisted, an effort to consolidate and strengthen the diocesan parish structure and pastoral resources. With these realizations, Catholics questioned the justice of turning their parishes into cash to be poured into the deep hole at the center of the diocese's battered budget.

Amid all of these staggering numbers, the sense of tradition, the history of efficacy and presence in churches, and the daily routine of sustaining a church occupation continued to convince parishioners that their parishes should remain inviolate. Financial realities were one thing, but the abiding history of sacred presence, as a power beyond worldly concerns, offered something else altogether. Legal questions surrounding parish closures would add yet another layer to the sense that Catholic presence and efficacy had entered a new level of contestation.

Catholic Gifts and Catholic Presence, or, Who Owns the Sacred?

"Since no sacred space is merely 'given' in the world, its ownership will always be at stake."[71]

The reverberations of "Christa's Bells," like Margery's story of the hand-placed stones of the Weymouth grotto and David's story of bringing Padre Pio to East Boston, spoke to the sense of ownership that contributed to the perception of inviolable presence in Catholic locales and objects. The same could be said of a small monument behind St. Jeremiah, which was built out of stones brought from individual parishioners' own yards.[72] All of these material objects participated in the metaphor of "living stones" that is so powerful in contemporary church reflection on architecture and aesthetics. In the official rendering, of course, the "living stones" are the people who make up the local and universal church. But in these cases, the actual stones, bricks, and sounds contained in some measure the lives of those who labored to place them. The line between a metaphorical and literal reading of the idea of "living stones" blurred as Catholic objects took on the weight of Catholics' memories and hope. These items gained resonance and value because they provided a link to predecessors both known and unknown. They provided a sense of history or continuity between past and present. As gifts constructed during years of increasingly lean church finances, these objects also reminded Catholics of the promises of lay ownership that accompanied church calls for generosity. Far from making them expendable "assets," the enhanced sense of lay ownership of church objects invested those objects with their meaning and power. It is not only the case, then, that one can indeed own the holy, but also that the character and history of ownership sometimes actually make holiness possible. A sense of ownership was one of the most resonant meanings of Catholic objects and locales as they found a way into the hands of the people of God. It was also among the most hotly contested.

Occupiers sought to affirm their ownership of Catholic objects and locales in any way they could. At Mount Carmel, the vigilers' idea for an exhaustive photo documentary of every donated item in the church—a task which, as the owner of a digital camera, I took up—aimed to take advantage of the church building's powerful link to the past. With this photo-documentary project the resisters wanted literally to show lawyers, judges, officials, and anyone who would look that every part of the church—its pews, the walls, the altar, its windows, a kneeler, the kitchen, an elevator, doors, and statues—was built on their and their ancestors' generosity and sacrifice.

Entanglements like these were among fears articulated by the authors of the new church design manual, *Built of Living Stones.* They had lay Catholics' emotionally resonant and legally complicated claims of ownership in mind when they warned pastors against the once-common practice of financing church improvements by allowing donated objects to become memorials. The warning against this "easy fundraising solution" hinted at risks that came to fruition in the resistance. Putting names on art or furnishings, the manual said, "can lead to future problems when there may be need to remove or alter the memorialized object."[73] The *Closing Manual* also included reflection on this problem, but offered a more directly judgmental perspective. Quoting a pastor who had closed a parish, the manual presented an economy of giving that many found hard to accept. "I was caught off guard," this pastor wrote,

> when people asked that the window, statue, etc. given 'in memory of a relative' be given back. I shared with them gently that the gift was 'given' to the Church—as a gift![74]

This pastor does not go on to say how his parishioners responded to this fantasy of the unencumbered gift, but experiences in Boston suggest that this message may not have been fully satisfying.[75] The anticipations, strategies, and animosities around the ownership of sacred locales and objects speak to the contested character of sacred presence that would emerge clearly in the fight over closed parishes in Boston.

Resisters' claims of ownership not only pitted them against the local archdiocese, but also entered them into national and international legal debates involving the U.S. Council of Catholic Bishops and the Vatican.[76] Questions about ownership of the churches came to a head after the archdiocese received a reprimand from the Vatican for its execution of the shutdowns under canon law. After this point, the archdiocese's confident description of the proper fate of parish assets (as well as its insistence on a disciplined accounting of parish goods) appeared more like wishful thinking than established policy. Questions of ownership radiated beyond Boston, and beyond the legal realm; they touched upon fundamental concerns about the relationship of gifts to their givers in the context of the sacred.

The story requires appreciation of a few subtleties in canon law. In 2005, after most of the parish shutdowns were complete, the chancery was told it had erred in its application of canon law in the process. This rebuke came from the Vatican's Congregation of the Clergy, which ruled in response to several closure appeals that the wrong canons had been applied in the shutdowns in Boston and elsewhere, causing the misappropriation of assets.[77] At stake was the proper recipient of the assets of closed parishes. Only when a parish becomes "extinct," meaning "no Catholic community any longer exists in its territory, or if no pastoral activity has taken place for a hundred years," do the assets and liabilities revert to the diocese. In most cases, the congregation of bishops insisted, the assets and liabilities should "follow the Faithful." In mislabeling merged parishes "suppressed," the archdiocese overreached, applied the wrong canon and seized the assets of closed parishes for itself.[78] The goal of this plan had been to give the archbishop discretion over the use of the assets of wealthy parishes. He sought to have the possibility of putting those assets to use for the good of the entire church in Boston rather than automatically sending them to the receiving parish, regardless of its financial status.[79] Despite these intentions, the Vatican ruled that the archdiocese had not followed canon law.[80]

The Vatican critique of Boston's process was designed in part to avoid charges of inconsistency in church policy about ownership of parish assets. In attempting to protect parish assets from creditors in the case of diocesan bankruptcies resulting from sexual abuse settlements, several dioceses around the country had argued that parishes belong to parishioners. It appeared that the unique deed at the North End's Sacred Heart was perhaps only a civil law equivalent of the kind of relationship between parishes and diocese that was now being forwarded in certain sectors of the church. In this argument, the bishop or archbishop (as corporation sole of the arch/diocese) is a title-holding steward, but not an owner of the property. In the case of charitable organizations, if a steward goes bankrupt, only assets not legally spoken for can be claimed by creditors. Parishes and their assets are protected from creditors because parishes are considered separate from the diocese.[81] Moreover, charitable gifts to the parishes should therefore be considered "restricted," meaning that those who gave to the parish intended their money to be used only for the good of the parish.[82] Even if there was no legal document specifying this restriction, the character of parishes as distinct public juridic persons under canon law meant that the gifts that sustained or furnished a parish were not part of the estate of the diocese.[83]

Among the officials making this argument was the president of the United States Conference of Catholic Bishops (USCCB), Bishop William S. Skylstad of the Diocese of Spokane, Washington. With his diocese under the protection of Chapter 11 bankruptcy, Skylstad sought to protect parishes from being claimed in award settlements for victims of clergy sexual abuse. In a letter distributed to the press, the Council of Parishes sought to ally itself with Skylstad against the Archdiocese of Boston, urging the head of the USCCB to enforce a clear policy in an upcoming annual meeting.[84] In the several secular court appeals of parish closures in Boston, the archdiocese claimed that Chapter 11 laws did not apply since there was no question of bankruptcy in the Boston church. By March 2008, the secular courts appeared to have avoided the question, arguing that the Constitution restricts it from interfering in matters relevant to a religious organization's internal disputes.[85]

At the same time, the Vatican reprimand and consequent adjustments to archdiocesan policy added another layer of protection to the church in Boston as it sought to illustrate consistency with various dioceses across the United States. In essence, the reprimand confirmed the Council of Parishes' position, and showed that the archdiocese was wrong in claiming closed churches' assets. But it also offered an opportunity for the archdiocese to make an internal correction by offering recourse to those who had made valid internal appeals. Before the Congregation for the Clergy's reprimand became public, the archdiocese asked pastors of receiving parishes to assent to the donation of the property of the closing parish to the archdiocese. Only pastors who had absorbed a parish with a valid appeal of the closure decision were given this option. In effect, as a review board noted, the policy punished those who had "obediently surrendered their churches and assets." Moreover, as critical observers noted, pastors' responsibilities of obedience to the ordinary made it unlikely they would go against the archdiocese's clear desire to have these parish assets as its own. By the time the news of the correction became public, all but one pastor had complied with the request to legitimate the diocese's acquisition of the assets it had tried illegitimately to gain. Most pastors donated the major portion of the funds they were due, keeping only a small amount for projects aiding the integration of parishioners from the closing parish.[86]

The Vatican's critique of Boston's process endorsed the argument of dioceses like Spokane without significantly altering the process in Boston. Ongoing legal arguments cite this error on the part of the Boston archdiocese, but the Vatican's correction could shield the archdiocese from external consequences.[87] In the Spokane case, a federal judge eventually agreed with the diocese's argument that parishes had control over their assets and ruled that the diocese could not legally sell parishes to pay abuse victims.[88] In response, victims' lawyers threatened to sue individual parishes, forcing the parishes to agree to pay a portion of the settlement.[89] As part of this agreement, the parishes and the diocese formalized their relationship by licensing each congregation as a separate nonprofit organization.[90] This gave parishes a portion of the debt, but protected them from being sold in similar cases in the future. In this agreement the question of the ownership of parishes had not been resolved, but it did contribute to a precedent of individual parishes contributing to sexual abuse settlements.[91] Most important for the Boston legal appeals, if the matter of ownership appears to have been adjudicated internally, then civil courts may be even less likely to want to appear to breach church-state separation.

Despite these setbacks for advocates of accountability, 2002's revelations about hush money paid to abuse victims had brought new scrutiny to diocesan budgets. The independent review board, again after the fact and to little effect, made use of this greater transparency to make the specific complaint that the archdiocese had transferred over twelve million dollars it had claimed in the shutdowns into the diocese's central fund to cover a budget deficit. This transfer meant that they could not be sure how funds from the reconfiguration were then used. The archdiocese had long insisted that the shutdowns would not be used to pay for settlement of sexual abuse cases. The board agreed that the sale of the chancery and other buildings to Boston College along with insurance payments had covered the cost of the settlements to date. As the board noted, however, the archdiocese borrowed significant sums from the Knights of Columbus in order to cover shortfalls that had resulted from decreased giving after the scandals. The infusion of shutdown cash into the central fund suggested that the archdiocese also used monies from the sale of closed parishes to cover shortfalls that were at least indirectly related to the sexual abuse crisis. More directly, the diocese reported nearly $10 million in expenditures in 2006 for abuse settlements, victim treatment, and other abuse-related costs.[92] As the committee complained, there was no way to determine how the shutdown funds had been used, and the promise that it would be put toward "ongoing support services for parishes" seemed intentionally vague.[93]

Boston's resisters kept an eye on these developments and contributed to them as well. Their willingness to think in practical, legal, and economic terms about the objects and locales of Catholic practice grew out of their embrace of a people of God ecclesiology. They saw awareness and manipulation of national and international debates about the legal status of parishes as a signature characteristic of an educated and savvy laity. Resisters routinely argued that the archdiocese had been poor managers of their assets.[94] Marian Walsh, a Catholic politician sympathetic to both the resisters of closure and the Voice of the Faithful, brought a bill to the state senate that would have required the archdiocese (and other religious groups) to submit an annual audit to the state. Walsh and thirty-five cosponsors in the senate thought that the church should not be free from the kinds of oversight the state required from non-religious charities. William Galvin, the Secretary of the Commonwealth and a parishioner at the closing Our Lady of the Presentation, was among the bill's supporters. He noted that since 2003, when O'Malley took over, the diocese had liquidated over $200 million worth of property. As a *National Catholic Register* article noted, "[t]here is little clear indication where that money has gone."[95] Hundreds of supporters from all around the diocese traveled to the courthouse in Boston to attend a hearing on the bill. This show of support notwithstanding, opponents of the bill (including lobbyists from the archdiocese and from other religious groups who complained about the costs of a yearly audit) the bill failed to make it out of the senate.

This inconsistency calls attention to stresses over the meanings and power of Catholic locales and objects. The conflict emerged out of a combination of rules of parish practice. Resisters' complaint that the archdiocese was simultaneously too businesslike and not businesslike enough emerged at the meeting point of two ways of practicing presence. Resisters embraced the rules that emphasized the sanctity and separateness of sacred goods from legal and business spheres while also taking up the competing claim that sacred presence is fundamentally in the people of God. Their embodiment of sacred presence, in a sort of Catholic version of democratic principles of representation, secured their ability and responsibility to manage the church. The sense that holy goods had been put to use in extricating U.S. dioceses from the sins of sexual abuse animated the efforts of resisters and bishops alike to reorient ownership toward the local people who funded parishes. They wanted sacred objects to be free of the conflicts and compromises of the legal sphere. And they felt that they were the ones—as the people of God in whom the presence of God resided—properly to protect the inviolable goods of their churches.

Presence and Efficacy in Priestless Churches

Inherited and internalized narratives about sacred presence, not simply unreflective attachment, kept these Catholics in their parishes. The vigils exposed these inherited idioms about the sacramental, memorial, and communal importance of particular objects and locales. But the resistance did not just call up familiar ways of thinking about objects and locales. It also required renewed engagement with the parishes and recommitment to the now-embattled objects. This demand intensified people's attachments and also brought differences and ambivalences within vigiling communities into relief. Catholics in resisting parishes across Boston experienced their churches anew in their occupation of them. They were there at different hours, for one thing. Night-and-day vigiling meant long stretches of time in church sanctuaries, lofts, vestibules, kitchens, crying rooms, basements, and front stoops. The vigilers were also there in physical positions other than the ordinary ones. They were there on their backs on the floor; they were high on ladders, moving saints, scrubbing walls, or replacing bulbs. New physical positions indicated different status positions too, as they climbed behind the pulpits, reached into tabernacles, and counted weekly collections. These unaccustomed times and movements gave resisting Catholics a chance to assert a new level of control over the tradition through its objects. They carried a theology of the church in their bodies.

Oftentimes these assertions indicated an enhanced sensitivity and alertness to church aesthetics. Within the first weeks of occupation, Gerald, a corrections officer who joined Annetta as an original Mount Carmel Survivors co-president, sent me walking up a dark flight of stairs leading from behind the altar to an alcove above the sacristy. When I finally found the string for the overhead bulb, I was surprised to find perhaps a dozen saints covered in dust clustered together next to piles of other refuse. These had been set aside over the course of the past few decades, and Gerald had made it his mission to restore some of them to their former niches in the church. In some cases this required major renovation work. Where drywall had covered up two altar-side niches, Gerald ripped it down and hoisted the saints back up. Gerald's renovation and repopulating of the altar did not stop with these two alcoves. On our first tour of the parish he showed me how he had brought a vividly realistic version of the crucified Jesus back to its original location at the front of the church. I later learned that one of the statues of Our Lady had also been liberated from its place in the underground hallway connecting the church basement to the rectory. As for the crucifix, Gerald told me that it had been called "depressing" by a previous pastor and had for that reason been cut down to fit in the small "saints' room" at the back of the church.[96]

At the forty-eight-year-old St. Jeremiah parish there were fewer goods left over from previous eras, but the manipulation of art and artifacts remained a way to make a claim on the church and enhance its religious potency. As if to highlight the end of priest's special mediating role in confession, the occupiers relocated a statue of the Blessed Mother that had sat above a confessional to a more prominent place in the sanctuary. There it received a new crown, a weekly bouquet, and the attention of a daily rosary group. This new position offered the possibility of an enhanced intimacy between the Blessed Mother and her devotees.

> It's a spiritual experience to be here at night I sleep down near the organ. And to wake up and see the crucifix or look up and see the Blessed Mother, it's a beautiful statue. It's very comforting. Not to say that the church doesn't have noises that go bump in the night, but it's very comforting.[97]

Unexplained nocturnal and daytime noises constantly occupied vigilers' attention and enlivened their conversations. These places were uniformly thought to be more religiously alive than others. Sleeping in a place normally reserved for the most reverential of postures did cause some mental dissonance, but initial fears wore off for vigilers over time, as they grew accustomed to their new environs and staked out comfortable spots for sleeping. Familiar routines provided comfort and promoted a deepened connection to the buildings. Art, for example, became accustomed before lying down for sleep to sitting for a few minutes in the back of the church, listening to music on his headphones, with only the soft glow of altar lights.

Like Art at St. Jeremiah, Mount Carmel's Gerald found pleasure in the chance to customize church aesthetics. Under his watch, Mount Carmel was lit only by the smaller alcove lights and soft bulbs around the saints, never by the more industrial fluorescent lamps that would become the norm after Gerald left the vigil. The gentle light put the church's best face forward. The soft glow of candles and angled spotlights did not show the deteriorating paint, the drywall (painted with streaks to look like marble) covering the former confessional boxes, or the bent window frames. Gerald's strong appreciation of this moody, dim aesthetic soon extended into other realms and became the source of the first major challenge the Mount Carmel Survivors faced.

Gerald had frequently mentioned to me his desire to restore the original altar to a pre-Vatican II format. He wanted to take away the second altar and restore the communion rail, pieces of which he had discovered while rummaging through discarded materials in the attic and basement. As people's appreciation for the new statues and the crucifix witnessed, his energy for this type of renovation could be infectious within the community. As a leader of the Survivor's group, Gerald's ideas carried weight within the community. More important, as a fit middle-aged man with the physical strength to move heavy items around the church, Gerald was able to make major changes in the building by himself. This work of restoring the church to its former glory had great appeal, freighted as it was with the disdain for former pastors' neglect.

But eventually Gerald's reforming impulses provoked a breach in the community. The problem was the plan to bring a group Gerald called "the singing nuns" to Mount Carmel for a Christmas concert to benefit the vigil. At first people were enthusiastic about the plan. As Annetta relayed the story, however, it soon became apparent that for Gerald, the nuns represented something more than beautiful caroling. After doing some research on the web, Annetta's husband Mark had discovered that the nuns were Sisters of Mary the Immaculate Queen, a Tridentine Latin Rite group with a motherhouse at Saint Michael's Convent in Spokane, Washington. Centered on the propagation of "the traditional Catholic faith," and with a special focus on Our Lady of Fatima, the group advocates a return to the pre-Vatican II liturgy.[98]

Annetta became alarmed. "The religion is not yours to change," she told supporters of the nuns, suggesting that the nuns were after the property in order to make missionary inroads in New England. In preparation for their arrival, Gerald proposed to move the statue of Our Lady of Mount Carmel from her central spot on the altar. "She's the icon," Annetta told him. "You can't take Our Lady off the altar." From her report, a meeting on the issue as the scheduled Christmas concert approached turned into a shouting match, with Gerald and a few others storming out in protest of the group's decision to cancel the concert and revoke the nuns' invitation. The conflict revealed an ambivalence within the community at Mount Carmel toward pre-Vatican II Catholicism, the borders of which were uneasily guarded.

Gerald, an active participant named Anne, and several others never returned to the occupation. Annetta defended her contribution to this schism with a critique of the nuns' traditional theology, their strict gender norms, and their overabundant notions of presence and efficacy:

> Does anybody want Vatican I? You think about the children, how are we going to get people into the church with that type of thing? With Anne saying 'I've been touched, I've been blessed?'[99]

Annetta's concern echoes the community's approach to the tumbled Madonna. Reports that supporters of the nuns had seen a statue's eyes blink and had witnessed an inexplicable flashing of lights caused Annetta to take a cautious stance: "I'm a realist. Yes, I saw the lights blinking, but you don't dwell on it." On other occasions, however, Annetta was more enthusiastic about the mysterious events in the church. At one point she mentioned she wanted to recount for me all the mysterious happenings parishioners had noted since the vigil began. This conversation never took place, but Annetta's interest in these events did occasionally moderate her skepticism toward the idea of special presence in the place.

It was not always clear what these presences meant. Describing the ups and downs after about a year in the occupation, she said that she sometimes felt "that Our Lady is holding me with one hand and beating me with the other." The simple dichotomies of their struggle with the archdiocese gave Annetta a way to clarify what she meant. "When one bad thing happens," she explained, "a good thing happens and holds me in the church."

As she went on Annetta attempted to remove blame from the Madonna and put it in the proper place:

> I'm not saying it's here, I'm convinced it's an evil spirit doing it, you know, the archdiocese . . . they're doing the devil's work and we're doing God's work. I'm convinced of that.[100]

The clear distinctions drawn in this description capture well the occupiers' vehemence in their rejection of the shutdown plan and the leadership behind it. But the intimacy of the original phrasing, where the power to comfort and punish resided in the Madonna, close to home, better conveys the challenge facing Boston Catholics as they struggled with the meanings of the Catholic past in light of the shutdowns.[101] The tradition seemed to give and take away presence, which in this case meant a comforting and galvanizing relationship with a powerful other, at the same time.

But Annetta's stance against the nuns remained firm. "Who are they," she wondered, "to come in here and take the church when we've been here one hundred years and are still trying to figure out who owns it?" This argument won out in the controversy with the nuns in East Boston. Many of Gerald's efforts to heighten the mystique, grandeur, and solemnity of the building were not carried forward by the remaining group. While they still sought to keep the church beautiful with extensive bouquets, seasonal lights, altar candles, and even major repairs, Gerald's more traditionalist aesthetic faded from the church. With Gerald's departure, for example, the group decided to scale back on some of the design changes he had made in anticipation of the Christmas concert. They removed from the altar the small statues of caroling children and their puppy standing in cotton snow near a gas lamp and set the scene up in a less prominent place in the back of the church. They also decided to return two expensive artificial Christmas trees, and, lacking the receipt, had to convince the seller that they were not stolen. Perhaps thinking of liability concerns, the group now operated almost all the time with the overhead lights brightly shining. Dangerous and messy wax candles were now replaced with electric candles or removed altogether.

The majority group did not completely erase Gerald's influence in the neighborhood or even over the church. Two of the nuns, who did end up coming to East Boston without the support of the Mount Carmel occupiers, ended up living in an apartment two blocks away, selling religious goods and hosting meetings in a garage provided by one of the ousted vigilers.

Their presence in the neighborhood served as a constant reminder of the breach in the community. It was also considered by some to be a threat to the vigil. For many months after they arrived, the nuns came to the church each morning. Even after being encouraged to keep them out, Nick, a sympathetic vigiler who occupied the early morning shift, routinely welcomed them and was able to appreciate their singing voices as he sat in the church vestibule watching the sun come up over the neighborhood. Even though he enjoyed being alone, he was so enthralled by this experience that he urged me to join him there early one morning.

The episode with the traditionalist nuns eventually faded from significance at Mount Carmel. While other resisting parishes may have found the controversy foreign to their experience of the church, the struggle in East Boston remained relevant to the broader issues about place and presence in the tradition. The nuns appeared in East Boston as reminders of a Catholic past when presence and inviolability still mattered. Across Boston, nuns were noticeably absent from the religious worlds of the resisters. Sister Janet Eisner, who co-chaired the independent reconfiguration review board, stood as a lone exception to this rule. Resisters took heart in particular in Eisner's presence on the board, hoping perhaps that a woman's perspective might shake up the decisions being implemented by the all-male hierarchy. But the nuns in East Boston represented something else. Their formal habits, which some resisters claimed to like seeing around in the neighborhood again, stood as a marker of purity. As signals of chastity (another word for inviolability) and Catholic distinctiveness, the nuns called up all the ambivalence attending Catholic change over the course of the latter half of the twentieth century.[102]

The suspicion that the nuns wanted to take over the building and use it for worship put those who opposed their theology and politics in a difficult position. Where the Boston hierarchy used language from the Second Vatican Council to justify the destruction of Catholic churches, here were different Catholic authority figures proposing to preserve the church in East Boston under loyalty to principles of Vatican I. The dilemma epitomizes the broader challenge of continuity and change with respect to sacred presence. Annetta's initial hope that she could use the threatened takeover by the nuns to wrest concessions from the archdiocese was perhaps too risky to enact. But the plan did signal the abiding attraction and potency of the notion of parish inviolability rooted in their embodiment of sacred presence.

Moments of absorption like Nick's with the nuns singing in the morning offered a pointed enhancement of religious life, even if the long hours of vigiling were a burden on the schedule or a strain on the family. Witnessing special events unnoticed in faster-paced times—the creaking building, the subtle shadows cast by lights, the sunlight streaking through at just the right moment, the teardrop suddenly appearing in the eye of a beloved statue—became a crucial part of a religious re-enlivening that the vigils inevitably were said to produce. The sheer control of Catholic objects and spaces, moreover, offered vigilers another powerful vehicle for expressing and testing their own orientations to objects and locales. Control entailed responsibility for church maintenance, for one thing. The duties of upkeep allowed otherwise uninvolved vigilers to participate in the resistance and to test and communicate the meanings of their attachments. Priestless churches were also a novelty for these Catholics. The grounds were theirs to manage and orient toward whatever ends they determined useful, valuable, or compelling. Contests over what was and was not appropriate in church revealed interesting loyalties and divisions among resisters.

With thin budgets and long quiet hours among the vigilers, church upkeep fell largely into the hands of volunteers. As a relatively old Boston church, Mount Carmel suffered in particular from numerous structural and cosmetic problems and demanded nearly constant attention. Much of the initial energy at Mount Carmel centered on improving the condition of the church. For the first few months and often even later, some new feature of the layout or a new cleaning or repair project were always the first things I was shown when I came to the church. I was repeatedly asked to appreciate, for example, the gleam of the recently scrubbed pews or the shine of Irene's Mop & Glo'd floors. Oftentimes, my entry into these upkeep projects—whether through simple appreciation of others' work or by my own labor—was a key component of getting to know individuals and becoming closer to the group. This is perhaps true because these projects were important validating markers for the vigilers. If the church hadn't been so neglected by the pastor, the closure never would have happened, they reasoned.

Furthermore, for some, the fact that they could be kept busy with repair work mitigated nervousness at having taken over the building. Sam, for example, repeatedly disowned religious motivations for his presence. To assert some religious claim on the parish, he said, would be hypocritical, since he had rarely attended mass before the closure. Instead, he claimed that he hung around only because it offered him the opportunity to help out as the maintenance man. As a retired machinist, he readily admitted that this new job simply gave him something to do during the day. Even though the work sometimes took him away from his wife Celia, who needed Sam and their car to travel the few blocks to their social club or three blocks to the church, he relished the praise and admiration heaped upon him by the vigiling women. Sam also loved to be in the church alone, tinkering. He fantasized to me about locking the church doors—so he wouldn't have to worry about intruders or visitors—and spending the whole day alone, working on projects.[103]

Others worked on the church out of simple boredom during long hours of quiet occupation or because they saw work on the church as a religious duty. Irene, in particular, was particularly scornful of those who simply sat around watching TV or gossiping during the vigil. For Irene, who was impatient with groups and had not been involved in committees or church organizations before the closure, the chance to roam around the church carrying out chores of her own determination proved to be a powerful tonic. Her constant scrubbing, painting, and streetside recruiting of visitors were accompanied by powerful denunciations of the pastor *and* of those in the vigil. They weren't taking advantage of this "payback" time, by which she meant the opportunity to offer her labor on the church as a gift to God.[104] Even if they weren't inclined to manual or evangelical tasks like Irene, the vigilers were eager to show that their presence offered an enhancement to what came before, and the material goods of the parish became a key vehicle for making that point. The worse the building's condition, the deeper the sense of justification the vigilers felt when they put things right.

Free rein over the parishes also spurred controversy among the vigilers over what was and was not acceptable church behavior. Vigiling groups were eager to maintain the sanctity of the buildings, but they also did not want to risk losing members or support because of disagreements on such matters. At Mount Carmel some vigilers asserted that the vestibule was a "neutral zone," where they could eat, swear, and smoke if the need arose. Nick urged his fellow resisters not to put a statue in the vestibule, but to keep the saints and their powers of moral surveillance where they belonged, in the saints' room.[105] While there was some opposition to this idea, leniency in the vestibule was the norm. When the cable TV package they bought turned out to include channels with sexually explicit movies, however, the group felt the need to announce that TV watchers should be careful to avoid these channels. Likewise, when a new group of visitors began bringing cups of coffee into the Sunday communion services, another announcement had to be made. Earlier, when an older woman suffering from dementia urinated in one of the pews and later attempted to brush her teeth in the holy water, the group felt itself unable to keep an eye on her, and had to make the difficult decision to ask her not to come back.

Priestless churches also enabled vigilers to experiment with the power usually reserved for the people in charge. One day I visited Mount Carmel to find that Irene had stepped up to the lectern at the church, and, with Sam getting the feel for the notes on a newly donated organ, began bellowing what she could remember of the words to several hymns into the microphone. Louisa openly cringed and halfheartedly offered some coaching. Since Irene never approached the microphone at a communion service, it was clear that this was not practice or training, but fantasy and fun. It reminded me of a scene I'd witnessed numerous times during my fieldwork across Boston: the people were hesitatingly, but excitedly taking over the buildings. The chance to stay up late talking in front of a dimly lit crucifix, to snap a photo of yourself or your child at the top of a majestic ambo, or to utter jokes and songs into a church microphone gave vigilers much needed exhilaration. Their presence in the buildings was more than the reverential, pious, and quiet presence that the term 'vigil' was meant to communicate. These experiments did not always sit comfortably with everyone in the occupation. Sam's eventual refusal to play any secular songs in church for fear that those hearing them walking by would be scandalized reflects this ongoing play with the boundaries of sacred space at work in the communities. The church hall, where Sam once danced around for laughs with women's lingerie over his clothes, was a different matter.

Questions of different zones of the occupation came up in Weymouth, too, where I heard subtle undercurrents of division in the group between those who considered the vigil a matter of being "upstairs" in the sanctuary, and those who concentrated their time and energy "downstairs" in the church hall. The difference between the prayerful quiet of the sanctuary and the social buzz of the basement prompted one parishioner to criticize the group's leaders as downstairs people. This charge implied showiness and glory-seeking, and spurred the accuser to nickname one of the leaders after the pope.[106]

A more public division over the appropriate management of priestless space emerged at St. Anselm parish in Sudbury. This community, located in a comfortable suburb north of Boston, experienced its most intense test as a community when almost half of the members voted in favor of a subgroup's proposal to screen *Our Fathers*, a made-for-TV film based on the book by journalist David France about the sexual abuse crisis in Boston. Two of the council members told me that they appreciated the film and its message, and that they cared deeply about the abuse crisis and its connection to the closings. Their concern, however, centered on the insistence of the supporters and the film studio that the graphic film be shown only in the sanctuary of the occupied church:

> As I watched the movie, I thought, two wrongs don't make a right. Because [the abuse] happened in the church, I can't support it being shown in the church. The church was desecrated once, let's not do it again. That's where I was coming from.[107]

Concerned that the supporters of the screening were overly focused on the issue of the abuse scandal and worried about protecting the boundaries of church decorum, these board members voted against the plan.

They proposed an alternative, however, suggesting that they could show the film in another part of the parish.

> Can we have it downstairs in the hall, or could we have outside or something like that? And they really said no. They felt that in order to really get their message home they felt they had to do it in the sanctuary of a church.[108]

The disagreement left lingering disappointments because the staunch victims' rights faction had been outvoted. But the community's strong endorsement of democratic decision-making meant that there was no major loss of members. Perhaps considering their ongoing negotiations with the archdiocese, the majority was willing only to go so far. This plot to show the film in the sanctuary weighed too heavily on the side of sheer aggravation of the archdiocese's central leadership. Across the occupations, radical proposals for the reformulation of sacred space—like allowing a film studio to make a publicity stunt out of the sanctuary, or even hiring a married priest to say mass—usually failed. Vigilers were always eager to prove themselves 'more Catholic' than the hierarchy. Maintaining standards over the use of sacred space became a way to assert superiority over the hierarchy who, they reasoned, just wanted to shut down the parish and desanctify it once and for all. It was also an assertion of the vigilers' desire to live their Catholic lives with intention and judgment.

Conclusion: Layered Versions of Practicing Presence

After two years of occupying their parish, the vigilers at Our Lady of Mount Carmel added another element to the display in front of the altar. Alongside the Madonna and her lights and flowers, Bill placed a brick reported to have been salvaged from the recent demolition of a closed suburban church.[109] Whether this brick was a symbol—a living stone representing the people of God—or a relic—somehow pure and purifying—for those who encountered it, its placement on the Mount Carmel altar could not have signaled more precisely the contrast between hierarchical expectations and the troubled enactment of Boston's shutdowns. For all the distancing from "brick and mortar" suggested by the planners of the closures, here an actual brick took its place alongside a moving Madonna who had helped launch a multiyear church occupation.

This brick mattered enough to find a place on Mount Carmel's altar for reasons well beyond certain Catholics' inability to change. The challenge of the ambivalent present life of the Catholic past shaped the resistance at Mount Carmel, St. Albert the Great, and other resisting parishes. But this challenge is also built into the tradition in the United States, as it continues to struggle with the application and meaning of the reforms of the Second Vatican Council. The desire for a delicate balance between change and continuity was not an accident, but a core component of the revision of the liturgy and teachings about presence in objects and locales. Reformers desired to channel presence and concentrate it in the celebration of the Eucharist and in the endorsement of presence in the people of God. In the practice of a parish, these changes did not mean that the lessons about reverence for church buildings and their efficacy had to be abandoned.

In the case of Boston's parish shutdowns, officials determined that progress required the sale of dozens of church buildings. As a rationale for this change, they highlighted the church's recent emphasis on the symbolic meanings of Catholic objects and locales. This change was itself thought to be in continuity with the ways of the early church and with a substantial, if sometimes muted, tradition across the centuries. But as these symbols were being built up and extended, people continued to understand that their churches were places where their prayers could have a special hearing and their ills might find unique relief. Presence and its efficacy in local places persisted in the church. This was evident in peoples' relationships to grottos, statues, relics, and stained glass and in their appreciation for the majesty and awe of their buildings. It also came out in resisters' and bishops' strained engagements with church and civil law, and with the question of the place of sacred locales in the marketplace. Officials in Boston, who certainly knew of their own special places in the church, feared the parallel histories that made these discomforting outcomes possible. This awareness became obvious during planning for the closures, when officials sought to cut off over-investment in objects and locales before "chaos" could "abound."[110] And it became obvious again as resistance to the closures began and chaos abounded.

Speaking of changes in post–World War II church architecture, one Catholic historian has suggested that the "most difficult aspect of the shift . . . has been to produce a change in lay Catholic opinion about the meaning of tradition."[111] In one sense, the resistance to parish closures confirms this assessment of an entrenched Catholic populace, locked into old ways of thinking about and moving within sacred places. Resisters' orientations toward their churches carried the imprint of years of training, before and even sometimes after the council, within which churches were uniquely holy ground.

But if presence and efficacy persisted in the latter half of the twentieth century, they were not unchanged. Instead of wholly replacing old forms with new ones, resisters had taken the new lessons about objects and locales and found in them, too, an endorsement of the special power and inviolability of the local church. In particular, the "people of God" ecclesiology took on adamantly local meanings, and the presence of God in the people came to seem inalienable from a particular people meeting in a particular place. People come and go from parishes, but having those kinds of changes forced upon them created a different breed of resentment. Consolidation felt like an untenable depersonalization of religion. The closures asked Catholics to give up the relationships with people and objects that had literally been religion for them. These relationships had gained their own form of presence, as the new dedication rite implied they would. Many were willing to give up these relationships, perhaps agreeing that they would only be altered, not irrevocably lost in the transition out of a parish. Others did not have this confidence. Presence in the "people of God" had become local.

Likewise, the emphasis on people's ownership of the tradition, an outgrowth of both the "people of God" ecclesiology and the church's intensifying need to encourage parishioner contributions, gave Catholics a sense that their churches contained something of themselves in them. One pastor's response to the *Closing Manual* and the shutdown procedures illustrated the kinds of teachings on ownership that made resistance feel like a legitimate Catholic option. "We're not doing any of that ritual stuff," he told me referring to the prescribed last masses,

> The property here . . . the sacred objects and things, that belongs to the people here. My feeling is, as long as I'm pastor here and we're not suppressed, if people want those objects I'm going to give them back to them.

This pastor disdained both the ritual transformation of objects and the disciplined accounting of them for future transfer or sale to benefit the church. He proposed instead to sell all the objects and have a "big barbecue" for the parish.

> I feel such an offense, you know, these people coming in here from the bank and putting stickers on the property that these people, that these *poor* people donated to [purchase and maintain]. I don't know how they sleep at night, these people.[112]

This pastor's vehemence along with O'Malley's references to his own suffering suggest that separating gifts from their givers entails more than laying out the moral and legal consequences. Giving created a sense of ownership and 'say' that was linked to appreciation of the gathered people as vehicles of God's presence. Accordingly, the giving was not ordinary giving, it was not the kind of giving that modifications in the laws about charitable donations can fully address. There were strings attached, of course. But some of these strings connected the gifts to the idea of the presence of God in the community past and present.

In some cases, these bonds were so firm that Catholics could not imagine the alienation of gift from giver. Some fantasized that the gifts—the church included—should be obliterated by the resisters rather than removed from them in service of a higher moral or legal purpose of which they wanted no part. At Our Lady of Mount Carmel the tired vigilers frequently wondered aloud about closing the parish down on their own terms by having a final Eucharist service and throwing a party. At one point this imagined celebration took on the moniker of a "fuck you party," a title evoking the sense of power it might restore to the hurt vigilers. Once in a while I heard suggestions that certain vigilers would rather throw rocks through the stained glass windows than have them removed and sold for the archdiocese's profit. On a less pained note, many others imagined preserving specific sacred goods in their homes if the resistance failed. Occupying communities at Mount Carmel, St. Albert's, St. Jeremiah's, and elsewhere made plans, should the archdiocese take over, to give any funds accumulated during the occupation to selected charities rather than to the archdiocese.

Engagements with the churches during the occupations intensified these commitments. People got to know churches and their furnishings better than they ever had before. They learned the parish's architectural histories, discovered the names of the artists of particular pieces of artwork, and even redesigned churches to fit their tastes. This labor took some of the mystique out of priests' former authority over the places. Because they bred familiarity, the occupations tested postures of reverence and attitudes of awe. But familiarity also endeared places to people in new ways. People found their particular spot to lay their bedrolls at night and cherished quiet hours alone amid art and grand architecture. The places got inside people as the people got deeper inside them. These engagements brought out differences in resisters' sense of place. There was no one single tendency or issue that informed all the resisters' relations to the places and objects they were protecting. Churches' presence and efficacy were inflected differently for different individuals and different communities. But the tradition of working, moving, and thinking about churches as if they offered something unique on the landscape meant that resisters had some reasonable justification for their surprise and confusion at the closures. The soothing ambitions of the *Closing Manual* and the predominant story of a new Catholic distance from objects and locales faced a daunting parallel history. Even if the vigilers highlighted the less attached aspects of their efforts, affinity and respect for their churches as locales of presence and efficacy were crucial pillars of the resistance.

4

"This is unrest territory:" Authority and Sacrifice in Resisters' Practice of the Parish

Introduction: "Where are you going to church?"

Among the community of Italian-American Catholics in the Jeffries Point section of East Boston, daily errands are rarely performed anonymously. In this one-square-mile cluster of triple-deckers and converted industrial buildings, chores on the streets augment Sunday mass as a chance to connect with neighbors, swap stories, and keep up with the news. Though the neighborhood's family-owned shops and offices have partly given way over the years to large retail chains, Jeffries Point's residents still find traces of familiarity and sociality in the streets. This is particularly true for the neighborhood's longtime residents, many of whom affiliate themselves with the one-hundred-year-old Italian national parish, Our Lady of Mount Carmel. As a national parish, Mount Carmel relied as much on visitors from outside East Boston as it did on those within walking distance. This trend toward remote affiliation along with gradual decreases in parish participation enhanced the connections between the churchgoers who stayed in the neighborhood: with fewer of them around, their awareness of one another and their need for one another grew. Their presence (or absence)—at mass, on the streets, at parish gatherings—could not easily be missed. With the closure announcement in the spring of 2004, Mount Carmel parishioners had additional reasons to keep track of one another. As they had at closing parishes across the diocese, parishioners at Mount Carmel were asked to move on to designated "welcoming parishes," where they would be invited to help create a new and perhaps more vibrant Catholic community.

Within a few days of the parish's official last mass and its tumbling Madonna, parishioners of Mount Carmel were presented with another possibility. A small group of them had decided that they would not leave the church, and invited any and all other parishioners to join them in resisting the closure. Discussion in the community about taking over the church had been spurred by the church occupations that were already under way at closing parishes in Weymouth and Sudbury, two of Boston's suburbs. Despite the example of these successful predecessors, plans for a takeover of Mount Carmel had not initially gained much traction. The community at Mount Carmel had been intrigued for a time by a proposal to convert the abandoned convent into a chapel supported by the pastor of the welcoming parish. After this possibility had fallen through, the community appeared to have resigned itself to walking away from the church. But when the October day for locking the church for good arrived, one parishioner simply decided he would stay overnight. Another joined him and began calling her friends to let them know that they didn't plan to leave.

Soon several dozen parishioners had joined the group, which began calling itself the "Our Lady of Mount Carmel Survivors." This provocative moniker—aligning resisters with victims of clergy sexual abuse, who were often called "survivors" and whose advocacy organization was called Survivors Network of those Abused by Priests (SNAP)—signaled, perhaps unwittingly, the Mount Carmel resisters' blunt approach to its relations with the wider community. Like their counterparts in Weymouth and Sudbury, the resisting Catholics in East Boston occupied the church twenty-four hours a day. The resisters rejected the closure decision and sought to convince the archdiocese to restore the parish. In the meantime, they would manage the buildings and direct the religious lives of those who stayed on. They changed the locks at the church, making several copies of the keys so that they could secure the building while one or two of them slept inside overnight. They hoisted mattresses into the upstairs choir loft and tucked a small refrigerator into a corner of the "saint's room" adjacent to the sanctuary. The vigilers kept a watchful eye out for representatives of the archdiocese, who they feared would attempt to kick them out. Later in the fall, the police removal of lingerers at two additional parishes after their last masses seemed to confirm the need for diligence with the keys and tight surveillance of the grounds. Vigilers kept "calling-trees" within close reach so that neighbors could be alerted of the need to rush to the church at any sign of threat. If they were going to get kicked out, they reasoned, they wanted to have enough "bodies" in the church to make their removal good theater for the many journalists who had also found their way onto the vigilers' speed dials. They stocked up on extra supplies of food and drink and settled in for a long standoff.

Resisters immediately began attending to the efforts of sustaining the community. To this end, they arranged for a continuous supply of consecrated hosts. As at St. Albert's and elsewhere, the hosts that arrived at Mount Carmel were provided by priests whose identities were kept secret to all but those with a need to know. Every so often, a go-between would arrive with a ciborium full of the consecrated wafers which would be deposited in the church tabernacle. The hosts provided by these spiritual benefactors would allow the occupiers to hold regular communion services as a replacement for Sunday masses. The Survivors also hosted fundraisers, social events, processions, and daily rosaries. Although a former group member's oversight and disorganization meant that the church did not have a valid canon law appeal, they did hire a lawyer to organize a legal case against the archdiocese in civil court. For those occupying the church, these were heady times. While the drudgery, legal setbacks, and internal conflicts experienced over the course of several years of church occupation would make the effort challenging, the thrill of taking over the church in opposition to the archdiocese never abated entirely.

Thrill came with scandal, of course, and this is where the intimate streets of Jeffries Point provide a telling example. After the closure announcement, formerly routine encounters among parishioners—at the supermarket or on the street—could become eruptive sites of conflict between occupiers and those who had moved on. These divisions meant that old friendships based on parish life together had to be revisited and reevaluated. Vigilers saw themselves as the bridge between the parish's past and its future. This claim put a charge into encounters with those who had moved on, and it was both satisfying and unsettling for the vigilers to relay them at the church afterward.

A lifelong Mount Carmel parishioner named Louisa was so disturbed and energized by one of these encounters that she told the story multiple times in one night, making sure that everyone had a chance to know the lines that had been drawn. The story begins in the teller line at the bank, with Louisa running into an old acquaintance, a woman whom she used to greet with "hugs and kisses."[1] After cordial hellos the two entered a discussion about church. "Where are you going to church?" the woman asked

Louisa. When Louisa told her she went to Our Lady of Mount Carmel, the woman immediately upped the ante: "They don't have a mass there, right?" Here Louisa drew on what she had learned as a resister to rebut this slight: "Well, they have a service, and if you know your canon law you know that it fulfills the obligation." The affirmation that a lay-led Eucharistic service satisfied Catholics' weekly obligation to attend mass in cases where a priest was not available was an important baseline for the communities of resistance. For Louisa, it signaled the orthodoxy of the occupation and should have prevented outsiders form being scandalized.

In this case, as in others, the discussion turned ugly. "That's not a church," Louisa's friend answered. At this point in the story, Louisa had captured her audience; this charge struck a nerve. Louisa's story was building momentum. With this statement of rejection, all of Louisa's illusions concerning her friend were swept away. It was what she called a "reversal." What was once friendliness was now acrimony, what was cooperation was now competition. The "hugs and kisses" of years past were revealed to have been corrupt, fake, vile. Personality played a role in the story's vividness as well. When she felt offended, Louisa could speak with bitterness and open hostility that was in this case magnetic and exhilarating.

The theme of reversal perfectly accompanied this change of tone. When the woman said Mount Carmel was not a church, Louisa replied that as she saw it, the *receiving parish* was not a church, but a home for hypocrites, church deserters. When she said Louisa should "move on," Louisa incongruously said she thought *she* should move on. The hurtful pettiness of this exchange did not stop Louisa from trumpeting it through the vigiling community. Even in their simplicity the reversals captured an important aspect of the vigilers' sense of scandal. The closure meant that the world had been turned upside down. As Louisa understood them, the rules for practicing parish had been violated in the request to shut the parish down. Her assailant's implicit assent to the breaking of those rules undermined the sacrifices that had made the parish and its traditions possible in the first place.

After one telling of the story another Mount Carmel resister named Irene picked up this idea of reversal and extended it to matters of commitment and integrity. "Why are people so angry at this church?" she yelled to everyone and no one in particular in the church hall. "Why?" Many of those who had left, like Louisa's critic, "used to come here even more than I did," Irene continued,

> but now they won't even step inside to say a prayer. So it's closed. You can still say a prayer! I don't understand it. I used to do my part, sign my checks. I wouldn't come to the parties, but they were *always* here. You'd think they'd really care.

Irene, who still considered herself an outsider in terms of her social commitment to the church, had nonetheless stayed on, not just signing checks, but also spending hours in the building as an occupier. It was deserters' presumed anger—not simple indifference or dismissal—that could begin to explain the reversal for Irene. It is true that there were those who were angry with the vigilers for having divided the community, but in Irene's interpretation, anyone who left after having been so committed had to be hostile. Otherwise, their absence made no sense. Another of Louisa's listeners reflected on the reversal with reference to the special character of a church. If Mount Carmel is not a church then "what is it . . . a barn?" Leonard asked. What had started out as a chance encounter in a bank had quickly lit the fires of speculation about the character of the sacred and the meaning of church, parish, and Church.

"A vigil is a sacrifice": Resistance, Power, and Belonging in Boston's Church Occupations

As Louisa's story of scandal and vindication illustrates, resistance among these Catholics was a complicated endeavor. The vehemence of both Louisa and her attacker, as well as Louisa's own search for affirmation at the church afterward, betrayed the fraught character of Catholics' relationships to their parishes and to church authority in contemporary Boston. Leonard and Irene's questions in response to Louisa's story were meant to be rhetorical, but they also contained an undercurrent of uncertainty and unease. The plausibility of Louisa's outrage, Irene's confusion, and Leonard's sarcasm did not emerge solely out of their forceful personalities and rich storytelling. It was grounded in the church's past, in the attitudes and postures toward the church that its members and leaders had urged upon those who frequented it.

In their resistance to parish closures Boston Catholics faced an old responsibility with a new intensity: the shutdowns provoked them to work out for themselves, for one another, and for observers their understanding of who they were in relation to the Catholic tradition. As they did so, the simple but forceful assertions that they were neither "sheep" nor "children," and the claim that they were normal Catholics carried remarkable weight. During my fieldwork among these vigiling parishes, I heard one or another version of these assessments more than any others. What it meant to be an average Catholic, and yet not a sheep or a child, in the context of the Boston Roman Catholic Church was taken as nearly self-explanatory. Indeed, this may not seem a complicated point: for too long, vigilers argued, the laity has kowtowed to the all too human leadership of the church, whether they were nuns, brothers, priests, or bishops. The long period of fear and groveling is over; a new, mature, independent laity is emerging and we are its vanguard. At the same time, we will not be marginalized from the tradition—we are reclaiming its center. These were the positive values of their rejections of how the archdiocese portrayed them (as religiously immature and marginal) and what it expected of them (willing compliance).

But the relationship among independence, maturity, and belonging was no simple matter for these modern Boston Catholics. In a situation of grievance, turmoil, and exploration, they tried on postures of opposition and of orthodoxy. For Louisa and her listeners, as for others involved in the resistance, hostility toward the church mingled with the search for comfort in familiar patterns. Comportment and discipline overlapped with rebellion and experimentation. Understanding these Catholics is not so much a matter of isolating these tendencies in order to get at one essential quality, but rather of thinking carefully about the combinations and their meanings as a part of modern Catholic practice.

"This is unrest territory."[2] Annetta offered this assessment of the Catholic community of East Boston on good authority. As the leader of the Survivors, she became a hub of information and controversy for the community. Annetta, who was in her early sixties when the shutdowns began, had an intimate understanding of the neighborhood's recent history. In addition to a career in senior care, she had been involved in church and community initiatives and in neighborhood arms of Boston political campaigns for decades. She had put four children through Catholic schools in the neighborhood and had been active in supporting the creation of a consolidated Catholic primary school after parish schools, including Mount Carmel's, closed in the 1970s. She had also been active in helping to prevent the closure of the community's Catholic high school in the mid-1990s.[3] So contest and controversy were not new for the community, nor were they foreign to Annetta's experience in it.

But the unrest of the parish shutdown posed new and more troubling challenges. With the parish closures, Annetta experienced and observed a profound dis-ease, a sense of division and disorientation unlike what she had witnessed before. If previous pressures had allied residents with one another against industrial encroachment or in defense of a community asset, with the parish shutdown the lines of division were far less clearly drawn.

So although the public face of Boston's resisters (presented happily to an initial crush and an eventual trickle of journalists seeking stories at the closed parishes) was usually polished and confident, there were layers to resisting Catholics' experience that made Annetta's more probing evaluation of the situation understandable. The closures and the resistance to them unearthed anxieties, untapped energies, and unleashed frustrations associated with being a Catholic in Boston. Working with notes and recorded conversations among vigiling communities, this chapter explores the contours of the unrest Annetta sensed and identifies it as an interpretive problem for the study of U.S. Catholicism and the study of religion more broadly.

If resisting Catholics were not asking precisely whether or not they were Catholic at all, the threatened loss of a parish and community did encourage consideration of *how* they were Catholic. This chapter tracks answers to this question in light of the divergent histories of Catholic sacrifice. Over the course of the twentieth century, Catholics were encouraged to devote themselves to the parish as it embodied the church's glory. In the latter half of the twentieth century, parishioners were enjoined to feel a sense of ownership of the parish as the home of the people of God. Although they had very different connotations, these differing sets of rules for parish life were not, in practice at least, mutually exclusive. Catholics found ways to combine these two sets of rules, especially as parishes seemed to become less and less secure over the latter half of the twentieth century. The emphasis in the post-Second Vatican Council church on continuity amid change gave this braiding legitimacy.

These combinations did not diminish attachment to the parish as the inviolable center of Catholic practice. By offering Catholics new ways to be devoted to the local parish, the new rules about parish practice only enhanced the significance of the place for those who continued to seek some connection with the church through parish life. As "willed suffering," sacrifice is always "for" something.[4] In the shifts and additions over the course of the twentieth century, Catholics continued to develop an understanding of sacrifice for the glory of the faith alongside idioms that linked sacrifice with ownership of the faith. In both cases, faith became manifest at particular parishes; faith was the faith at St. Albert's, Our Lady of Mount Carmel, and Our Lady of the Assumption.

This chapter hinges on the link between sacrifice (as a Catholic value embedded in the practice of parish) and Catholics' orientations to authority. The question of 'for what' the Church could (successfully or not) ask its members to sacrifice is ultimately a question about authority. As a project that relied on the willed suffering of Catholics involved, the shutdowns posed stark questions of authority. In resisting the parish shutdowns and the version of Catholic authority embedded in this call for sacrifice, the occupiers offered a response that drew on their past and the various versions of Catholic authority it contained. These combinations, which were in some cases strategic and in others more a matter of Catholic training and family experience, offer a window onto the resistance and its meanings for Catholic belonging and Catholicism as a part of American religious history.

A brief example will clarify this argument. Resisters' preference for the terms "vigil" and "vigilers" captures precisely the delicate maneuvering between competing ways of thinking about authority and sacrifice that typified their efforts. Evoking the tradition of overnight prayerful adoration of the Holy Eucharist, the term vigil suggested that resisters had embarked on a familiar, if no longer common, devotional ritual.[5] Since overnight vigils were mostly a vestige of an older Catholicism, the term aligned resisters with a deep past. It suggested a time when reverence for churches and for the presence of Christ within them were paramount in Catholic practice. It spoke too of sacrifice, comportment, and discipline, not rebellion or unruliness. "A vigil is a sacrifice," Annetta said as she summarized her commitment to the parish.[6] The phrase communicated the resisters' deep commitment to their cause without at the same time suggesting variance from Catholic traditions. Embrace of sacrifice, as a historic vehicle to American Catholic distinctiveness, had aligned Catholics with the shared moral world of Catholic abundance. The 'goods' of Catholic life—strong connections with others, family bonds, moral discipline and mutual support—relied on Catholics' acceptance of the authoritative calls to sacrifice announced in parishes across the twentieth century. It had been lifted up as Catholics' defining feature; they could consider themselves unique for not having turned away from this duty. Framing the vigil as sacrifice carried this sense of duty forward.

But another Catholic discourse about sacrifice also emerged in the latter half of the twentieth century and also informed the meaning of the vigils. In this narrative sacrifice was tied not so much to Catholics' distinctiveness from or contrast to America, but more to their alignment with the modern affirmation of the primacy of conscience. This theme, a keynote of the Second Vatican Council's *Gaudium et Spes* ("The Pastoral Constitution on the Church in the Modern World," 1965), did not imply simply doing whatever one wanted. Far from offering a free pass to selfishness guided by "blind choice," relying on conscience puts demands and constraints on individuals. More than mere "internal impulse" conscience is the "law written by God" on the heart, "which is fulfilled by love of God and of neighbor."[7] Following conscience, then, does not do away with sacrifice, but more clearly alerts people to the internal and universal laws they are bound to obey.

In embracing "conscience," resisters joined the tradition of those late nineteenth-century liberal "Americanizers" and "modernizers," who committed themselves to putting Catholicism in deeper conversation with America in order to revive the tradition, help it adapt and grow, and divert the constant undercurrent of U.S. anti-Catholicism. In the process these reformers opened up the possibility of Catholic self-reliance, attentiveness to personal experience as a source of religious insight, and encouraged active and open dialogue with non-Catholics about theology, education, and politics.[8] When the Second Vatican Council opened the church to those who had shepherded these ideas across the twentieth century (while systematically linking them to medieval and early church sources), it smoothed the way for Boston's vigilers to link their surface disobedience to a deeper Catholic tradition of obedience to conscience. These combinations emerged in three categories of resisters' practice and narrative. Resisters' takeover of the churches, their reflections on departed parishioners, and their evaluations of Catholic obedience among the previous generations all illustrate the ways resisters lived inside the key theological tensions of the contemporary church.

"They're protesting us!" Claiming the Churches & the Center

The occupations were most remarkable for the immediate distance they created between the parishes and the church's leadership. Vigiling parishes were in a curious relationship with parishes of the ideal type—they were in constant connection with the traditions and objects of Catholic practice, but they were also curiously unreal *as parishes*, in that they were absent the constituting authority of the church. They were no longer listed as parishes in the archdiocesan register, yet they continued to attract varying numbers of Catholic worshipers every Sunday and throughout the week. This hybrid status offered room to test out varying orientations to the rules of parish practice. Among the parishes I studied, none had been without a resident pastor before and none of the pastors stayed behind with the vigilers. However beloved or reviled their pastors had been, and however involved the laity had been in the management of the church before its closure, the vigilers' sudden control over the ritual and material aspects of parish life was starkly new and exhilarating.

The question of what to do once the churches had been secured posed many options for the vigilers. Along with daily rosaries, communion services were at the center of the vigilers' ritual lives. Held at least weekly, these formal lay-led gatherings took the place of official masses at many of the vigiling parishes. These services mirrored a typical mass in many aspects, including readings from the scriptures, a comment on those readings, singing, prayers of the faithful, the recitation of the Lord's Prayer, and the kiss of peace. In place of the mass's Eucharistic Prayer (during which a priest oversees the consecration of bread and wine), communion services included a simpler communion rite. Without a priest to perform the consecration, in a communion service lay leaders retrieved previously consecrated hosts from the tabernacle for distribution to the congregation.

No one in Boston suggested that these services, when officially sanctioned, are not a legitimate part of the Roman Catholic life of prayer and worship. In part designed to enable trained lay people to assist priests in distributing the Eucharistic bread and wine during mass, church legislation regarding communion also explains that lay ministers can distribute previously consecrated hosts to Catholics if an "Ordinary" minister and a full mass is unavailable.[9] In light of priest shortages and with pockets of inspired lay Catholics eager to enhance their role in the ritual life of the church, these services had become part of the fabric of worship at some U.S. parishes.[10]

But in the context of Boston's shutdowns the services provoked controversy for two reasons. They operated outside of the sanction of the local Ordinary, and by extension, outside of the church. But in sustaining these groups of Catholics, the services endowed the occupations with a

Catholic weight and resonance that would otherwise have been missing. The consecrated hosts were essential to this project. Through the network of resisting Catholics, the communities received hosts that had been consecrated for this purpose by priests in good standing. These priests were known only by a few of the key insiders who actually arranged for the pick-up and drop-off of the hosts. Occupiers took seriously the notion that sympathetic priests had put their jobs at risk in nurturing the occupations. The promises of legitimacy that came with these hosts assured resisters that they had the sympathy and support of at least some of those with access to the traditional powers of the church to sanctify life and worship. Even if their providers thought the particular closures were warranted, their willingness to give spiritual succor made them revered benefactors among resisting communities.

Occupiers were proud of being able to keep the light alongside the tabernacle lit as an indication of the continuous presence of the body of Christ in their closed churches. The communion services helped occupied parishes replicate the life of the parish before the closure. Within the parish clusters, then, the services drew potential new members away from the receiving churches. The services were very close in form, length, and content to a mass. Noting these similarities, Catholics who might otherwise have moved on to receiving parishes instead took themselves (and their donations) to the resisting churches.

If the services undercut the smooth execution of the shutdown plan, archdiocesan officials also suggested that they dangerously misled Catholics and even threatened them in the afterlife. In a visit to Mount Carmel to celebrate the community's first Easter mass in four years, Bishop Robert Francis Hennessy said that he felt obligated to tell the congregation that what happened at the church on Sundays was "not a good thing" and that it put their eternal souls "at risk." Afterward, when questioned by a journalist on this point, I overheard him make repeated and desperate efforts to clarify that he spoke of the risk of not attending mass, not any risks associated with supporting the vigil.[11] If Catholics who were attending only the communion services thought that they were fulfilling their obligation, officials wanted to make it clear that they were not. If they attended only these communion services, resisters had essentially abandoned their Sunday obligation and risked the punishments in the afterlife that came with this sin. Any exceptions to the Sunday obligation that could legitimately be invoked for "grave" and urgent causes were not applicable in this case.[12]

Resisters differed with the hierarchy at precisely this point. Where the archdiocese insisted that no one had been deprived of the Eucharist, as there were other Catholic churches readily available, the occupiers made the case that the archdiocese *had* deprived them of the Eucharist by removing their priests and closing their churches. The occupiers' growing expertise in church law joined with their unshakeable commitment to the sanctity of each parish to make this opinion persuasive for many. But the legitimating authority of the church imperiled these delicate arguments. Without the church's direct approval, it was hard to make the case on legal grounds that the services were Catholic.

But resisting Catholics wanted their services to have the weight of Catholic legitimacy. Accordingly, they emphasized their appreciation of the communion services as satisfying worship more than they pointed out differences of interpretation in the rules governing the distribution of the Eucharist. Even if the services technically didn't fulfill their Sunday obligation, resisters were willing to take that risk in the belief that their occupation and the services fulfilled other demands of Catholic living, such as loyalty to a community and its memories, or the application of the people of God ecclesiology. Add the undisputed legitimacy of the hosts, and resisters felt that they had successfully navigated the tricky terrain of perpetuating Catholic life without a priest or a sanctioned mass. For the less confident among them, there was no reason that resisters could not augment their time at communion services with masses either at the receiving parish, at another parish, or through watching the mass on TV.

This combination of caution and creativity was a fundamental characteristic of the occupations. "That's one thing we are absolutely vigilant about here," a St. Jeremiah resister told me. "We are not going to do anything that is outside the canons and traditions of the Catholic Church. We are claiming our tradition."[13] They wanted to stay on the right side of tradition, but were willing to put their interpretations of it up against those of the reconfiguration's leaders. One active resister, a self-trained biblical historian and liturgist from a parish slated for closure, made it his mission to educate and train potential communion service leaders at at least one parish. Having given communion services at his own parish before the closures were announced, he had the confidence and persuasiveness to convince the sometimes hesitant vigilers to take up the role in their own parishes.[14] His knowledge of scripture and early church history were crucial to his case.

With help from the experts in their midst, vigilers also often discussed alternative models of the parish. In particular, the idea of a roving pastor attached to several parishes and attending to each of them on a rotating basis had profound appeal. Lay people could run their own parishes. The success of the communion services was a primary source of confirmation for this claim for Karen, a twenty-five-year parishioner and middle-aged lawyer at St. Albert's:

> Part of the thing that I felt was beautiful was the empowerment of having lay people do as much as they could do, and just the whole idea had never occurred to me; it had never occurred to me that lay people could bless each other. Duh! So part of it was just seeing how much people could do, and how special people could make things.[15]

Celia, who was close to being homebound and watched the mass on TV every day, expressed a similar point. Celia, recall, was a former Holy Name Society and Mother's Club member who had recently celebrated her sixtieth wedding anniversary at Mount Carmel. She frequently told me that the services run by the group's lay liturgical leader were just as good as those the pastor had offered before the closure.[16]

Such enthusiasm notwithstanding, the parishes in vigil that were granted officially sanctioned weekly masses by diocesan priests immediately jumped at the opportunity. The presence of a priest not only brought the sanctity and power of the consecration back to their church, but also spoke to vigilers as an implicit acknowledgement of their power and even legitimacy.[17] But 'getting a mass' was an accomplishment of some, not all, of the vigiling parishes. The unevenness of this policy left those without a mass wondering about the differences: while sanctioned masses were sometimes understood as a gesture of good faith on the part of the archdiocese, vigilers without masses wondered at the criteria and charged that the hierarchy was essentially holding the Eucharist hostage.[18] When it came to finding means to redress these inequalities, Catholics in vigils were torn between displaying their resilience as orthodox Catholics and taking the risk of setting into motion a repressive response from the leadership. Defiant in their rebuttal of the new Catholic maps laid out in the reconfiguration, the services still spoke to Catholics' basic appreciation for the liturgy and its traditional forms.

Gender and ritual leadership was another vexing issue. Of the several vigiling parishes I visited, two regularly had women presiding at communion services.[19] Debate over this issue captured some of the communities, with some vigilers hoping to push for greater gender equality and others hesitant to overstep. For Karen, having a former Protestant minister and the familiar sacristan as the only leaders of the communion services kept the community too closely bound to the pattern established by tradition. Her aspiration for a more radical approach, and her envy of those parishes that had not been "caught" in the old rule expressed the tension within the vigiling communities between defiance and orthodoxy.[20]

Widespread hesitation among vigilers to invite married priests to say mass in occupied parishes also brought the resisters' pragmatism and orthodoxy into sharper relief. The idea of married priests arose in these communities in large part because of the publicity work of a member of a closed parish in Natick who was a supporter of the Council of Parishes. Angela, 57, advocated a group called Celibacy Is The Issue (CITI), which sponsors and supports priests who have left their clerical state by marrying, but who want to continue to provide priestly services to Catholics. Through word of mouth and their website, www.rentapriest.com, CITI appeals to alienated or uneasy lay Catholics, particularly those searching for a Catholic blessing for their second marriages. On the website, Catholics are encouraged to search "God's Yellow Pages" to find local married and affiliated retired priests who "make house calls" and provide "non-judgmental" "spiritual and sacramental ministry." Priests are priests for life, they remind us, and they have a duty to respond to Catholics' calls for ministry. In addition, CITI asks Catholics to call upon them to say masses in the growing number of "priest-less parishes," assuring them that a recent canon law dissertation concluded that church law allows Catholics to call upon married priests. The Council of Parishes' moderate support of masses with married priests did not catch fire outside of this clearinghouse.[21]

Discussions about the names resisters would accept for themselves further illustrate Catholics' navigation between the competing pulls of the oppositional and the orthodox. Given the active effort of archdiocesan officials and some pastors to portray them as a marginal minority worthy of sympathy but not capitulation, one of the resisters' priorities was to be known as average Catholics. But since a majority of Catholics had seemingly moved on without struggle from their closed parishes, the resisters faced a difficult task. They had to acknowledge their differences from the majority without at the same time setting themselves too far from the center and aggravating possible sympathizers. It was not easy to know just what an average Catholic was. There were some very fine lines to be walked as they considered their position in relation to other lay Catholics and the church's local, national, and international leadership.

One of the most consistent descriptions vigilers used was a negative one: they repeatedly asserted that they were "not that religious." What individual resisters meant by this varied. One leader deflected the title of "leader" by telling me that there were many others who went to mass everyday to whom she "couldn't hold a candle" in terms of religiousness.[22] When an East Boston vigiler berated his fellow vigilers for turning the church into a gossip hall, he deflected possible reproach and intensified the critique by disowning more than average religiousness.[23] Typically such denials were meant to defray suspicions of fanaticism and affirm the resisters' stability and validity in light of both public scrutiny and Catholic orthodoxy. In Weymouth, parishioners' loyalty to their former pastor presented a risk. Many there thought the closure had a sinister underside; they considered it a recrimination against their pastor's success. Others shared this opinion, but worked to counteract misunderstanding. Ryan spoke glowingly about the pastor as a "special person," but then made sure to add that he considered himself "far from a fanatic."[24] Braden, the group's public relations expert, made a similar point one evening when he let me know there was no merit to the "pied piper" critique of the parish that emerged because of the abundant enthusiasm of the occupiers for their departed pastor, Father Coyne. As evidence, he noted that he had once offered his vehement disagreement to Father Coyne related to an issue from the pastor's homily.[25]

He also told me that at least some members of the parish council differed with Father Coyne on an issue that had come up before the list of closing parishes had been finalized. The disagreement arose when a group on the council wanted to organize the people of St. Albert's to descend upon another parish one Sunday before the closures in a demonstration of St. Albert's size and strength. They planned to arrive unannounced for a Sunday mass in order to fill the rival parish's lot with their cars and pack its pews with their bodies. They were confident they would outnumber the parish's own parishioners, and hoped that this overwhelming display of size and organization would help convince the other parishes to keep St. Albert's off the closure list. Braden told me that Father Coyne sought to moderate this guerilla tactic, but would not enforce his will on the group if they chose to go forward with it. Although this critical-mass-at-mass event never took place, Braden's message to me was that the group was not operating under the beguiling sway of a single charismatic priest-hero.[26] It is almost certain, however, that the vigil at St. Albert's never would have started without Father Coyne's popularity and his message of lay Catholic empowerment.[27]

The need to attract enough participants was another reason for affirming a moderate stance. To a large extent the vigils thrived on being able to draw in fellow Catholics and retain parishioners. It was not coincidental that St. Albert's, the vigil group with the largest number of participating members, was the first vigiling parish to receive a reprieve from the archdiocese. If a significant portion of the parish had not embarked on the transition into the welcoming parish, the archdiocese was more likely to consider reversing its decision or moderating its stance.[28] Although resisters would dispute this reasoning when it came to the archbishop's willingness to hand out masses to the larger groups and not to others, there was a clear desire on the part of all the vigil communities to attract and retain crowds.[29] Vigiling groups carefully counted bodies in church and at events. Because the communities were so vulnerable, small oscillations in the numbers could signal disaster. At the same time, resisters were happy to deflect criticism from the smaller vigils with reference to Jesus' promise that "Wherever two or three are gathered together in my name, I am with them."[30] Even with this teaching behind them, vigilers naturally desired expansion.

Clearing up possible misconceptions about what it meant to be involved in a vigil, then, was an important part of attracting the people needed to sustain the effort. The very idea of a vigil was delicately crafted to emphasize the devout, respectful, and sober discipline of the effort. Resisters made persistent efforts to stay "on message" and they eagerly welcomed news cameras into their churches almost any time, but especially during prayer services or in the late evening when they would be setting up their picturesque sleeping bags. One vigiler described the mandate handed to the resisters by the parish council in the following way:

> They made sure to emphasize that it was a prayerful vigil and an eternal vigil and stuff like that. It wasn't a protest, it was a vigil, and some of the other parishes maintain an angrier stance about everything that went on, and that just wasn't here, we were practicing our religion, but we didn't have that anger, we just wanted to share our love of God and love of each other.[31]

The distinction between protest and vigil was crucial for many of the resisters. This was a sensitive issue. When word got back to St. Jeremiah's that the vigilers had been called "vigilantes" by people at the receiving parish, resisters were vehement in their rejection of this wordplay. At Mount Carmel, Annetta expressed similar frustration when she read a bulletin article written by the pastor of the receiving parish designating the vigilers "protesters." The real situation, she urged, was that "they're protesting *us*."[32] A woman at St. Albert's made a similar point, adding that she had evolved toward a proper orientation: "the more I came here the anger went away . . . a lot of people called it a protest, but it wasn't, it was all about just kind of finding our own spot."[33]

While the resisters wanted the vigils to be peaceful and respectful, they also wanted them to be enjoyable, attractive, and fulfilling. All the communities I got to know aimed to sustain a range of activities and provide opportunities for religious and social activity among their members. Hospitality hours, dances, pot luck dinners, fundraising dinner dances, and other parties checkered the communities' calendars. At least three of the closed parishes restarted religious education courses for adults and children.[34]

Charity and other outreach activities also remained a part of their parish life. Almost all the resisters reported that they got to know their fellow Catholics much better and had entered into a more rewarding community experience than before the closure. One joked that the vigilers would have to sue the archdiocese for therapy after the vigil ended because they would no doubt suffer from withdrawal.[35] Even filling hours in church as a member of a day's vigiling team could be uniquely rewarding, as St. Jeremiah's website bulletin announced under the question "Can You Vigil?":

> **Vigiling is FUN!** If you have not vigiled at St. Jeremiah, you have no idea what you are missing! This is the time to make new friends and renew old acquaintances. You do not just have to sit and pray. You can bring along your hobby, a book, your business work, the kids or just relax! There is a TV, a radio and a computer (in fact, we are looking to upgrade to a new computer). Every hour or two is an important, significant contribution for our cause. We welcome new faces and look for our old friends. Why not give it a try? Please sign up on the vigil board or call. . .[36]

Embedded in this call for assistance in the difficult task of sustaining the church occupation after twenty months is the familiar assertion of being normal. While prayer was a central component of all the parishes' practice, it was important to maintain and highlight the full range of options open to anyone involved with the resistance.

Empty Seats: Struggling with Those Who Moved On

Resisters saw their occupations and their opposition to the shutdowns as a clean break from a version of Catholic sacrifice that had sentenced Catholics to a bleak existence as passive followers. Accordingly, they considered abandonment of the parish at its closure to be an implicit embrace of permanent servitude. The zealousness of this conviction was not diminished by the acknowledgment that many of those who left probably moved on out of nothing more than indifference. In the resisters' calculus, indifference, while perhaps tempting, was paramount to fatalism, which was just shy of blind obedience.

Ronald, the leader of Mount Carmel's communion services, expressed this reasoning at the pulpit after relaying a range of unhappy news items including a legal setback at another occupied church and the retirement of an abuser bishop in Iowa. Lay Catholics who had moved on from closed parishes and continued to drop money in the basket without asking questions only exacerbated the church's problems.[37] Resisters had made it their challenge to reject fatalistic or passive suffering associated with the past while retaining the powerful idioms of church glory and ownership embedded in the notion of Catholic sacrifice. They were not necessarily free of these tendencies themselves, which meant that their critiques of those who moved on were by turns sympathetic and harsh. They considered leaving to be a vestige of a deeply damaging resignation to the power of tradition. It was faulty, unnecessary sacrifice.

Resisters' interactions with those who had left the parishes instead of joining in the resistance elicited reflection on the meanings of Catholic sacrifice as it related to practicing parish. Encounters like Louisa's at the bank stirred controversy in resisting communities precisely because they brought questions of authority and belonging into the light of day. Reflecting on this encounter, Annetta diagrammed for me the fates of the scattered members of Mount Carmel Parish. She divided the once-united parishioners into five post-shutdown categories—those who resisted the closure, those who joined the receiving parish, those who went to another parish, those who stopped attending church altogether, and former resisters who had dropped out. Some in the latter category had joined up with the schismatic traditionalist nuns who had come to East Boston at the invitation of another vigil participant. These fractures and the emotional intensity of each of these decisions prompted Annetta to suggest that the Catholics in East Boston really needed a psychologist to make sense and provide healing.[38]

According to Annetta, her own sister, who was a Mount Carmel parishioner who had moved on after the closure, critiqued Annetta with reference to the authoritative voice of parish rules. "The parish should have been saved first," her sister said during one of their long painful conversations about the shutdowns and the proper response to them. Since Annetta had not been active in the parish in the years leading up to the closure, her sister had blamed Annetta and other aloof or alienated parishioners for the closure: "You didn't go to church like you should have gone," was the message Annetta received.[39]

This critique cut deep, and perhaps contributed to Annetta's tendency to argue that she took up the resistance more as a matter of "justice" than of religion.[40] The contrast here is really between Catholics' advocacy, primarily after the Second Vatican Council, on the primacy of conscience and the older tradition in the church which prioritized obedience as a vehicle to Catholic distinctiveness. Annetta's sensitivity to the hurt and confusions linked to the closure suggest that the disavowal of religion did not tell the whole story. On a number of occasions I saw Annetta turn away from a frustrating conversation and head into the church to "say a prayer."[41] She also often attributed happy developments in the vigil to the support of Our Lady.[42] If these orientations to prayer and the miraculous do not supersede motivation based on "justice," they do illustrate Annetta's willingness to draw on a range of explanations and strategies to sustain and nurture her work in the occupations.

The narrative of a Weymouth parishioner about her experience with a friend who had left the church suggests that East Boston was not the only unsettled place in the archdiocese. Catharine, the woman who had secured her favorite saint's image for a window dedicated to her husband at St. Albert's, told me of a painful encounter with a departed friend as we talked over coffee in the church basement. After the vigil started and she had moved on to another parish, this friend and Catharine tried to stay in touch. "She was lovely," Catharine told me, but their conversations slowly had become a source of great stress since the closure. It became so tense between them that Catharine eventually had to ask her friend not to call her anymore if she was going to insist on "saying negative things" about "the church," by which Catharine meant calling the vigil into question. Catharine explained her involvement in the vigil to her friend by asserting that Catholics had a right and a responsibility to be happy:

> I have to do what I feel to make myself feel happy. And I am very happy. And I like to be happy because being happy I think is very very important, and I think that if you are happy people around you will be happy too.

For Catharine, leaving the church would have violated this dictum about happiness. If her friend insisted on being unhappy, that was just a legacy of restrictive upbringing and a narrow vision of Catholic validation through suffering. The challenges from her friend continued despite Catharine's request. Eventually, Catharine felt she had to take a more forceful approach. Catharine told me that she got "a little agitated" with her friend and finally thought she had convinced her that they should avoid the topic in order to preserve their friendship.

Shortly after this exchange, and before they had a chance to reconcile, Catharine's friend died. This added a new sadness to an already painful rift, and Catharine recalled feeling unsettled and "a little guilty."

> So I went into church and prayed, and I said 'maybe if you can get to her and tell her that I really didn't mean to hurt her feelings.' I didn't raise my voice or anything like that. I just told her that this is what I think, [that what] I'm doing is right.

The hope for divine mediation combined with Catharine's own justifications to shield her from excessive guilt. Beginning with the anxiety of a strained relationship and culminating with a sense of guilt only imperfectly relieved, Catharine's experience of this break with the past was not uniformly happy. Division over the proper practice of the parish lingered in her reflections on this event and on other departed friends.

Fractured relationships were punctuated by the church's empty seats. Catharine often surveyed the church by noting absences:

> I can just see them in my mind even as I look at the altar. I think, and I look over at their seat, and I say, 'Oh my gosh, Cynthia,' and 'Where is she? She's gone, she's gone, she's going to another church.' Carole? She would sit here, because everyone would sit in certain seats. She was a Eucharistic minister for twenty-five years. And I feel so bad that they're gone.

People's former preferences for "certain seats" were a glaring reminder of the divisions that the closures had unwittingly exposed. Part of Catharine's lament resided in missing old friends, whose "views on things" she liked. The lost comfort of familiar faces was a sorrow for many resisters. The vigilers at St. Albert's honored their beloved pastor by leaving a large picture of him on the celebrant's chair on the altar.

According to vigilers like Catharine, those who left were enthralled by the ways of the past. In particular, the vigilers thought those who had moved on were captivated by a previous time during which calls for lay suffering and sacrifice were heeded without question or critique. What was troubling was that these people were once indistinguishable from the vigilers present—they had sat across from her during mass, distributed Holy Communion to her, and offered her their thoughts on matters of the day. They also seemed to have listened as attentively as Catharine had to their progressive pastor who had created a resurgence in the parish in recent years. But in leaving they had opted for a tradition Catharine considered retrograde. On one hand, this choice for the past was baffling, almost incomprehensible for those who stayed on. "I'm surprised at some of them," Catharine explained, "because I thought that they believed just as much as I did."[43]

On the other hand, the vigilers could not deny that across the archdiocese (if not also in their own parishes) the orientations to authority that they asserted were of the past were not actually past: the majority of Catholics in closed parishes had moved on as they had been asked. Explaining the differences between themselves and their departed fellow-parishioners was a challenge not readily solved by the accusation of anachronism. Mount Carmel's Celia told me that friends she encountered outside of the resisting community could not understand her involvement with the group. "They think you're crazy, probably, but I don't care," Celia said. Celia's brother Victor took part in activities both at the receiving parish and at the occupied Mount Carmel. This gave Celia perspective on the variety of possibilities available to people who, as she said of Victor, still had their hearts at Mount Carmel, but also wanted to maintain former roles and old friends. For Celia, critics who said "You're wasting your time" in trying to get Mount Carmel reopened missed the point. For Celia, Mount Carmel was the only parish she ever knew. Parish and religion had become intertwined to the extent that an official decree of church closure had no weight. To those who said she was wasting her time, Celia offered a simple reply: "As long as you can walk in, it's not considered closed." While she certainly hoped the church would be reopened, that result was less important than continuing to practice the rules of the parish as she had embraced them at Mount Carmel.[44]

At St. Albert's, where a large number of parishioners—perhaps the largest proportion of any occupied church—stayed behind to participate in the church occupation, resisters like Catharine puzzled over those who had moved on. If leavetakers were the exception at St. Albert's, their presences were not wholly erased in the thoughts of those who stayed behind. Just as they resided in Catharine's mind's eye as she sat at communion services, they were a shadow behind her thoughts as she justified her position. The proximity of this dangerous past urged resisting Catholics like Catharine to express more forcefully their vision of a reliable past, a stable present, and a promising future. What was once thought to have been a shared orientation to the practice of a parish was now in need of re-articulation and justification.

Obedience, Freedom, and the Ambivalence of the Previous Generation

One of the most common ways to accomplish this task involved the search for an acceptable Catholic maturity. Ideas and language about childishness and adulthood and meanings of these words within families pervaded the resisters' language. As co-leader of the Council of Parishes, Peter Borré urged that all the members were doing was refusing to be treated like "doltish children."[45] This charge captured well the tone of the resistance across the archdiocese. In a suburb outside of Boston, a vigiler whose daughter had suffered sexual abuse by a priest at another parish drew a typical distinction grounded in the metaphors of maturity:

> I have no problem with being under Rome and being under the Archdiocese of Boston. I just don't want to be treated like a kindergarten child. And this is the way we are being treated.[46]

There were tensions, however, over whether having been treated "like a child" warranted more sweeping rejections of the leadership. This is why resisters sometimes extended the dismissal of childhood metaphors into a more elaborate reversal of positions. Annetta reported feeling like the true "priest" while the receiving pastor with whom she was trying to negotiate was more like a "child." On another occasion she compared this priest to the group's precocious thirteen-year-old member, saying that he "doesn't think" before he acts.[47]

For these Catholics, the laity were now the adults, and the men leading the botched reconfiguration were the children. Archbishop O'Malley's entry into the seminary during his early teens spurred resisters' suspicions about his emotional intelligence, rationality, and street wisdom. It was as if O'Malley's capacity to develop an adult approach to real problems had been stunted by his early admission to the priesthood. When I asked Braden if he thought theology helped explain the differences between them and the hierarchy, he said he wished it was that easy. If it was a matter of two normally developed people in conversation, Braden reported, he could easily imagine the two groups coming to a valid resolution, but, he went on, "You can't reason with them."[48]

The common invocation of a parent-child theme added a more specific and intimate frame of reference to the resisters' claims about maturity and immaturity. At the communion celebration of a parish's sixth month in vigil, one speaker argued that their success was a result of their "adult faith." To illustrate this, he narrated a parable of two dark-eyed parents seeking an explanation for their blue-eyed child: it feels awkward, yes, but the child is ours. The recessive trait of an adult faith "was always there" he reminded the group. "We are about rediscovering the Catholic DNA, those qualities of faith that allow us to act as adults with one another."[49]

Discussion of another suburban parish's beloved prodigal son mural witnessed to a reversal with a more ambivalent undercurrent. Any too-firm assignment of positions on the scale of childishness and maturity, particularly in the context of familial metaphors, made Christian teachings of human brokenness and neediness less readily comprehensible. Abiding idealizations of the family—and also the church family—as the exemplary site of wise authority and unconditional and forgiving love made lay Catholic attempts to break out of traditional roles a complicated affair.

Thus vigilers at St. Jeremiah reported continually rethinking who, in their struggle with the archdiocese, played which part in the parable. In one sense, the resisters wanted to be the son, gladly welcomed home by the church as a loving father; in another, as another vigiler described it, they were the ones waiting for the church to come back to their own steady hearth.[50] At St. Albert's another resister's age metaphor captured this same mixed sensibility. Explaining that a lot of people seem to have left the church rather than remain obedient "old-fashioned Catholics," Nora sought the right words to position the vigilers and the others who stayed behind. Citing an unnamed source inside the archdiocesan offices, Nora told me that "they pray, in the chancery, for people to go to church and accept." "They just want people [who say], 'We're going to close? Yes, Father. Who's going to turn the lights out?'" Describing how she could easily understand why her children left the church, this woman went on to try to locate the vigilers on a parent-child continuum:

> What we did threw them off in that respect. It's like a mother of teenagers . . . because teenagers throw you off, but a [mother of a] two-year-old, [just says] 'you'll do it because I said so. Because I'm the mother and *I* said so. You don't have to know the reason, I'm not going to explain it to you. You just do it because I said so.[51]

Nora settled on teenagers as the exemplary comparison because they can "throw a parent off" in a way toddlers supposedly cannot. At the same time, it is significant that Nora did not claim "adulthood" in this conversation. If pressed, she might also want to use that label, but here it is revealing that the in-between status of the teen best captured her point.

Not willing to do something just because the church said so, the resisters claimed that they had been infantilized by their treatment during the reconfiguration. This charge had a particular salience in Boston, where the clerical child abuse and cover-up scandal had indelibly underlined children's unique vulnerability to religious authorities. The common argument that the reconfiguration was a "new form of abuse" put the laity in the position of innocent children in need of better care. In their pursuit of a form of workable Catholic belonging, the resisters fashioned themselves as both neglected children and capable adults.

If the resisters' reflections on adulthood and childishness put rebelliousness in tension with belonging, a similar combination attended the resisters' defense against the charge of passivity. When I asked them whether they felt pressure to be obedient, two women at St. Albert's drew on alternate teachings from within the church as justifications of their current opposition. For Karen, the St. Albert's lawyer who was also very involved in Voice of the Faithful, the archdiocese was requesting "blind obedience," which cut against what she understood as the Catholic idea of the "primacy of the informed conscience." Drawing a distinction between obedience in matters of "dogma or theology" and obedience in matters of management and process, she argued that the vigils were not at all about questioning the former. She went on to elaborate on the primacy of conscience by way of example:

> The one thing that the Catholic Church supposedly would say, [is:] If Hitler comes along to you and says, 'You're going to put babies in the furnace,' the

> Catholic conscience is supposed to say, 'No, I'm not.' And not be one of the ones that says, 'Oh, well, Bishop Hitler told me to put babies in the furnace so I've got to do it.'[52]

The word "Bishop" here brings the rejection of acquiescence home with a force befitting many of the vigilers' sense of scandal. In particular, the implicit, hyperbolic, but unapologetic comparison of church closures to genocide and the bishop to Hitler reveals the vehemence of the vigilers' dismissals of the concept of Catholics as sheep. Karen's thinking is an orthodox manifestation of post–Vatican II Catholic teachings on conscience; the extremity of her comparison comes from the intensity of the harm caused by the closure of her church.

Karen's vehemence was not unique. Play at the edges of scandal gave resisters confirmation of their freedom from quiet acquiescence to church authority. After the archbishop offered his self-pitying reflection on the closing process, Annetta wondered out loud if maybe it would be better if the agonies of the process did kill him.[53] At another point, Annetta wondered if O'Malley would suffer the fate of a medieval heretic and have his "head chopped off" on an upcoming visit to Rome.[54] Like Karen's "Hitler" reference, Annetta's hyperbolic comparisons were sometimes reckless, but she occasionally recanted and blamed her exhaustion and frustration for her outbursts. Sometimes fellow resisters policed one another in my presence. In one instance, during the last days of Pope John Paul II, a woman at St. Albert's joked that all the news reports said that Catholics were flocking to their churches, but they never said what they were praying for. Braden, always alert as a public relations professional, jumped in to moderate this comment with disavowals of antipathy toward the dying pope.[55]

This was not always the case. When I mentioned my plan to try to preserve the anonymity of those I wrote about, Annetta told me that she didn't "really care." Harsh criticism of the hierarchy rarely warranted softening or apology. Explaining her willingness to own her comments, Annetta told me that she had "called the archdiocese bastards" before and she would "still call them bastards" again.[56] Nor did resisters apologize for critiquing the archbishop's demeanor. Girard suggested that O'Malley's "cold" personality was the reason Rome brought him to Boston to undertake the consolidation. Annetta added to this by recounting O'Malley's stone-faced response to her during a meeting.[57] Others compared Boston's hierarchy to an organized crime cabal, a communist dictatorship, ruthless businessmen, and an unfeeling Washington bureaucracy.[58] In the fall of 2005, occupiers couldn't resist reveling in news reports that the archbishop suffered from an ear infirmity. His seeming unwillingness to listen to the occupying communities made jokes among fellow resisters on this occasion an easy proposition.[59] Photoshopped images of the archbishop with a Yankees hat replacing his bishop's mitre also got some laughs in the midst of the home team's battles with the so-called "evil empire" in the fall of 2004.[60]

Testing the boundaries of irreverence was only one aspect of Karen's "Hitler" reference. The more fundamental point was the reclamation of a Catholic ideal for use in explaining the occupations as an act of true Catholics. Karen's reference to the primacy of conscience extended the people of God ecclesiology into the church occupations. For her part, Karen's co-vigiler Elizabeth described another Catholic teaching that determined her inability to accept the decisions of the leadership: stewardship.

> Being responsible stewards means that you don't give [your church] to people who squander it, you don't give the assets to people who don't behave responsibly, who send predators into parishes, who can't deal with their human resources. Who can't deal with the cash assets that you give them, who are not sufficiently honest that they will tell you what's going on, you have to make sure that what you do is going to make the world a better place.

Crucially, for Elizabeth this tradition of stewardship was embedded deeply in the tradition, which required both good conscience and good stewardship—knuckling under, as she put it, would have been "just totally antithetical to what they taught us."

"What they taught" Elizabeth, however, was widely varied as her anxiety over her first night sleeping in the church reveals. Nervous on a number of levels, Elizabeth outlined for me and several of her co-vigilers her range of emotions and her strategies for getting through. Describing her "traditional Catholic upbringing" she reported that sleeping in church or arriving to mass without a head covering would have been considered "disrespectful." Elizabeth had long since abandoned head coverings at mass, but the occupation brought her back to the time when such rules of the parish had been dramatically overturned. Other fears and memories were activated in this process, leading Elizabeth to report that she felt as though she were "violating all the rules [she] was taught as a child." In addition to a command for reverential comportment in church, these violated rules included the implicitly sexual prohibitions of sleeping with "strangers" and the civic duty to obey the law, in this case against trespassing. The idea that overnight vigilers were "sleeping together" was a much repeated joke across the resisting communities. The mock jealousies and real embarrassments that such jibes caused hinted at the exciting and serious sense of defiance that the vigils nurtured.

If stewardship was one legacy, then clearly there were others competing for Elizabeth's loyalty as well. She emphasized, for example, her diligence in maintaining precise liturgical standards in her role as cantor for the occupied church. This basic liturgical scrupulosity, which was widely shared among the vigil communities, had the dual function of systematizing the ongoing ceremonies (thereby avoiding alienating possible vigil members) and displaying to the archdiocese their loyalty and non-confrontational stance in matters of faith.[61] Although it clearly put them at odds with the chancery's interpretation of proper Catholic practice, it was important that the vigilers be able to consider their routines unimpeachable by the standards of the church.

Elizabeth's strategy for getting through her first night conveys this double heritage. As she tossed and turned on the floor, she recalled saying a little prayer:

> 'OK, Lord, we know I'm doing this for the right reason, but I'm a little apprehensive about this. But St. Augustine said 'my heart will not be happy until it rests in you.' And tonight is probably about as close as I'm going to get to that! So please forgive me and help me to sleep.

When she would wake up in the middle of the night, she said, she would ease her mind and bolster her commitment by looking up at the red light near the tabernacle and saying "Lord, you're here, and I'm here, and we're together." Both asking for forgiveness and asserting a special intimacy, Elizabeth captured the necessarily mixed character of the resistance.[62]

Even the public assertions of outspoken critics exemplified this kind of combination. When denouncing the archdiocese, a Council of Parishes leader liked to reference Ezekiel 34, particularly the sections urging prophesy against "Israel's shepherds" who incur the Lord's wrath for their abuse of their flocks: "You have fed off their milk, worn their wool, and slaughtered the fatlings, but the sheep you have not pastured." (Ez 34:3, NAB).[63] It is not difficult to understand the appeal of this passage for the resisters. Ezekiel's author captures the resisters' major complaints about the reconfiguration. The opening clause's references to the shepherd's food and clothing express the resisters' sense that the hierarchy is both exploitative and detached from real life. "They're living in this luxury, with chandeliers and gold and sinking-in carpeting and all this and they don't know what it feels like to be an average person, struggling," as one vigiler put it to me.[64] This common anticlerical barb against opulence gained momentum in Boston under the Cardinal Law administration. Despite the leadership's protests to the contrary, the possible windfall from the reconfiguration reinforced the sense that the chancery and the Vatican were lavish retreats from reality. For the resisters, the slaughtered "fatlings" in the Ezekiel passage represent the parishes targeted and devoured by the archdiocese because of their real estate value or because they were thriving with independent-minded priests.

In making such references, the resisting Catholics asserted their loyalty and special affinity with God, while suggesting that the neglectful middle managers would be left out of the fold, going hungry. Here, the resisters have willingly become sheep again, but now they are sheep under the exclusive management and special providence of the Lord. Like the ideas of the primacy of conscience and stewardship, this strategy aimed to separate the flawed reconfiguration process and the character of church bureaucracy from the essence of the faith. As Peter Borré urged during a Council of Parishes "media day," the resisters might be passionate, but they were not "just say no" people.[65] Resisters repeatedly reported that their problem was not precisely with the church, but with hierarchy's misuse of their power within it. Indeed, they claimed to embody the tradition more than the decision-makers at the top, who displayed un-Catholic hubris in their willingness to close down their important communities. "They've lost any connection they had with God," an East Boston vigiler told me.[66]

Specifically, resisters called upon the idea of Christ's humble ministry and the early church's modest scale as a validation of their own communities in contrast to the official church's apparent distance and blind power. A middle-aged suburban woman captured the feeling across the resisting communities:

> You look and you say, what would Jesus have done? He started a small Christian community. He would have loved this. He wouldn't have loved, I don't think, the idea of the pray, pay, and obey Catholic. He wouldn't have loved the cathedral-type churches. He would have been more comfortable with the people. You know, walking beside them in whatever they're doing. Saying 'Wow, this is good, this is encouraging,' not closing them down.[67]

But because the resistance was caught somewhere between the restorative and the revolutionary, the separation of religion from church could only go so far. Starting an independent American Catholic Church or breaking off into a separate religious entity were appealing fantasies in the darker moments of the struggle, but discussions of these radical steps were essentially nonstarters. Though some resisters imagined changing the church from the ground up, this was not a universal or immediate goal, and there were no obvious means to accomplishing it.

Most saw the church as essentially intractable, with patience, prayer, or the miraculous as their only recourses for change. Annetta joked that it would take a statue starting to walk down the aisle in order to get the attention of the hierarchy.[68] Eliza, who did fervently hope that their resistance could change the church from the bottom up, compared her rosaries of the 1980s—prayed for the fall of communism in Russia—to those she prayed in the vigil for the "revolution" she hoped for in Boston.[69] They did not seek to detach from the church, but rather sought ways to restore the glory of the church in their parishes and meaningful ownership of the church in the congregation.

Eliza offered this vision of the church to the cardinal in a conversation she had with him about the status of St. Jeremiah's. Not wanting to get into the particulars of their disagreement, Eliza summarized the conversation. "Suffice it to say, I said, basically, 'What would Jesus do?'" The power of this invocation of Jesus' spirit was irresistible. The cardinal, Eliza said, "changed his decision and he did what was right." The lesson of this exchange for Eliza was that "the hierarchy gets in the way" and "they misinterpret" Jesus' message. Women in particular, Eliza said, "have always been the teachers of our faith," and the protectors of children and parishes.

Eliza's willingness to name the "grassroots" as the church also played into the parish's momentous division during the months leading up to the shutdown. Eliza narrated the story as a moment of fracture between opposing camps of the parish council. In this narrative, the crucial point in the conversation came when Eliza had rejected one councilman's appeal that the parish should follow its "shepherd," the pastor, into the new parish. "I looked at him straight in the eye and I said, 'I *am* following my shepherd and his name is Jesus.' And that's when our parish split." This split sent some members to the receiving parish and kept some in the parish as an occupying vigil. In framing the divisions at the parish as crystallized in this moment of decision, Eliza's narrative offered a clear picture of the resisters' sense of good and bad Catholicism. Eliza understood that her elimination of the role of the hierarchy threatened to carry her outside of the Catholic Church, and she even admitted that someday she might convert, saying "Who knows?" But she also insisted that "The bottom line is, I'm Catholic. It's who I am." The local essence of the church for Eliza aligned defense of the parish with defense of the faith.

In support of this view, Eliza, who was a lawyer and had trained at a Catholic law school, took the idea of the "universal Church" and read it in terms of the local foundations of church and the principle of subsidiarity. "We are universally related and we are universally united with our belief," Eliza admitted. But she went on to cite the maxim of famous Boston politician Tip O'Neill. "'All politics are local,'" Eliza quoted, applying this insight to the church and its laws:

> They have the hierarchy that comes down and all of that stuff, but the parish is a juridic person. It is like the family, the core of the church, the family is the core of society. So even though there is a universality up here, it all begins at the bottom. And this is the foundation, and when this crumbles, so does everything else come tumbling down. That's what happened as a result of the inequity in Boston.

According to Eliza, the Boston hierarchy had "usurped and twisted" the idea of the universal church in the shutdowns, particularly in their application of canon law.[70] For their part, the representatives of the archdiocese continued to remind Eliza and Arlene that they had been "disobedient" and that reconciling that fact with any adjustments to the closure decree was going to be very difficult.[71]

If the idea of a better future within the church seemed attractive but distant, the hope for recovery of a purer past was similarly forlorn. Even if, as one resister put it, many Catholics had hardly even heard of the archdiocese before the sexual abuse crisis and the reconfiguration, there was no real way to go back to such seemingly free times.[72] Stephanie, a young Charlestown resident who had taken up leadership among resisters at St. Catherine of Siena, asserted that she saw herself as "a member of the church in Charlestown" while "not necessarily buying into the whole archdiocese thing." This hopeful separation shared a wistful quality with the remembrance of a time before the archdiocese's reach extended to the area, especially as she acknowledged that Charlestown's new priest-administrator in charge of managing the local reconfiguration was clearly a "company man." Regaining a lost distance, then, was perhaps more a vain hope than a serious possibility. "Change will come," she affirmed,

> It's going to have to come. If it doesn't come the church is going to die because people aren't going to stand for it anymore. And I think reconfiguration created that, and they had no idea. And now they've created this monster, and there's no going back. People aren't going to turn a blind eye and just be sheep anymore.[73]

Stephanie's statements move in competing directions. Both watching and hoping for change and asserting a liberating distance, she captures precisely the core frustration of Boston's resisting Catholics. Divesting the faith from the church obscured the ambiguity of the resistance.

For the resisters, there were some appealing elements to the Catholic past, but also some that they thought worthy of being kept at a safe distance. They shared the hopes of the Catholic reformers of the twentieth century for a tradition that could be rooted and solid without giving up on innovation and change. It often happened that a single reality or memory was by turns attractive and disconcerting. For some vigilers, the mystery and majesty of the Latin rite played this dual role. The lost presence of nuns and their habits was a similarly complicated transition for others. The notion of the parish as a fortress amid a hostile culture was yet another. Even more fundamentally, however, resisters faced the challenge of positioning themselves in relation to the legacy of sacrifice as it shaped the rules for practicing parish.

On this score resisters faced a challenge in the authoritative narrative of the past embedded in the archdiocese's justification of the shutdowns. Reconfiguration literature pointed to a far distant or even cosmic past as a way of pitting the eternity of church against the fleeting nature of individual churches. This strategy is common, according to anthropologist Michael Herzfeld, who argues that power's "most palpable embodiment in bureaucratic practice consists in yoking the timelessness of the state to the pace and timing of specific interactions."[74] As we saw in the previous chapter, officials also took up more proximate histories in their efforts to shepherd Catholics through the transitions into new parishes. In the hands of those supporting the shutdowns, previous generations—their challenges as immigrants, their willingness to sacrifice for the parish and for their children—were exemplary of the spirit of sacrifice that was again necessary in this new time of trial.

This harkening to ancestors and their sacrifices was a powerful invocation. But resisters' recollections of the sacrifices of the past were not uniformly adulatory. While many among the resisters had a history of personal and family giving to their churches over the years, the sacrifices of the past and their meaning in the present now took on a double character. On one hand, family histories of sacrifice signaled commitment and inspired pride. Among resisters, such feelings did not necessarily encourage further sacrifice, but instead anchored them in the churches for which they and their families had sacrificed as good Catholics. In this case, the sacrifices of the past were a warrant for the current resistance and a validation of their Catholicism. Because it entailed a level of ownership, the idea that the church is the people of God further validated this interpretation of sacrifice.

On the other hand, resisters found the sacrifices of the past embarrassing. Catholics had given too much, too easily, and had failed to ask questions. In this understanding sacrifice entailed more than providing for the upkeep of the church (which was laudable), it extended to Catholics' acquiescence to church authority (which was shameful). It was difficult to extricate the sacrifice of time and money for the parish from the sacrifice of the will, abandonment of the instinct to question, and the embrace of obedience. With the closures, the supposed gullibility and trust of previous generations were coming back to bite their progeny. The sacrifices of the past had laid the groundwork for suffering in the present.

These two sides of sacrifice were further complicated by the tendency to remember the past as it was refracted through family histories. This natural inclination to remember with the help of lived relationships inserted the complications of family life and generational change into the vigilers' orientations to the tradition. The puzzles of intimacy and distance in parent-child engagements added another wrinkle to resisters' thinking about the past as it related to their current vulnerable position in the church. Occupiers' parents were routinely remembered as staunchly obedient *and* as inspirations for dissent. The past looked more complicated when it was viewed as family legacy and not merely institutional or community history.

Catharine hinted at the meanings of sacrifice and its relationship to church authority in a narrative of her upbringing that wove together institutional and family history. Like so many others, Catharine told me that she had been raised with Catholic parents who acquiesced to the church without fail. Perhaps because the sexual abuse crisis was so close to hand, the most popular anecdote in this vein was the narrative of just complaint and misplaced blame. Any child who reported a problem with a religious teacher or church official was immediately presumed by unsympathetic parents to be the actual guilty party. Catharine offered a succinct summary of this common narrative:

> I went to parochial school. If we did anything in school, it was your fault. And when I think about it, there was no balance. It was: 'They were right and you did something.'

Her mother "believed whatever they did was right" and trained Catharine and her siblings growing up in Quincy with the same attitude. These lessons did not fade. Even after Catharine had been married, lost her parents, had her own children and grandchildren, and had become a widow, she thought of herself as continually formed by these teachings. "I was being brought up that way until recently," she told me.

Now, with the reconfiguration, the hierarchy was demanding the same kind of obedience from the laity as that which resisters' thought had started the problems in the first place. But the qualities of the people had changed, the narrative continued, and the vigils were precisely exemplary of their new level of education, organization, and independence. Resisters to Boston's church closures often built stories of personal transformation into their self-description. Occupying a middle space between their deferential parents and their (mostly, presently) indifferent children, the vigilers often described their former selves as blind to or simply alienated from the true possibilities of their tradition. If they used to suffer willingly, now they stood up for themselves.

Perhaps related to this story of personal change, vigilers' parents and grandparents took on another position with a more intimate quality. As individuals within families, the people of the previous generations were often considered the seedbeds of the current dissent. Catharine's reflections on her mother in relation to the church and to herself are typical of this ambivalence.[75] The weight of Catharine's recollections rested on the idea that nothing in her upbringing prepared her for such a moment of opposition and self-assertion. At the same time, she insisted that her mother, if she were alive, would have been "very upset" by the closures.

Since this wasn't precisely an endorsement of the vigil, Catharine gathered evidence from her mother's parenting style to confirm and extend this interpretation. For Catharine’s mother, if the kids “weren’t happy, she wasn’t happy.” In addition to tireless effort, this commitment to happiness required a lenient approach: “She said if you sit a child in a chair and just tell him to sit still, that’s not a kid. As long as they’re not climbing up the curtains, who cares, as long as they’re happy?” This narration of her mothers’ attitude in mundane affairs followed immediately on the heels of a description of Catharine’s daily experience with the occupation. Again this description centered on happiness:

> When I say my prayers, and when Frank [St. Albert’s lay leader of Eucharistic services] says those words and he says those little things that he reads in the morning, it just . . . I just feel so good. When the service is over, he’s made my day; I started my day off right. When I get up in the morning, I get dressed, I get washed, I have breakfast with my daughter, I come here. I look forward to it, because I know I am going to get something when I get here, and when I leave here I’ll feel good. That makes my day. And then when I am finished with here I drop Eleanor off, I get home, I get changed, and I just put the music on, and I start cleaning, and I am as happy as can be. And that makes me happy. I just think being happy is very very important.

The morning service at the occupied church gave Catharine great pleasure and offered an important organizing principle to her day.

But the relentlessness of Catharine’s happiness refrain speaks to the anxieties the vigils produced for many about the place of sacrifice in the tradition. Similar language and speculations at other moments about her mother’s unease with the closure suggest that it is not too much to see Catharine—in the course of our conversation—seeking release from these anxieties by turning to her mother, or at least the traditions of that generation, for approval. It was as if Catharine worried that the resistance was the equivalent of climbing up the curtains; were the occupations straying too far from the reasonable constraints of the past? Had rejecting the sacrifices called for in the shutdowns violated the rules of practicing parish? Perhaps acknowledging the regularity and routine of the rest of Catharine’s day was a way to confirm that the occupation had not derailed her entirely from normal, responsible, and simple living. Catharine’s insistence on the value of happiness aimed to liberate her from a restrictive upbringing without alienating her from the past.

Another approach to the anxiety produced through the rejection of sacrifice was to turn the tables. Instead of affirming Catholics’ right and responsibility to be happy, one could appropriate sacrifice as the defining feature of the resistance. Resisters tried both of these approaches. Annetta was particularly adept in the appropriation of sacrifice for her cause. After a disappointing conversation with the archbishop about ending the occupation, Annetta explained her view of the relationship between suffering and the physical, emotional, spiritual, and financial demands of the vigil:

> I told him we are suffering, and we will keep on going, suffering. . . . That's what the vigil is all about. It's not a vigil. It's actually a suffering by sleeping on the floor, by crying, by saying the prayers, by trying to maintain a church.[76]

It became one of Annetta's most repeated lines. With characteristic bravado, Annetta ventured onto the archbishop's theological terrain and tried to wrest away his most potent term. If they rejected the suffering associated with the sacrifice of parishes for the good of the diocese, they did not cede the terrain of redemptive suffering entirely. This was a powerful turn in part because it undercut critiques of the vigils as sheer selfishness. More fundamentally, the resisters' tendency to identify the vigil with sacrifice while also embracing it as an expression of Catholics' right to follow their conscience speaks to their delicate relationship to the Catholic past.

Again, parents were a crucial testing ground for these combinations. The place of Catholic parents in the memory of resisters animated my conversations with Arlene, Eliza, and Patrick at St. Jeremiah. All three agreed that their parents would be right there alongside the resisters if they were still alive during the shutdowns. Arlene noted that her mother's "way of treating priests and the entire hierarchy" signaled that she valued Arlene's childhood parish (and its Polish ethnicity) over particular leaders. "Growing up, that's what we learned: a priest doesn't make a parish. It's the community, it's the people in the community." Eliza added to this solidarity with the previous generation by elaborating on her parent's deep involvement with her childhood parish. "Our parish was the center of family life, it was the center of everything." Her parents even managed church clubs and "did everything that needed to be done at the church." While Eliza felt sure that her parents would have approved of the resistance, she nonetheless considered their combination of very "devout" Catholicism and a willingness to stand up to church authority to be an unusual aspect of her origins. Though Eliza's parents wouldn't have unthinkingly blamed her for problems with her Catholic school teachers, they nonetheless lived with what Eliza saw as a "funny" mix of rules for parish practice.[77]

Understanding the legacies of these "funny" mixes posed challenges and enlivened the reflections of those in the vigiling communities. Like Eliza's effort to claim her devout parents as progenitors of resistance, Catharine bolstered her defense of the compatibility of Catholicism and personal happiness by embracing a decentralized version of Catholic authority. At the time I got to know her, Catharine was still in mourning for her husband, who had died several years before. She routinely told me of his charms and once asked me if I thought that they would still be husband and wife in heaven.[78] The occasion for this question was a conversation we were having about purgatory, which she described as "very close to heaven." She went on to express her enthusiastic agreement with Father Coyne on the idea that there is no hell. "That isn't the way God works," she explained, "he won't punish us." This led to a reflection on the connections between this world and the next. "I really want my husband to be my husband," she said, while admitting "It sounds crazy." When I said that I didn't know the answer, Catharine told me of the former pastor's reply when she had asked him the same question. Instead of answering, he turned the question around and asked her whether *she* thought they would still be married in heaven: "I said 'Yes, I do.' And he said, 'Well, that's it.'" That gentle and evasive response was refreshing for Catharine, who respected the pastor's willingness to admit that he didn't have all the answers. Catharine also appreciated that Father Coyne did not patronize her by giving her an answer that would just make her feel good.

But this reply also left Catharine free to nurture her longings for reunion with her husband. Under this pastor's care, Catharine did not have to abandon her hopes to a firm orthodoxy or even to a nuanced explanation of how the afterlife might work. When I asked if the pastor had asked a lot of his parishioners, Catharine said no: he wanted people just to "be themselves."[79] Not all former pastors of resisting parishes nurtured this kind of radical version of the people of God ecclesiology and the primacy of conscience. And not all the resisters would have accepted the looseness of Catharine's reflection on the afterlife. But Catharine's willingness to think with Father Coyne about the damning obedience of the past captured a widely held conviction that the rules of sacrifice had changed and that the occupiers, in their resistance, were helping implement that shift.

Conclusions: Belonging in Church

Art, like several of the people I got to know in the resisting communities, had not considered himself a deeply devoted Catholic at the time of St. Jeremiah's shutdown. In fact, when he learned of the suppression of his parish, Art was not even an active member, only returning to the church for occasional special ceremonies, such as weddings, confirmations, or baptisms of his friends' children. He had left the parish indefinitely after discovering that both a longtime acquaintance and that same man's son twenty years later, had been abused by priests in Massachusetts. As we sat in the crying room that had become the vigilers' unofficial office, Art recalled his own vulnerability to a childhood coach, and told me how he watched with deepening empathy as his friend spoke publicly about his family's horrors.

As he learned of the secrecy and neglect typifying the responses of the Cardinal Law administration, Art decided that he "didn't need this anymore." He could no longer attend mass. Art remembered thinking "I can go off and say my prayers to God" and "try to do my own good work." While he said he "wondered" at God's "ways" and puzzled at how priests—whom he called God's "own people," and God's "fingers down here"—could commit these crimes, Art said he "never lost faith in God." Standing apart from the church, however, gave Art a moderate sense of satisfaction, particularly because he was able to withhold his contributions. While he didn't get involved in any active or vocal opposition to the church, the financial "dent" and his absence from the pews stood for Art as what he called his "protest sign."

This stance became untenable for Art, however, once the closure of the parish began to unfold. His outsider position and his assertion of independence changed after the parish ended up on the suppression list. When Art saw the pastor's black flag waving from the flagpole signaling the bad news, he experienced a trace of guilt, wondering if maybe he had been there—if he and others like him had just stuck around—they would not have had to close. Art's sense of guilt shifted as the shutdown process unfolded. Attending the one of the community's two "last masses," he had a moment of clarity:

> I just—I felt really sad that after all these years the place is closing. And I was thinking back to my kids' baptism and leading up to my daughter's wedding, and I just saw all these people. You know I was sad myself, but I saw all these other people who were *really* sad, like they were losing their

> best friends, you know? And it was kind of a light that went off, that it's not really about me, you know me and God, but it's [that] God brought all of us together to be a community, and help each other and work with each other and be friends with each other, and I had walked away from that for the last two or three years.[80]

This experience of a 'light going off' had inspired Art to remarkable commitment in the occupation. Not only did he stay over at the church two nights a week, but he also took on the additional job of janitor, regularly cleaning the church basement and bathrooms. When I returned to St. Jeremiah in 2008, Art was still filling these slots.

The complex braiding of older and newer Catholic versions of authority and sacrifice enacted in the resistance to parish closings suggest a need for closer attention to the relationships among power and belonging in religious worlds. Interpretations along these lines would put broadly political elements (such as overt oppression and intimate domination) in deeper conversation with the elements of generational ambivalence, willful embrace of suffering, and signs of existential comfort or anxiety in religious worlds.[81] Art returned to the church after having left for several years because the resistance offered a new way to belong in the church. It was not only that the church had control over him and his sense of self, but also because he recognized that there was terrain within the occupied church—which was also drawing on tradition to claim to be the church itself—to work out a more satisfying and supportive community life and to remain in touch with important memories. The decision was also informed by a sense of responsibility to the legitimate claims for sacrifice that connected the parish to the church and members of the parish to one another as a distinctive locale of connection on the American landscape. The various orientations toward sacrifice and authority that the resisters tested out in the occupations help illuminate the contours of their belonging. Rather than merely breaking the rules, the occupations involved working within the "more or less confining field of possibilities for expression" in their tradition.[82] This put them in the middle of stresses in the contemporary church about the relationship of continuity to change.

The diverse ways that belonging was contested, expressed, and negotiated by different people in Boston can be seen in their decisions about language and naming, in their occupation of the church buildings, in their reflections on obedience, and in their attitudes toward the previous generation and those who left the community after it was officially closed. These,

I argue, are vivid and readily comprehensible—although complicated—manifestations of belonging and its challenges. The occupations help turn attention in the study of contemporary Catholicism toward the question of what those who stand apart are standing on—toward the "present-life of the past."[83] In the study of contemporary Catholicism, this charge translates into a call for a renewed interrogation of belonging.

5

Openings

In 2008, a woman named Diane responded to an advertisement I had placed in the archdiocesan newspaper seeking stories, photos, and records from people whose parishes had closed.[1] Although Diane did not make a habit of reading the *Pilot*, a friend noticed my ad and suggested she call. Diane had considerable experience with Catholic Boston's dark season. At the time of the Boston shutdowns, she was serving as principal of a Catholic elementary school, St. Andrew the Apostle in Jamaica Plain. The parish connected to the school had closed in 2000, just two years before the world learned that it been one of the parish homes of notorious serial abuser Father John J. Geoghan.[2] Diane entered St. Andrew's school in 1995. She later learned that parents had seen her arrival at the school as a harbinger of a forthcoming shutdown, but Diane was unaware of any such plan. For several years she built up the enrollment of the school. But the numbers started to drop after the parish closed. The receiving parish had its own school, and in this diversifying neighborhood there was no natural feeder of new families.

After the "painful" process of closing the parish, Diane and several parents decided to take the school's fate into their own hands. In 2004, this "core group" made the decision to close up shop on their own, without input from the archdiocese. This way, Diane reasoned, they could give the school a send-off "with the dignity it deserved." Diane remembered talking about enabling parents and children to keep their own dignity as they said a gradual goodbye to the school. The language of mourning promoted in the diocesan closing manual echoed in Diane's experience. The closure was a "grieving process." "It was almost like someone who died": cleaning out the school after the last day was like "cleaning a body" or clearing out the house of a dead relative. As she locked the door for the last time, Diane remembered taking a long look at a large crucifix she had added to the school shortly after her arrival. As the only religious item at the school, the crucifix had become a kind of special emblem for the school's children. They had decided they would leave on the lights illuminating it as they left.

While Diane was going through this controlled but nonetheless "difficult" process, the archdiocese had named her parish of twenty-three years, St. Frances X. Cabrini in Scituate, to the list of those that would close in 2004. Diane responded differently to this latest upheaval. Like some others I got to know in Boston, Diane could not bring herself to attend St. Frances's last mass. If in her professional role she labored to ritually mediate the school shutdown, she sought no such closure at St. Frances. The shutdown was "too painful"; Diane could not fathom participating in "something to mark 'It's over.'"

Despite these powerful feelings, Diane did not join the group of fellow parishioners in the takeover of St. Frances. "It was over," she explained; the thought of joining the vigil simply "never occurred" to her. After reflecting on her complete lack of interest in the occupation, Diane decided that she understood church differently from her friends who were still occupying St. Frances four years later:

> The church is a vessel, there's nothing in it. A vessel is only used to carry things, and I don't mean to use those kinds of metaphors, but that's the closest I can come. It's a shell. It doesn't carry anything in it. I know that the people there believe strongly that it does, but to me it doesn't. There's no priest there, there's no sacraments there.

This was the orientation to churches that reconfiguration officials hoped Catholics would adopt. It is not a building that ties Catholics together, but the valid and licit performance of the sacraments with and by the people of God. Leaving a beloved building might be hard, and people will have diverse ways of expressing their grief. But there's nothing essential in a church. Closure is possible.

Diane rejected more than just the idea of going back to St. Frances. She also could not bring herself to join a new parish. As a "strong Catholic," Diane was at a loss to explain her hesitation. She knew that she did not consider the vigilers' Eucharistic service to be a satisfactory version of

Catholic practice. She knew that they had consecrated hosts, but without a priest and without a full congregation, the rite just didn't have the same meaning. Noting that some of the vigilers had not previously been regular churchgoers, Diane suspected that the idea of a vigil had some peculiar attraction to "people on the fringe of parishes." A true parish was more organic, in Diane's understanding. But a new parish just did not seem right either. Diane had long been involved at a nearby Catholic retreat center, and she soon found herself regularly attending mass in the small chapel there. But this decision did not sit easily with Diane, who from her childhood in Boston had always defined her Catholicism by her parish membership. With its small, self-selected, and always changing congregation, the retreat center resembled the vigiling community in ways that also made her uncomfortable.

When the retreat center mass was cancelled one week, Diane decided this was her opportunity to re-enter parish Catholicism. She decided she would try the mass at the parish in Cohasset, where most of the St. Frances parishioners had arrived after the shutdown. The visit did not last long: "I went in and I started weeping. I mean this was stupid. I couldn't stop. And I left." This sense of religious disorientation stayed with Diane for years. When I spoke with her it had been almost four years since the shutdown and she still hadn't found her way into another parish community. The shutdown had prompted new and fundamental questions. If she had gone to mass and taught CCD (Confraternity of Christian Doctrine) classes in the past "almost without thinking," now her Catholicism became much more a matter of asking "Why am I doing this?" Parish participation and the Sunday obligation both came in for new scrutiny in light of the loss of her parish: "Am I free from going [to Sunday mass] if they take my parish away? And if I am, then I can really not feel guilty about not going, but make a conscious choice that this is what I want to do." Diane knew that losing their parish did not exempt Catholics from their Sunday obligation. But the loss of the parish seemed to loose Diane from the bonds that had been religion for her in the past.

Even for Diane, then, who was too young to remember pre-Vatican II liturgy, and who agreed (at least theoretically) with the teaching promoted in the shutdowns about the fundamental emptiness of church buildings, the loss of a parish rattled the very foundations of her understanding of the tradition. It was not as if Diane was reveling in her newfound ability to question authority. Her tears in the Cohasset receiving parish and her ongoing uncertainty about the retreat center mass suggested a profound struggle and confusion about the idea of Catholicism without St. Frances.

Tracking the Departed

The question of parishioners' destination after the shutdown of their parish remained difficult to answer in the years following 2004. Word of mouth in resisting communities inevitably suggested a large number of former parishioners who had not found a new parish. In 2005, shortly after the vigil began at St. Jeremiah, Arlene told me that a former parishioner made a point of walking in front of the church each evening to "peek" in at the rosary group about to start their prayer. Even when invited she refused to come in, but she continued to walk by every night. Arlene chose to interpret this reticence to rejoin (even after the group had secured a regular mass) as the result of a guilty conscience for not having initially supported the vigil.[3] Both Eliza at St. Jeremiah and Annetta at Our Lady of Mount Carmel had confidence that these now-hidden communities would return should their parishes be restored.[4] In 2005, when I asked the pastor of an East Boston receiving parish if his sacramental numbers had grown after the shutdowns, he let me know that they had, but that it was hard to determine the reason. The original numbers were very fluid, and other parish closures and the departure of an older pastor made it difficult to track the source of new participants.

He did know that resisters at Mount Carmel were not helping matters. They had undermined even greater growth at his parish by creating a discouraging atmosphere in the neighborhood. Just as vigilers felt judged in the presence of those who moved on, non-resisters felt indicted by the community holding on to the church. The pastor said that Mount Carmel occupiers had spread the word that anyone who joined the receiving parish was "a Satan worshipper," with the pastor himself cast as the devil. The neighborhood had become charged with the energy of religious division. When Mount Carmel's non-resisters "set foot outside of their house they're being accosted" with questions about their abandonment of the parish. The pastor thought that this hostile environment helped explain why so many stayed away from the receiving parish. "They don't want to get involved, so they just stay home."[5] In the case of St. Albert the Great in Weymouth, the occupying community was itself so large that the hope for a return of the departed was less urgent. When St. Albert's reopened with a pastor after the independent review board recommended the closing be reversed, some parishioners who had not joined the vigil came back. But the parish did not return to its pre-closure numbers. Resisters blamed the loss of the dynamic Father Coyne for the drop-off.[6] Sacred Heart in the North End had become a chapel, so they still had officially sanctioned masses to keep their original community more or less intact.

Despite Diane's reticence, it seemed likely that closed parishes would get some of their original membership back if they were to reopen. A 2006 *Globe* analysis of the results of a Medford shutdown reported that a receiving pastor counted about 400 of the closing parish's 800 parishioners in the receiving parish. The rest "are no longer affiliated with any parish."[7] An archdiocesan estimate in 2007 put the rate of transfer to a new parish at about 80%, meaning 800 could not be accounted for.[8] One aggrieved parishioner in Medford, who reportedly "felt abandoned by the archdiocese" after the closings, expressed frustration that his parish did not resist. "'At the time, I felt that the archdiocese was going to do the right thing and help people,' he said. 'Now, I think I made a mistake.'" This lament about naive obedience echoed in the report of the board assigned to review the financial aspects of the shutdown. This was the meaning of their complaint that parishes who had not opposed the shutdown by making a valid canon law appeal were officially excluded from getting their improperly seized assets back from the archdiocese.[9] In an atmosphere of continuing uncertainty about the future of Catholic locales, the benefits of obedience were far from certain.

Knowing of these uncertainties among the departed, resisters circulated stories like Diane's in their communities. They hoped that people like her were out there, quietly watching their efforts and secretly hoping for their success. If they themselves could not occupy a church, maybe they would come back if the vigil proved successful and the church was reopened. In some cases this hope may have been a fantasy. Diane expressed her conviction that she would never be able to go back to St. Frances, even if it were reopened. The vigiling community "owned" the parish now, and since they hadn't asked permission from Diane or anyone else to take over, she felt they weren't fighting for her, but for themselves. But Diane's religious disorientation after the shutdown made the lines between resisters and those who "moved on" seem less indelible.

Freedom, Authority, and Modern Catholics

On the face of it, the resistance to parish shutdowns established a clear dividing line for Catholic conversations about church authority: parishioners at closing parishes would either attend the welcoming parish or join a rebellion against that directive. The shutdowns were indeed a fundamental testing ground for the legitimacy of the church's calls for sacrifice from its members. But behind the scenes, as in the retelling and reception of Louisa's bank-line encounter and in Diane's questions about religious life after St. Frances, questions of church authority or power relations among parishioners and chancery officials gave way to more fundamental puzzles about what it meant to belong in the church.

Questions of who had say over church buildings or parish finances were only one piece of this puzzle. The resistance unearthed questions about the meanings of local traditions, the power of particular places on the landscape, the durability of relationships, and about the pace, sustainability, and temper of modern life. These questions make up the contours of Catholic belonging as much or more than the questions of power struggle that so often dominate Catholic scholarly and popular writing. Understanding contemporary Catholicism requires a willingness to push beyond the narrative that links a normatively modern Catholicism with struggles over the place and significance of the "voice of the faithful." In other words, power struggles in the contemporary U.S. church, of which the resistance to parish shutdowns is one of many, should be assessed for more than their commentary on the rise or fall of church "democratization."

Another way to make this point is to suggest, with anthropologist Lila Abu-Lughod, that instances of resistance should be interpreted by scholars not only for what they say about human freedom or agency, but also for what they suggest about the reach and meaning of authority in a particular context. Evidence of resistance in lived worlds can be used "strategically" by scholars to learn more about various "forms of power and how people are caught up in them." Taking Michel Foucault's famous dictum and inverting it, Abu-Lughod suggests a new formula as a way of explaining this tactic: instead of "where there is power there is resistance" Abu-Lughod suggests that "where there is resistance there is power." The shift enacted here reorients scholars away from exclusive attention to the action of resisters in the interstices and toward analysis of the new or alternative structures of power into which resisters locate themselves *in the act of* resistance.[10] In other words, resistance is not exclusively a sign of the fracturing of power and the triumph of "agents," but is also an opportunity to better understand the inflections and reach of power. Abu-Lughod's analysis of resistance as "diagnostic of power" directly critiques the tendency among scholars to celebrate resistance among those they study. The resistance in Boston—with its long hours and persistent demands for justification, 'catches Catholics up'—as Abu-Lughod might say—into different realms of belonging.

More recently, Saba Mahmood extended this analysis in ways that are very helpful for the study of contemporary American Catholicism. Her study of pietist Muslim women in Egypt prompted Mahmood to reflect on the limits inscribed by the norm of "freedom" that sits behind most feminist and liberal scholarship. This ideal of freedom means that these projects are not just analytical, but also "politically prescriptive." Despite Abu-Lughod's desire to avoid the romance of resistance, Mahmood argues, her broad and eager use of the category "resistance" too readily situates actors on a teleological path toward progressive politics. Too much scholarship is "encumbered by the binary terms of resistance and subordination," within which the practices and desires of those studied are forced to fit within one or the other of these categories of action. The problem is that much of what humans do in the world, and especially perhaps in religious worlds, does not map readily onto this grid. These realities suggest the need to decouple the notion of agency from progressive politics. Agency, Mahmood argues, "is entailed not only in those acts that resist norms, but also in the multiple ways one *inhabits* norms."[11]

In its own ways the study of U.S. Catholic history has taken up this kind of critique. Representative projects have sought to understand the actions of Catholics in light of their desires to create viable communities and live ethical and good lives. Instead of seeing American Catholics' agency as either subsumed under the weight of church authority or flourishing in realms beyond that authority, scholars have noted the variety of ways Catholics have inhabited the norms of the church in their pursuit of stability, meaning, and belonging. Thus John T. McGreevy can write of the puzzle of reputedly "lax" Italian Catholics hurling projectiles at Protestant missionaries who entered their neighborhoods in the 1920s and 1930s. This kind of attack witnessed neither submission to nor resistance of church authority. Instead it carried out a particular and locally meaningful way of living within Catholic norms. A similar sensitivity allows Robert A. Orsi to write of figures like St. Jude as "cultural double agents," whose volatile character offers Catholic women the chance to work on the world and on themselves "in an oscillating dialectic between 'fantasy' and 'reality,' self and other, objective and subjective, past and present, submission and resistance." In their prayers to St. Jude the women whose stories Orsi relays inhabit Catholic and gender norms; they do not move decisively toward or away from "freedom." James T. Fisher's study of Irish Catholics' internal struggles over the character of dock work in the ports of New York and New Jersey offers sobering insight into the powerful Catholic "code of silence" that repeatedly undermined mid-century reform efforts. In a book about ecologically attuned Catholic sisters, Sarah McFarland Taylor writes of the sisters' work creating "new ways to reinhabit their community lands." In the process, she notes, the "sisters are also creating more sustainable ways to 'reinhabit' the spiritual landscapes of Catholic tradition and vowed religious life."[12]

Despite these counterexamples, the study of American Catholicism suffers from a tendency to write American Catholic history as a long but steady journey toward "freedom." Factors of "modernization" such as the rise of "conscience" as the source of authority in personal decision-making, the shedding of old attachments to special places and neighborhoods, and the enhanced role of lay Catholics in the management of everyday church affairs give off an overpowering glare. Within this frame of reference, historical developments and contemporary events are assessed as the inevitable stories of the maturation of the church. There are good reasons for attending to changing sources of authority in Catholics' moral worlds. The rise of individual "conscience" in decisions to use birth control and the rejection among Catholic sisters of male church leaders' calls for obedience are perhaps the clearest examples of an embrace of "freedom" among Catholics.[13] And as we have seen, resisters in Boston drew on the church's embrace of individual conscience to justify their occupations. But American Catholics' troubled conversations about issues of sex, sexuality, and gender threaten to prevent scholarly appreciation of Catholics' other concerns.

Likewise, it is reasonable also to expect that the church's future will be guided by increasingly assertive lay leadership. Along with other organizations, Voice of the Faithful, which began in the wake of the sexual abuse crises of the early 2000s, has made a forceful push toward church democratization and transparency. But this organization's prominence in Boston (despite recent decreases in membership) has made difficult any interpretation of parish closures that does not see the resistance to shutdowns as something different from another chapter in the struggle for Catholic freedom from constraint.

This limitation comes to light in a representative article about the Boston shutdowns from the *Washington Post.* The article quotes Jim Post, then president of Voice of the Faithful, summarizing the situation by suggesting that Catholics have "learned to say 'No' to bishops here in Boston." It goes on to cite Catholic historian James O'Toole. His suggestion that the struggle in the Boston church is about "the collapse of institutional authority" seems essentially to reiterate Post's point. But certainly O'Toole would appreciate the ways the resistance to the shutdowns likewise underscores Boston Catholics' renewed *longing* for certain kinds of authority, and not just their own. Such are the perils, perhaps, of lending scholarly authority to short-form media outlets. While the article—to its credit—acknowledges some vigilers' traditionalism (in refusing to hire married priests, for example), it does not explore the links between tradition and authority that would complicate Post's description of the vigils as an "ecclesiastical Boston Tea Party."[14] The rise, among scholars, clerics, and laypeople alike, of the label "Vatican II Catholic" further clouds understanding of the ways that Catholics, especially (but not only) those who grew up before the Second Vatican Council's efforts to update the church, interact in a variety of complicated ways with modernization.[15]

Timothy Kelly's thorough study of Pittsburg Catholicism from 1950–1972 is a more drawn-out analysis of lay Catholics' thirst for religious democratization and freedom. Kelly amplifies a recent tendency in American Catholic studies to de-center the 1960s and the Second Vatican Council in the story of twentieth-century Catholic change.[16] He argues that by the 1950s Catholics in Pittsburgh had already begun to move away, against their bishops' hopes and expectations, from anti-modern practices. He shows declines in devotionalism, endogamy, and fixation on sin. Catholic women moved assertively into the public sphere. In light of advances in science, Catholics gradually abandoned their need for and confidence in miracles. The decreasing popularity of processions and massive public gatherings suggested the waning of the era of triumphant Catholic separatism. Social justice began to replace devotionalism as Catholics' top religious priority. Driven by increased economic mobility, Catholics' access to suburban homes helped satisfy their need for a "culture less unnerving and condemnatory."[17] Lay Catholics no longer looked exclusively to the church for guidance amid the threats of "materialism," which included commercialism, unbridled capitalism, communism, and indecency. In some ways these declines were a product of initial successes. All of these factors plus the church's inability to provide enough priests and sisters to work in Catholic schools added to the trend away from Catholic isolation.

Kelly wants us to see that lay Catholics were ahead of their bishops when it came to change. "[C]ontemporary Catholics did not perceive the Council's changes to be so much a shock to the unchanging Church that they had inherited from their parents, but rather as official recognition of the currents of change already underway." Lay Catholics not only knew what was coming, they actually paved the way for its implementation. But the swell behind this moment of transformation soon dissipated. Momentum from these changes joined economic and other social factors to distance Catholics from engagement with the church. In general, the gains of the long era of reform were quickly given away, and a more conservative hierarchy began to reign in church democratization. Lay Pittsburg Catholics were still more likely than their bishops to embrace church democratization, but they were not assertive enough or sufficiently involved to push this agenda forward in the 1970s and 1980s. In this reading, the sexual abuse crisis and intensifying priest shortages of the early twenty-first century awakened a sleeping giant. For Kelly, lay leadership toward reform in the 1950s provides a model for the newly attentive Catholics of the contemporary period.[18]

Kelly's approach establishes a useful but troubling binary. In rejecting interpretations which identified the reforms of the 1960s as a "shock," Kelly offers another extreme. Reforms not only weren't a shock for the laity, they were overdue official adaptations to ways of being religious they had already embraced. The approach allows Kelly to highlight the limits of top-down approaches to Catholic change. It also provides him and his readers a useful past by confirming that contemporary Catholics' moves toward democratization are not novel, but have ancestral roots.[19] Kelly does show parishes fighting and even dividing over reforms in the 1960s and 1970s. Some parishes and their pastors did everything they could to hold off change. Those rejecting the reforms may not have been shocked by them. Regardless, they were a minority, and Kelly sees them fading from view (outside of the ranks of the hierarchy) in the late twentieth and early twenty-first century.

But the large majority of parishes did not divide over the implementation of Second Vatican Council reforms of liturgy and church management. Kelly's sense that people were more than ready for change offers one explanation. The stories emerging from the parish shutdowns in Boston, occurring as they do at some distance from the time of the implementation of the changes, offer another possibility. The Catholics I got to know in Boston had a much more complicated relationship to the modern. The resistance highlighted the vexed points of contact between past and present that have shaped the U.S. church since the mid-twentieth century. Dilemmas about the relationship between Catholics' past and present were built into the tradition that Catholics encountered in the late twentieth century.

Catholics found ways to begin to answer these dilemmas precisely in the plurality of rules they had encountered for "practicing parish" over the years. For them, changes in the church with respect to ecclesiology, sacred presence, and sacrifice were additive rather than comprehensive. Catholics took up ways of thinking about parish practice that developed after the Second Vatican Council and added them to rules they had been taught or that had lingered on in parish life from before the Council. These combinations (by turns strategic and unwitting) of sometimes competing orientations to tradition determined resisting Catholics' stance on the shutdowns.

This analysis does not undermine the story of lay Catholic preparedness for change in the 1950s and 1960s.[20] But it does suggest that the narrative of American Catholic "modernization" may benefit from a willingness to bracket expectations (and hopes) of an innate lay Catholic desire for freedom. There are precedents in other fields as well for the kind of shift I am calling for here. Historians of sixteenth-century European religion have begun to undermine the constraints imposed on their work by terms like "Reform," and "Counter-Reform." Challenges to "declension" as the story of Puritanism in America have opened up new ways to see the variety and vitality of Protestant piety amid change. And historians of religion in the nineteenth and twentieth centuries continue to make efforts to escape from under the weight of "secularization."[21] The dominance of these terms has simply made it too difficult to understand or even see manifestations of religious life outside of their foreordained outcomes. Noting this difficulty, historians have set out to unseat these terms, to launch new investigations of the past without the glare of prevailing storylines. They have not rejected dominant narratives altogether. Simply opening a space for alternate stories has enabled a much richer understanding of the past.

Resistance to parish shutdowns suggests that the study of American Catholicism is ready for a similar shift. Kelly himself provides data that supports an alternate reading of the meanings of the changes of the Catholic 1960s and 1970s. In the process of demonstrating declines in Catholic devotionalism and lay preparedness for the adjustments that resulted from the Second Vatican Council, Kelly cites a 1970 survey of participants at a

Catholic retreat center. Among respondents were two groups: retreat participants and a set of lay "leaders" not necessarily associated with the retreat center. The survey, which the retreat center hoped would help explain the recent halving of their participants, asked respondents to state what kind of retreat they preferred and what kinds of devotions they would like to participate in while on retreat. Kelly is primarily interested in the latter question about devotions. As he summarizes: "The results suggest strongly that the retreatants remained far more interested in devotions generally than did the lay leaders." Since the number of retreatants was shrinking, the data confirms a wider point: Pittsburgh's Catholics were losing their attachment not just to retreats, but to devotional practices more generally. "Even when active lay Catholics were interested in retreats, they did not wish to participate in devotional rituals."

But there is another story buried in the 1970 data Kelly provides. Among those who responded to the question about what kind of retreat they would like, lay leaders and retreatants clustered most heavily around the same answer: they both preferred a retreat that was a blend of "new & old." Instead of noting this common search for some kind of combination of old and new forms of Catholic practice, Kelly highlights the areas of difference between leaders and retreatants. Relatively few leaders agreed that they would prefer a "traditional" retreat, and a correspondingly low number of retreatants wanted a "modern" retreat. In other words, only a fading remnant of the church clung to American Catholics' recent past. But the common, if inchoate aspiration of leaders and retreatants for a "blend" of old and new may have been the more interesting and telling set of answers.[22] Alertness to this zone of overlap may help explain the fall-off Kelly notes from the 1970s through the 1990s in lay energy and enthusiasm around initial reform impulses. The aspiration for continuity amid change remained a puzzle to be solved. Parish shutdowns brought this puzzle to the surface.

But this challenge, which is about the way the past lives in the present, is not only relevant for post–Second Vatican Council U.S. Catholicism. The church has long been an institution that "can and cannot change." John T. Noonan illustrates the ongoing dilemma of reconciling the church's "deposit of faith" with changing moral contexts through an evaluation of Catholic "development" across centuries in moral teachings on slavery, usury, religious freedom, and divorce.[23] In a more sociological and contemporary register, historian John T. McGreevy has suggested that the key contemporary challenge for the church is "to distinguish permanent truths from contingent applications."[24] Boston's parish shutdowns enabled investigation of this Catholic challenge as it was felt in relation to sacred places and in communities. This pressure had been felt before. French Catholics during the years of the revolution barged through closed church doors and even led masses in the absence of a priest. As in Boston in 2004, it was women who were most likely to be leaders and participants in these efforts to reclaim local Catholicism in the face of ecclesial and national struggles in France. These lay Catholics, who essentially rejected priest shortage as an end to local tradition, fell on both sides of the debates about church and state then roiling the French nation.[25]

Like French peasants sympathetic to the revolution barging through church doors and calling for the return of their priests, parish shutdowns call out for an augmentation of what we can say about Catholics' "braided" modern history. In this understanding of Catholic change, twentieth-century U.S. Catholics did not move easily along a prescriptive "modern" religious path. U.S. Catholic encounters with modernity were fitful, ambiguous, and complex.[26] This way of talking about Catholic modernity parallels developments in other fields of American religious history. Historian Leigh Schmidt has described the complicated exchanges that determined the relationship between pre- and post-Enlightenment attitudes toward the sense of hearing and religious presence. Instead of describing religion as suffocated by and absent from Enlightenment critique and practice, Schmidt explains that there were actually ongoing exchanges between secular and religious ways of inquiring, experiencing, and knowing. These exchanges were reciprocal and complex, with questions and ambitions moving back and forth, all the while accruing new complications or adjustments related to the needs of a given community or individual. Divides between secular and religious, popular and elite, pre-modern, modern and postmodern were crisscrossed by a continual flow of "gifts"—questions as well as modes of inquiry, performance, or display—and were therefore less firm than their defenders (and historians) sometimes liked to claim.[27]

A similar tangled reality shaped the struggle over church closings in Boston. The exchanges between Catholics and their pasts resembled the "half-planned poachings, mediations, and transmutations" of Schmidt's eighteenth-century scientists, magicians, and religious practitioners.[28] The struggles in Boston were not a matter of modernists versus anti-modernists in the church; both resisters and those supporting the shutdowns, and individuals within these groups, cobbled together satisfying, strategic, and sometimes conflicting ways of practicing sacrifice and presence. Combinations and contradictions that might have been casual or overlooked in times of relative calm posed challenges when Catholics had to put themselves on one side or other of the plan to shutdown churches. Explanations that rely on a straightforward division in post–Second Vatican Council U.S. Catholicism along the lines of "restorationists" and "progressives" will always tend to miss the more interesting stories of combination and ongoing play in individuals and communities among competing ways of being Catholic and being a Catholic in the contemporary United States.

In the case of the parish shutdowns, resisting Catholics had an ambivalent relationship to the prescriptively modern religious trajectory that has been established for them: they not only slipped out of its bounds in their defense of their parishes, but they also found ways to accuse others (the architects of the shutdowns, those who obeyed the closure plan) of falling short of an authentic modern Catholic paradigm. More than just being caught up in it, they embraced a modern paradigm and announced this with authority and eagerness to those who would listen, but this was a different modern than that offered by the archdiocese in its effort to explain the shutdowns. It was difficult sometimes to pull apart the intertwined threads making up resisters' Catholicism. But if you listened carefully, you could hear the message in comments like those of Mount Carmel's communion service leader Ronald: after explaining the need for the church to "update" by acting more like a democracy and by allowing priests to marry, he noted that these complaints had "nothing to do" with the vigil at Mount Carmel.[29] The same braided modern sensibility rests behind Eliza's admission that while the community's opening of a preaching role for women warmed her heart, such subversions of Catholic rules were "not why we got into this."[30]

Occupiers' embrace of "the modern," then, does not tell the whole story. Evaluations that said the occupiers were simply attached to their parishes suggested as much. This suggestion, which sat behind the idea that good Catholics should move on as instructed, had several implications, but one of the most potent was to link resisters to an embarrassing pre–World War II Catholic past, when immigrant Catholics were supposed to have clung desperately to their neighborhood "enclave" churches instead of integrating themselves confidently into broader U.S. social, political, and cultural arenas. If attachment was understandable, it was also a disordered remnant from this bygone era: modern Catholics, the archdiocese implied, are not attached to objects and locales. In identifying the historical sources for Catholics' resistance to parish closures (even if only to ridicule them) this critique contained some truth, but in its extreme form, the evaluation not only mangled the Catholic past, but also flattened the resisters' relationship to that past and their connection to their churches. While they wanted to (and did) claim to be modern Catholics, the occupiers also witnessed to the abiding power and attraction of older ways of "practicing parish." This was as true in Boston's suburbs as it was in its urban places. By doing so, ironically, they became more modern than the modernizers.

The Architectonic of Occupied Churches

Exploration of a Boston Catholic "architectonic" opens one possibility for progressing in the direction of a more supple and subtle understanding of American Catholic modernity. Anthropologist James W. Fernandez uses this term to describe both the organization of space as it orients people to their histories and knowledge and the feeling a space has "by virtue of the enlivening activity that takes place within it." In short, architectonic means "the feelings and meanings that a given space may evoke." According to Fernandez, description of the activity that takes place in architectural spaces enables understanding of the architectonic.

Focusing on an "unsettled" Fang community in contemporary Gabon, Fernandez describes the community's effort to build and occupy a new chapel as an "architectonic response to the various dissolutions, decenterings, and dampenings" of the spatial and social order of Fang life. As part of Bwiti, a Fang revitalization religion, the chapel offers people a respite from the pressures of secularization and the "glare" of the colonial world, a place for connection to their ancestors, and a reaffirmation of cosmic order and origins. In their ritual movements in and through the place, the Fang can "redistribute in a kinesthetic form modes of being which have gone awry." It is a "breathing space" for the "religious imagination in touch with its roots." The chapel does not orient the Fang solely toward their pasts. The place embodies a "syncretism" in its openings to activity related to the disparate temporal and spatial realities of Fang tradition, evangelical Christianity, and "mercantilism." Especially in this last set of practices, the chapel "partakes of the modernity toward which so many Fang desire to move." Fernandez sees the openings to modernity as "compensating," by which he means they are relatively superficial counterbalances to the more fundamental orientation of the place toward the production of meaning over value.[31]

The work of occupying Boston's churches gave the places a distinct architectonic. As occupied places, the churches had to be remade—they were invested with new meanings and feelings related to the struggle for reopening. The physical presence of "bodies" in the churches—which even after four years vigilers could never be sure was totally unnecessary—gave the places a whole different set of meanings than the ones that had been planned for them. The bodies immediately subverted the attempt to place the buildings into the logic of the real-estate marketplace. Approaching the status of a commodity, they became instead citadels against the commercialization of the landscape. It was of course their potential power as commodities, which occupiers often highlighted by speculating about the value of certain parts of the physical plant, which made this subversion meaningful. Occupiers' willingness to sell off parts of the church property (other than the church itself) aimed to convince observers of their reasonableness. They were ready to partake of modernity, but they wanted say in how that should be accomplished. Vigiling bodies also transformed older meanings and feelings associated with the places. Just setting foot in the places as an occupier initiated the transformation. No longer sites of the official church, these places were remade into sites of struggle as a good in itself. This is why occupiers could so often refer to their effort as a work of justice. Again, it was churches' potential to once more become a part of the official church which made the work of justice meaningful.

There were other architectonic remakings of occupied churches as well. Vigilers' eyes, unaccustomed perhaps to undistracted survey of the buildings, fixed upon items in the church they had never seen or appreciated before. Murals, plaques, statues, windows and other objects were reinscribed with meaning in light of the occupation. These objects, originating in the distant or recent past, tied occupiers to history in ways that had not been possible before. Sore arms and backs carried meanings too. Body aches from scrubbing layers of dirt from church floors or maneuvering heavy statues from one place to another reminded vigilers of their new positioning as caretakers of a valuable past.

In the atmosphere of contest and doubt under which the vigils operated, the architectonic of occupied churches was fragile. When a vigiler at Mount Carmel dropped a heavy antique statue of Saint Gerardo, the individual and the community faced the risk of a profound disorientation. Vigilers observed closely Sam's painstaking reconstruction of the statue from the dozens of fractured pieces, just as they reached out to ease the self-recrimination of the one who had dropped the saint. When a plainclothes police detective made his presence known during the vigilers' conspicuous lingering after St. Jeremiah's last mass, the excitement of the illicit rippled among the community and inaugurated the occupation as a work of justice. Later, when a member of the receiving parish barged into the occupied St. Jeremiah's to size up the altar for transport to another locale, a profound unease gripped the stunned observers.[32] Vigilers' success in turning away these fractures of the architectonic of their occupied churches only added to the places' meaning and power in their lives.

But the architectonic of Boston's occupied churches consisted of more than the simple affirmation of the occupation. As Fernandez suggests, architectonics imply a "multiplicity of meaning." Like any cultural form, occupied churches were "a reservoir of many potential modes of being and ways of valuing." The various meanings and feelings evoked in the occupied churches were "not necessarily consistent or compatible with each other." But holding on to the churches sustained the possibility of holding these various realities together in the pursuit of "some coherence."[33]

Among the many activities at the occupied churches, three stand out as exemplary of the multiplicity of meanings alongside the pursuit of coherence in troubled Catholic Boston. The first is the continuous flow of consecrated hosts into the church and its tabernacle, and from there into occupiers' bodies. This activity, common to all the occupied churches, contained a variety of meanings. The hosts provided the perfect opportunity for occupiers to be simultaneously inside and outside the tradition. This made them absolutely crucial to the effort. When occupiers at St. Jeremiah learned that the consecrated hosts had been taken out of the tabernacle by an unfriendly visiting parishioner, Eliza described it as a "knife through our hearts."[34] The consecrated hosts were this powerful because they carried both the weight of resisters' claims against the church and their desire for reunification with it. Forced to sneak the body of Christ into their communities, vigilers could see, touch, and taste in the hosts an indictment of a church that would undermine Catholics' access to this unifying sacramental heart of the tradition.

Distributed by lay Eucharistic ministers who put themselves in direct competition with priests' simultaneous actions at other nearby parishes, the hosts provided an opportunity for resisters to affirm their commitment to the democratization of the church: lay people have as much right to distribute the host as an archdiocese-sanctioned priest. But of course lay people were not consecrating these hosts themselves. The activity of bringing the hosts into the churches, then, served as a metonymic action. In most cases barred from actually hosting a priest, the communities imported priests into the church in the form of the act of consecration that everyone agreed they alone could perform on the wafers. In at least this matter, the resisters wholly embraced the kind of thinking about "essential" differences between lay and clerical Catholics promoted in the second and third chapters of the Second Vatican Council's constitution on the church. The "sacred power" reserved to priests held sway in the occupied churches. The hosts acted in two registers. They were both a statement of lay empowerment and an endorsement of the kinds of power the church reserved to its elite members. Given the vigilers' pursuit of reunification with the church, the latter affirmation conveys the underlying coherence sought through and in the occupations.

Vigilers' sleeping bodies pointed in more than one direction as well. A necessary part of starting an occupation, sleeping in church did not necessarily continue across the communities' four years and running of vigil. But sleeping in church remained a polyvalent emblem of the architectonic resisters sought to create in these remade church buildings. Borderline sacrilege and certain breach of decorum in a normal church, sleeping in an occupied church worked on practical and theological levels to remake churches as sites of particular meanings and feelings. Practically speaking, sleeping in church simply prevented the archdiocese from retaking the building unopposed. Having Catholic bodies cozily tucked into pews or on the floor beneath the baptismal font promised at least to provide the occupiers—in case of hostile takeover—with the benefit of news coverage of vigilers ripped from sleeping bags and shoved into police cruisers. The violation of the old rules of comportment offered another set of meanings. It affirmed Catholics' freedom from the rules of a more staid and formal tradition. This was the meaning behind the playful aspects of this practice, including jokes about the sexual encounters vigilers would have at night and the jockeying for position close to a particular statue, image, or window.

But sleeping in church pointed primarily toward the revitalization of forgotten and discarded tradition. The practice gave weight to the idea that occupiers had really embarked not on a protest, but on what they sometimes called a "perpetual" or a "prayerful" vigil. This language pointed Catholics toward the traditional practice of "perpetual adoration." In this devotion, which flourished in U.S. parishes in the early and mid-twentieth century, Catholics (usually men, who ostensibly could be alone in church without fear) would take shifts sitting before a consecrated host reserved and displayed in a monstrance for this purpose.[35] Sleeping in church remade churches as the sites of a blend of old and new. If this combination was more contradictory than seamless, it is nonetheless indicative of Catholic uneasiness with the modernizing telos of increasing freedom, liberation from authority, Americanization, and gradual release from the power of presence.

The recitation of the rosary, which was a new and common practice among all the vigiling communities, reshaped the churches in a similar way. Vigilers understood the restoration of this declining practice as a mark of the divine sanction upon their efforts. Vigilers asserted control over the tradition by transforming the buildings to better accommodate their own sense of the meaning and power of the rosary. The tumbled Madonna at Mount Carmel received those prayers from her new central position on the altar. The vigilers at St. Jeremiah in Framingham made sure to position their own Madonna within the line of vision of the evening rosary group. Noting that a certain bishop had expressed admiration for the community's rosary recitation, St. Jeremiah's Arlene claimed the Blessed Mother as a guardian of the church and the vigilers: "Us and the Blessed Virgin versus the Archbishop, I'll take those odds."[36] At St. Albert's in Weymouth, occupiers initiated a different architectonic in their reorganization of space. They had rosary recitation as well, but there the prayerful could look up to see, propped up on his former altar chair, a large picture of their pastor, Father Coyne. A note accompanying the photo read "Fr. Coyne's chair is empty, but his spirit is still with us." At another spot on the altar, alongside a basket for petitions to be included in the liturgy, resisters had placed another receptacle for "letters for Fr. Coyne." The church had been remade to honor and continue the relationship among parishioners and their beloved pastor.

The vigils offered Catholics a certain freedom to organize their churches and, in the process to remake the meanings and feeling of their Catholicism; they chose to use that freedom to find new and deeper ways live inside the tradition. While certainly in part a pursuit of "freedom" from hierarchical decision-making, the resistance to parish closures was much more than this. To return to Mahmood's terms, the occupations remind us that "agency" is entailed not just in the rejection of norms, but in the ways that Catholics—in the act of occupying a church—inhabit Catholic norms. The vigilers' resistance to parish closures brought the contours of modern Catholic belonging into relief. Their opposition to the closures and their remarkable takeover of their religious lives prompted them to explore what it means to be a part of the church today.

I have in part answered the question of how to understand those occupying their churches by frequently referring to them not just as "vigilers," or "friends" or "survivors" of a particular parish (as they also called themselves), but also as "resisters." Analysis of resistance in this situation is unavoidable given the direct opposition these Catholics posed to the plan to close their parishes. By putting what they sometimes referred to as "bodies" in closed churches, they added resistance to the ambitious plan for progress through parish shutdowns. But the Catholics in closed churches were not just brakes adding friction to "the system;" they offered a theology of parish in their occupations. But they were not simply agents of change, as their responsibilities to orthodoxy showed. Neither agency nor rebellion precisely describes their stance. Resistance, Boston's Catholics showed, is more than a sign of human freedom or a diagnostic of power: it can also be a test or experiment with belonging.

Appreciating the connections between resistance and belonging in Boston enhances what we can say about Catholics' braided modernity. One can "belong to" or "belong in (or with)" a place or tradition. These opposing aspects of belonging suggest different modes of being in the world. The first, "belonging to," has connotations of objectification, subjection, and submission. The other, "belonging in," speaks to a condition of comfort, mutual respect, and a modicum of control. Catholics' protection of their parishes brought both of these aspects of belonging into relief. Sometimes despite themselves, Catholics belonged both "to" and "in" the church and their churches. Ongoing encounters with changing notions of sacrifice and presence were the means through which resisters forged their modes of being Catholic. In this way the closures were an opening, not only for those who resisted, but also for people like Diane, who became disoriented upon losing her church, and for those who defended the shutdowns. Everyone involved, if they were to make sense of the upheaval, had to venture onto the precarious terrain of the recent past.

The idea of an architectonic implies not only the organization of space, but also the feeling of a space brought about through the "enlivening" activity of people moving inside and around it. It is not only people who come alive, but also the places through the people's action. As Michel de Certeau writes, "haunted places are the only ones people can live in."[37] This suggests a dialectic of liveliness: people and place gain life in an ongoing and reciprocal exchange. As the place comes to life in the religious imagination, the people too experience their own revitalization, which is itself a call to further imagining.[38] Caring for churches in contemporary Boston called upon Catholics to offer some positive response to the lives—of the church, its saints and ancestral benefactors, those who suffered secretly and rejoiced publicly in its shadow, the neighborhood—they had in their hands through their histories and their choices. Occupations were not so much a denial of the reality of loss and death as they were an attempt—inside the radiating power of parish and church—to remake reality as something livable and humane.

Epilogue

In 2004, Carla, Sacred Heart's former business manager, left behind the drama surrounding the proposed shutdown of her North End parish only to enter into a new and even more pressing round of tragedies. "I had a lot of things happen," she told me in 2009. "My mom had a major heart attack, my father died from lung cancer, my sister's husband, [aged] thirty-four, was killed in a car crash . . . then I had breast cancer. So who cares about the stupid church!" After the discovery of the San Marco Society deed helped subvert the plan to shut down Sacred Heart, the parish became a chapel. A newly appointed pastor and an assistant at nearby St. Leonard's—now the only full-fledged parish in the North End—offered masses, oversaw operations, and managed the finances of Sacred Heart. The chapel had four weekly masses, including a nine o'clock mass on Sundays, which was offered in a mix of Italian and English. The parish of Sacred Heart, which officially no longer existed, still had a formal canon law appeal making its dubious and costly path through the Vatican judicial system. The appeal argued that the shutdown of Sacred Heart as a parish was unjust. When the appeal process began, parishioners hoped it would result in the restoration of Sacred Heart as a full parish. Denied at the level of the Congregation for the Clergy, Sacred Heart's petitioners spent another $16,000 to have their Vatican lawyer take the case before the Supreme Tribunal of the Apostolic Signatura, the highest juridical office at the Vatican.[1]

But by 2009, Carla didn't care anymore about the appeal. While in earlier years even seeing the document had made her "nauseous," now it sat innocuous and untouched in a cabinet in her new office. Carla remained business manager of St. John School, which was now overseen by St. Leonard's instead of Sacred Heart. She had secured her sister-in-law the job of business manager of the new parish. Carla was showing her the ropes, instructing her in the art and science of completing parish financial books according to archdiocesan standards. St. John's enrollment was up, and a recent economic downturn had spared the school from an expensive plan to consolidate it with others in the region.

Amid this work, and still feeling the effects of her chemotherapy, Carla's "passionately angry" response to the archdiocese's approach during the closure process had been profoundly muted. A moment of revelation during confession at Boston's Saint Anthony's Shrine helped Carla move away from her anger. Carla recalled telling her confessor the whole story of the shutdown, naming Bishop Lennon and Cardinal O'Malley, and excoriating their bulldozer approach to Sacred Heart. When the Franciscan hearing her confession reminded her that O'Malley and Lennon would have to answer to God on "Judgment Day," Carla experienced a change of heart. It was not so much the thought of divine retribution that consoled Carla, although that did help. But she was even more moved by the fact that one of O'Malley's fellow Franciscans would willingly admit, however obliquely, that the cardinal had botched the shutdowns. This brief glimpse of a tiny fissure in the church's monolithic bureaucracy restored to Carla her sense of equilibrium. She realized the matter was now out of her hands, and she also saw that the "Panzer tank" of archdiocesan power was not without its vulnerable spots. Catholic officials' insularity was not total.

The new priests appointed to help take care of Sacred Heart were another balm. "The right personnel was key"; having two priests of Italian background helped assure a successful transition to chapel status. Carla sensed that others in the community shared her new sense of calm. The priests are "such nice guys" that "everyone seems content." The pastor may have ingratiated himself to the Sacred Heart Catholics when he became the lone pastor in Boston to deny the cardinal's request that receiving parishes hand over the assets they gained from the closing parish. He determined that the Sacred Heart money should remain untouched, at least until the appeal had gone through. Even the old-timers, who Carla had been sure would never set foot in St. Leonard's, were now making their way to the new rectory—even "coming out with their canes . . . in the snow"—to request masses and be in the presence of priests. Carla even sensed that anyone who had been angry enough to leave had soon "come back." Sadness during the first year over not being able to host the school children's first communion at Sacred Heart had given way to acceptance of the policy. This and other initiatory rites could only be celebrated at an official parish, but Sacred Heart could still host wedding masses and funerals. Initial frustration that bubbled up when the pastor-administrator decided to pool the collections of Sacred Heart with those of St. Leonard's had also evaporated. For her part, Carla's recent concern for the "general parishioner" had given way to the more immediate concerns of a grandmother. With the possibility of a school merger looming, Carla did not have the energy or the desire to raise the alarm: she just wanted the school to remain unchanged long enough for her four granddaughters to graduate. Even recent news from the pastor about the mysterious emptying of Sacred Heart's approximately two-million-dollar account at the chancery did not seem to move Carla beyond a modest curiosity.[2]

Carla felt sure that Sacred Heart would not be made a parish as she had once hoped, but she was also confident that the place did not face imminent closure. The rectory holding her former office now housed *Memores Domini*, celibate Catholic laymen who lived in community as members of the fifty-five-year-old "Communion and Liberation" movement. Although Carla didn't notice them much around the neighborhood, the group had favor in Rome, and Boston's cardinal certainly had them in his sights.[3] In 2009 O'Malley celebrated the Easter Vigil with the group. He blogged about it and presented pictures of himself sitting down to dinner with these favored evangelists of the faith. He did not note that their celebration took place in Sacred Heart's former rectory.[4] Such firm bonds, and a reported papal endorsement of their installation in the North End, gave Carla confidence that the chapel would not be shuttered.

If life at Sacred Heart had stabilized, uneasiness continued in other parts of Boston. By the fall of 2009, Catholics at five parishes were still staging their occupations. St. Therese in Everett, St. Frances Cabrini in Scituate, Our Lady of Mount Carmel in East Boston, and St. James the Great in Wellesley had been occupied by parishioners for five years, since October of 2004. St. Jeremiah in Framingham had been occupied since May of 2005. At St. Jeremiah resisters had secured a weekly mass just a few months after their 2005 shutdown. Their unique success in this regard opened the door for additional rapprochement with the archdiocese. In 2007, they agreed to share their church with Boston's dispersed congregation of Syro-Malabar Catholics, a branch of the Eastern Catholic Church with ties to St. Thomas, the legendary apostle of India. In hosting the Syro-Malabar Catholics and their priest, resisters saw an opportunity not only to solidify their access to a weekly mass, but also a chance to add legitimacy to their claims that they had never stopped being a parish despite the closure decree. They also understood that opening their doors to this community of first- and second-generation Indian-Americans could breed goodwill between themselves and the archbishop, who had repeatedly affirmed his commitment to nurturing Boston's newer immigrant Catholics. In the assessment of the group's co-leader Eliza, the move helped the parish gain "a lot of good faith with the archdiocese." But the "warmer" relationship and the presence of the Syro-Malabar priest did not convince St. Jeremiah's resisters to abandon their round-the-clock occupation. Eliza admitted that staffing the overnight shifts had become more difficult, but she carefully affirmed the continuation of the vigil despite the challenges. If a night or two saw the church left alone, St. Jeremiah's cautious and savvy group of resisters were not letting anyone know.

Smaller signs of distrust and disappointment lingered as well. When a Syro-Malabar festival attracted a Boston bishop to the building, Eliza felt the sting of her own group's continuing distance from the church. Eliza said she approached the priest one day after mass with tears in her eyes. When he inquired, she had to admit that she felt sad that the bishop would agree to come "for your congregation [but] not for ours." When the day arrived, the bishop made a point afterward of walking downstairs to visit members of the resisting group. Eliza imagined the bishop's initial wariness and his surprise when "nobody bit his head off" during the brief chat. Eliza took this opening, along with an additional cordial encounter with the bishop at another Syro-Malabar event, as hopeful signs of good things to come. The fact that both the Syro-Malabar group and the resisting group had a profound devotion to Mary gave Eliza the sense that the Blessed Mother was "looking out" for the resisters. While it was clear that Eliza thought the parish, if fully restored, could survive without the Syro-Malabars, she believed that they were sent to St. Jeremiah's for a reason. Without the Syro-Malabars as a buffer, the resisters never would have been able to "cross that chasm" dividing them from the hierarchy.[5]

But Eliza was not resting on hopes for the overwhelming eruption of goodwill in their relations with the archdiocese. In early 2009, she had become one of the lead authors of a memo originating in Boston's Council of Parishes called a "Request for Mediation." This document sought to shift the terms and venue of the debate over parish shutdowns. Aware of the strong likelihood that the resisting parishes' internal church appeals would eventually fail at the highest level of the Vatican court system, the signatories sought help from another department of the Roman Curia. Addressed to the Reverend Monsignor Pietro Parolin, then the Undersecretary for Relations with States, the request targeted the branch of the Curia responsible for the pope's diplomatic and political relations.[6] In effect, the petitioners suggested that the church hierarchy ignored injustices in parish shutdowns at the risk of full-blown disaster in the U.S. church. In the words of the petition, "in America our Church is at the 'tipping point' of permanent damage and irreversible decline." Calling for a temporary stop to shutdowns and to the canon law appeals process, the document warned that "Vatican-mandated mediation with the undersigned parishioners regarding the future of their parishes" was a "last resort."

It was not the resisters' last resort, the document made clear, for they "have been steadfast for the past four-and-a-half years, and show no signs of weakening." Instead, the pressure was squarely on the church, which needed to act promptly in order to avoid further embarrassment or worse. The alternatives to mediation were clear and profoundly un-Catholic according to the petitioners: once the Vatican courts had denied resisters' last appeal, Cardinal O'Malley would have two equally distasteful choices. He could continue to wait out resisters ("a strategy of temporizing with no exit strategy") or he could send in the police to forcibly remove resisters from their churches. Facing "continuing vigil stalemates" or the "wholesale arrests of Catholics," the church in Boston called out for an alternative. The appeals process meant that conversations between O'Malley and the resisters in Boston had come to a halt. But with dimming prospects abroad, resisters now thought this was precisely the level on which compromise and collaboration for the greater good needed to take place.

The problem reached beyond Boston. The petition was signed not only by various resisting parishioner groups there, but also by Catholics representing parishes in dioceses around the country. Boston's Council of Parishes had established the foundations for this broader collaboration early on in the process. At first, resisters simply reveled in the attention they received from the national media and occasional letters of support from Catholics around the country. But soon other dioceses began initiating their own sweeping shutdown processes, and voices of solidarity and congratulation became calls for guidance in the strategies of resisting closure. Just as Boston resisters had taken their cue from Catholics in nearby Worcester, parishioners in the dioceses of Syracuse, New York, New Orleans, Toledo, and Springfield, MA, emulated the Boston vigils in opposition to closure decrees.

The diocese of Toledo, Ohio, announced its plans to shut down twenty-one parishes in 2005. People at St. James, a parish in the rural town of Kansas, anticipated the closure of their church and took over in April. One day in March 2006, an elderly woman occupying the church alone was confronted by a diocesan maintenance man, who reportedly bullied the woman out of the church after blowing out the votive candles and unplugging the phone. Ousted from their church, the community continued to pray together in a nearby Methodist church. They also spent over $100,000 on a civil lawsuit claiming ownership of the property. Unlike the Boston resisters, they did not seek reinstatement as a parish, only "use and enjoyment" of the property. After lower courts rejected their arguments, the Ohio Supreme Court refused to hear the case on appeal in May of 2009.[7]

New York made its shutdown decisions in January of 2007, after a three-year process of consultation and assessment. Ten parishes would be shuttered and eleven more merged into other parishes, their buildings remaining open as "chapels." In this case, new parishes were opening in the diocese's wealthy northern suburbs while churches in Manhattan and the Bronx felt the brunt of the consolidation.[8] In February of that year, parishioners of East Harlem's Our Lady Queen of Angels Church decided to stay inside the church, beginning more than two weeks before their official closing date. The church immediately became the site of a tense standoff. Archdiocesan officials holed up in the sacristy while parishioners gathered in the sanctuary to pray, shout, and sing. As the day wore on, additional parishioners brought in supplies and added to the occupying force. Soon, archdiocese-hired security guards were locking doors and lining up inside the church. At one point, a vice-chancellor emerged from the sacristy to re-read the closure decision from the pulpit. Police and media waited outside the church. Vigil leaders from this predominantly Latino church addressed the media, laying out their case and demanding a meeting with Cardinal Edward Egan.

No meeting was forthcoming. On the second day of the occupation, police and news reporters found their way into the building. With police acting as the go-betweens, church officials in the sacristy informed the parishioners that arrests were imminent. Many left in the face of this threat, but several stayed behind. They were arrested and taken out of the church. The vigil had lasted only thirty-six hours. But the resisters did not go away. In March 2007, Queen of Angels parishioners hounded Cardinal Egan after he helped celebrate mass at another Manhattan parish. Hearing cries of "Egan, Egan, open our church!" and seeing a rush of protesters, the cardinal—to the delight of the *New York Post*—fled to the rectory and then "used a tunnel to the church school to make an escape in a waiting car."[9] Parishioners continued in 2010 to gather in front of Our Lady Queen of Angels for weekly communion services.

Ill-fated occupations also unfolded in New Orleans, where in April of 2008 the diocese proposed to shutter 33 of its 142 parishes. Two of these, Our Lady of Good Counsel and St. Henry's, resisted with vigils. In addition to highlighting the difficulties of life in New Orleans after Hurricane Katrina, media coverage of these events described resistance to parish shutdowns as a national dilemma with Boston as the epicenter. Part of the reason for this focus was the presence in New Orleans of Peter Borré, the active co-president of Boston's Council of Parishes. As he had in New York and elsewhere, the seventy-two-year-old retired energy consultant offered his advice and support to resisting parishes and remained the media's go-to voice of opposition.[10]

But there was little anyone, no matter how experienced and well connected, could do in the face of diocesan willingness to turn to the police. After a little more than three months in their churches, New Orleans vigilers were arrested and their churches shuttered. In January 2009 a New Orleans filmmaker released a documentary about the shutdowns, with specific focus on resisting parishes. The dramatic finale of the video is a slow motion black-and-white TV news clip showing two parishioners being escorted out of Good Counsel in handcuffs. Gregorian chant drowns out the tumult as policemen guide the cuffed men (who had planned to be arrested in the presence of the media) through a throng of photographers and observers. This ironic spin on the classic "perp walk" fades into a panning shot of a crucifix followed by a local newspaper proclaiming the archbishop's "peace" in his decision to evict.[11] Borré planned to use the video as a tool of leverage in his efforts to start a more productive conversation with the Vatican. He had already made several trips to the Vatican, and would make several more, in his role as advocate for resisting parishes. These efforts (which he once called "Special Ops") included meetings with officials and hand delivery of documents and petitions from Boston and other parts of the country.[12]

New Orleans and Boston were not alone in seeing arrests in closing parishes. A 2007-2008–vigil in Syracuse, New York, also ended with police action after officials got word that a "nonpriest had taken communion wafers to the church."[13] In Adams, Massachusetts, a small town with three parishes in the diocese of Springfield, parishioners at St. Stanislaus Kostka took over their church in December of 2008. As of December 2010, the occupation of this historically Polish parish continued while the diocese pursued its plan to shrink from 120 to 98 parishes.[14]

Amid these struggles, in the spring of 2008, the American church was making preparations to host the new pope, Benedict XVI. Seeing this visit as an opportunity to highlight the cause, Borré founded a national group made up of parishioners from six dioceses where shutdowns were under way. This "Coalition for Parishes" included parishioner groups from Boston, Toledo, New York, Buffalo, New Orleans, and Camden, New Jersey.[15] The Coalition of Parishes' wide membership formed the foundation upon which Catholics could frame the shutdowns as an issue of national importance. In addition to the Catholics from St. Stanislaus in Adams, parishioners from eight parishes in the diocese of Scranton and one in the diocese of Allentown, Pennsylvania, joined the cause. An additional parish group from Cleveland, Ohio (where Bishop Richard Lennon, the architect of the Boston shutdowns, proposed cutting 50 of 224 parishes), joined as a signatory on the Request for Mediation. In Cleveland, as in Detroit, officials argued that closures were required in order to redirect priests out of the city and into the growth suburbs.[16]

The Coalition of Parishes was not the only source of help and information. A lay Catholic organization called FutureChurch, which had been founded in 1990 in northeastern Ohio, took up the cause of defending what resisters called "vibrant parishes." In addition to materials aimed to foster discussion about the ordination of women, "optional celibacy" for priests, and lay ministry, online shoppers at the organization's website could order a packet of documents entitled "Save Our Parish Community." The folder included essays by Coalition of Parishes members, studies, a media kit, statements about parish life and ministry, as well as prayer resources and practical guides to organizing an official canon law appeal. The $12 package also included a "Crisis Kit" for those "unexpectedly faced with closing or merging."[17] In the meantime, other dioceses were proceeding with shutdowns and mergers in a more gradual fashion. Pittsburgh closed or merged over one hundred parishes between the early 1990s and 2000.[18] By 2009, Detroit was still in the midst of a five-year process called "Together in Faith," which included steady consultation and a more open-ended approach to the pace and timing of church shutdowns. Significant declines were also evident in the diocese of Green Bay, Wisconsin, which went from 212 to 160 parishes beginning in 1990. Twenty-one of those were lost starting in 2005.[19] In January 2009, the Albany diocese announced plans to close or merge over thirty parishes.[20]

As the Request for Mediation acknowledged, in many cases shutdowns were inevitable. But overly aggressive dioceses seemed ready to repeat Boston's mistakes in their application of canon law. Punning with recent geopolitical events, they chided these bishops as "veritable weapons of Mass destruction." According to the letter, desperate bishops in these dioceses proposed to turn parishes into diocesan "*bancomats.*" Nodding to tradition and demonstrating their sophistication, the petitioners put key words like this in Italian or Latin. In this case, they wanted to send home the point that American bishops were looking at parishes at their own cash machines. In the process the bishops threatened to violate canon law, but also, according to the petitioners, undermined Pope John Paul II's 2004 endorsement of parishes as "the first and foremost place" of Catholic encounter with the church. The petitioners reminded Parolin that the pope had affirmed their central point: "The Diocese should always be understood as existing *in and for its parishes*," not the other way around. This citation downplayed the pope's suggestion in the same address that bishops adopt and execute a "unified pastoral plan" aimed at the "revitalization of the parish community," a description of episcopal duties which would echo in the rationales for consolidation through targeted parish shutdowns.[21] But resisters wanted officials to know that the "'command and control' approach" they detected in "Allentown, Boston, Buffalo, Cleveland, New York, New Orleans, Scranton, and Springfield" threatened permanently to alienate Catholics from the church.

While beginning with reassurances about resisters' orthodoxy, the letter ended with dire warnings about the future of the church in America. A recent study by the *Pew Forum on Religion and Public Life* helped the petitioners make this argument. Catholicism suffered the "greatest net losses" of all American religions; almost a third of Americans had been raised Catholic but only a quarter of Americans remained Catholic in 2008.

Noting that the study counted 22 million "former Catholics" in America, the resisters suggested that this massive block of the disaffected had undermined Catholic officials' hopes for the 2008 presidential election. The letter implied that if these former Catholics had been more deeply in the fold they would have voted in tune with the public political pronouncements of their bishops. Important and heavily Catholic states like Ohio, Pennsylvania, and Michigan could have upended the victories of pro-choice Democrats like Barack Obama. If this argument operated in bad faith (it was not at all clear that resisters in Boston shared the conservative political positions of America's most outspoken bishops), it nonetheless offered evidence worthy of the undersecretary's attention. If the Secretariat truly cared about shaping America's political culture, it should be worried about further alienating U.S. Catholics. Moreover, if the church thought that Latino Catholics would make up the difference, the authors of the petition had news: Latinos were leaving the church too. According to the study, the fleeing Latinos were joining Protestant and unaffiliated ranks. This analysis downplayed the consistent total number of Catholics as about one-quarter of the U.S. population (mostly due to Latino immigration). But it served as a warning against taking these people and their donations for granted and dangled the possibility of overwhelming Catholic dominance on the U.S. landscape.[22]

If loss of influence was one possibility, even more serious prospects loomed. Perpetuating the process of shutdowns could readily push otherwise devoted Roman Catholics further into "cafeteria Catholicism." The memo suggested that the 2002 revelations about abuse and cover-up caused many Catholics to abandon their "pray-and-obey" instincts. But Americans' abandonment of the "traditional" was also a matter of modernization and economics. As citizens of one of the world's "contemporary developed countries," many Americans could no longer accept the church's "geriatric mode of governance." But this was just a beginning. Invalid closures—shutdowns or mergers involving parishes of "spiritual and material vibrancy"—threaten "irreversible damage" to the "moral authority, the material well being, and the future prospects of **Roman** Catholicism in America." As the bold type suggested, unseated Catholics were very likely simply to give up all allegiance to Rome and the entire Catholic hierarchy. American bishops' "path of parish destruction" left "wreckage" from which a "new form of Catholicism" would emerge. The letter attempted to put the potential losses in world-historical perspective:

> To deprive unjustly America's parishioners of their spiritual sanctuaries, especially during these somber times, carries the strong likelihood that convulsive changes will be set in motion, on the scale of those which fractured the Roman Catholic Church during the 11th and 16th centuries.

Envisioning "communities of displaced parishioners who are ready to retain their core Catholic beliefs, and equally ready to renounce their allegiance to the hierarchies," the letter argued that officials, not parishioners, would be responsible for schisms in the church. If the church was willing to accept a smaller church as a necessary result of "purification," resisters in the United States implied it would have more than a few feckless progressives to contend with. It risked losing its entire American church.

For the crafters of this letter, vigiling communities in Boston were the proof that such visions could be realized in America. These communities, after all, had survived outside of the official church for several years. What they lacked in size they made up for in perseverance, knowledge, and faith. But the communities' patience and durability actually made the precise opposite point. Despite what some of the leaders of the group may have hoped (or hoped they could wield as a threat), Boston's occupiers did not show signs of breaking off from Rome. Ironically, the fact that occupiers had waited so long and spent so much money and time hoping for a return to the fold undermined the key threat of the Request for Mediation. Of course the church might lose these people as devoted Catholics if they went ahead with the shutdowns, but they had already lost so many in the United States without a perceptible decrease in their overall numbers that it was hard to imagine officials in Rome calculating a need for reversal based on this persuasive but very small minority. They were far more likely to make sure that future shutdowns would go more smoothly than Boston's and expect that soon Catholics would come around to seeing the benefits of fewer parishes, even if it meant sacrificing some healthy and beloved communities. Moreover, if resisters saw the offense of parish shutdown as a last straw, officials may have noted Catholics (including the resisters) returning to the fold after the abuse crisis and given such possibilities little credence.

When the resistance began in 2004, few imagined that parishioners would be in their churches for more than a few months. As resisters spent thousands to push their canon law appeals through successive steps, occupying Catholics had additional reasons to hold on. But delays may have been part of a strategy on the other side as well. Although Vatican courts are notoriously slow, it was likely in this case that delays in offering a final ruling on the appeals were part of a coordinated plan to avoid putting Cardinal O'Malley in a difficult pastoral position. If the court had not yet ruled out the parishes' appeals, O'Malley could continue to tolerate vigils. By holding off, he could portray himself as both respectful of the church legal process and pastorally sensitive. Resisters saw this caution as stubborn bureaucratic stonewalling. After an initial wave of reversals and counterproposals ended in 2005, none of the resisting parishes had succeeded in engaging the diocese in pursuit of a solution. Once the decisions came through, the vigils would be marked definitively as not only illicit but also scandalous, in that they would be causing people to lose the faith. O'Malley would have to act. Keeping the cases in limbo at the Vatican increased the likelihood that the occupations would waver and collapse on their own. For East Boston's Mount Carmel, which had no valid canon law appeal, the cardinal may have been waiting to act in order to avoid singling out one parish.

The official delays and the vigilers' persistence seemed to offer resisters at Mount Carmel some reward in late 2009 when a wealthy benefactor died. The deceased, who Ronald told me was not a regular of the occupying group, stipulated that Mount Carmel should receive $100,000 from his estate. Mount Carmel's "Survivors" immediately turned this gift into an opening salvo in what they hoped would be a renewed dialogue with the archdiocese. They felt the money along with recognition of overcrowding at one parish and structural deterioration at another might convince the archdiocese to reconsider the shutdown. According to Ronald, the pastor at the receiving parish seemed to be warming to the possibility, since he saw Mount Carmel's former convent as a possible site for religious education classes.

As Ronald himself admitted, however, rescinding the closure would require an admission of error, and it seemed unlikely that officials would be willing to swallow that pill just to gain a pastor some additional teaching space. If the nearby parish of Our Lady of the Assumption really was about to fall off its hillside perch, then it was far more likely that they would simply close that place too and attempt to channel its small community elsewhere. Volunteering Mount Carmel as that place seemed to Ronald the best possible solution. He was even willing to reopen Mount Carmel as a territorial parish, since, as he put it, the "Italian is over" as a viable base for an ethnic parish. With Latinos making up an increasing percentage of East Boston's population, the idea of opening Mount Carmel as a trilingual territorial parish seemed the best promise for longterm vitality.[23] As they had been so many times before, resisters were waiting to hear back from the archdiocese on these possibilities.

At the same time that these possibilities presented themselves, the archdiocese had to figure out what to do with the body of its former leader, Cardinal William H. O'Connell. As a part of its scramble to pay abuse settlements in 2004, the archdiocese had sold a major parcel of its chancery property to Boston College. Included in the sale was the land upon which O'Connell's crypt rested, inside a chapel he had had built for that purpose at St. John's Seminary. At Boston College's request, the archdiocese had agreed to unearth the cardinal and re-inter his remains somewhere else. When distant relatives of O'Connell protested, the church found itself in another charged battle involving the meaning and power of Boston's Catholic past.

Even the dead were coming back to haunt the archdiocese by pointing out its inability to escape the expectations of its glorious past. O'Connell's biographer James O'Toole noted that the late cardinal had "helped define standards for the [Boston] community as a whole, upholding traditional values against the onslaughts of the modern world, defending stable truths in a time of relativity and change." The cardinal, despite a radically diminished standing in the church and among his own clergy during the last two decades of his cardinalate, "never lost his skill at public drama, at creating a symbolic role for himself in personifying the church of his age."[24] It seemed he still had his touch even in death. Amid the archdiocese's financial desperation, parish closures and occupations, and now scrutiny over the fate of a cardinal's body, O'Connell's early twentieth-century proclamation of Catholic ascendancy in Protestant-dominated Boston—"the Catholic remains"—takes on new meanings.

Despite her own expectations, Carla moved on from the North End's Sacred Heart and welcomed the healthy relationship that seemed to be emerging between St. Leonard's current pastor and the former Sacred Heart parishioners. These people still had their church (as a chapel), and the bright intensity of the loss of parish status had dimmed. Carla, at least, also saw that illness and death are close at hand and sometimes trump everything else in life. Her tale highlights a dark wisdom buried inside archdiocesan officials' messages of unity, maturity, and rebirth in their efforts to inculcate the proper Catholic response to parish closure: this wound will heal as attention shifts to other of life's miseries. Perhaps life's joys could have the same effect. This 'life-goes-on' truism no doubt would apply as well for the resisters who continued to occupy churches in Boston at the end of 2010. For this reason, it makes sense that very few in Boston are still paying attention to the occupations. The occupations are quiet affairs, even routine. Although they are reminded by church officials in occasional newspaper quotes that their occupations must end, nothing seems imminent. They could very easily fade from view and be lost to history.

But the resisters have opened a clearing in which we might well linger. For one thing, contemporary American Catholicism looked different than we have come to expect as it moved—in the bodies and minds of resisters—in and around Boston's occupied churches. Resisters' commitment to memory and durability against the demands of the market and calls for efficiency and flexibility exposed widening holes in the already well-worn notions of Catholic "Americanization." At the same time, resisters' pragmatism and irreverence, as well as their claims to authority in the church, subvert easy assumptions about Catholics' rigidity and uniformity. Moreover, in the lights of the occupied parishes in Boston, the church's recent ambition to combine continuity and change appeared as something more than an abstract theological puzzle; church closures and resistance to them exposed the vexing and painful challenges such formulations can entail in a life. Occupiers offer a different story as well about the sources of authority and vitality in the church, suggesting the continuing relevance of Catholic claims about the potency, reliability, and intensity of the sacred as a part of the material surroundings of everyday life in cities and suburbs. On a broader scale, the resisters challenge us to pause as we embark on projects that will reshape America's lived environment. They remind us of the threats to history and memory amid the urge for change embedded in free-market capitalism and new forms of information technology.

But at bottom, resisters open the even more fundamental question about how to live at the fraught intersection of past and present. Such questions are pronounced in contemporary U.S. Catholicism, but they are not unique to it. All of us have to discern and decide, especially when something we love seems to be disappearing, how to make sense of the past as it invades or shapes our efforts to forge meaningful lives. The problem of when to "let go" and when (or how) to "hold on" is a matter that popular psychological bromides and statistics cannot resolve. Even powerfully ingrained religious narratives sometimes fail to resolve this puzzle. These matters cut to the very core of who we are and how we live. Resisters' engagement with those questions present an an opportunity to understand our own inevitable confrontations with loss, and our inevitable hopes for something else.

Notes

Acknowledgments

Index

Notes

Introduction

* Unless otherwise indicated, all newspaper articles were accessed through www.lexisnexis.com.

1. Brother Fidelis DeBerardinis sexually abused altar boys in the parish from 1968–1973. John Ellement, "Franciscan brother charged with molesting four altar boys," *Boston Globe*, August 15, 2002, A30; Robin Washington, "Friar guilty of molesting altar boys 30 years ago," *Boston Herald*, May 27, 2004, 030.
2. Susana (F-68) and David (M-72), September 7, 2006, Our Lady of Mount Carmel (hereafter "OLMC"). With a few exceptions for those in obvious positions of leadership that are a matter of historical record, I have changed the names of the people I quote. When I have their ages, I have included it in the footnote for the first citation of that individual after an indication of sex (e.g., F-68). I haven't changed the names of their parishes, or organizations, or any other details. As I told them in our conversations, it is likely that some of those within the communities of resistance will recognize one another despite the use of pseudonyms. Anonymity did not concern most of those I spoke with, as they were willing and in some cases eager to have their names attached to their opinions and actions. I decided to use pseudonyms both to help prevent unforeseen harm and to encourage freer interpretation. The project includes no composites and quotes only passages that are recorded verbatim, either in my field notebook or in transcripts of my conversations with these Catholics. Passages quoted from field notes are cited with date and location.
3. The Council of Parishes said Catholics had been subject to a "new form of abuse" in a news release in 2005. This phrase peppered resisters'

statements throughout the resistance. One of the earliest public usages in this case was found in the Boston Globe. Council of Parishes, "Council of Parishes calls on archbishop to halt parish closings process and expand reconfiguration committee," press release, April 10, 2005, http://www.councilofparishes.org/releases/041005.html. Eileen McNamara, "Unanswered prayers," *Boston Globe*, October 3, 2004, B1; Washington, "Friar guilty," *Boston Herald*.

4. Rev. Cletus J. Dello Iacono, OFM, JCD, "Jubilee Address," in *Our Lady of Mount Carmel Church, East Boston Diamond Jubilee, 1905-1980* (program book), 9.
5. Roman Catholic Archdiocese of Boston, "2003 Parish Pastoral Statistics," http://web.archive.org/web/20080327053704/http://www.rcab.org/Parish_Reconfiguration/PastoralStats2003.html. Mass attendance became a more important statistic than parish families when it became clear that membership and participation in weekly liturgy were different matters for modern Catholics.
6. Roman Catholic Archdiocese of Boston, "Parish Reconfigurations (1985–2003)," http://web.archive.org/web/20080327065436/http://www.rcab.org/Parish_Reconfiguration/reconfiguration.html Two new Spanish-language parishes were established during this time. For a rich overview of the consolidations, demographic shifts, vocation shortages, and budget crises during the 1980s and 1990s, see Thomas H. O'Connor, *Boston Catholics: A History of the Church and Its People* (Boston: Northeastern University Press, 1998), 302–313.
7. Jason Lefferts, "Loss of churches will be archdiocese's gain," *Lowell Sun*, June 11, 2004; Christopher Scott, "Heartbreak for four Lowell parishes," *Lowell Sun*, June 27, 2004; Denise Lavoie, "A dozen more churches slated to close in Boston," *Boston Globe*, May 26, 2004; Martin Finucane, "Boston Church announces parish closures," *Associated Press Online*, May 26, 2004.
8. "Religion news in brief," *Associated Press Online*, March 30, 2006,
9. John T. McGreevy, *Parish Boundaries: The Catholic Encounter with Race in the Twentieth-century Urban North* (Chicago: University of Chicago Press, 1996); Eileen M. McMahon, *What Parish Are You From? A Chicago Irish Community and Race Relations* (Lexington: University of Kentucky Press, 1995); James O'Toole, *The Faithful: A History of Catholics in America* (Cambridge, MA and London: Belknap Press of Harvard University Press, 2008), 95.
10. John Cosgrove, "Religious Congregations as Mediators of Devolution: A Study of Parish-Based Services," in *Social Work in the Era of Devolution: Toward a Just Practice*, ed. Rosa Perez-Koening and Barry Rock, 331–350 (New York: Fordham University Press, 2001), 342.

11. The outside structure of South Boston's Peter and Paul Parish was preserved in its conversion to luxury condos. Some were dismayed that it did not offer low-income housing. Denise Lavoie, "Churches selling as luxury condominiums," *Associated Press Online*, June 13, 2004. On architectural concerns see Michael Paulson, "Preservationists fear church closings," *Boston Globe*, March 28, 2004, A1.
12. Paula Kane describes the early twentieth-century Catholic orientation toward both separation and integration as an aggressive subculture. Paula Kane, *Separatism and Subculture: Boston Catholicism, 1900–1920* (Chapel Hill: University of North Carolina Press, 1994). For white Catholic responses to African-American migration to the Northeast and upper Midwest see McGreevy, *Parish Boundaries*.
13. Gerald Gamm, *Urban Exodus: Why the Jews Left Boston and the Catholics Stayed* (Cambridge, MA: Harvard University Press, 1999), 267.
14. Reed Ueda and Conrad Edick Wright, eds., *Faces of Community: Immigrant Massachusetts, 1860–2000* (Boston: Massachusetts Historical Society, distributed by Northeastern University Press, 2003). O'Connor, *Boston Catholics*, 307–311.
15. Gamm, *Urban Exodus*, 262.
16. Karen Terry et al., "The Nature and Scope of the Problem of Sexual Abuse of Minors by Priests and Deacons" (Washington, DC: United States Conference of Catholic Bishops, 2004), 27. http://www.bishop-accountability.org/reports/2004_02_27_JohnJay/index.html.
17. Michael Paulson, "Diocese gives abuse data," *Boston Globe*, February 27, 2004, A1. The archdiocese used the standards for defining accusation and abuse outlined by the "John Jay report" (as the Karen Terry et al. study was often called because of its association with the John Jay College of Criminal Justice).
18. The rates of disclosure to anyone, across genders, was 26%. Disclosure rates to the police were 4%. Almost 10% of priests ordained in 1970 were accused of sexual abuse. Terry et al., "Problem of Sexual Abuse of Minors," 24, 27, 70, 78, 80, 106.
19. Kevin Cullin & Stephen Kurkjian, "Most plaintiffs accept $85 million church deal," *Boston Globe*, September 10, 2003.
20. Ron Goldwyn, "Bishops 'shameful,'" *Philadelphia Daily News*, February 28, 2004, 03. Rachel Zoll, "Abuse cost for Catholic dioceses tops $1 billion," Associated Press Online, June 10, 2005.
21. Ralph Ranalli, "Boston's internal inquiry presses on," *Boston Globe*, January 7, 2004, B6.
22. Laurie Goodstein, "Diocese are moving ahead on abuse, audit finds," *New York Times*, January 7, 2004, A1.

23. James Muller and Charles Kenney, *Keep the Faith, Change the Church: The Battle by Catholics for the Soul of their Church* (New York: Rodale Inc./St. Martin's, 2004). The group grew primarily among well-educated and suburban Catholics.
24. Erin Williams, "Boston archdiocese statistics," *Patriot Ledger*, March 29, 2006, 19. The archdiocesan head count takes place each year over the course of several weekends in October. 2003 saw 15.2% attendance. The appeal raised $10.3 million in 2003 and $10.8 million in 2004. Michael Paulson, "Church raised $10.8 million in 2004," *Boston Globe*, March 4, 2005, B4. Some suspected that increasing counts in parishes were a result of exaggerated counts to boost parish image in order to stave off closure.
25. Michael Paulson, "Refocused church seeking donations," *Boston Globe*, December 22, 2002, A1.
26. O'Connor documents the efforts of Cardinals Medeiros and Law to implement "planning" initiatives and organizational restructuring for a cash- and priest-strapped archdiocese. See O'Connor, *Boston Catholics*, 283–328. In 2000, before the sexual abuse crisis, Cardinal Law had suggested that additional closures would be unnecessary. During his tenure (1985–2003) forty-five parishes were closed. "It would be my hope now," the Cardinal said, "that we could put the issue of parish reconfiguration, with the exception of those few instances where planning is in progress, behind us. . . . Now that we have dealt with the question of reconfiguration for the foreseeable future, it is time for all of us to be focused on the far more significant task of planning for mission." Cardinal Bernard Law, "Address to the Convocation of Parishes," March 11, 2000. www.rcab.org. See also Stan Doherty and Eileen Doherty, "Informal Statistical Study (Part II)," August 17, 2004. www.futurechurch.org/Doherty.pdf. This study of parishes in the Roman Catholic Archdiocese of Boston before and after parish closures was performed by two lay Catholics at St. Albert the Great Parish.
27. These groupings or "clusters" had been organized precisely for this purpose in the mid-1990s. Gamm, *Urban Exodus*, 268.
28. In early July 2004, Portland, Oregon, became the first U.S. diocese to declare bankruptcy as a result of sexual abuse claims. The Roman Catholic Diocese of Tucson, Arizona, filed for Chapter 11 protection in September of 2004. News that the Diocese of Spokane would file came out in November of that year. While the archdiocese initially downplayed the problems in the archdiocesan budget, resistance and agitation among Catholics spurred the archbishop to put the relationship between diocesan finances and the closure plan in sharper view. In April 2006, for example, O'Malley suggested that the closures might have helped prevent Boston

from having to file for Chapter 11 protection. Janet I. Tu and Stuart Eskenazi, "Archdiocese in Portland declares bankruptcy," *Seattle Times*, July 7, 2004, A1; Virginia de Leon, "Bankruptcy for diocese," *Spokesman Review* (Spokane, WA), November 11, 2004; Michael Paulson, "O'Malley sees a test of values," *Boston Globe*, April 21, 2006, A1.

29. Kellyanne Mahoney, "Closure suggestions wrench city parishes," *Boston Globe (City)*, March 21, 2004, 9.
30. Bella English, "It's parish against parish," *Boston Globe (South)*, March 7, 2004, 1. English uses the "off the island" analogy. English extended the analogy later, in "Keeping the faith," *Boston Globe*, June 22, 2004, E1. Boston parishioners in closed parishes repeated this analogy frequently.
31. Rev. Joseph M. Hennessey refuted the speculation about ruthlessness, citing his own cluster, where they initially refused to vote against any parish, but eventually, under pressure from the archdiocese, relented and named two parishes that the archbishop could close, if he "sees fit for the common good of the entire archdiocese." "Parishes bonding," *Boston Globe (South)*, March 14, 2004, 10 (letter). This refusal was also the case in the Weymouth cluster. A cluster of two including St. Susanna and St. Mary church in Dedham was another cluster that refused to make any recommendation.
32. Michael Paulson, "37 parishes are notified they might face closing," *Boston Globe*, May 6, 2004, B3.
33. Later, this same pastor memorialized the day with a poem called "Black Tuesday, May 25, 2004." The poem appears in "St. Jeremiah's Parish, 1958-2004: Remembrance," a memorial booklet distributed in advance of the last mass. The booklet features pictures of the church and its stained glass, reflections by lay people and the pastor, prayers, and an image of the congregation. The film, which was brought out by Element Productions and called *Closed on Sundays*, was produced by Charlestown resident Rudi Schwab. Resisters from around the archdiocese later gathered for a premier screening in Cambridge, Massachusetts, on April 22, 2005. Clips and a trailer for the film, including a dramatic suppression notice delivery scene can be viewed at www.youtube.com.
34. Michael Paulson, "Pope names Law to ceremonial position in Rome," *Boston Globe*, May 28, 2004, A1; "Law to get $5,000 monthly stipend," *Boston Globe*, June 6, 2004, B2.
35. Even before the closures, VOTF executive director Steven Krueger was recommending a democratized process of decision-making and the full disclosure of financial conditions in the archdiocese before closing parishes was considered. Secretary of State William Galvin suspected that the archdiocese already had a "list," and considered the plan for a

three-month consultation about closures at the level of parish clusters to be little more than a shield from critique. See "When churches close," *Boston Globe*, December 29, 2003, editorial; Michael Gustin, of the Weston-Chelmsford branch VOTF, aired a common critique after the closures, endorsing lay-run parishes as a better option than closing churches that would otherwise be in the black. See "Voice of the Faithful's plan for churches," *Lowell Sun*, July 4, 2004, letters to the editor.

36. Kathy McCabe, "Sadness grips closed churches, but some gear for appeals," *Boston Globe*, May 30, 2004, 1; Mark Fontecchio "Weymouth church ready to fight back," *Patriot Ledger*, June 10, 2004, 11; Joanna Massey, "Two parishes say they'll fight to stay open," *Boston Globe*, May 30, 2004, 1.

37. Mark Fontecchio, "St. Albert parishioners may stand up with sit-in," *Patriot Ledger*, August 14, 2004, 17.

38. Rev. Stephen S. Josoma of St. Susanna in Dedham, the Rev. Robert J. Bowers of St. Catherine of Siena in Charlestown, the Rev. Ronald Coyne of St. Albert the Great in East Weymouth, and the Rev. David Gill of St. Mary of the Angels in Roxbury were among the most vocal critics of the closure. By March 2008, none of their parishes had closed. In 2005 St. Susanna's earned a three-year reprieve with Father Josoma as pastor. In late 2004, Father Bowers resigned from St. Catherine's in exchange for a renewed cluster process for the parish with its two partner parishes in Charlestown. Under new leadership, St. Catherine's eventually joined efforts with St. Mary's and awaited further discussions about consolidating all three parishes into a single Charlestown parish. In September 2004, St. Albert the Great closed and lost its pastor, Father Coyne. The parish was occupied by parishioners for ten months and reopened by the archbishop with a new pastor in 2005. The closure of St. Mary of the Angels was rescinded in June 2005. The parish retained Father Gill.

39. Philip J. Murnion and Anne Wenzel, *The Crisis of the Church in the Inner City: Pastoral Options for Inner City Parishes* (New York: National Pastoral Life Center, in cooperation with the Conservation Co. and Lilly Endowment Inc., 1990), 47.

40. Judith Gaines, "Occupation over, church conflict goes on," *Boston Globe (City)*, June 27, 1993, 25; Dan DeLeo, "Parish shutdowns: before St. Albert's there was St. Joe's," *Patriot Ledger* (Quincy, MA), September 4, 2004, 1.

41. The leaders were Sister Janet Eisner, the president of a local Catholic university, and Peter Meade, head of the board of Catholic Charities and an executive vice president for an insurance company. The committee became known as the Meade-Eisner Commission.

42. In at least one of the smaller vigils, resisters discreetly discontinued the overnight aspect of the occupation. The passage of time and their confidence that an alarm system would give them time to reoccupy should the archdiocese seek to retake the church gave them faith that they could safely relieve overburdened occupiers of the chore of sleeping in church.
43. Among the occupied parishes, St. Albert's reopened as a parish, St. Anselm became a rectorate, Infant Jesus-St. Lawrence became a chapel, St. Bernard was merged with another parish, and the other five remained occupied as of December 2010. Several of these five were granted occasional or regular masses by the archdiocese. Among other parishes on the original closure list, several had been taken off the closure list either to remain parishes, to become chapels of nearby parishes, or to receive delayed or indefinitely postponed closure dates. Blessed Takeri Tekakwitha, Plymouth, St. James, Stoughton, St. Florence, Wakefield, St. Mary of the Angels, Roxbury, St. Isodore, Stow, St. Thomas the Apostle, Salem/Peabody remained parishes. Mary Star of the Sea, Quincy, St. Joseph, Lincoln, and Sacred Heart, Boston (North End) became chapels or alternate worship sites attached to other parishes. Holy Trinity, Boston (South End) and St. Susanna (Dedham) remained open with possible closure looming. St. Catherine of Siena, Charlestown, Mary Immaculate (Newton), and Sacred Heart Lexington were merged (or slated to be merged) with other parishes instead of closing. St. Peter, South Boston, St. Joseph, Woburn, St. Pius X, Milton, and Sacred Heart, Watertown had closing dates either rescinded or never assigned. Thanks to Peter Borré of the Council of Parishes for much of this summary. See also Michael Paulson, "Status unclear of parishes converted into chapels," *Boston Globe*, August 7, 2005, B1; Ralph Ranalli "Awaiting closure," *Boston Globe (West)*, June 10, 2007, 1; Matt Viser, "Two parishes still open, but future in doubt," *Boston Globe (West)*, August 25, 2005, 10.
44. Michael Paulson, "Resistance widens to parish closings," *Boston Globe*, May 8, 2005, A1.
45. These numbers are referenced as the "archdiocesan estimates" in Ralph Ranalli, "Awaiting closure," *Boston Globe (West)*, June 10, 2007, 1. The number 4,000 is just under 15% of the 28,000 estimated to have been members (active or not) of the closing parishes.
46. As of December 2010, occupations continued at St. James, Wellesley, Our Lady of Mount Carmel, East Boston, St. Jeremiah, Framingham, St. Therese, Everett, and St. Frances Xavier Cabrini, Scituate. Michael Paulson, "Big tab still rises at shut churches," *Boston Globe*, January 18, 2008, A1.
47. John T. McGreevy, "Faith and Morals in the United States, 1865–Present" in *Reviews in American History* 26, no.1 (1998): 244; Robert A. Orsi,

The Madonna of 115th Street: Faith and Community in Italian Harlem, 1880–1950 (New Haven: Yale University Press, 1985), 219ff.; David D. Hall, *Worlds of Wonder, Days of Judgment: Popular Religious Belief in Early New England* (Cambridge, MA: Harvard University Press, 1990).

48. Thomas Rzeznik, "The Church in the Changing City: Parochial Restructuring in the Archdiocese of Philadelphia in Historical Perspective," *U.S. Catholic Historian* 27, no. 4 (Fall 2009): 75, 90. For pastoral advice about ritually mediating closures see Michael A. Weldon, O.F.M., *Struggle for Holy Ground: Reconciliation and the Rites of Parish Closure* (Collegeville, MN: Liturgical Press, 2004); Philip J. Murnion and Anne Wenzel, *The Crisis of the Church in the Inner City: Pastoral Options for Inner City Parishes* (New York: National Pastoral Life Center, in cooperation with the Conservation Co. and Lilly Endowment Inc., 1990). For another qualitative study, see Peter R. D'Agostino, "The Archdiocese of Chicago: Planning and Change for a Restructured Metropolis," in *Religious Organizations and Structural Change in Metropolitan Chicago: The Research Report of the Religion in Urban America Program* (Chicago: University of Illinois, 1996).

49. Rev. James Burns, Ph.D., spearheaded the "Parish Transitions Project" at the Center for the Study of Religion and Psychology, Albert and Jessie Danielsen Institute, Boston University. Burns and others at Boston University organized a major project seeking to explore the "emotional and spiritual consequences of closing and reorganizing Roman Catholic parishes in Boston and elsewhere." The research included surveys and interviews with priests and parishioners in closing Boston parishes. The results of this work await publication. See www.bu.edu/danielsen/research/project/previous-research-projects; personal correspondence, June 7, 2010.

50. Ralph Ranalli, "Awaiting closure," *Boston Globe (West)*, June 10, 2007, 1.

51. One might think here too of the common practice among fieldworkers in the study of religion of telling their readers about a moment of boundary confusion or fleeting personal transformation amid fieldwork. See for example, Robert A. Orsi, *Thank You St. Jude: Women's Devotion to the Patron Saint of Hopeless Causes* (New Haven: Yale University Press, 1996), xxi; Susan Friend Harding, *The Book of Jerry Falwell: Fundamentalist Language and Politics* (Princeton: Princeton University Press, 2000), 33; Thomas A. Tweed, *Crossing and Dwelling: A Theory of Religion* (Cambridge, MA: Harvard University Press, 2006), 181–82. My choice to sit in the vigil had elements of this confusion, but was more deliberate than the spontaneous utterances reported by others.

52. Usually these conversations were conducted one-on-one, but a significant number of them included two or more resisters. They were often

prearranged, but they were more like directed conversations than interviews. I tried to strike a balance between maintaining disciplined attention to my developing questions and allowing Catholics' own concerns to guide our conversations. In addition to these prearranged conversations, on occasion I would ask if I could turn on my recorder if a topic or event during the normal course of the occupation sparked a particularly interesting conversation. The recordings range from ten or fifteen minutes to nearly two hours, with most lasting about forty-five minutes. I recorded conversations with a few Catholics on more than one occasion. I informed those I spoke with that I was doing research and received their verbal consent for use of recordings. I kept these audio recordings and transcripts of them as digital files on my personal computer. I have preserved them on my hard drive and an external backup drive. They remain in my sole possession and any future uses will be only for the purposes of extending research analysis. Catholics in the resisting communities knew that I was a researcher. I introduced myself that way to those I met and also with more formal inquiries I sent to pastors and communities' lay leaders. In the early days of the occupations it would have been easy to mistake me for a representative of the media, as the vigils attracted scores of reporters from around the archdiocese. Over time, however, as the media interest faded, my presence became more noticeable.

53. See for example Joanne Passaro, "You Can't Take the Subway to the Field!": 'Village' Epistemologies in the Global Village," in *Anthropological Locations: Boundaries and Grounds of a Field of Science*, ed. Akhil Gupta and James Ferguson (Berkeley: University of California Press, 1997).

54. See George Marcus, "The Uses of Complicity in the Changing *Mise-en-scene* of Anthropological Fieldwork," *Representations* 59: 1997, 85-108.

55. Gamm, *Urban Exodus;* Paula Kane, "Architecture as Apologetic: Boston's Catholic Churches and Architects of the Early Twentieth Century," in *Faces of Community: Immigrant Massachusetts, 1860–2000* ed. Reed Ueda and Conrad Edick Wright (Boston: Massachusetts Historical Society, distributed by Northeastern University Press, 2003), 133. Jay P. Dolan, introduction to *The American Catholic Parish: A History from 1850 to the Present, Volume 1*, ed. Jay P. Dolan (New York, Mahwah: Paulist Press, 1987), 3; Joseph J. Casino, "From Sanctuary to Involvement: A History of the Catholic Parish in the Northeast," in *The American Catholic Parish*, 9–116. For a recent endorsement of bishops' responsibility for parishes see John Paul II, "Address of John Paul II to the Bishops of the Ecclesiastical Provinces of Dubuque, Kansas City in Kansas, Omaha, and St. Louis (U.S.A.) on Their '*Ad Limina*' Visit" November 26, 2004, www.vatican.va.

56. Susana, September 7, 2006, OLMC.
57. A council is one way the Catholic Church has for advancing official teachings and decrees. A council meets with the approval of the pope, and with the pope presiding and offering final approval of the bishops' conclusions. Its conclusions apply universally to the church. See Gertrud Kim, O.S.B., "Roman Catholic Organization Since Vatican II," in *American Denominational Organization: A Sociological View*, ed. Ross P. Scherer (Pasadena, CA: William Carey Library, 1980), 84–85.
58. As my description begins to suggest, the actual breakdown in the reception of the Council among Catholics cannot be captured by this binary. One must take into account, for example, the fact that there are various texts in the Council, some of more importance, weight, and controversiality than others. Moreover, a variety of ways of talking about continuity and fracture emerged. On the far critical end of the spectrum were a group of traditionalists who considered the Council opposed to tradition, considering the popes who enacted its changes to have been guilty of schism and heresy. For them, the church is in a "*sede vacante* situation"—the seat of the pope is actually empty of a true pope. Others inclined in this direction do not go so far as to say the papal chair is empty, but still reject the dogmatic weight of the Council, insisting it is merely of "pastoral" legitimacy. Critics of the Second Vatican Council also came from the liberationist left. In particular they accused the Council of sacrificing the poor on the altar of class harmony. Others, like French theologian Jacques Maritain, who originally supported the Council, started to worry in writing soon after the Council about having unleashed a revolutionary frenzy of uncontrollable and ultimately destructive change. Many proposed to accept the Council, but interpreted it in ways that downplayed its reform and highlighted its continuity with tradition. Paul VI, Pope John Paul II, and Cardinal Joseph Ratzinger (later Pope Benedict XVI) are among those most often cited as holding up the "continuity" interpretation of the Council. In various documents and statements they advanced the idea that a sophisticated understanding of the Council would read it strictly in light of tradition. Paul VI's encyclical on human sexuality, *Humanae Vitae* (1968), stands as a key document affirming the "continuity" interpretation. Paul's encyclical rejected the recommendations of a commission at the Council to soften the rules against Catholics' use of artificial birth control. See Daniele Menozzi "Opposition to the Council (1966–84)," in *The Reception of Vatican II*, ed. Giuseppe Alberigo, Jean-Pierre Jossua, and Joseph A. Komonchak (Washington DC: The Catholic University of America Press, 1987), 325–348. John W. O'Malley, *What Happened at Vatican II* (Cambridge, MA and London: Harvard University Press, 2008), 2–6.

59. See for example Karl Rahner, "Towards a Fundamental Theological Interpretation of Vatican II" *Theological Studies*, 40, no. 4 (1979): 716-727; A variety of responses from prominent individuals sympathetic to the "break" interpretation can be found in William Madge and Michael J. Daley *Vatican II: Forty Personal Stories* (New London, CT: Twenty-Third Publications, 2003); John W. O'Malley has been a leading Catholic historical voice for recognizing the shift of tone—the attitude with which the church engaged the rest of the world—as marking a profound transformation and break from the past. O'Malley, *What Happened at Vatican II*, 11–12.
60. Xavier Rynne, *Vatican Council II* (Maryknoll, NY: Orbis Press, 1999), 8. Some questions, notably clerical celibacy, artificial contraception, reform of the Roman Curia, and the character of the newly formed Synod of Bishops, did not make it to the floor for discussion. Still others passed relatively easily through the period of debate and into official teaching. Still others demanded long weeks of debate. John W. O'Malley, *What Happened at Vatican II* 6–7.
61. Xavier Rynne, *Vatican Council II*, 10. See also O'Malley's description of "the long nineteenth century," a "beleaguered" period for church leaders in their encounters with social, scientific, theological, and philosophical change. For Catholics, this "long nineteenth century" ended not in 1900, but in 1962, with the opening of the Council. O'Malley, *What Happened at Vatican II*, 53–92.
62. For an analysis of this realization as an impetus for change in the church, see Stephen S. J. Schloesser, "Against Forgetting: Memory, History, Vatican II," *Vatican II: Did Anything Happen?*, ed. David G. Schultenover (New York: Continuum Press, 2007), 92–153.
63. Rynne, *Vatican Council II*, 31; O'Malley, *What Happened at Vatican II* discusses the history councils, the relationship of conciliar decisions to papal authority, and debate over church canons related to these issues. O'Malley, *What Happened at Vatican II*, 25–33.
64. Pius XII, *Humani Generis* ("Concerning some false opinions threatening to undermine the foundations of Catholic doctrine," 1950). See Rynne, *Vatican Council II*, 15.
65. Henri de Lubac, "Internal Causes of the Weakening of the Sense of the Sacred," in his *Theology in History* (San Francisco: Ignatius Press, 1996), 223–240.
66. Second Vatican Council, *Nostra Aetate* ("Declaration on the Relation of the Church to Non-Christian Religions," 1965) and *Dignitatis Humanae* ("Declaration on Religious Freedom," 1965).
67. O'Malley, *What Happened at Vatican II*, 8–9; John T. Noonan, *A Church That Can and Cannot Change: The Development of Catholic*

Moral Teaching (Notre Dame: University of Notre Dame Press, 2005); John T. McGreevy, *Catholicism and American Freedom: A History* (New York: W. W. Norton, 2003), 293. O'Malley identifies three fundamental issues, including "development," "the relation of center-to-periphery" or "authority," and the "style" or "model." He cites John Courtney Murray, the American Jesuit theologian of church-state relations, who describes "development" as "*the* issue under the issues." Although it does not speak directly to the experience of the Council, my research revealed that the question of "development" was most central to the conflicts in Boston, with issues of authority and tone emerging primarily in connection to the question of continuity and change. For the language of "development" as a way to think about Catholic change, most theologians turn to the 1845 text by John Henry Newman, "An Essay on the Development of Christian Doctrine."

68. Jerome M. Hall, "Intelligent and Active Participation: The Liturgical Press," *U.S. Catholic Historian*, 21, no. 3 (Summer 2003), 43–48. For an in-depth study of the liturgical movement in the United States, see Keith F. Peckler, *Unread Vision: The Liturgical Movement in the United States of America, 1926–1955* (Collegeville, MN: Liturgical Press, 1998).
69. Rynne, *Vatican Council II*, 16–17, 61–76. Jay P. Dolan, *The American Catholic Experience: A History from Colonial Times to the Present* (New York: Doubleday, 1985). For a short and helpful summary of Virgil Michel and "reform," see Joseph P. Chinnici, O.F.M., *Living Stones: The History and Structure of Catholic Spiritual Life in the United States* (Maryknoll, NY: Orbis Press, 1996), 177–185. On Dorothy Day see James T. Fisher, *The Catholic Counterculture in America, 1933–1962* (Chapel Hill: University of North Carolina Press, 1989), 1–99.
70. O'Malley, *Vatican II: Did Anything Happen?*, 2–3.
71. Rynne, *Vatican Council II*, 22; James C. Livingston, Francis Schussler Fiorenza, Sarah Coakley, James H. Evans, *Modern Christian Thought, Volume II: The Twentieth Century*, 242.
72. Rynne, *Vatican Council II*, 8; O'Malley, "Introduction," in *Vatican II: Did Anything Happen?*, 5. On complications entailed in the idea of a "majority" in favor of change see Giuseppe Alberigo "The Christian Situation after Vatican II," in *The Reception of Vatican II*, ed. Giuseppe Alberigo, Jean-Pierre Jossua, and Joseph A. Komonchak (Washington DC: The Catholic University of America Press, 1987), 9.
73. O'Malley, *What Happened at Vatican II*, 11.
74. Livingston *et al.*, *Modern Christian Thought*, 237.
75. In *Habits of Devotion*, James O'Toole and his coauthors suggest a need for greater attentiveness, in the study of "lived" Catholicism, to the "routine"

rather than the "unusual" and "exotic." This is a move they see as a necessary complement to Robert A. Orsi's focus on "vivid but exceptional practices." This distinction downplays the intensity of Catholics' everyday life (death, loss, deep personal connections and fractured relationships, sin, guilt, and relief cannot be construed as "unusual," but are certainly "intense"). But the move toward study of routine does assist in the production of the "long historical view" in the effort to make sense of Catholics' response to change in church and society across the twentieth century. James M. O'Toole, "Introduction," in *Habits of Devotion: Catholic Religious Practice in Twentieth Century America* (Ithaca, NY: Cornell University Press, 2004), 2–3. Robert A. Orsi, *The Madonna of 115th Street*, and Orsi, *Thank You, St. Jude*.

76. Just as the word "Church" appears capitalized in the official documents of the Roman Catholic Church and elsewhere, the phrase "people of God" often appears as "People of God." The historical discipline has been split on the question of capitalizing "church" (when referring to the specific branch of Christianity called Roman Catholicism) and "people" in the phrase "people of God." In order to follow contemporary academic standards and to avoid conflating the Roman Catholic Church with the entire Christian religion, I have chosen not to capitalize "church" when referring to the Roman Catholic Church. I have decided to retain the pattern with "people of God." As a proper name of sorts, "God" is capitalized. Context has proven sufficient in most cases to distinguish the church as institutional Roman Catholic Church from church buildings.
77. Jay Dolan, *The American Catholic Experience*, 438–440; O'Malley, *What Happened at Vatican II*, 11.
78. Among the most notable changes in practice in the middle decades of the twentieth century were a sharp decrease in devotions such as novenas and Eucharistic adoration, a decline in public processions and feast-day events, and a stunning drop-off in the formerly robust sacrament of penance. Out of these declines emerged new or rediscovered forms of Catholic practice, including charismatic (Pentecostal) Catholicism and contemplative prayer. The best single source for understanding a wide array of changes in Catholic practice in the United States is *Habits of Devotion: Catholic Religious Practice in Twentieth-Century America*, ed. James M. O'Toole (Ithaca: Cornell University Press, 2004).
79. Komonchak, "Interpreting the Council," 22; O'Connor, *Boston Catholics*, 266. Paul VI's *Humanae Vitae*, which countered the recommendation of the council's committee on birth control, stands as a primary example with momentous implications. See Leslie Wheelcock Tentler, *Catholics and Contraception: An American History* (Ithaca, NY: Cornell University

Press, 2004); Joseph A. Komonchak, "*Humanae Vitae* and Its Reception: Ecclesiological Reflections," *Theological Studies* 39 (1978): 221–257.

80. Thomas H. O'Connor, *Boston Catholics*, 268–269. Dolan, *The American Catholic Experience*, 428–433.
81. Pius VI, *Lumen Gentium*.
82. My observations and a census I conducted at three occupied churches revealed that Catholics in resisting parishes were mainly of a generation that had grown up and moved into young adulthood either before or during the Second Vatican Council. Out of the 155 Catholics who participated in the census, the average age was 60.5 (born in 1948). 72.25% of the respondents were 50 years old or older (born in 1958 or earlier), 60.5% were 60 or older (born in 1948 or earlier), and 30.9% were 70 or older (born in 1938 or earlier). Forty-nine were men (32%) and 100 were women (67%). Six respondents did not list their sex. "Parish Census," Our Lady of Mount Carmel, East Boston Three Year Vigil Anniversary Communion Service, October 27, 2007; St. James the Great Wellesley, Three Year Vigil Anniversary Mass, October 14, 2007; St. Jeremiah, Framingham, Sunday Mass, March 2, 2008. As a group, participants in the census were younger than everyday vigil participants.
83. The connections were sometimes quite direct. In the mid-1950s Cardinal Cushing opened the way for Monsignor Francis J. Lally, an expert on urban planning and the editor of the archdiocesan newspaper, to become chairman of the Boston Redevelopment Authority, the agency largely responsible for planning neighborhood renewal projects in Boston. O'Connor *Boston Catholics*, 296. Thomas H. O'Connor, *Building a New Boston: Politics and Urban Renewal, 1950–1970* (Boston: Northeastern University Press, 1995), 217–220.
84. Chinnici helpfully documents nineteenth-century Catholic efforts to separate religious from social Americanism. If Catholics could prove they had not "Americanized" religiously, they could avoid critiques from Rome associated with this label while still opening a way for accommodation and adaptation to American social life. Joseph P. Chinnici, *Living Stones: The History and Structure of Catholic Spiritual Life in the United States* (Maryknoll, NY: Orbis Books, 1996 [1989]), 119–136. The distinction would remain significant in the middle and late twentieth century. See, for example, Margaret M. McGuinness, "Let Us Go to the Altar," in *Habits of Devotion*, 207–208.
85. On hyphenated religion or the "triple melting pot" of "Protestant-Catholic-Jew" see Will Herberg, *Protestant, Catholic, Jew: An Essay in American Religious Sociology* (Chicago: Chicago University Press, 1955). On postwar American "spiritual revival" see also Joseph P. Chinnici, "The Catholic

Community at Prayer, 1926–1976" in *Habits of Devotion: Catholic Religious Practice in Twentieth-Century America*, ed. James M. O'Toole (Ithaca, NY: Cornell University Press, 2004), 53. On Catholic participation in and enthusiasm for the Cold War fight against Communism see Mark S. Massa, *Catholics and American Culture: Fulton Sheen, Dorothy Day, and the Notre Dame Football Team* (New York: Crossroads, 1999), 57–81; for a more specific study of Cold War Catholicism, see James T. Fisher, *The Catholic Counterculture in America, 1933–1962* (Chapel Hill: University of North Carolina Press, 1989), 131–167. On suburbanizing see Massa, *Catholics and American Culture*, 99–100. For a contemporary sociological look at suburban Catholicism, Andrew M. Greely, "The Catholic Suburbanite," in *The American City: A Sourcebook of Urban Imagery*, ed. Anselm L. Strauss (Chicago: Aldine Publishing Co, 1968), 421–426 [originally in *The Sign* 37 (February 1958)]. See also O'Connell, *Boston Catholics*, 266–68.

86. Edward T. Linenthal and David Chidester, "Introduction," in *American Sacred Space* (Bloomington: University of Indiana Press, 1995), 1-42.
87. Catherine Bell, *Ritual Theory, Ritual Practice* (New York: Oxford University Press, 1992), 98.
88. Danièle Hervieu-Léger, *Religion as a Chain of Memory*, trans. Simon Lee (Cambridge, UK: Polity Press, 2000), 167.

1. The Pasts Living in People

1. Augusto Ferraiuolo, *Religious Festive Practices in Boston's North End: Ephemeral Identities in an Italian American Community* (Albany: State University of New York Press, 2009), 77.
2. Thomas O'Connor, *Building a New Boston: Politics and Urban Renewal 1950–1970* (Boston: Northeastern University Press, 1993), 291. Paula J. Todisco, *Boston's First Neighborhood: The North End* (Boston: Trustees of the Public Library of the City of Boston, 1976), 53–55.
3. North End parishes St. Mary's and St. Stephen's were closed in 1992. A historic landmark, St. Stephen's building would remain open as a chapel of ease, administered officially by St. Leonard's. St. Leonard of Port Maurice became a territorial parish in 1992.
4. Ralph, (M-mid-50s), Phillip, (M-mid-50s), Carla (F-59), August 24, 2004.
5. Lord et al. cite United States immigration reports to conclude that between 1898 and 1910 Massachusetts "received 132,820 immigrants from Southern Italy, and 22,062 from the North." Robert H. Lord, John E. Sexton, and Edward T. Harrington, *History of the Archdiocese of Boston in the Various Stages of its Development, 1604–1943*, v. III (New York: Pilot Publishing, 1944), 220.

6. James M. O'Toole, "Prelates and Politicos: Catholics and Politics in Massachusetts, 1900–1970," in *Catholic Boston: Studies in Religion and Community, 1870–1970*, ed. Robert E Sullivan and James M. O'Toole (Boston: Roman Catholic Archbishop of Boston, 1985), 16; Lord et al., 194. Lord et al. describe the ways Italian immigration had been construed as a religious problem: "There is no denying . . . that the Italian immigrants furnished an unusually difficult problem for the church. More than with almost any other incoming Catholic stock, it seemed hard to draw them into normal contacts with the church here, or to induce them to attend to their religious duties with the fidelity and regularity that American Catholics have commonly shown. Many an alarming report on this subject appeared in our Catholic press. Hosts of the newcomers, it was said, did not know even the rudiments of their faith; had never received any instruction . . . had never received any Sacrament save Baptism. Hardly one in a hundred, it was affirmed, attended mass, at least with any regularity. Most of them, it was charged, had abandoned their religion in the Bay of Naples, or, if they retained any, seemed to express it only in emotionalism, or in occasionally going to Mass on the feast of some national Saint. There was even talk of 'the apostasy en masse of the Italian immigrants.'" Citation is from Rev. A. Palmieri (*Il grave problema religioso-italiano negli Stati Uniti* (Firenze, 1921), 8ff.), who, Lord notes, cites these and many similar cries of alarm, but deals with the problem objectively. Lord et al., 221–222. See also O'Connor, *Boston Catholics*, 166.
7. O'Toole, "Prelates and Politicos," 19; Susan S. Walton, "'The Good Sisters:' The Work and Position of Catholic Churchwomen in Boston, 1870–1940," in Sullivan and O'Toole, *Catholic Boston*, 90, 98–100; Peter R. D'Agostino, "The Scalabrini Fathers, the Italian Emigrant Church, and Ethnic Nationalism in America," *Religion and American Culture* 7:1 (Winter 1997): 131.
8. Donna Merwick, *Boston Priests, 1848–1910: A Study of Social and Intellectual Change* (Cambridge, MA: Harvard University Press, 1973), 64, 108.
9. Lord et al., 189–90; Paula Kane, *Separatism and Subculture*, 4–5; James O'Toole "Here and There: Looking at Catholicism in New England," *U.S. Catholic Historian* 18, no. 3 (Summer, 2000): 16–17.
10. Walton notes that the Catholic Immigration Bureau established a Sunday school in Sacred Heart Parish in the North End in order to offset the influence of Protestant proselytizing and offer to the Italian children "moral and religious inspiration from these Irish Catholic role models which presumably they lacked among their Italian parents and neighbors." Walton, "The Good Sisters," 101.

11. Leonard Bacigalupo, O.F.M., *The Franciscans and Italian Immigration in America* (Wappingers Falls, New York: Mount Alvernia Friary, 1973), 31; Lord et al., 225.
12. Out of 26,000 residents of the North End in 1880, approximately 1,000 were Italians. The period between 1880 and 1900 was tumultuous for the North End, with many upwardly mobile Irish leaving for Beacon Hill and the Back Bay. By 1900, the North End housed approximately 15,000 Italians. Stephen Puleo, *The Boston Italians: A Story of Pride, Perseverance, and Paesani, from the Years of the Great Immigration to the Present Day* (Boston: Beacon Press, 2007), 7–8. On devotions at St. Leonard's see Bacigalupo, *Franciscans and Italian Immigration*, 31–33.
13. The marriage registers of St. Leonard of Port Maurice from its early years show an overwhelming preponderance of Italian surnames. RCAB Archives, Marriage Register, St. Leonard of Port Maurice Parish.
14. Puleo, *The Boston Italians*, 6–7.
15. Lord et al., 224. See also Oscar Handlin, *The Uprooted: The Epic Story of the Great Migrations that Made the American People* (Philadelphia: University of Pennsylvania Press, 2002 [1951]), 122.
16. "About 30 percent of new parishes founded in New England between 1880 and 1930 were ethnic (national) parishes, compared with a mere 9 percent between 1850 and 1880." Kane, *Separatism and Subculture*, 5.
17. Kane, *Separatism and Subculture*, 13–14.
18. For this and the following see Patrick W. Carey, *People, Priests, and Prelates: Ecclesiastical Democracy and the Tensions of Trusteeism* (Notre Dame, IN: University of Notre Dame Press, 1987), 214–15. For a concise summary of the legal origins of corporation sole and a defense of "subsidiarity" see Mark E. Chopko, "Parish Structures: Identity, Integrity, and Indissolubility," *Church Magazine* Summer, 2009, www.churchmagazine.com.
19. Jay P. Dolan, *The American Catholic Experience: A History from Colonial Times to the Present* (New York: Doubleday, 1985), 111, 114–116.
20. The "Romanism" of bishops like Martin Spalding, Francis Kenrick, and Patrick Lynch was one manifestation in America of the nineteenth-century Catholic revival in Europe. See John T. McGreevy, *Catholicism and American Freedom: A History* (New York and London: W. W. Norton Company, 2003), 26–28.
21. But just as in the case of lay trustees the ordinary as corporation sole held the property in trust for the good of the church. This definition of the relationship of parishes to dioceses in civil and canon law (parish real estate and non-real assets as trusts held by local ordinaries for the good of the parish) meant that parish assets were not of dioceses, but of parishes for whom the diocese held them in trust. As we will see, this

would become a crucial firewall in legal efforts to protect parish assets from dioceses' creditors, including the many victims of sexual abuse who came forward in the early 2000s. When dioceses pleaded bankruptcy, victims' lawyers indentified parishes and their property as diocesan assets that should be made available for their clients. The difference between the local ordinary as trustee and as owner also proved a thorny issue during Boston's shutdowns, where the diocese improperly tried to claim the assets of parishes instead of allowing those funds to move with the parishioners to their new parish.

22. Lord et al., 225; Bacigalupo, *Franciscans and Italian Immigration*, 31.
23. Lord et al., 225.
24. Kane, *Separatism and Subculture*, 13–14.
25. For "two Johns" references see Lawrence McCaffrey, *The Irish Catholic Diaspora in America* (Washington, DC: The Catholic University of America Press, 1997), 183; Garry Wills, *Why I Am a Catholic* (Boston and New York: Mariner Books, 2003), 219; Rebecca Sullivan, *Visual Habits: Nuns, Feminism, and American Postwar Popular Culture* (Toronto, Buffalo, and London: University of Toronto Press, 2005), 126; Jay P. Dolan writes that by the time of the Second Vatican Council, Catholics in America were "comfortably American," but that the changes in the church now made them uncertain what it meant to be a Catholic. Jay Dolan, *The American Catholic Experience*, 427–428. Andrew Greeley has been the leading voice describing a postwar American Catholic laity ready for democratization, updating, tolerance, social justice, and freedom of conscience and religion. The appeal of the "Catholic imagination" and its "sacramentality" is what keeps Catholics in a church whose hierarchy they have generally moved beyond. See Andrew Greeley, *The Catholic Revolution: New Wine, Old Wineskins, and the Second Vatican Council* (Berkeley and Los Angeles: University of California Press, 2004), 107–108. For relatively early and perceptive historical analyses of these transitional years see Phillip Gleason, "The Crisis of Americanization," in *Contemporary Catholicism in the United States*, ed. Phillip Gleason (Notre Dame, IN: Notre Dame University Press, 1969), 3–32; David J. O'Brien, *The Renewal of American Catholicism* (New York: Oxford University Press, 1972), 51–108. See also Joseph P. Chinnici, "The Catholic Community at Prayer, 1926–1976" in *Habits of Devotion: Catholic Religious Practice in Twentieth-Century America*, ed. James M. O'Toole (Ithaca: Cornell University Press, 2004).
26. Merwick, *Boston Priests*, xi, 75–76.
27. Archbishop John Ireland of St. Paul, Minnesota, was a particularly strong advocate of Americanization in the latter years of the nineteenth century.

He and some of his episcopal colleagues actively sought theological dialogue with Protestants, enthused about American democracy, sought compromise on issues related to Catholic and public schooling, and urged the elimination of ethnic Catholic difference. Ireland's "liberal" confreres included Cincinnati Archbishop John Purcell, Father Thomas Ferrell and Father Edward McGlynn of New York, Father Patrick F. McSweeney of the Poughkeepsie plan, and Father Thomas Bouquillon of the Catholic University. McGreevy, *Catholicism and American Freedom*, 118–122. Enthusiastic reception of a French translation of Walter Elliott's biography of Father Isaac Hecker, the American founder of the Paulists, brought the "crisis" to a head and spurred the papal condemnation of the "heresy" of Americanism.

28. R. Scott Appleby, *Church and Age Unite!: The Modernist Impulse in American Catholicism* (Notre Dame, IN: University of Notre Dame Press, 1992), 7–8.
29. McGreevy, *Catholicism and American Freedom*, 121–22.
30. Leo XIII, *Longinqua Oceani* ("On Catholicism in the United States"), 1895. Leo XIII, *Testem Benevolentiae* ("Concerning New Opinions, Virtue, Nature, Grace, with Regard to Americanism"), 1899. On "self reliance" in contrast to "obedience" as a spiritual issue in the Americanist crisis of the 1890s, see Joseph P. Chinnici, *Living Stones: The History and Structure of Catholic Spiritual Life in the United States* (Maryknoll, NY: Orbis Books, 1996 [1989]), 120.
31. Here I am indebted to the analysis of a similar case found in Robert A. Orsi, *The Madonna of 115th Street: Faith and Community in Italian Harlem, 1880–1950* (New Haven: Yale University Press, 1985), 61–63.
32. See D'Agostino, "The Scalabrini Fathers," 126; Kane, *Separatism and Subculture*, 8–9.
33. Merwick, *Boston Priests*, 67. Quotations from "The Good Parish," *The Pilot*, February 2, 1867, 4.
34. Lord et al. write that the group gave the title over to the Scalabrinian priest Father Zaboglio. Lord et al., 225–226.
35. This part of the deed was quoted in "AG gains oversight of assets at parishes," *Boston Globe*, August 19, 2004.
36. O'Brien, *The Renewal of American Catholicism*, 63. Appleby, *Church and Age Unite!*, 235. On the connection between Americanism and modernism see Appleby, *Church and Age Unite!*, 181–182.
37. O'Brien, *The Renewal of American Catholicism*, 64. Chinnici, *Living Stones*, 126–127.
38. The Vatican approved the "national parish" solution to church growth in 1897. It became an official part of canon law in 1918. James O'Toole, *Militant and Triumphant: William Henry O'Connell and the Catholic Church*

in Boston, 1859–1944 (Notre Dame and London: University of Notre Dame Press, 1992), 148. O'Brien, *The Renewal of American Catholicism*, 63; Orsi, *The Madonna of 115th Street*, 61–63.

39. O'Toole, *Militant and Triumphant*, 77–78, 147, 171. See also O'Connor, *Boston Catholics*, 215–218; Kane, *Separatism and Subculture*.
40. Kane shows that early-twentieth-century Boston Catholics endorsed Catholicism (as illustrated in communalism, the church's stance on progressive social reform, and its public processions) as the seedbed of principles for effective and moral national governance. Kane, *Separatism and Subculture*, 30, 38, 47.
41. Michele McPhee, "'Disgusted' Eastie churchgoers boiling mad over lost donations," *Boston Herald*, March 11, 2005.
42. Val (M-62), June 18, 2005.
43. After a few months of rotating overnight shifts in the church, resisters at Mount Carmel reasoned that the peace of mind secured through round-the-clock church occupation could more easily be secured through the installation of an alarm system. The expense of installing the system easily outweighed the costs of round-the-clock occupation—sleepless nights, high heating bills, over-exertion, and increased potential for accidents in the church.
44. "East Boston: Boston 200 Neighborhood Series," (Boston: Boston 200 Corporation, 1976), 6.
45. Boston Landmarks Commission, "East Boston: Exploring Boston's Neighborhoods" (City of Boston 1995), 2; "East Boston: Boston 200 Neighborhood History Series," 6. The presence of settlement houses speaks to the presence of a significant working-class Catholic population who were considered by settlement house missionaries to be in need of training and assistance.
46. Roy Rosenzweig, "The Parks and the People: Social History and Urban Parks," *Journal of Social History* 18, no. 2 (Winter 1984): 292.
47. Thriving in the North End, the Scalabrinians soon set their sights on other mission fields. Sacred Heart was not only a successful parish, but also became a platform for the expansion of their missionary goals. By 1892, the parish had begun to send missionaries from North Square into other neighborhoods with significant Italian populations around Boston. Their mission sites included East Boston. Lord et al., 228.
48. On financial challenges at the outset, see Rev. Liberti (letter, 16 November, 1907). RCAB Archives, Parish Correspondence. (Letterhead reads Francis F. Sanella, Pastor.)
49. OLMC Archives-NY, "East Boston Reports 2; East Boston: Moral Reports," "Financial Reports."

50. Kane, *Separatism and Subculture*, 322; O'Connor, *Boston Catholics*, 202–203. Pius XI's endorsement of Catholic Action as a closely supervised lay initiative opened the way to the flowering of lay organizations in the United States in the 1930s. See Jeremy Bonner, *The Road to Renewal: Victor Joseph Reed & Oklahoma Catholicism, 1905–1971* (Washington DC: Catholic University Press of America, 2008), 5.
51. OLMC Archives-NY, "Dedication of Our Parochial School: Entertainment September 21, 1930." (folder title "Historical Item").
52. Val, June 18, 2005, OLMC. Robert A. Orsi, "'The Infant of Prague's Nightie': The Devotional Origins of Contemporary Catholic Memory," *U.S. Catholic Historian* 21 no. 2 (2003): 13. See also James M. O'Toole, *The Faithful: A History of Catholics in America* (Cambridge and London: Belknap Press of Harvard University Press, 2008), 115–116, 176–177; O'Connor, *Boston Catholics*, 247–249.
53. Richard Sennett, *The Corrosion of Character: The Personal Consequences of Work in the New Capitalism* (New York: W. W. Norton and Company, 1998), 9–31.
54. Sennett, *The Corrosion of Character*, 10.
55. Roman Catholic Archdiocese of Boston, *Archdiocese of Boston Parish Closing Manual: Rebuild My Church, version 1.0*, May, 2004, 18. [hereafter "*CM*"]
56. Sennett, *The Corrosion of Character*, 133.
57. Father Willard, August 22, 2006 Sacred Heart (East Boston).
58. Val (M-62), June 18, 2005, OLMC.
59. Sennett, *The Corrosion of Character*, 133.
60. In some locales, the "family pew" was seen as a hindrance of post-Vatican II efforts to bring Catholics into greater participation with the mass. The common pre-mass scene of pastors imploring people to move up to the front illustrates the conflicting values at work in the church. See Bonner, *Road to Renewal*, 205.
61. Rev. A. J. Schulte, *Consecranda: Rites and Ceremonies Observed at the Consecration of Churches, Altars, Altar-Stones, Chalices, and Patens* (New York & Cincinnati: Benzinger Brothers, 1956 [1907]). These manuals were derived from the Roman Pontifical. The 1956 manual implements only slight changes. Bishops' Committee on the Liturgy, *Rite for the Dedication of a Church and an Altar: Provisional Text* (Washington, DC: National Conference of Catholic Bishops, 1978) (hereafter "*RDCA*"). The 1978 manual is a translation of a 1977 document produced by a liturgical committee designated for the task in Rome. The group first met in 1970, under the auspices of the Sacred Congregation of Rites and "working with the Consilium for Implementing the

Constitution on the Sacred Liturgy, the Sacred Congregation for Divine Worship (as it was then called), and by the Sacred Congregation for the Sacraments and Divine Worship (as it is now called)." Members included Pierre Jounel, Ignazio M. Calabuig, O.S.M., Andre Rose, O.S.B., Domenico Sartore, and Rosella Barberi. Thomas G. Simons, *Holy People, Holy Place: Rites for the Church's House* (Chicago: Archdiocese of Chicago Liturgy Training Publications, 1998), 26.

62. In the introduction to *Consecranda*, H. J. Heuser, the editor of the *American Ecclesiastical Review*, noted that Schulte had admirably carried forward work begun in a series of articles in the *Review* designed to clarify "ecclesiastical functions." Heuser also discusses the manual's ability to prevent clumsy and delayed performances that might be "a source of irreverence and disedification to the critically disposed spectator." H. J. Heuser, "Introduction," *Consecranda* (1907), xi–xii. On the uniquely "practical" bent of the American liturgical movement see Jerome M. Hall, "Intelligent and Active Participation: The Liturgical Press," *U.S. Catholic Historian*, 21, no. 3 (Summer, 2003): 49, 53.

63. Simons, *Holy People, Holy Place*, 23; Ignazio M. Calabuig, O.S.M., *The Dedication of a Church and an Altar: A Theological Commentary* (Washington, DC: United States Catholic Conference, 1980), 12; John Allyn S. M. Melloh, "The Rite of Dedication," *Assembly* 10, no. 2 (Nov. 1983): 229; Field, "The Rite of Dedication: History, Theology, Celebration," *Environment and Art Letter* (March 1994): 5.

64. O'Brien, *The Renewal of American Catholicism*, 66.

65. Robert A. Orsi discusses some reformers' violent attitude toward devotional objects associated with a pre–Second Vatican Council tradition as one manifestation of Catholics' obsession with remembering and imagining the Catholic past. Robert A. Orsi, "'The Infant of Prague's Nightie': The Devotional Origins of Contemporary Catholic Memory," *U.S. Catholic Historian* 21, no. 2 (2003).

66. Brian Repsher, *The Rite of Church Dedication in the Early Medieval Era* (Lewiston, NY: Edwin Mellen Press, 1998), 17, 134; Simons, *Holy People, Holy Place*, 18; James Field, "The Rite of Dedication," 4.

67. Repsher, *Rite of Church Dedication in the Early Medieval Era*, 121.

68. P. Jounel says that if they could find relics, "most" bishops "wanted to place some relic of a martyr in their new place of worship." *The Church at Prayer: An Introduction to the Liturgy*, v. 1, ed. Aimé Georges Martimort, trans. Matthew J. O'Connell (Collegeville, MN: Liturgical Press, 1987), 217. By the time of the Second Council of Nicea in 787 consecrated churches were required to have relics embedded in or below their altars. Thaddeus Ziolkowski, *The Consecration and Blessing of Churches: A*

Historical Synopsis and Commentary (published dissertation) (Washington, DC: Catholic University Press, 1943), 14, 32; Ruth Horie, *Perceptions of Ecclesia: Church and Soul in Medieval Dedication Sermons* (Turnhout, Belgium: Brepols) 2006, 50.

69. Schulte, *Consecranda* (1907), 29. The 1956 version asks only that two candles be kept burning overnight. Schulte, *Consecranda* (1956), 25.
70. Schulte, *Consecranda* (1956), 9.
71. Schulte, *Consecranda* (1956), 2.
72. After the rite of consecration "the Mass then begins as usual, as if nothing had happened before that." Melloh, "The Rite of Dedication," 229.
73. The consecrating bishop could opt out of the mass, or could choose only to assist the mass after he had finished the consecration. Schulte, *Consecranda* (1956), 132.
74. Psalms 6, 31, 37, 50, 101, 129, 142.
75. Repsher, *Rite of Church Dedication in the Early Medieval Era* describes the consolidation of the rites of dedication at this time.
76. Repsher, *Rite of Church Dedication in the Early Medieval Era*, 142. This is a translation of a ninth-century version of the rite. Gregorian water is a combination of water, salt, wine, and ashes and was used in the lustration of the altar.
77. Calabuig, *The Dedication of a Church and an Altar*, 13.
78. Foster identifies the origins of this rite in a Celtic practice of claiming territory, and cites Corinthians 3:11 and Psalm 86. Michael Smith Foster, "The Sacred in Relation to a Church Building: A Canonical Evaluation" (Washington, DC: JCL Dissertation, Catholic University of America, 1988), 22.
79. Ziolkowski, "The Consecration and Blessing of Churches," 2.
80. Calabuig, *The Dedication of a Church and an Altar*, 29.
81. Schulte, *Consecranda* (1956), pp. 51–119.
82. On the Liturgical Press and its part in the liturgical movement in America, see Hall, "Intelligent and Active Participation," 37–56.
83. Botz edited *Sponsa Regis*, the publication from which the "Popular Liturgical Library" pamphlet cited here was drawn. He was also, with Mary Anthony Wagner, OSB, the first director of the Benedictine Institute of Sacred Theology at the College of St. Benedict in St. Joseph, Minnesota. His works include *The Benedictine Brother* (Collegeville, MN: St. John's Abbey Press, 1954), *Thanksgiving after Holy Communion* (Collegeville, MN: Liturgical Press, 1959), *Blessed Old Age* (Collegeville, MN: Liturgical Press, 1961), *Runways to God: The Psalms as Prayer* (Collegeville, MN: Liturgical Press, 1979). See Richard Oliver,

O.S.B, "St. John's and the American Benedictine Academy," *The Abbey Banner: Magazine of St. John's Abbey* 4, no. 3 (Winter, 2004): 15. Coleman James Barry *Worship and Work: St. John's Abbey and University, 1856–1980* (Collegeville, MN: Liturgical Press, 1980), 262, 268, 281, 380. On Botz's relationship to influential reformer Godfrey Diekmann see Kathleen Hughes, *A Monk's Tale: A Biography of Godfrey Diekmann, O.S.B.* (Collegeville, MN: Liturgical Press, 1991), 24, 56, 78. Diekmann helped craft the document that would establish the foundation for the Second Vatican Council's *Sacrosanctum Concilium* ("The Constitution on the Sacred Liturgy" (1962)).

84. Botz, "Meaning of the Altar," in *Blessing Church, Altar, School: A Group of Four Liturgical Pamphlets* (Collegeville, MN: Liturgical Press, 1958), 3, 5.
85. Botz, "Meaning of the Altar," pp. 6–7.
86. Botz, "Meaning of the Altar," pp. 10–11.
87. Botz, "Meaning of the Altar," p. 12.
88. Repsher, *The Rite of Church Dedication in the Early Medieval Era*, 28–29.
89. O'Connor, *Boston Catholics*, 247–50.
90. On traditional lay distance from the sanctuary see O'Toole, *The Faithful*, 113.
91. Annetta (F-62), field notes February 27, 2005, March 6, 2005, OLMC.
92. Danièle Hervieu-Léger, *Religion as a Chain of Memory* (New Brunswick: Rutgers University Press, 2000), 128–130.

2. Divergent Histories

1. OLMC Financial Reports, NY; OLMC Bulletins 1993–1997.
2. Catharine, November 30, 2004. The windows are also featured in Bella English, "They're throwing us away," *Boston Globe*, August 26, 2004.
3. Catharine, November 30, 2004, SAG.
4. "Surrounded by the Saints" is the title on one page of the SAG "Golden Jubilee Parish Album," 2000, SAG Parish Archives.
5. John T. McGreevy, *Catholicism and American Freedom: A History* (New York: W. W. Norton and Company, 2003), 292–293.
6. Stephen Schloesser, "Against Forgetting: Memory History, Vatican II," in *Vatican II: Did Anything Happen?*, ed. John O'Malley (New York: Continuum Press, 2007), 92–153.
7. Orsi, "The Infant of Prague's Nightie," *U.S. Catholic Historian.* See also Joseph P. Chinnici, "The Catholic Community at Prayer, 1926–1976" in *Habits of Devotion: Catholic Religious Practice in Twentieth-Century*

America, ed. James M. O'Toole (Ithaca, NY: Cornell University Press, 2004), 9–88.

8. "Parish Census," Our Lady of Mount Carmel, East Boston; Three Year Vigil Anniversary Communion Service, October 27, 2007; St. James the Great, Wellesley, Three Year Vigil Anniversary Mass, October 14, 2007; St. Jeremiah, Framingham, Sunday Mass, March 2, 2008.

9. According to O'Toole, confession disappeared "almost completely in the 1970s." James M. O'Toole, "In the Court of Conscience: American Catholics and Confession, 1900–1975"; on Marian devotions, see Paula Kane, "Marian Devotions since 1940: Continuity or Casualty?" Both appear in *Habits of Devotion: Catholic Religious Practice in Twentieth-century America*, ed. James M. O'Toole (Ithaca, NY: Cornell University Press, 2004), 89–130 and 131–186. See also O'Connor, *Boston Catholics*, 289–91.

10. The Official U.S. Catholic Directory showed 2,556 priests in Boston in 1975, 2,502 in 1978, 2,203 in 1987, 1,665 in 1999, and 1,408 in 2006. The number of sisters showed an even more precipitous drop, going from 6,080 in 1967 to 5,092 by 1977, 4,005 in 1987, and 2,646 in 1999. Decline in the number of brothers started earlier, going from 388 to 200 between 1960 and 1975. But their numbers rose to 265 in 1987 before declining sharply thereafter. *Official Catholic Directory* (New York: P. J. Kennedy, serial). O'Connor, *Boston Catholics*, 289–290.

11. Busing was of particular relevance in Boston. For Archbishop Medeiros's moderate, but nonetheless controversial, support for court ordered busing see O'Connor, *Boston Catholics*, 299–301. For a more specific look at the Roman Catholic Archdiocese of Boston's stance on these issues during the 1950s, 60s, and 70s see O'Toole, "Prelates and Politicos," 42–65. See also Anthony Lukas, *Common Ground: A Turbulent Decade in the Lives of Three American Families* (New York: Vintage Books, 1985), and Ronald Formisano, *Boston Against Busing: Race, Class, and Ethnicity in the 1960s & 1970s* (Chapel Hill: University of North Carolina Press, 2004 [1991]), Louis P. Masur, *The Soiling of Old Glory* (New York: Bloomsbury Press, 2008), 1–53. For another take on busing see Michael Patrick MacDonald, *All Souls: A Family Story from Southie* (Boston: Beacon Press, 1999), 74–106.

12. Dolan, *The American Catholic Experience*, 421–454.

13. The number of students in Catholic colleges is one indicator of these shifts. In 1916, Dolan notes, there were 8,304 students and by 1950 there were 112,765. Dolan, *The American Catholic Experience*, 399. Among a sample of Catholics surveyed in 2005, "Vatican II Catholics," (those who attended school mostly in the 1950s and 1960s) were "most likely to have

attended a Catholic elementary school, high school, or college or university for at least some of their schooling." Catholic high school education was particularly common for this generation. This education correlated with greater financial success. Mary Gautier, "Does Catholic Education Make a Difference?" *National Catholic Reporter*, September 30, 2005. www.natcath.org.

14. There were 286 diocesan and parochial high schools and elementary schools in Boston in 1967, up from 283 in 1960 and 211 in 1940. By 1970 the number had fallen to 271. It was at this point that a major consolidation took place; by 1975 there were 204. Declines continued over the next thirty years. By 1999 the number stood at 136, and by 2006 there were 111. This was part of a national pattern. In 1972, Catholic schools in United States were closing at a rate of more than one per day. Enrollments had dropped 18% over the previous three years, and there was a 42% drop projected for 1980. *Official Catholic Directory;* James E. Glinski, "The Catholic Church and the Desegregation of Boston's Public Schools," in *Boston's Histories: Essays in Honor of Thomas H. O'Connor*, ed. James M. O'Toole and David Quigley (Boston: Northeastern University Press, 2004), 249. See also O'Connor, *Boston Catholics*, 290–92.
15. Wanger describes flourishing devotions in Catholic Boston under Cardinal O'Connell (archbishop from 1907–1944) with an increasing volume of daily and weekly communions, the expansion of Eucharistic Adoration as well as other devotional societies, especially the Holy Name Society. Thomas E. Wanger, "Catholic Religious Life in Boston in the Era of Cardinal O'Connell," in *Catholic Boston*, 239–272. O'Connor reports continued vitality in the 1950s. O'Connor, *Boston Catholics*, 247–50.
16. Chinnici, "The Catholic Community at Prayer, 1926–1976" 86–87. See also Hervieu-Léger, "What Scripture Tells Me," 26.
17. Dolan reports that a 1974 survey showed that 50% of Catholics attended church regularly compared with 71% in 1963. Non-attendance, he notes, doubled during that period. Dolan notes that mass attendance increased somewhat in the 1970s. Mass attendance in the United States was still among the highest in the world by the mid-1980s, when approximately 50% still attended on an average Sunday. Chaves and Cavendish used headcounts to report that approximately 26% of Catholics attended mass regularly in 1994. A 2004 poll indicated that about 30% of Catholics reported weekly mass attendance, with another 32% claiming they attended mass almost every week or at least once a month. Nationally, there were no statistically significant changes in mass attendance between 2000 and 2007. The archdiocesan sample headcounts may be more reliable than poll indications, especially those which entail an interview

rather than private reporting, which tends to over-report attendance. Hadaway, Marler, and Chaves suggest that attendance numbers should actually be counted at about half the rate of the most frequently cited polls. Dolan, *The American Catholic Experience*, 433–34; E. J. Dionne, Jr., "America and the Catholic Church: Conflicts with Rome and Within," *New York Times*, December 24, 1986, A1; Mark M. Gray, "The CARA Catholic Poll Digest: Measuring Mass Attendance Q & A," (Washington, DC: Georgetown University, Center for Applied Research in the Apostolate, 2006); Mark Chaves and James C. Cavendish, "More Evidence on United States Catholic Church Attendance," *Journal for the Scientific Study of Religion* 33 no. 4 (1994): 376–381; Mark M. Gray, Paul M. Perl, and Tricia C. Bruce, "Marriage in the Catholic Church: A Survey of United States Catholics" (Washington DC: Georgetown University, Center for Applied Research in the Apostolate, 2007), http://cara.georgetown.edu/MarriageReport.pdf; C. Kirk Hadaway, Penny Long Marler, Mark Chaves, "What the Polls Don't Show: A Closer Look at United States Church Attendance," *American Sociological Review*, 58 (1993): 741–752.

18. O'Connor, *Building a New Boston*, 10, 13–14.
19. O'Connor, *Building a New Boston*, 32, 72, 77.
20. John T. McGreevy, *Parish Boundaries: The Catholic Encounter with Race in the Twentieth-century Urban North* (Chicago: University of Chicago Press, 1996), 20, 24.
21. *Official Catholic Directory*. The city of Boston includes Boston, Dorchester, Roxbury, Brighton, Charlestown, East Boston, and South Boston.
22. From 1820 to 1846, the number of Catholics in the Boston diocese grew from approximately 3,500 to 32,000. By 1868 the number expanded to about 350,000. In the 1890s Catholics numbered approximately 750,000. By 1900 there were approximately 1 million Catholics in the diocese. Merwick, *Boston Priests*, x, 5; Lord et al., *History of the Archdiocese of Boston*, 18; Kane, *Separatism and Subculture*, 2; *Official Catholic Directory*. Joseph J. Casino, ("From Sanctuary to Involvement: A History of the Catholic Parish in the Northeast," in *The American Catholic Parish*, ed. Dolan, 106,) counts significantly lower numbers, but roughly similar rates of growth.
23. "The suburban population grew more than four times faster than the central city population in America during the 1950s, so that 13 million more Americans moved to the suburbs than to the cities in the decade. Suburban population growth constituted 76% of metropolitan area growth in the 1950s." Timothy Kelly, "Suburbanization and the Decline of Catholic Public Ritual in Pittsburgh," *Journal of Social History* 28, no. 2 (1994): 321. See also Joseph J. Casino, "From Sanctuary to Involvement," 84–101 and the *Official Catholic Directory*. Kelly reports that nationally,

suburban parishes generally had more parishioners than urban parishes. See also Gamm, *Urban Exodus;* O'Connor, *Boston Catholics*, 310–312.

24. Other parishes, especially after changes in U.S. immigration policy in 1965, became the home parishes of growing numbers of Spanish, French-Creole, Vietnamese, and Chinese-speaking Catholics. On the assets for institutional stability of centralized, hierarchical organization see Gerald Gamm, *Urban Exodus;* Peter R. D'Agostino, "The Archdiocese of Chicago: Planning and Change for a Restructured Metropolis," in *Religious Organizations and Structural Change in Metropolitan Chicago: The Research Report of the Religion in Urban America Program* (Chicago: University of Illinois, 1996); Thomas Rzeznik, "The Church in the Changing City: Parochial Restructuring in the Archdiocese of Philadelphia in Historical Perspective," *U.S. Catholic Historian* 27 no. 4 (Fall 2009).
25. O'Malley uses the phrase "center-periphery relationship" to describe one of three key underlying problems approached at the Second Vatican Council. John W. O'Malley, *What Happened at Vatican II?* (Cambridge, MA and London: Harvard University Press), 9–11, 137, 173–176, 269, 298, 302–305, 308.
26. O'Malley, *What Happened at Vatican II?*, 178.
27. Joseph A. Komonchak, "The Local Realization of the Church," in *The Reception of Vatican II*, ed. Giuseppe Alberigo, Jean-Pierre Jossua, and Joseph A. Komonchak (Washington DC: The Catholic University of America Press, 1987), 79–80.
28. O'Connor, *Boston Catholics*, 312–313.
29. City of Weymouth, "A Short History Lesson," http://www.weymouth.ma.us/history/index.asp Weymouth's 1960 population was 48,177. U.S. GenWeb Genealogical Site for the Town of Weymouth, MA, "Population in Censuses," http://plymouthcolony.net/weymouth/#census. Weymouth's population in 1999 was 54,397. City of Weymouth, "About Weymouth (from the Town's Master Plan)," http://www.weymouth.ma.us/about/index.asp.
30. Newspaper clipping, publication unknown, May 2, 1951, St. Albert the Great Parish Correspondence Files, Roman Catholic Archdiocese of Boston Archives (hereafter "SAG Parish Correspondence").
31. Cardinal Cushing was not available, but promised to attend the benediction. A Newton bishop would offer official witness to the ceremony. Chancellor Furlong to Father Connors (letter), January 29, 1954, SAG Parish Correspondence.
32. Baptismal records, St. Albert the Great Parish.
33. On parish councils and their challenges in the face of pastoral authority see Daniel Callahan, *The New Church: Essays in Catholic Reform* (New York: Charles Scribner's Sons, 1966), 104–123.
34. St. Albert the Great Parish Council Board to Cardinal Medeiros (letter), February 25, 1971, SAG Parish Correspondence; Rev. Msgr. Thomas H.

Kennedy to Rev. Msgr. Joseph F. Maguire (letter), March 23, 1971, SAG Parish Correspondence; Msgr. Joseph F. Maguire, Secretary to Rev. Msgr. Thomas H. Kennedy (letter), March 29, 1971, SAG Parish Correspondence.

35. SAG Parish Bulletins, November 24–25, 1973, December 1–2, 1973, December 15–16, 1973, April 13–14, 1974.
36. O'Connor, *Boston Catholics*, 291–293.
37. James T. Patterson, *Grand Expectations: The United States, 1945–1974* (New York and Oxford: Oxford University Press, 1996), 639, 783–784; SAG Parish Bulletins, May 4–5, 1974, May 24–25, 1975.
38. SAG Parish Bulletin, May 31-June 1, 1975.
39. SAG Parish Bulletin, December 11–12, 1976.
40. SAG Parish Bulletins, November 8–9, 1975; June 24–25, 1980.
41. In 1971–72 the parish paid about $2,100, or nearly 25% of its annual assessment of just over $8,700. In the 1972–73 fiscal year the assessment rose to over $9,600 and Mount Carmel's contribution went down to about $1,300. By 1973–74, payments were down to less than $1,000 and by 1974–75 payments dropped to less than $400, or just 4% of the assessed amount. Father Little to Cardinal Medeiros (letter), Nov 25, 1974, OLMC Parish Correspondence.
42. Annetta (F-62), who now had a close eye on the parish financial situation, made this assessment of the church financial condition on June 27, 2005, OLMC.
43. Rev. Cletus J. Dello Iacono, OFM, JCD, "Jubilee Address," in *Our Lady of Mount Carmel Church, East Boston Diamond Jubilee, 1905-1980* (program book), 2.
44. Ibid., 9.
45. Ibid., 11–12.
46. Ibid., 12–13.
47. Rev. Norbert De Amato, OFM, "My Parish," Updated, 1984, OLMC Archives-NY.
48. The letter refers to Law's letter of March 1994 called "You Shall Be My Witness." Letter insert in OLMC Bulletin, "From the Pastors of Our Lady of the Assumption Parish, Most Holy Redeemer Parish, St. Mary Star of the Sea Parish, Our Lady of Mount Carmel Parish, Sacred Heart/St. John the Baptist Parish," OLMC Parish Bulletin, November 16, 1996.
49. SAG Parish Bulletin, October 3, 1999.
50. SAG Quarterly Financial Report, July-September, 2001.
51. Peter Steinfels, *A People Adrift: The Crisis of the Roman Catholic Church in America* (New York: Simon & Schuster, 2003), 47.
52. Mary Gail Frawley-O'Dea, "The History and Consequences of the Sexual Abuse Crisis in the Catholic Church," *Studies in Gender & Sexuality* 5, no. 1 (Winter 2004): 11–30; Thomas Doyle, "Roman Catholic Clericalism,

Religious Duress, and Clergy Sexual Abuse," *Pastoral Psychology* 51, no. 3 (January 2003): 189–231.

53. Bernard Cardinal Law to "Dearly Beloved in Christ" (letter), OLMC Parish Bulletin January 1 and 2, 1994.
54. "Transcript excerpts: 'I really did not believe there was a systemic problem,'" (Deposition of Cardinal Bernard Law, August 13–14, October 11, 16, 2002) *Boston Globe*, November 20, 2002, A17.
55. Steinfels notes that he compared the dimensions of clergy sexual abuse in the Church to "a biblical plague" on the front page of the *New York Times* in 1993. A confidential paper, circulated in the Bishops' Conference of 1985, also raised the issue and urged that sexual abuse by clergy and its cover-up was already an acute and alarming problem across the U.S. church. Steinfels calls 1985–1993 the "years of transition" during which Catholic officials were "dragged kicking and screaming into dealing with the issue" of clergy abuse. Cardinal Law was among those who were critical of early proposals to reform the U.S. church's approach to abusive employees. Steinfels, *A People Adrift*, 24–25, 44, 47–48.
56. St. Albert's Parish Bulletin, April 28, 2002.
57. St. Albert's Parish Bulletin, June 30, 2002.
58. St. Albert's Bulletin, September 29, 2002.
59. St. Albert's Bulletin, November 10, 2002.
60. David, Sept. 7, 2006, OLMC.
61. "A statue of limitations," *Boston Globe*, July 11, 2004, 4; "Unanswered Prayers," *Boston Globe* October 3, 2004, B1.
62. David, Sept 7, 2006, OLMC. Father Francis did not respond to my mailed requests to meet with him.
63. Vatican II, "Decree on the Apostolate of Lay People," *Apostolicam Actuositatem* ("Decree on the Apostolate of Lay People") November 18, 1965 in *Vatican Council II: The Conciliar and Post Conciliar Documents* ed. Augustine Flannery, O. P. (Northport, NY: Costello Publishing, 2004), 766.
64. John W. O'Malley, *What Happened at Vatican II?* (Cambridge, MA and London: Harvard University Press, 2008), 11, 50, 85, 186, 296.
65. Annetta, May 2005, OLMC.
66. Ralph, August 24, 2004, SH.
67. Thomas O'Connor, *Building a New Boston: Politics and Urban Renewal 1950–1970* (Boston: Northeastern University Press, 1993), 71, 126.
68. Lawrence W. Kennedy, *Planning the City Upon a Hill: Boston Since 1630* (Boston: University of Massachusetts Press, 1994), 157–158. Kennedy notes that Boston's struggles continued into the 1950s as its economy stagnated and the population decreased by 100,000.
69. Paula J. Todisco, *Boston's First Neighborhood: The North End* (Boston: Trustees of the Public Library of the City of Boston, 1976), 52.

70. O'Connor, *Building a New Boston*, 211–212.
71. Todisco, *Boston's First Neighborhood*, 84–85.
72. O'Connor, *Building a New Boston*, 126, 138.
73. See Patterson, *Grand Expectations*: 335, 383; Thomas J. Sugrue, *The Origins of the Urban Crisis: Race and Inequality in Postwar Detroit* (Princeton, NJ: Princeton University Press, 1996), 48–52.
74. O'Connor, *Building a New Boston*, 133–34, 139, 190–91, 215; Kennedy, *Planning the City Upon the Hill*, 187.
75. Herbert J. Gans, *The Urban Villagers: Group and Class in the Life of Italian-Americans (updated and expanded edition)* (New York: The Free Press, 1982).
76. Todisco, *Boston's First Neighborhood*, 52; Puleo, *The Boston Italians*, 242.
77. Ralph, August 24, 2004, SH.
78. Ivan Strenski, *Contesting Sacrifice: Religion, Nationalism, and Social Thought in France* (Chicago: University of Chicago Press, 2002), 175–176.
79. Strenski, *Contesting Sacrifice*, 4.
80. Strenski, *Contesting Sacrifice*, 176.
81. McGreevy, *Catholicism and American Freedom*, 154.
82. "E. Boston waterfront project stalls: Massport, companies dispute reasons for setback at Pier One," *Boston Globe*, June 1, 2007, C1; "Eastie is the 'gateway to the city,'" *Boston Globe*, November 7, 1993, 2.
83. "East Boston: Boston 200 Neighborhood Series," 10; Alan Lupo, Frank Colcord, Edmund P. Fowler, *Rites of Way: The Politics of Transportation in Boston and the U.S. City* (Boston: Little, Brown, and Company, 1971), 34–35.
84. Lupo, Colcord, and Fowler, *Rites of Way*, 34.
85. Lupo, Colcord, and Fowler, *Rites of Way*, 34–37; "East Boston: Boston 200 Neighborhood Series," 10.
86. Father Ryan to Bishop Daily (memo), Oct. 29, 1976, Our Lady of the Assumption Parish Correspondence, Roman Catholic Archdiocese of Boston Archives [hereafter "OLA Parish Correspondence"]; Father Loughlin to the Most Rev. Lawrence J. Riley (letter), Aug 8, 1972, OLA Parish Correspondence; Father Louglin to Thomas J. Finnegan, RCAB Chancellor (undated memo), OLA Parish Correspondence.
87. Frank E. Fairbairn to Rev. Joseph Smyth, Personnel Director Archdiocese of Boston (letter), April 14, 1972, OLA Parish Correspondence.
88. Father Loughlin to the Most Rev. Lawrence J. Riley (letter), Aug 8, 1972, OLA Parish Correspondence. Two other Catholic schools in the neighborhood had been consolidated into one in 1970.
89. Father Louglin to Thomas J. Finnegan, RCAB Chancellor (undated memo), OLA Parish Correspondence.
90. For the nationwide "urban crisis" of the 1970s and its impact on schools, see James T. Patterson, *Restless Giant: The United States From Watergate to Bush v. Gore* (Oxford: Oxford University Press, 2005), 37–44.

91. Michael F. Groden to Rev. DeBenedictis, OFM (letter), May 12, 1970 OLMC Parish Correspondence; also see OLMC Archives-NY, "East Boston: Diocesan Plans."
92. Bacigalupo to Msgr. Finnegan (letter), May 20, 1970; Finnegan to Bacigalupo (letter), May 28, 1970, OLMC Parish Correspondence.
93. Although Archdiocese Director of Education Father John Boles was not entirely confident that the plan would work, he argued that the communities should have another chance to succeed. Father Boles to Bishop Daily (memo), Oct. 2, 1973, OLMC Parish Correspondence.
94. The church came up $7,000 short on its assessment of $25,000. Bishop Daily to Rev. Michael F. Groden, Archdiocesan Planning Office for Urban Affairs (letter), December 2, 1974; Father Little to Cardinal Medeiros (letter), Nov. 25, 1974, OLMC Parish Correspondence.
95. The Office of Urban Affairs "agreed to continue its support of the East Boston Central Catholic School by leasing property and investigating areas of possible funding to help out in that part of the school budget, listed as fund raising, in the amount of $16,000.00." Vice Chancellor Rev. Richard P. Little to Rev. Centrella (letter), Dec. 13, 1974, OLMC Parish Correspondence. In 2007, the school claimed to be the only successful multiparish collaborative school still functioning in the Archdiocese of Boston, http://www.ebccs.org/.
96. Annetta and Mark were among resisters who led in the planning efforts for the new school. Annetta recalled that their role included insisting that the pastors not have all the decision-making power on the new school board. November 11, 2007, OLMC.
97. Lukas, *Common Ground;* Formisano, *Boston Against Bussing;* Louis P. Masur, *The Soiling of Old Glory* (New York: Bloomsbury Press, 2008), 1–53.
98. MacDonald, *All Souls*, 79–106.
99. Father Ryan refers to Palladino as a "very militant lady." Ryan to Fathers Daily, Shea, and Little, Re: "BUD LAUGHLIN's being on our side. . ." (undated memo), 1974, OLA Parish Correspondence. For more on Palladino, see Lukas, *Common Ground*, 137.
100. Ryan to Fathers Daily, Shea, and Little, Re: "BUD LAUGHLIN's being on our side. . ." (undated memo), 1974, OLA Parish Correspondence.
101. Bishop Daily to Cardinal Medeiros (memo), Nov. 18, 1976, OLA Parish Correspondence.
102. Anna F. Porrazzo to Bishop Daily (letter), Nov. 4, 1976 OLA Parish Correspondence.
103. Miss Lena Matera to Cardinal Medeiros (letter), Nov. 8, 1976, OLA Parish Correspondence.
104. Mrs. Jennie Ioro to Bishop Daily (undated letter), OLA Parish Correspondence.

105. Mr. and Mrs. Richard Goggin (undated letter); Mrs. Edward McKenna to Bishop Daily (letter), Nov. 16, 1976, OLA Parish Correspondence.
106. Ms. Eleanor K. Welch to Bishop Daily (letter), Nov. 8, 1976, OLA Parish Correspondence.
107. Ms. Anne Marim to Bishop Daily (letter), Nov. 11, 1976, OLA Parish Correspondence.
108. Mrs. C. Staffier (letter), Nov. 12, 1976, OLA Parish Correspondence.
109. Bishop Daily to Cardinal Medeiros (memo), Nov. 22, 1976, OLA Parish Correspondence.
110. Bishop Daily to Father Ryan (memo), Dec. 7, 1976, OLA Parish Correspondence.
111. Christine MacDonald, "A statue of limitations," *Boston Globe*, July 11, 2004, 4.
112. In 2003, OLMC's sacramental index stood at 77 (27 baptisms + 40 funerals + (2 x 5 marriages)). OLA's sacramental index of 60 (39 baptisms + 15 funerals + (2 x 3 marriages)) included more baptisms but far fewer funerals than OLMC. OLA had about 500 people attending mass each weekend compared to Mount Carmel's 300.
113. Val, June 18, 2005, OLMC. Annetta, June 18, 2005, OLMC.
114. October 14, 2007, OLMC (I discussed this with St. Albert's resisters who visited Mount Carmel's three-year occupation anniversary).
115. Margery, September 22, 2004, SAG. For a history of the abiding power of Gothic architecture in U.S. Catholic history see Paula Kane, "Getting beyond Gothic: Challenges for Contemporary Catholic Church Architecture," in *American Sanctuary: Understanding Sacred Spaces*, ed. Louis P. Nelson (Bloomington: Indiana University Press) 2006. Paul VI, *Nostra Aetate* ("Declaration on the Relation of the Church to Non-Christian Religions"), 1965.
116. Ignazio M. Calabuig, O.S.M., *The Dedication of a Church and an Altar: A Theological Commentary* (Washington, DC: United States Catholic Conference, 1980), 29.
117. These phrases come from the "address" printed in the 1907 consecration manual. Rev. A. J. Schulte, *Consecranda: Rites and Ceremonies Observed at the Consecration of Churches, Altars, Altar-Stones, Chalices, and Patens* (New York and Cincinnati: Benzinger Brothers, 1956 [1907]).
118. Rev. George Edwin Stuart, IV, S.T.B., J.C.L., "The Meaning of Sacred Status in the 1917 and 1983 Codes of Canon Law" (PhD diss., Catholic University of America, 2001).
119. John Allyn S. M. Melloh, "The Rite of Dedication," *Assembly* 10, no. 2 (Nov. 1983): 230.
120. Lines 9 through 29. Line 9 establishes the relationship between church building and Church: it reads "Here is reflected the mystery of the Church." Lines 10, 15, 20, and 25 begin with a description of the Church as "fruitful,"

"holy," "favored," and "exalted," and are followed by stanzas elaborating on these designations. Lines 34–50 of the new prayer begin with the words "Here" or "From here" and begin stanzas describing actions—either sacraments or acts of mercy performed by the people—that take place in the church, including baptism, the Eucharist, prayer, justice, and funeral masses. Prayers reproduced in Melloh, "The Rite of Dedication," 230.

121. James Field, "The Rite of Dedication: History, Theology, Celebration," *Environment and Art Letter* (March 1994): 8.

122. Dedication, one canon lawyer reported, is an overarching term used for the withdrawal of a place from profane use. Both consecration and blessing fall under the category of "dedication." Consecration was considered a more solemn rite appropriate for permanent separation, while blessing was a less elaborate ceremony applicable to temporary chapels. The terms were often used interchangeably, even in the Roman Pontifical. Thaddeus Ziolkowski, *The Consecration and Blessing of Churches: A Historical Synopsis and Commentary* (published dissertation) (Washington, DC: Catholic University Press, 1943), 3. The revision of canon law in 1983 echoed the new rite's modification of this differentiation.

123. Melloh, "The Rite of Dedication," 229, 232.

124. Melloh, "The Rite of Dedication," 232.

125. Catholic Church, *Environment and Art in Catholic Worship* (Washington: National Conference of Catholic Bishops, Bishops' Committee on the Liturgy, 1978), #14. [Hereafter *EACW*].

126. Melloh, "The Rite of Dedication," 230. Crichton describes action as the key difference as well: "In the new Order, the church does indeed remain a 'sacred place,' but it is sacred as a symbol and as, the prayer goes on to say, on account of what goes on in it." Crichton offers an evolutionary take on the movement of ritualized space. There was a time when "man in the early stages of his religious development thought of the whole of reality as sacred, but, as he came to realize that there were forces hostile to the sacred in the world, he fenced off places" that became "the shrine of the god" untouchable for all but priestly hands. J. D. Crichton, *The Dedication of a Church: A Commentary* (Dublin: Veritas Publications, 1980), 7.

127. *EACW*, #14.

128. Ibid.

129. Bishops' Committee on the Liturgy. *Rite for the Dedication of a Church and an Altar: Provisional Text*. Washington, DC: National Conference of Catholic Bishops, 1978, iii.

130. *EACW*, #29.

131. Ibid., #35.

132. Thomas G. Simons, *Holy People, Holy Place: Rites for the Church's House* (Chicago: Archdiocese of Chicago Liturgy Training Publications, 1998), 1.

133. *EACW*, #41.
134. National Conference of Catholic Bishops/U.S. Conference of Catholic Bishops, *Built of Living Stones: Art, Architecture, and Worship* (United States Conference of Catholic Bishops, 2000), #16. [Hereafter *BLS*]
135. Ibid., #22, 25.
136. Ibid., #25; the text here quotes Pope Leo the Great (*Sermo.* 74, 2: PL 54, 398).
137. Ibid., #26.
138. Ibid., #25.
139. Ibid., #258. "Mystery" was an important term in the Second Vatican Council definition of the Church. Paul VI's opening address to the second session of the council spelled this out: "The Church is a mystery. It is a reality imbued with the hidden presence of God. It lies therefore, within the very nature of the Church to be always open to new and ever greater exploration." This use of "mystery" pointed toward the value of ecumenism. Paul VI, Vincent Arthur Yzermans, Jane E. McCarthy, Archbishop Leo Binz, *The Church in the World: Inaugural Address of Pope Paul VI at the Second Session of the Second Vatican Ecumenical Council 29, September 1963* (St. Paul, MN: North Central Publishing Co., 1963) See also Avery Dulles, S.J. *Models of the Church, Expanded Edition* (New York: Image Books, Doubleday, 2002 [1978]) 10.
140. *BLS*, #260.
141. *Boston Pilot*, November 29, 1920.
142. *Boston Pilot*, February 27, 1954.
143. Dello Iacono, "Jubilee Address," 3.
144. St. Albert the Great Parish Bulletin, December 1–2, 1973.
145. St. Albert the Great Parish Bulletins. On Fatima: June 14–15, 1975, May 6–7, 1977; On the Medal Novena: April 26–27, 1975, June 21–22, 1975, October 18–19, 1975.
146. See also Jeremy Bonner, *The Road to Renewal: Victor Joseph Reed & Oklahoma Catholicism, 1905–1971* (Washington DC: Catholic University Press of America, 2008), 169.
147. For the grim entailments of Catholic subsidiarity in twentieth century urban America see also James T. Fisher, *On the Irish Waterfront: The Crusader, the Movie, and the Soul of the Port of New York* (Ithaca: Cornell University Press, 2009); McGreevy, *Parish Boundaries.*

3. "What do we have?"

1. Louisa and Ella (F-62), March 1, 2006, OLMC.
2. A priest at Mount Carmel's "receiving parish" explained to me that those who had not moved on were the ones who refused to believe the

naturalistic explanation. They thought that the Madonna had "jumped" and, believing it was a miracle and a sign, refused to leave. Father Willard, August 22, 2006, Sacred Heart (East Boston).

3. Roman Catholic Archdiocese of Boston, *Archdiocese of Boston Parish Closing Manual: Rebuild My Church, version 1.0*, May, 2004, 1. [hereafter "*CM*"]
4. The *Globe*'s Thomas F. Mulvoy, Jr., suggested that "Archbishop Seán, as he has asked to be called . . . brings a touch of the exotic to the scene in his Capuchin Franciscan friar's brown robe and sandals." "'What will Lake Street think?' no longer: from the puritans to a new passing," *Boston Globe*, December 14, 2003, p. 11. See also Peter DeMarco, "For many Catholics, a positive impression," *Boston Globe*, July 2, 2003; Michael Paulson, "A humble Franciscan steps into the eye of the storm," *Boston Globe*, July 2, 2003.
5. Marcella Bombardieri, "At B.C., students watch with optimism, awe," *Boston Globe*, July 31, 2003, A17.
6. David Mehegen, "A new archbishop/voices of Catholic Boston," *Boston Globe*, July 30, 2003, B4.
7. "A humbler church" (editorial), *Boston Globe*, December 6, 2003, A12.
8. Most Reverend Seán O'Malley, "Remarks of Archbishop O'Malley on Parish Reconfiguration," May 25, 2004, in *CM*.
9. The General Instruction of the Roman Missal, VIII: 326–334. http://www.vatican.va/roman_curia/congregations/ccdds/documents/rc_con_ccdds_doc_20030317_ordinamento-messale_en.html.
10. *CM*, 30.
11. Ibid., 44.
12. Ibid., 43.
13. Ibid., 44.
14. Ibid., 34.
15. Ibid., 39.
16. The website says this poem was "written by Evelyn Sweeney-Toner in 2004 after hearing the news that her parish was closing during the Reconfiguration Process," http://rcab.org/Parish_Reconfiguration/HomePage.html.
17. *CM*, 30–31.
18. Ibid., 50.
19. Ibid., 35.
20. Ibid., 50.
21. The manual notes that this optional rite was reprinted from "Archdiocese of Chicago Liturgy Training Publications," *Liturgy* 90 (February–March 1996).
22. *CM*, 66.

23. Ibid., 67–68.
24. Ibid., 68.
25. Ibid., 2.
26. *CM*, 134–35.
27. Trying to coerce "community" out of the ranks of the uprooted is particularly dubious: "What is *not* replaceable or recoverable are the existential rights people have over their own destinies. This is the ultimate value." Michael D. Jackson, *Minima Ethnographica: Intersubjectivity and the Anthropological Project* (Chicago: University of Chicago Press, 1998), 127.
28. Such convictions were behind the deep offense Eliza (F-53) reported after opposing counsel suggested that the St. Jeremiah appeal was just about keeping their churches. March 2, 2008, SJ.
29. Ronald (M-54), February 12, 2007, OLMC; Eliza, June 13, 2006, SJ.
30. Ralph, August 24, 2004, SH.
31. Art, July 2005, SJ.
32. Louis, July 21, 2005, SJ.
33. *CM*, 30.
34. Abigail (F-62), September 22, 2004, SAG.
35. December 4, 2004, SAG; This story or a similar one had also been captured by Paula Kane in "Is that a beer vat under the baldochino?: From antimodernism to postmodernism in Catholic sacred architecture," *U.S. Catholic Historian* 15 (Winter 1997).
36. Date unknown, OLMC.
37. Michael Paulson, "Anguished O'Malley explains fiscal crisis," *Boston Globe*, November 14, 2004, A1.
38. When I presented a portion of my research to a group of VOTF members at St. Albert's, members of the audience rolled their eyes at the mention of O'Malley's comment on his pain. March 11, 2008, SAG.
39. Ralph, August 24, 2004, SH.
40. On social Catholicism and the Catholic "family ideal" see John T. McGreevy, *Catholicism and American Freedom: A History* (New York: W. W. Norton and Company, 2003), 154. For basics on the Christian Family Movement see Jay P. Dolan, *The American Catholic Experience: A History from Colonial Times to the Present* (New York: Doubleday, 1985), 395–96. Marriage encounter, a movement brought to this country in the late 1960s and designed to strengthen Catholic marriages and prepare engaged couples for Catholic marriage, awaits a thorough general history. See Dolan, *The American Catholic Experience*, 431; James T. Hennesey, *American Catholics: A History of the Roman Catholic Community in the United States* (New York and London: Oxford University Press, 1983), 317; Roger Fortin, *Faith and Action: A History of the*

Catholic Archdiocese of Cincinnati (Columbus: Ohio State University Press, 2002), 365; Ann Shepard Feeley Swaner, "Marriage Encounter and the Catholic Theological Response to Contemporary Marriage" (PhD diss., University of Iowa, 1984).

41. March 2, 2008, SJ.
42. David O'Brien, director of properties for the Boston Archdiocese acknowledged that housing was a "logical potential reuse" of churches, but also said that the archdiocese hoped "to attract buyers with community interests, such as congregations from other denominations." Nicholas Grudin, "Selling old churches for worldly use," *New York Times*, sec. 11, col. 1, January 23, 2005.
43. Thomas C. Palmer, Jr., and Chris Reidy, "Sixteen churches for sale worth $28 million," *Boston Globe*, November 18, 2004.
44. Christine Tolfree, "Lawrence, Stoughton, and Beverly parish properties offered for sale," *Boston Pilot*, June 3, 2005. Also see Tolfree, "Church property sale finalized, five more under agreement," *Boston Pilot*, May 27, 2005. The archdiocese also got credit in the media for appointing a strong advocate of financial transparency in charge of the sale of closed church buildings. Stephen Kurjian, "Lay figure to head church sale panel," *Boston Globe*, November 24, 2004.
45. Among the first six properties sold, two went to faith communities, one to Tufts University, and three were to be used as housing. Christine Tolfree, "Church property sale finalized, five more under agreement," *Boston Pilot*, May 27, 2005. By June of 2005, the Archdiocese had put 31 parishes closed in reconfiguration on the market, sold one, and reached purchase and sale agreements on nine. Christine Tolfree, "Lawrence, Stoughton, and Beverly parish properties offered for sale," *Boston Pilot*, June 3, 2005.
46. Paysha Stockton Rhone, "Neighbors want sale of church investigated," *Boston Globe*, City 5, January 28, 2007.
47. Laura Crimaldi, "Special investigation: photographer snaps $1.8 million in Eastie church deal," and "What is the Universal Church of the Kingdom of God?," *Boston Herald*, January 5, 2007, p. 2.
48. Paysha Stockton Rhone, "Neighbors want sale of church investigated," *Boston Globe*, City 5, January 28, 2007; "Church makes airwaves," BBC News, August 3, 2000, http://news.bbc.co.uk/1/hi/uk/864623.stm.
49. Peter Borré, Co-chair Council of Parishes, to Most Reverend Pietro Sambi, Apostolic Pro-Nuncio to the United States of America (letter distributed by email to author), January 7, 2007. The PRFOC noted that the bidding history on the property revealed that the archdiocese had turned down another evangelical group's $2 million bid on a larger parcel of the property before accepting the photographer's bid.
50. PRFOC, 6.

51. The archdiocese's "final report" disowned all "impropriety" but admitted that it should have put a restrictive covenant on the property. It also noted that they would not have sold to the eventual owning church group at the higher price because of their "anti-Catholic positions." James P. McDonough, chancellor, "Report to the Archdiocesan Financial Council: Sale of St. Mary Star of the Sea Church/Rectory/Hall-East Boston," September 6, 2007, p. 3. html. The archdiocese also released a document describing policy for the sale of church buildings. This document included "anti-flip" measures and explanations of what would be considered "appropriate and acceptable" prospective uses of a church building. One rule specified that buildings sold for use as housing could not in the future be used as houses of worship without the approval of the archdiocese. The document was a response to the troubled deal in East Boston. Roman Catholic Archdiocese of Boston, "Roman Catholic Archbishop of Boston, A Corporation Sole's Policy on the Sale of Church Buildings." http://web.archive.org/web/20080327033616/www.rcab.org/Parish_Reconfiguration/HomePage. .
52. This 1995 episode caused significant controversy in Brazil, and the video appeared on CNN, where the announcer explained how the "pastor" kicked and abused a statue of Our Lady of Aparecida, the Patron Saint of Brazil, for ten minutes, asking "Can God really be compared to this ugly thing?".
53. Celia, September 10, 2006, OLMC; Susana and David, September 7, 2006, OLMC.
54. Susana, September 7, 2006, OLMC.
55. David, September 7, 2006, OLMC.
56. McAuliffe's mother, Grace Corrigan, used the term "Christa's bells" in an article documenting memorial efforts on Christa's behalf. The bells were purchased with funds raised in a "church drive." Joseph P. Kahn, "A spirit endures: new book, mother's work keep Christa McAuliffe's memory alive," *Boston Globe*, September 7, 1993, Metro 1. Franco Ordonez, "Parishioners sue to keep church open," *Boston Globe*, May 14, 2005, B1.
57. At a talk in Brighton as the shutdowns were getting started, the archbishop offered his critique of consumption with a barbed joke highlighting Franciscan poverty in contrast to Jesuit worldliness. He said he likes to tell the story of a Franciscan and a Jesuit who walk "out of a church and walk down the street and were approached by a young man who said 'Fathers, what novena do I have to make to get a BMW?' And the Franciscan said, 'What's a BMW?' and the Jesuit said 'What's a novena?'" Seán O'Malley, "Handing on the Faith" (lecture), September 17, 2004, St. John the Evangelist, Wellesley, MA. http://escholarship.bc.edu/church21_webcast/5/.
58. Ralph, August 24, 2004, SH.

59. See also Charles Taylor, *The Secular Age* (Cambridge, MA: Harvard University Press, 2008), 57–61.
60. Ralph, August 24, 2004, SH.
61. Stephanie (F-30), May 28, 2006, Saint Catherine of Siena Parish, Charlestown, MA [hereafter "SCS"].
62. Ralph reported that Sacred Heart had a million dollars in the archdiocesan depository, a sum the resisters had offered to donate to the archdiocese in exchange for keeping their parish open.
63. Eva (F-30), June 21, 2005, OLMC.
64. Dorothy, December 4, 2004, SAG.
65. Severe shortfalls are cited in O'Malley's October 21, 2005 letter, "Financial Transparency Letter from Archbishop O'Malley." Michael Paulson, "Citing deficit, archdiocese eyes substantial budget cuts," *Boston Globe*, March 24, 2005. Roman Catholic Archdiocese of Boston, "Archdiocese of Boston Financial Report: Financial Transparency Review," 10. Now they reported a cumulative deficit of $46 million, the largest of any diocese in United States history. Pam Belluck, "Boston Archdiocese opens books," *New York Times*, April 20, 2006, A1. Part of the deficit, the archdiocese eventually reported, stemmed from the jubilee-year debt forgiveness offered by Cardinal Law to debtor parishes in the year 2000.
66. Roman Catholic Archdiocese of Boston, "Archdiocese of Boston Financial Report: Financial Transparency Review," (PowerPoint presentation), 10, www.rcab.org. O'Malley referred to the deficit spending as "bleeding" in Pam Belluck, "Boston Archdiocese opens books," *New York Times* April 20, 2006, A1.
67. Michael Paulson, "Big tab still rises at shut churches," *Boston Globe*, January 18, 2008, A1. The article seemed to be aimed at stirring new controversy over the occupied parishes by specifying that these cost the archdiocese "$10,000 a month . . . or about $350,000 to date." PRFOC "Final Report," 4.
68. The $62.7 million number comes from Michael Paulson, "Big tab still rises at shut churches," *Boston Globe*, January 18, 2008, A1. He suggested the original windfall was expected to be "several hundred million." The Parish Reconfiguration Financial Overview Committee reported that the expectations were more modest, saying that it was thought they "might reach $200 million."
69. "If we hadn't had the money from reconfiguration, we might be considering bankruptcy, I don't know. We'd be in much worse shape, obviously." Sean O'Malley in "O'Malley sees a great test of values," interview transcript, *Boston Globe*, April 21, 2006.

70. Associated Press State and Local Wire, "Archdiocese sells land to move administrative offices to suburbs," May 25, 2007.
71. Chidester and Linenthal, "Introduction," *American Sacred Space*, 15.
72. Eliza (personal communication), March 2008, SJ.
73. *BLS*, #246.
74. *CM*, 8.
75. Anna Della Monica, an organist at St. Mary's, Salem, captured the conflict over gifts and their meanings at closing parishes: "We gave these gifts to God," she told a film-maker. "They are taking it, they are stealing the gifts." *Hand of God*, Frontline PBS, January 16, 2006. http://www.pbs.org/wgbh/pages/frontline/handofgod/view/
76. "Struggles over the ownership of sacred space," Chidester and Linenthal write, "inevitably draw upon the commitment of larger constituencies that hold an investment in the contest." Chidester and Linenthal, "Introduction," *American Sacred Space*, 16.
77. In a letter obtained unofficially and published on the web, Cardinal Dario Hoyos Castrillon notified Cardinal Skylstad of the United States Conference of Catholic Bishops of this mistake and asked him to inform United States bishops of proper procedure. Instead of Canon 123, which speaks of the "extinction" of a parish, the Congregation said that Canons 121 or 122, which speak of the merging and dividing parishes and the creation of new "juridic persons" in those processes, were applicable in almost all cases of so-called parish suppression. The letter appeared at http://www.freerepublic.com/focus/f-religion/1667106/posts on July 17, 2006.
78. Cardinal Castrillon was the Prefect of the Congregation of the Clergy. The archdiocese said that the decision was "communicated verbally to archdiocesan officials at a series of meetings in Rome." Michael Paulson, "Vatican stops diocese in taking parish assets," *Boston Globe*, August 11, 2005, A1.
79. Ibid.
80. By the time the Vatican offered its critique, the damage had already been done and no further recourse was allowed. Only eight territorial parishes that had made a valid appeal within the proper timeframe were affected by this adjustment, and all but one of their receiving pastors assented to the original distribution of assets. PRFOC, "Final Report," 4.
81. Legal title in the name of the diocese or corporation sole does not erase the distinction between parish and diocese as separate entities. For detailed analysis of the legal issues involved in the bankruptcies related to sexual abuse claims see Catherine Pierce Wells, "Who Owns the Local Parish?" *Seton Hall Legislative Journal* 29, no. 2 (2005). I also draw on this article for the legal analysis below.

82. Discerning intent of gifts poses challenges for the courts, which turn to canon law to gauge internal rules about giving and the relationship between parish and diocese. Some charitable gifts have specific express restrictions on them, such as funds raised for a specific repair job to a church building or those raised to buy furnishings or equipment. The question of legal restrictions attached to general weekly parish collections is not clear. Separate collections for the archdiocese originating in the parish were a different matter. In 2006, the archdiocese asked the attorney general to apply the legal doctrine of *cy pres*, allowing the transfer of almost three million in restricted funds from closed parishes to go to designated successor parishes. *Cy pres* means that charitable gifts given for a specific purpose that can no longer precisely be carried out should be applied to a new purpose that is as close as possible to the original one. Welcoming parishes were considered the closest possible replication of the original intended use of these funds. The funds included bequests, scholarships, money for masses purchased on behalf of the deceased, and unspent assets designated for parish work related to the "Promise for Tomorrow" campaign, which had begun in 2000. States News Service, "Attorney General Martha Coakley agrees to plan to redistribute funds to closed parishes," August 17, 2007; see also Michael Paulson, "Church asks to redirect $3m given to shut parishes," *Boston Globe*, January 3, 2007, A1; "Transferring restricted funds from closed parishes to welcoming parishes (the *Cy Pres* process)," Roman Catholic Archdiocese of Boston, March 6, 2008.
83. Daniel Jay Marcinak, "Separation of Church and Estate: On Excluding Parish Assets from the Bankruptcy Estate of a Diocese Organized as a Corporation Sole," *Catholic University Law Review* Winter 2006, 583–633. Marcinak concludes that the legal status of corporation sole "creates a statutory trust and incorporates canon law," in a way that allows the First Amendment to prohibit liquidation of parishes under Chapter 11, 589. Nicholas P. Cafardí, "The Availability of Parish Assets for Diocesan Debts: A Canonical Analysis," *Seton Hall Legislative Journal* 29, no. 2 (2005): 361–373; Mark E. Chopko, "Parish Structures: Identity, Integrity, and Indissolubility," *Church Magazine* Summer, 2009, www.churchmagazine.com.
84. Council of Parishes, "Council of Parishes Letter asks Bishop Skylstad to Reaffirm the Rights of Parishes Under Canon Law" (news release,) June 15, 2005; Letter from Peter Borré and Cynthia Dysher to Bishop Skylstad, June 14, 2005.
85. Wells, "Who Owns the Local Parish?" 397–98, n. 64.
86. Going against the recommendation of the PRFOC, an independent lay financial review board, the archdiocese decided not to extend the option

of keeping or surrendering assets to pastors from all the receiving parishes. PRFOC, "Final Report," 4.

87. Franco Ordonez, "Parishioners sue to keep church open," *Boston Globe*, May 14, 2005, B1.
88. Janet I. Tu, "Judge: Spokane diocese can't sell parishes," *Seattle Times*, June 16, 2006, B1.
89. John Stucke, "Abuse victims may sue parishes," *Spokesman Review* (Spokane, WA), June 16, 2006, C10.
90. John Stucke, "Parishes, diocese to formalize relationship," *Spokesman Review*, April 21, 2007, Idaho edition, A8. An association of parishes and the victims of sexual abuse agreed to a payment plan within which parishes would raise $10 million of a total $48 million for settlements. Parish property was used to secure the $10 million commitment. The reorganization included the plan for incorporating parishes as separate individual nonprofits. John Stucke, "Four asked Skylstad to resign," *Spokesman Review*, April 21, 2007, Idaho edition, A1. A somewhat different arrangement helped the diocese of St. George's in Newfoundland settle abuse claims without losing its parishes. In 2005, after sixteen years of legal battles, the diocese was forced by Canada's supreme court to sell all its properties, including churches, in order to pay thirteen million dollars in settlements for clergy sexual abuse inflicted beginning in 1961. The diocese did not sell the properties to an outside buyer, but instead put them into a trust, from which it then bought the properties back with assets raised through diocese-wide fundraising efforts. "Diocese buys back property sold in abuse case," *The Globe and Mail*, June 1, 2006, A11.
91. Matt Miller, "The lessons of Spokane," *Daily Deal/The Deal*, April 30, 2007. In its settlement, the Davenport, Iowa Diocese secured a contribution from four parishes where the most serious abuses had taken place. Matt Miller "Davenport to file $37M plan," *Daily Deal/The Deal*, February 1, 2008.
92. "Archdiocese cuts $2 million from deficit," *Boston Globe*, April 26, 2007.
93. PRFOC, "Final Report," 2–3.
94. Annetta, June 15, 2005, June 27, 2005, July 5, 2005, OLMC; Edith, September 14, 2005, SAG; January 17, 2005, Our Lady of the Presentation, Brighton.
95. "Digging in to stay and pray," *National Catholic Register* August 26, 2005. http://natcath.org/NCR_Online/archives2/2005c/082605/082605a.php.
96. November 18, 2004, OLMC.
97. Eliza, May 15, 2005, SJ.
98. For information on these Marianist Catholics, see Michael Cuneo, *Smoke of Satan: Conservative and Traditionalist Dissent in Contemporary American Catholicism* (New York: Oxford University Press, 1997).
99. December 2004, OLMC.

100. October 18, 2005, OLMC.
101. See also Michael P. Carroll, *Madonnas that Maim: Popular Catholicism in Italy Since the Fifteenth Century* (Baltimore: Johns Hopkins University Press, 1992).
102. Ella told me she heard the nuns singing in the church and that they sounded "like angels." September 1, 2005, OLMC.
103. June 20, 21, 2005, July 7, 2005, August 18, 2005, OLMC.
104. June 15, 2005, OLMC.
105. Nick, June 16, 2005, OLMC.
106. May 6, 2005, SAG.
107. Theresa, July 30, 2006, SA.
108. Alec (M-45), July 30, 2006, SA.
109. The brick was from St. James, Medford. August 23, 2005, OLMC.
110. This was Bishop Richard Lennon's warning to pastors who kept sloppy books. *CM*, 2.
111. Paula Kane "Have We No Language of Our Own? Boston's Catholic Churches, Architects, and Communal Identity," in *Faces of Community: Immigrant Massachusetts, 1860-2000,* edited by Reed Ueda and Conrad Edick Wright, Northeastern University Press, 2003," 139.
112. Father Ames, September 10, 2004, SCS.

4. "This is unrest territory"

1. Louisa (F-63). This story and the responses to it that follow were recorded in my field notes on January 11, 2006.
2. May 2005, OLMC.
3. Monica R. Young, "St. Dominic Savio High to be closed in June," *Boston Globe*, January 15, 1993.
4. Robert A. Orsi describes sacrifice as an idiom of relative freedom and an assertion of control over life that was otherwise vulnerable for the poor East Harlem Catholics he studied. Robert A. Orsi, *The Madonna of 115th Street: Faith and Community in Italian Harlem, 1880–1950* (New Haven: Yale University Press, 1985), 203.
5. See Margaret M. McGuinness, "Night and Day: Eucharistic Adoration in the United States, 1900–1969" *U.S. Catholic Historian* 19, no. 3 (Summer 2001), 21–34.
6. Annetta, August 23, 2005, OLMC.
7. Second Vatican Council, *Gaudium et Spes* ("The Pastoral Constitution on the Church in the Modern World," 1965) 16-17.
8. See R. Scott Appleby, *Church and Age Unite! : The Modernist Impulse in American Catholicism* (Notre Dame, IN: University of Notre Dame Press, 1992).

9. Thomas Richstatter, O.F.M., "Mass and Communion Service: What's the Difference?" *Catholic Update* (undated), www.americancatholic.org. St. Susanna in Dedham, for example, held lay-led communion services on a regular basis.
10. A July 15, 2007, report from an archdiocesan review committee urged the Cardinal to consider broadening the use of communion services in the archdiocese in order to mitigate problems related to the priest shortage and avoid additional rounds of church closures. Michael Paulson, "Archdiocese facing priest shortage," *Boston Globe*, July 15, 2007, B1.
11. Bishop Robert Francis Hennessy, "Easter Sunday homily" (lecture), March 23, 2008, OLMC; see also Roman Catholic Archdiocese of Boston, "Statement on St. Jeremiah Vigil communion service" May 20, 2005.
12. A 2004 instruction on practices surrounding the Eucharist specifies the authority of the Apostolic See and the local bishops over the practice of the sacred liturgy. Only grave and urgent causes warrant the use of extraordinary ministers and communion services. Such services are never to be confused with the mass. Roman Catholic Church, "*Redemptionis Sacramentum: On Certain Matters to Be Observed or to Be Avoided Regarding the Most Holy Eucharist*" (April, 2004), www.holysee.org.
13. Eliza (F-51), May 15, 2005, SJ.
14. Arlene (F-48), Eliza, and Patrick (M-47), June 13, 2006, SJ.
15. Karen (F-54), September 16, 2005, SAG.
16. September 9, 2007, OLMC; Anniversary party, June 27, 2005, OLMC.
17. At St. Jeremiah's in Framingham the occupation and a weekly mass coexisted for many months while the vigilers continued to seek reopening and pursued their lawsuit against the archdiocese. The willingness of the archdiocese to offer occasional masses in the occupied churches was another example of the institutional "regulation of spontaneity" that Hervieu-Léger describes in the context of Catholic charismatic movements. Hervieu Léger, "What Scripture Tells Me," 28. See also O'Brien, *The Renewal of American Catholicism*, 66.
18. Council of Parishes, "Celebration of Easter Mass at Shaw Park in Natick, Organized by Friends of Sacred Heart in Natick" (news release), March 26, 2005, http://www.councilofparishes.org/releases/032605.html.
19. St. Anselm, Sudbury, and St. Jeremiah, Framingham. Others may have done so as well.
20. Karen, September 16, 2005, SAG.
21. Council of Parishes, "Celebration of Easter Mass at Shaw Park in Natick, Organized by Friends of Sacred Heart in Natick," March 26, 2005.
22. Bridget (F-68), May 27, 2006, SAG.
23. Mark, date unknown, OLMC.

24. Ryan, Jan 21, 2005, SAG.
25. February 2, 2005, SAG.
26. February 2, 2005, SAG.
27. A sign-in book that was placed in the church's narthex during the vigil bore the signatures and comments of hundreds of appreciative parishioners who poured out their love to Father Coyne in his absence. One of the most popular expressions in notes to Father Coyne was "You're the Best!" which I discovered was the way Father Coyne had always addressed the parishioners of St. Albert's. "St. Albert the Great Welcome Book."
28. The occupations at Our Lady of Mount Carmel, St. Frances Xavier Cabrini (Scituate), St. James (Wellesley), and St. Therese (Everett) were among the smaller groups. By March 2008, they had not received any official change in status. Resisters at Mount Carmel had rejected a deal to reopen as a chapel because the proposed mass times (late evening and mid-afternoon) wouldn't have attracted sufficient crowds. St. Albert the Great, St. Anselm (Sudbury), Infant Jesus-St. Lawrence, St. Jeremiah (Framingham), and St. Bernard's (Newton) were generally larger groups. By 2008 all of these except St. Jeremiah had been at least temporarily removed from the closure list. St. Jeremiah had received a weekly mass during the time that its canon and civil appeals were pending.
29. For dispute of the favoritism toward larger groups see Council of Parishes, "Celebration of Easter Mass at Shaw Park in Natick." March 26, 2005 (press release) http://councilofparishes.org/news.html.
30. At a meeting of the Council of Parishes, a representative from Infant Jesus-St. Lawrence reported that they were "being told they were closing because of their small numbers" and countered with this quotation, February, 2005.
31. Karen, September 16, 2005, SAG.
32. Annetta, February 13, 2006, OLMC.
33. Paula, September 16, 2005, SAG.
34. St. Anselm (Sudbury), St. Jeremiah (Framingham), St. Albert the Great (Weymouth). Others may have offered these as well.
35. Kathleen, February 16, 2005, SAG.
36. St. Jeremiah "E-newsletter," January 12, 2007.
37. Ronald (M-54), February 12, 2007.
38. January, 2005, OLMC.
39. Annetta, March 8, 2007, OLMC.
40. May 2005, OLMC.
41. Ibid.
42. August 23, 2005, OLMC.
43. Catharine, November 30, 2004.

44. Celia, October 25, 2005.
45. Peter Borré, Council of Parishes meeting, Infant Jesus-St. Lawrence Church, Brookline, MA, February, 2005.
46. Abigail (F-62), September 22, 2004, St. Albert the Great Parish, East Weymouth, MA [SAG].
47. Peter Borré, who was also at this meeting, helped Annetta find this comparison as she puzzled over the right term of contrast. Annetta, June 18, 2005, OLMC.
48. Braden (M-52) Feb 2, 2005, SAG.
49. Brian, Feb. 27, 2005, SAG.
50. Josephine (F-54), June 29, 2005, SJ; Patrick also mentioned this on occasion. He took pride in having discovered the painting covered in dust and restoring it to the altar where he enjoyed the ways it caught the sunlight at certain times of day. May 15, 2005, SJ.
51. Nora (F-60), September 16, 2005, SAG.
52. Karen, September 16, 2005, SAG.
53. Annetta, December 2004, OLMC.
54. Annetta, June 5, 2005, OLMC.
55. Braden, February 2, 2005.
56. Annetta, December 2004, OLMC.
57. September 12, 2005, OLMC. Girard (M-42), OLMC (field notes).
58. Church as "mafia:" May 6, 2005, SAG; at a February, 2005 Council of Parishes meeting, the leader read a quote from the *Boston Globe* comparing the Catholic Church in America to organized crime. At a rally just outside of the chancery walls, Council of Parishes co-chair Peter Borré played Reagan to O'Malley's Gorbachev: "Archbishop O'Malley, tear down this wall!" The tents set up in the square in front of Our Lady of Presentation School evoked the Great Depression by aligning the tent cities with that era's Hoovervilles. The first and second in command in the Archdiocese each had a section of the square named after him: "Lennonville" and "O'Malleyville." Our Lady of the Presentation School Rally in Oak Square, Brighton, MA, June 10, 2005.
59. One vigiler read aloud an email from another non-OLMC resister about body parts that "atrophy" through lack of use. September 22, 2005, OLMC.
60. October 2004, SAG.
61. Elizabeth, for example, explained their evolving approach to the gospels during communion services: "Technically, you cannot have a lay person 'proclaim' the gospel; you can 'read' the gospel, but you can't 'proclaim' it. So that's why, in a prayer service, we don't do an alleluia before the gospel. The alleluia is the sign that the gospel is going to be 'proclaimed.'"

Research and consultation with the former pastor and with other sympathetic priests helped them come to this resolution. Elizabeth (F-53), September 16, 2005, SAG.

62. Elizabeth, September 16, 2005, SAG.
63. Peter Borré, Council of Parishes Co-chair, used this passage on several occasions. In May of 2005 he substituted a reading of this passage for a closing prayer at a Council of Parishes meeting in Wellesley. On another occasion he used it in a public speech denouncing the reconfiguration in Brighton. June 10, 2005.
64. Abigail, Sept. 22, 2004, SAG.
65. Council of Parishes meeting, Infant Jesus-St. Lawrence, February, 2005.
66. Rich (M-40), June 28, 2005, OLMC.
67. Theresa (F-59), March 31, 2005, St. Anselm Parish, Sudbury, MA [SA].
68. Annetta, date unknown, OLMC.
69. Eliza, May 15, 2005, SJ.
70. This was a reference to the canon law mistake of the archdiocese in using parish "suppression" canons instead of parish "merger" canons.
71. Arlene, Eliza, and Patrick, June 13, 2006, SJ.
72. Raymond, date unknown, OLMC.
73. Stephanie (F-30), SCS.
74. Michael Herzfeld, *The Social Production of Indifference: Exploring the Symbolic Roots of Western Bureaucracy* (New York: Berg-St. Martin's Press, 1992), 162.
75. Recall too Annetta's comment that the unhappy neighbor's grandmother was "turning over in her grave" as a result of her granddaughters' unsupportive attitude toward the vigil. Others, like OLMC resisters Louisa and Val, told me that their parents were deeply saddened by the closures, but were homebound and therefore did not come to services at the closed churches.
76. Michael Levenson, "Request to Reopen Church Denied," *Boston Globe*, December 20, 2004.
77. Arlene, Eliza, and Patrick, June 13, 2006, SJ.
78. Catharine may have been referring to Mark 12:25 ("When they rise from the dead they will neither marry nor be given in marriage but will be like angels in heaven") when she expressed her anxiety to her pastor and, later, to me. She told me that after she had asked her pastor, she decided that she wouldn't ask anyone ever again. She renewed her vow to leave the topic after our conversation. Catharine, January 18, 2005, SAG.
79. Catharine, January 18, 2005, SAG.
80. Art (M-52), July 11, 2005, SJ.
81. In his advocacy of a "structural, historical anthropology" Sartre argued that the familiar categories of Marxist historiography such as alienation

and reification must also be recognized as categories of human experience, not just as structural processes. Sartre's use of the term "praxis" as "the project which throws [one] toward the social possibilities in terms of a defined situation" suggests the kind of attention to the interactions of rules and experience that I attempt here. Jean Paul Sartre, *Search for a Method*, trans. Hazel E. Barnes (New York: Knopf, 1963 [1960]), 169, 175.

82. Miller uses this apt phrase to describe Maurice Merleau-Ponty's orientation to meaning and history. James Miller, "Merleau-Ponty's Marxism: Between Phenomenology and the Hegelian Absolute," *History and Theory* 15 no. 2 (May 1976): 115.
83. Walter Johnson, "On Agency," *Journal of Social History* 37, no. 1 (2003): 119.

5. Openings

1. Diane (F-49), March 19, 2008.
2. Of Geoghan's scores of victims across three decades in Boston, seven were young boys at St. Andrew's when he served there in the late 1970s. Written warnings from the boys' aunt had fallen on deaf ears at the chancery. Instead church officials trusted medical reports proclaiming Geoghan cured after a year of psychiatric treatment. Geoghan was reassigned to parish duty in 1982 and again in 1984 after facing renewed abuse charges. It wasn't until 1998 that the church defrocked Geoghan. "Church allowed abuse by priest for years," *Boston Globe*, January 6, 2002.
3. Arlene (F-47), August 21, 2005, SJ.
4. Annetta (F-62), June 15, 2005, OLMC; Eliza (F-54), August 19, 2009, SJ.
5. Father Willard, August 22, 2006, Sacred Heart (East Boston).
6. Edith, September 14, 2005; Edward, May 6, 2005 predicted the church would "croak" without Father Coyne. The group almost rejected the reopening agreement on the basis of its exclusion of a return of Father Coyne.
7. "Search for a spiritual home: Consolidations leave some feeling displaced," *Boston Globe*, July 30, 2006. The same article quoted Kathleen Heck, the archdiocese's coordinator of the shutdowns, suggesting that in this parish "about half the parishioners have moved on" to a new parish. She admitted that about 35% needed greater outreach and support from the archdiocese in making the transition.
8. Ralph Ranalli, "Awaiting closure," *Boston Globe (West)*, June 10, 2007, 1. The number 4,000 is just under 15% of the 28,000 estimated to have been in one of the closing parishes.
9. PRFOC, "Final Report," 4.

10. Abu-Lughod shows young Bedouin women resisting one form of disciplining power in ways that precisely catch them up in another realm of subjection. In the process we learn about the contours of both. These women have adopted western forms of dress in opposition to their mothers' more traditional dress, thus freeing themselves from one realm of subjection and entering another based on the male gaze. Some would analyze this situation by trying to determine whether their move to western dress shows their freedom or some kind of self-delusion. What Abu-Lughod shows us is that it is much more interesting to ask instead about the ways that their moves illuminate the changing realms of power at work in these women's lives. Lila Abu-Lughod, "The Romance of Resistance: Tracing Transformations of Power through Bedouin Women," *American Ethnologist* 17 no. 1 (1990): 42.
11. Saba Mahmood, *The Politics of Piety: The Islamic Revival and the Feminist Subject* (Princeton, NJ: Princeton University Press, 2005), 9.
12. John T. McGreevy, *Parish Boundaries: The Catholic Encounter with Race in the Twentieth-century Urban North* (Chicago: University of Chicago Press, 1996), 13. Robert A. Orsi, *Thank You St. Jude: Women's Devotion to the Patron Saint of Hopeless Causes* (New Haven: Yale University Press, 1996), 210. James T. Fisher, *On the Irish Waterfront: The Crusader, the Movie, and the Soul of the Port of New York* (Ithaca: Cornell University Press, 2009), 34, 292; Sarah McFarland Taylor, *The Green Sisters: A Spiritual Ecology* (Cambridge, MA and London: Harvard University Press, 2007), 3, 14, 63, 77, 118, 123.
13. Leslie Wheelcock Tentler, *Catholics and Contraception: An American History* (Ithaca, NY: Cornell University Press), 2004, 268; Amy L. Koehlinger, *The New Nuns: Racial Justice and Religious Reform in the 1960s* (Cambridge: Harvard University Press, 2007); McFarland Taylor, *The Green Sisters*. Prominent women religious voiced resentment and protest at the initiation of a "visitation" of U.S. congregations by Vatican officials in the summer of 2010. Joan Chittister, O.S.B. compared the visitation to an "inquisition" and decried in particular the plan for the vistators' final report to remain hidden, even from the communities themselves. Joan Chittister, "Apostolic Visitation? Why Bother? Why be Bothered?" *National Catholic Reporter* June 23, 2010.
14. "Boston Catholics learn a few lessons," *Washington Post*, August 15, 2005.
15. Komonchak, "Interpreting the Council: Catholic Attitudes toward Vatican II," in *Being Right: Conservative Catholics in America*, ed. Mary Jo Weaver and R. Scott Appleby (Bloomington: Indiana University Press, 1995).
16. Timothy Kelly, *The Transformation of American Catholicism: The Pittsburgh Laity and the Second Vatican Council, 1950–1972* (Notre Dame, IN: University of Notre Dame Press, 2009). See also Joseph P. Chinnici,

O.F.M., "The Catholic Community at Prayer, 1926–1976" and James M. O'Toole, "Introduction," in *Habits of Devotion: Catholic Religious Practice in Twentieth-century America*, ed. James M. O'Toole (Ithaca, NY: Cornell University Press, 2004).

17. Kelly, *The Transformation of American Catholicism*, 85.
18. Kelly, *The Transformation of American Catholicism*, 296–299.
19. The same is true of Patrick Carey's reading of the "tensions of trusteeism." Patrick W. Carey, *People, Priests, and Prelates: Ecclesiastical Democracy and the Tensions of Trusteeism* (Notre Dame, IN: University of Notre Dame Press, 1987). For a less uncannily 'modern' version of this history, see Mark E. Chopko, "Parish Structures: Identity, Integrity, and Indissolubility," *Church Magazine*, Summer 2009, www.churchmagazine.com. Chopko shows that trustee arrangements were as much a matter of practical survival in an anti-Catholic nation as they were a result of a nascent democratization movement in the church.
20. Joseph P. Chinnici, O.F.M., has also highlighted, on a national scale, the preparedness of many Catholics for more collective, collegial forms of prayer. He describes a "pedagogy of participation" as the key of Catholics' formation in the period 1926–1960. The liturgical movement and the hierarchically guided initiatives of Catholic Action were largely responsible for this training and preparation. He discusses this preparation as "'latent' forces" in history, which emerged forcefully and clearly with the "grammar and words" drawn from the Second Vatican Council. Chinnici also describes conflicts and fissures that developed in the reception of the Council's transformations, especially after the social and cultural upheavals of 1967, when other conflicts—especially related to race, gender, and sexuality—began to impinge powerfully on Catholics' sense of themselves as Americans. "The Catholic Community at Prayer, 1926–1976," in *Habits of Devotion*, 39–51.
21. John W. O'Malley, *Trent and All That: Renaming Catholicism in the Early Modern Era* (Cambridge, MA: Harvard University Press, 2000); David Hall and Ann Brown, "Family Strategies and Religious Practice: Baptism and the Lord's Supper in Early New England," in *Lived Religion in America: Toward a History of Practice*, ed. David D. Hall (Princeton, NJ: Princeton University Press, 1997); Ruth Harris, *Lourdes: Body and Spirit in the Secular Age* (New York: Viking Penguin, 1999).
22. Kelly, *The Transformation of American Catholicism*, 224–225.
23. John T. Noonan, *A Church That Can and Cannot Change: The Development of Catholic Moral Teaching* (Notre Dame, IN: University of Notre Dame Press, 2005).
24. John T. McGreevy, *Catholicism and American Freedom: A History* (New York: W. W. Norton, 2003), 293.

25. Nicholas Atkin and Frank Tallett, *Priests, Prelates, and People: A History of European Catholicism since 1750* (Oxford and New York: Oxford University Press, 2003), 54–55, 61–62.
26. Robert A. Orsi, *Between Heaven and Earth: The Religious Worlds People Make and the Scholars Who Study Them* (Princeton, NJ: Princeton University Press, 2005), 9. See also Paula Kane, "Getting beyond Gothic: Challenges for Contemporary Catholic Church Architecture," in *American Sanctuary: Understanding Sacred Spaces*, ed. Louis P. Nelson (Bloomington, IN: Indiana University Press), 2006.
27. This argument counters the notion that the Enlightenment ushered in a smooth transition from an enchanted past to a disenchanted present. Schmidt describes instead the "modern braiding of presence and absence." Leigh Schmidt, *Hearing Things: Religion, Illusion and the American Enlightenment* (Cambridge, MA: Harvard University Press, 2000), 36. See also David D. Hall, "Review Essay: What Is the Place of 'Experience' in Religious History?," *Religion and American Culture* 13, no. 2 (Summer 2003): 249.
28. Schmidt, *Hearing Things*, p. 8.
29. Ronald, September 28, 2009, OLMC.
30. Eliza (F-53), June 13, 2006, SJ.
31. James W. Fernandez, *Bwiti: An Ethnography of the Religious Imagination in Africa* (Princeton, NJ: Princeton University Press, 1982), 377–378, 408, 411–412.
32. May 15, 2005, SJ.
33. Fernandez, *Bwiti*, 377, 391.
34. Eliza, May 15, 2005, SJ.
35. Margaret M. McGuinness, "Let Us Go to the Altar: American Catholics and the Eucharist, 1926–1976," in *Habits of Devotion* (Ithaca, NY: Cornell University Press, 2004), 203, 217.
36. August 21, 2005, SJ.
37. Michel de Certeau, *Practice of Everyday Life*, trans. Steven Rendall (Berkeley: University of California Press, 1984), 108.
38. I am indebted here to Elaine Scarry's reflections on the relationship of ethics and beauty. See Elaine Scarry, *On Beauty and Being Just* (Princeton, NJ: Princeton University Press, 1999), 90.

Epilogue

1. Ten other Boston-area closure appeals were finally denied at the Apostolic Signatura in May 2010. Sacred Heart's appeal may have taken a different route through the process, since the building remained open as a chapel.
2. Carla (F-64), September 22, 2009 [telephone conversation].

3. “He sings, he smokes, and he’s their American rep,” *National Catholic Reporter*, September 9, 2005, 9–10. The “Communion and Liberation” website includes four letters and one address from John Paul II to the movement celebrating various anniversaries in the movement’s history. John Paul II spoke at movement meetings in 1979 and in 1982. www.clonline.org. George Weigel, *Witness to Hope: The Biography of Pope John Paul II* (New York: HarperCollins, 1999), 328.
4. “Christ is Risen,” *Cardinal Séan’s Blog*, April 17, 2009, http://www.cardinalseansblog.org.
5. Eliza, August 19, 2009, telephone conversation with author.
6. http://www.vatican.va/roman_curia/secretariat_state/documents/rc_seg-st_12101998_profile_en.html. Accessed September 15, 2009. In August of 2009, Parolin was promoted to archbishop as a part of his transfer to a new assignment. He would now be the papal ambassador to Venezuela. *National Catholic Reporter*, August 18, 2009, http://ncronline.org/blogs/ncr-today/pope-sends-top-diplomat-deal-chavez, accessed September 15, 2009.
7. “Diocese locks doors on parishioners,” *Toledo Blade*, March 7, 2006, www.toledoblade.com; “Court rejects appeal in closed-church case,” *Toledo Blade*, May 7, 2009; for a narrative of the lockout, see www.stjameskansas.org.
8. “Archdiocese of New York announces realignment decisions,” Roman Catholic Archdiocese of New York, Press Release, January 19, 2007; “Members of churches set to close seek advice from those who have been there,” *New York Times*, January 27, 2007; “Upstate, drop in Catholics leads to drop in churches,” *New York Times*, February 10, 2008.
9. “Egan flees the masses,” *New York Post*, March 27, 2007.
10. “Boston church group shares tough tactics to keep parishes open,” *New Orleans Times-Picayune*, June 13, 2008, www.nola.com. In 2006, Borré mounted an unsuccessful bid to win a seat on the Boston City Council. His promotional literature, which he handed out at events at the occupied Our Lady of Mount Carmel, highlighted his work on behalf of shuttered parishes in the 1st District, including St. Catherine of Siena and East Boston’s Mount Carmel. “New hats in the ring,” *Boston Globe*, April 11, 2006, B1.
11. Craig Kraemer, *Swimming against the Holy See*, 2009, available for purchase and online at Kraemer’s blog: http://churchclosingsinneworleans.blogspot.com.
12. “New Orleans Catholics ask pope for new archbishop,” *National Catholic Reporter*, February 3, 2009, www.ncronline.org. Peter Borré, personal correspondence with author, September 23, 2009.

13. "Upstate, drop in Catholics leads to drop in churches," *New York Times*, February 10, 2008, www.nyt.com.
14. "Postcard from Adams," *Time Magazine*, January 8, 2009, www.time.com; "In a quiet rebellion, parishioners keep the faith, and a vigil," *New York Times*, January 6, 2009; "Keeping the faith: St. Stanislaus Kostka fights closing," www.iberkshires.com, April 8, 2009; "MA Catholic diocese to close 22 more churches," WBZ News, August 28, 2009, www.wbz.com.
15. In Camden, plans were under way for a radical reduction that would cut the number of parish churches from 124 to 66 over a two-year span. In Buffalo, restructuring translated into a reduction of parishes from 275 to 204 between 2005 and 2009. Toledo went from 157 to 131 parishes in 2006. "In U.S. pained and uncertain church awaits pope," *New York Times*, April 14, 2008. "N.O. church closures follow national pattern," *The Times-Picayune*, April 26, 2008.
16. "Threatened Catholic parishes seek support from the suburbs," *Cleveland Plain Dealer*, August 26, 2009.
17. www.futurechurch.org, accessed September 14, 2009.
18. Kelly, Timothy, *The Transformation of American Catholicism: The Pittsburgh Laity and the Second Vatican Council, 1950–1972* (Notre Dame, IN: University of Notre Dame Press, 2009), 298.
19. "Green Bay diocese to cut 21 parishes," *Green Bay Press-Gazette*, April 15, 2005. "N.O. church closures follow national pattern," *New Orleans Time-Picayune*, April 26, 2008; "Cleveland diocese not alone in closing churches," www.wkyc.com, accessed September 16, 2009.
20. "Diocese to close, merge worship sites," *Albany Times Union*, January 8, 2009.
21. John Paul II, "Address of John Paul II to the Bishops of the Ecclesiastical Provinces of Dubuque, Kansas City in Kansas, Omaha, and St. Louis (U.S.A.) on their '*Ad Limina*' Visit," November 26, 2004, www.vatican.va.
22. "Summary of Key Findings," *U.S. Religious Landscape Survey*, Pew Forum on Religion and Public Life, February 2008, religions.pewforum.org.
23. Ronald (M-57), September 28, 2009 (telephone).
24. James O'Toole, *Militant and Triumphant: William Henry O'Connell and the Catholic Church in Boston, 1859–1944* (Notre Dame, IN and London: University of Notre Dame Press, 1992), 2, 5, 229. On the controversy over O'Connell's body, see "City tells B.C. to revise its plan: new dorms opposed on Brighton land," *Boston Globe*, February 22, 2008; "Tumult over a resting place: land deal riles cardinal's kin," *Boston Globe*, March 9, 2008; "Church seeks to move body of O'Connell," *Boston Globe*, September 18, 2009.

Acknowledgments

This book is a result of curiosities launched many years ago in two departments of religion. I am thankful to those who brought me into the academic study of religion at Colorado College, especially Doug Fox and Sam Williams. A grant from Colorado College to observe life at two Rocky Mountain monasteries opened a door to a life's worth of work on the questions of modern American Catholicism. I have Ira Chernus, Fred Denny, Sam Gill, Bob Lester, and Lynn Ross-Bryant to thank for making the religious studies department at the University of Colorado a stimulating and convivial place to learn. The wonderful department they built at CU remains one of my own cherished sites.

I am grateful as well for the help of Bridgett Woodall, the archivist at the archdiocesan headquarters in Boston, and Friar Ronald Bofeta and others at the Franciscan Missionary Union, Immaculate Conception Province, on Thompson Street in New York. My editor, Sharmila Sen at Harvard University Press, made the difficult process of getting the text into print look easy—a true gift. I was also assisted by the press's Ian Stevenson and Heather Hughes. I am grateful too for the care and reflection given this project by two anonymous readers.

Several groups and individuals at Harvard University encouraged my research and challenged my thinking. Colleagues from the North American Religions Colloquium based at Harvard Divinity School made incisive and helpful comments on portions of this work. During my time as a part of it, this group succeeded in creating an environment consisting of equal parts gracious encouragement and bracing challenge. I want particularly to note the thoughtful critiques and warm collegiality of Brandon Bayne, Wallace Best, Lauren Brandt, Ann Braude, David Charles, Heather Curtis, Curtis Evans, Linford Fisher, Marla Frederick, Rachel Gordan, David Hall, David Hempton, Bill Hutchison, Hillary Kaell, Z Kermani, Robert Orsi, Tovis Page, Jim Reed, Jon Roberts, Stephen Shoemaker, Josef

Sorett, Adrian Weimer, and Eliza Young Barstow. Members of Harvard's Ethnography of Religion Workshop also helped create a fertile environment for the development of this project. A grant funded by William and Virginia Hutchison welcomed me to Harvard. A second Hutchison Fellowship, offered in memory of Bill, got me through a summer of research and writing. I will always remember and admire Bill for his sincere interest in his students, his optimism and warmth, and his incredible breadth of knowledge. Others I met in Cambridge, especially Michael Cohen, Jesse Elison, Michael Evans, Karen Evans, Joe Mudd, Vanessa Mudd, Chris Railey, and Mara Willard, remain reliable and deeply cherished sources of both intellectual challenge and genuine recreation.

Fordham University has provided a congenial setting for the refining of this work toward publication. In particular, I would like to thank Terrence Tilley, Christine Firer Hinze, Mark Massa, S.J., for opening avenues of practical support for this work at Fordham. James T. Fisher, with characteristically self-effacing generosity, stepped in at a crucial moment with insightful and, as it turned out, essential commentary related to the framing of my arguments. Over the past few years I have also been fortunate to become a part of the Religion in America Seminar at Columbia University. The members of this lively and insightful group helped me move the project toward broader themes in American history of religion.

Among those who read the work more closely at various stages, I would like to thank in particular David Hall, Michael D. Jackson, and Robert Orsi. David has been a sure and true guide of Christian history and the broader study of religion. I particularly appreciated David's willingness to deploy frequently his remarkable skill for zeroing in on the essential (and often very difficult) question. His directness with me over the years has made this a better book and me a better scholar. Michael continues to share liberally of his gift for posing matters in a way that is at once stunningly far-reaching and immediately relevant. His ability to detect and plainly describe the richness of everyday encounters still inspires me. Michael's commitment to understanding people 'where they live' points to a deeply ethical source and end for scholarship and philosophy. Bob has been especially generous and supportive. He exemplifies a mode of research, teaching, and conversation that is creative, deeply humane, and relentlessly well grounded. Bob took great care and showed astonishing kindness in an effort to sharpen my prose and arguments over the span of many years. He endured my worried complaints and occasional spiraling with equanimity, compassion, and a steady dose of hard truth. Through guidance, example, and friendship he has helped me immeasurably to become a better scholar and teacher. The effort continues. I am, of course, responsible for the shortcomings of this work.

I must also thank my family. Tim Moore has been extremely generous and supportive of me and the work I do and of our larger family 'project.' His unflinching confidence in us is a true gift. Keasha and Art Palmer sacrificed tremendously and improbably in support of this work. Their good humor and kindness, and their devotion to their granddaughter have enhanced my life and hers as well. I want also to thank Jamie Moore, Richard Brouillet, Emily Brouillet, Sara Moore, and Chris, Jylene, Matt, and Anita Seitz for their love and their confidence in me; it is felt despite the miles between us. My parents, Neal and Barbara Seitz, have provided remarkable and steady support and care throughout my life. They remain my models of good-natured and thoughtful generosity and my exemplars of the hard work and joy of constructing a family hearth. As important, their lifelong curiosities—especially about religion, art, and history—certainly laid the foundation for mine. Over the past two-and-a-half years, my daughter Tavia has opened my heart and mind beyond what I could have imagined. I hope her enlivening imprint on me is felt in these pages. In many ways Brenna Moore lived through this project with me. She is to be credited above all others for helping me to think through and with this research. What's more, she has been a true champion in our efforts to build a home and two academic careers. Brenna's combination of scholarly insight, infectious confidence, and buoyant humor carried me through this effort. *No Closure* is dedicated to her.

Finally, I want to offer a special note of thanks to the people I got to know in the occupied parishes of Our Lady of Mount Carmel, East Boston, St. Albert the Great, East Weymouth, and St. Jeremiah, Framingham. Knowing that my analysis might not match precisely with their understandings, occupiers in these churches nonetheless opened their doors and their stories to me with graciousness and good humor in the midst of trying times. In these closed-but-open churches and all across Boston—at St. Catherine of Siena Parish in Charlestown, at engaging gatherings of the Council of Parishes, at boisterous rallies in Oak Square, and in the narrow streets of Sacred Heart's North Square—I encountered Catholics who, in opening their histories, memories, and hopes to me, enlivened mine.

Index

Harvard University Press is a member of Green Press Initiative (greenpressinitiative.org), a nonprofit organization working to help publishers and printers increase their use of recycled paper and decrease their use of fiber derived from endangered forests. This book was printed on recycled paper containing 30% post-consumer waste and processed chlorine free.